STRENGTH
of SPIRIT

Susanna De Vries

STRENGTH
of SPIRIT

PIONEERING WOMEN
OF ACHIEVEMENT
FROM FIRST FLEET
TO FEDERATION

MILLENNIUM BOOKS

First published in 1995 by
Millennium Books
an imprint of E.J. Dwyer (Australia) Pty Ltd
Unit 13, Perry Park
33 Maddox Street
Alexandria NSW 2015
Australia
Phone: (02) 550-2355
Fax: (02) 519-3218

National Library of Australia
Cataloguing-in-Publication data

De Vries, Susanna.
    Strength of spirit : pioneering women of achievement
    from First Fleet to Federation.

    Includes index.
    ISBN 1 86429 038 2.

    1. Women – Australia – Biography. 2. Women pioneers –
    Australia – Biography. 3. Pioneers – Australia –
    Biography. I. Title.
994.0099

Cover design by Axis Design Works
Text design by NB Design
Typeset by Egan-Reid Ltd
Printed in Hong Kong

10 9 8 7 6 5 4 3 2 1

99 98 97 96 95

INSCRIPTION

In books lies the soul of the whole Past Time; the articulate audible voice of the Past, when the body and material substance of it has altogether vanished like a dream.

– Thomas Carlyle

DEDICATION

To my husband, Jake, who took some of the photographs and provided enormous moral support while I was writing and to my friend Sylvia Mary Alison, whose important role in the founding of Prison Fellowship (which now operates worldwide) reminds me of the Christian faith and vision of Mary McConnel.

Many of the paintings and photographs in this book are from private collections whose owners are thanked for their kindness in allowing them to be reproduced. Thanks are also due to Christie's, Sotheby's, Joel's and Lawson's Auctioneers for supplying transparencies. Many thanks also to Marusia Maccormick, whose assistance with researching and writing the stories of Ann Caldwell and Truganini was invaluable. Grateful thanks to Dr John Thearle of the Department of Child Health, University of Queensland, for additional information concerning the work of Mary McConnel in the founding of the Children's Hospital, and to her descendants, Duncan McConnel of Cressbrook and Dr David McConnel of Brisbane. Finally, my thanks to Carol Floyd, my dedicated editor and publisher; to Anthony Dwyer, managing director of E J Dwyer, who expressed faith in the project from the start; to designers Norman Baptista and Axis Design Works and, lastly, for the constant support for this book from my agent, Selwa Anthony.

Contents

Introduction

The stories in this book are both a homage to, and a celebration of, the lives of twenty extraordinary Australian women from our past. These heroic women captured my imagination due to their courage and strength of purpose. I have tried to present a portrait of intelligent, determined and talented women, who confronted a harsh and male-dominated land and succeeded in their chosen fields, despite stringent social constraints against any form of female achievement or personal expression in the late eighteenth and the nineteenth century.

The challenging circumstances of Australia's first century of white settlement produced women, white and Aboriginal, just as brave and determined as any of our explorers, pioneers, stockmen, outlaws and sporting heroes. Unfortunately Australia has not honoured these women sufficiently and few memorials, statues or museums celebrate their achievements.

In marked contrast to Australia's cavalier treatment of outstanding women, Americans have founded museums to celebrate pioneer 'wagon women' who opened up the West. Even Phar Lap the racehorse is better known to most Australians than women like Mary Watson, Lucy Osburn, Mary Penfold, Mary McConnel and Georgiana Molloy. The French venerate the names of Joan of Arc and Marie Curie; every Spaniard knows about Dolores Ibarruru, heroine of the Spanish Civil War; Britons know about the exploits of Flora MacDonald, Florence Nightingale, Grace Darling and Edith Cavell; the Dutch honour Kenau Hasselaer, a woman who rallied the populace against Spanish invaders.

Australian women were just as brave and determined as their male equivalents, so why are there so few Australian heroines? (In 1993, television mogul Bruce Gyngell complained to the press that the only widely known Australian heroine was Caroline Chisholm whose face has, ironically, been removed from Australian banknotes, and later that year a newspaper survey proved that he was right.)

This book aims to make some of our female heroes better known to all Australians and presents their stories illustrated by paintings and prints of the correct period found by the author in private and public collections. These women are role models: their lives are as varied as their backgrounds and as their reasons for coming to Australia.

Some, like Lucy Osburn, Australia's Florence Nightingale, rejected marriage to devote their lives to raise the abysmal standards of nursing and care of destitute children (we owe much to Lucy Osburn for the fact that Australian nurses today are seen as some of the best in the world). Mary Watson, who died of thirst while fleeing in an iron tank from Lizard Island, emigrated because her father lost his money and the family home.

For stories of Aboriginal women living between 1788 and 1888, we have to rely on brief entries in memoirs, letters and diaries of white government officials, settlers or governors. Walyer, Truganini and Fanny Cochrane Smith lived through a civil war as savage as today's conflicts in Bosnia or Rwanda. Walyer (an Aboriginal Boadicea) rallied a small band of her people and used her knowledge of the bush to

L. Sonny Poole. This Heidelberg School artist depicts with sympathy an attractive young woman, possibly a widow, with her children at a time when widows received no pensions and many took in washing or sewing to survive. Private collection, courtesy Leonard Joel/Lauraine Diggins Fine Art, Melbourne.

fight a guerrilla war against Europeans, who hunted down and killed the Tasmanian Aborigines as though they were foxes or vermin.

The name of Truganini is famous, but for the wrong reasons. Truganini, or Truganuna as today's Tasmanian Aborigines say her name was pronounced, was not a queen; nor was she the last of the Tasmanian Aborigines. In fact other Aborigines outlived Truganini on islands in Bass Strait and in Tasmania, yet so great had been the persecution of her race by Europeans that after her death Aboriginality was ignored or kept a family secret.[1]

Truganini's life has unfortunately often been sensationalised. She was not the 'good looking sealer's moll' and archtraitor as described by Robert Hughes.[2] Truganini was infinitely more complex and in the interest of historical integrity deserves more balanced treatment. Aboriginal women were seen by European men as sexually available and exploitable. This stereotype was also extended to convict and working-class women in the first hundred years of European settlement.

'Damned Whores', the 'Convict Taint' and Female Stereotypes

Esther Johnston, Mary Reibey and Sarah Wentworth struggled all their lives against the 'convict taint'. The stereotyped epithet 'damned whores' dogged all convict women, their daughters and women in unmarried relationships. An enormous and impoverished Irish migration, fettered and free, also imported the traditional Irish burden of sexual guilt and the concept of women as inferior beings,[3] fit only to cook, rear children and cut peat.

Female convicts in the first years of settlement were often forced by circumstance to take up their former occupation on the streets and alleyways of Australian cities. A cynical and uncaring government had failed to provide them with sufficient accommodation and, arriving in depressed times, they found no employment, so were often forced to live with male convicts to survive, or to sell themselves in prostitution. To remedy the shortage of women in colonial Australia, the British Government often imposed heavier sentences on female offenders in England than on their male equivalents. Unfortunate women like Esther Julian (Johnston) were transported for shoplifting a piece of lace and were intended by the government to provide sexual gratification to male convicts in the hope that this would keep them from rioting, bestiality and homosexuality.[4] Degradation at the hands of men started on the convict ships for these convicted women and girls, making the decision by Mary Reibey (transported for stealing a horse) to dress as a boy on the convict ship taking her to Sydney wholly understandable.

Not only were women despised and degraded by their gaolers and by the male convicts, they were doubly punished for their misdeeds. While men could serve their term and earn their passage back to Britain by working as sailors, women could not do this and, lacking the money for the fare back home, were, in effect, transported for life. The stigma of 'damned whore' shackled female convicts and ex-convicts as firmly as any leg irons, even throughout the Victorian period as Mary Reibey, Esther Johnston and Sarah Wentworth were to discover. It was an age of stereotypes and in male eyes women fell into two categories—the Madonna or the whore.

The belittling of former convict women, regardless of radical changes in their personal circumstances, or their economic and social position, would haunt many women. The 'convict taint' dogged Mary Reibey all her life and extended to her children and grandchildren, even though one of them eventually became Premier of Tasmania. Mary's attractive and accomplished daughters were virtually excluded from 'polite society'. Many townsfolk were happy to do business with Mary but refused to accept her socially. Sarah Cox Wentworth had a similar experience (see Chapter One).

The situation of free women migrants was also difficult. Caroline Chisholm was outraged to see how single women or widows[6] who emigrated of their own accord were treated little better than female convicts. Many of these free women had been recruited from British workhouses or orphanages by 'bounty hunters' who received a commission on the numbers they could persuade to emigrate with false promises of work and lodgings on arrival.

In 1834 the ship *Strathfieldsay* arrived at Hobart. On 19 August the *Colonial Times* ran an article describing how several thousand men waited for the women to disembark. The police were outnumbered and the women were forced to walk ashore through an avenue of screaming, jeering men, who leered at them and pawed those closest to them. Some 'stopped the women by force and addressed them in the most obscene manner . . .' Terrified of pack rape in the streets, some of the women became hysterical. The male convicts pursued the women to their billets and remained outside that day and through the night, banging on doors and windows trying to break in.

The convict women whose stories are related here were forced by circumstance and adversity to be stronger, more determined and more fearless than their counterparts in Europe as they had to overcome the Australian male's deep-seated prejudice against women. They lived in a ruthless, greedy and male-dominated society dedicated to making money and grabbing land.

Australian women who accompanied pioneering husbands out of love or duty faced danger, disease and isolation unknown anywhere else in the English-speaking world, except for the prairies of America and Canada.[7] But conditions

Mary Nye's life was ruined when her husband was transported for taking home a hen's egg found in a country lane. Convicted of stealing Mr. Nye was sentenced to be transported to Van Diemen's Land for seven years. To be with her husband, Mary committed a trifling offence so she too could be transported to Tasmania. But she never found her husband. Lacking the funds to return when she had served her sentence, she spent the rest of her days in poverty and loneliness. Photograph from Queen Victoria Museum & Art Gallery, Tasmania.

in Australia differed from America: there were few migrants fleeing religious intolerance like the Pilgrim Fathers had, and there was a grotesque imbalance between the sexes. In the earliest years of Australian settlement men out-numbered women in country areas by between ten or twenty to one and in the city by four to one. This imbalance has left Australia with the unpleasant legacy of one of the highest rates of male alcoholism in the world and a high rate of violence against women. It spawned the cult of mateship and ockerism and the idea that 'having a good time' consisted of watching sport, drinking with mates and rolling home drunk.[8]

Anne Summers' influential book *Damned Whores and God's Police*[9] described the division of colonial women by men into two categories—'damned whores' (a term first used by Lieutenant Ralph Clarke who wrote how '. . . those damned whores the moment they got below fel [sic] a fighting one another) and 'God's police' (a term coined by Caroline Chisholm in her 1847 pamphlet *Emigration and Transportation Relatively Considered*). By 'God's police' Chisholm meant wives rather than whores—'respectable' married women or 'Madonnas' who did not work outside the home and whose concerns centred around what the Germans termed *Küche, Kinder, Kirche*—or kitchen, children and church. Chisholm saw 'God's police' acting as a civilising influence on their husbands and sons.

Former governess Charlotte Waring embraced both stereotypes at different times in her life. After her husband's death she married one of her husband's friends who then revealed his true nature as a violent and highly disturbed alcoholic. Charlotte fled with her children from the family home and her second husband, as was his legal right, gained control of her money and property. Charlotte found herself regarded as a 'damned whore', or member of what the French call the *demimonde* or fringes of society. Living alone with her young children to educate, she had to battle the patronising and patriarchal attitudes of Alexander Berry, the arrogant executor of her first husband's estate. Charlotte spent years in poverty appealing to the courts to try and obtain money that had been left to her perfectly legally. It was only extreme adversity that made her write the first book written for Australian children.

This 'damned whore' epithet could be applied to any colonial woman who stepped outside the sphere allotted to the 'angel of the hearth'. A few women rebelled against this narrow role but the majority of middle-class women were content to stay home ministering to the comforts of fathers, brothers and husbands.

Charlotte Waring's experience demonstrates how women were deprived of control over their lives, children and their property by a legal system which favoured men and turned any woman who dared leave her husband on grounds of cruelty, or alcoholism or infidelity into a whore. Clothes, jewellery, land, money, babes in arms—all belonged to the husband in case of separation or divorce.

Georgiana McCrae sought a legal separation from a husband who had lost all her money and denied her the right to use her enormous artistic talents professionally. In Melbourne in the 1850s, legal separations or divorces were not yet standard legal practice and Georgiana was advised it would be too difficult to obtain one. She remained financially dependent on her children all her life and failed to fulfil the promise of a brilliant artistic career.

The Victorian theory of 'separate spheres'[10] laid down separate roles for men and women in marriage. The indissolubility of marriage was reinforced by churches of all denominations, which insisted that woman's role as helpmate and intellectual inferior was ordained by God. No matter how bad the marriage, nineteenth-century religious and civic authorities enjoined women to be meek and long-suffering 'in this vale of tears'. These sentiments were fervently espoused by the happily married Georgiana Molloy until the death of her only son by drowning marked a turning point in her relationship. She conquered the depression which followed her son's death by immersing herself in her passion for botanical research, leaving her husband to moan about buttons not sewn on, clothes unwashed and mountains of laborious, time-consuming housework undone.

Angels of the Hearth

Influential Victorian writers such as Thomas Gisborne and, on occasions, John Ruskin, took a condescending view of women. These authors saw women as feeble, inferior 'angels of the hearth' who should be devoted to and filled with admiration for men. Ruskin surrounded himself with adoring young women like Adelaide Ironside whom he instructed in the elements of drawing, but firmly believed that genius and high intelligence were male preserves. The Victorian male often saw himself as a combination of God and Sir Galahad and demanded to be treated accordingly.

American, British and Australian nineteenth-century women were constantly told by male doctors that they were mentally inferior. Some doctors thought that because women's skulls were smaller they had smaller brains. Dr Henry Maudsley, founded of London's Maudsley Psychiatric Hospital, in an article on the 'Theory of Reproductive Energy' in the British *Fortnightly Review* in 1874 proposed the theory that women who taxed their brains too much might become sterile! No universities wanted to award them degrees until the 1880s, so their access to well-paid work was blocked. No-one seemed to query what would happen to university-educated men. Any educated, independent woman with opinions of her own was deemed 'unfeminine' and hence unmarriageable. A 'she-dragon' was how Alexander Berry described his opponent in the law courts, the determined and highly intelligent Charlotte Waring, when she sought to obtain control of her own money.

University education was denied to women for most of the nineteenth century. Fashionable 'young ladies' were not encouraged to use their brains to think or ask questions about society. Instead they were taught accomplishments—copperplate writing, drawing, needlework, singing, piano, dancing and sometimes French—but no science of philosophy. It was generally believed that men of standing 'would not marry clever women'. Nineteenth-century men were intended to confront a challenging world while middle-class women remained docile, cared for children and played the piano—that instrument of respectability which was carted off to the bush to symbolise civilisation and the home as men's haven against the world.

Men kept most colonial women busy raising large families (on average one child was born every eighteen months to women at this period: as soon as the woman finished breastfeeding she bore another child). Authors like Gisborne and Hannah More (a traitor to her sex if ever there was one) saw the 'angel of the hearth' as 'contributing daily and hourly to the comfort of husbands, parents, brothers and other relations . . . in sickness and health'.

Gisborne felt too much education would make women argue against their husbands and warned young women against becoming too educated. He invoked the New Testament: 'Wives, submit yourselves to your own husbands, as to the Lord'.[11] He also issued dire warnings to intelligent or adventurous women of the wrath to come of they dared to question the Scriptures or their husbands' orders.[12]

Gisborne's doctrines proved prejudicial to enterprising women like Lucy Osburn. When they tried to achieve reforms or assert their independence, Sister Osburn and other strong-minded women often had their characters assassinated by male colleagues. Colonial men, like their British counterparts, formed a solid front to preserve the status quo and keep women at home. Ruskin, who was widely read, saw himself as a guardian of public morality and wrote at length on woman's role. (It seems bizarre to see Ruskin in the role of marriage adviser or counsellor as, horrified by the sight of his wife's naked body, he proved unable to consummate his own marriage. He made Effie Ruskin's life a misery and she left him to marry a Pre-Raphaelite painter.[13]) In his influential book *Sesame and Lillies* Ruskin laid down firm rules for female conduct in marriage. He described how 'woman's intellect is not for invention . . . but for sweet ordering, arrangement and (domestic) decision . . . protected from all danger and temptation'[14] and in the same book described how a 'wife is not for self-development but for self-renunciation'.

In 1841 author Sarah Ellis wrote:

> Love is woman's all, her wealth, her power, her very being. Man has an existence distinct from that of his affections . . . his public character, his ambition, his competition with other men. In women's love is mingled the trusting dependence of a child.[15]

Faced with such advice one can only marvel at the bravery of some of the women in this book, who sought to achieve something more than the 'trusting dependence of a child'.

The damaging belief that women were childlike, intellectually inferior and the chattels of husbands and fathers held sway in Australia (with its distorted imbalance of males to females) much longer than in Europe and America. Australia was a pioneering society: in the bush, women's ability to escape from masculine control was severely limited. Travel was doubly hazardous due to the number of escaped convicts who became bushrangers and preyed on female travellers and Aboriginal women.

The Henry Lawson 'mateship' ethos was founded on the absence of women other than as a sexual convenience. The harshness of bush life would eventually be described from the woman's point of view by author Barbara Baynton, in whose short stories women are maltreated by the men in their lives and often meet dreadful fates at the hands of bush husbands and passing swaggies.

Alcohol played its part in the degradation of working-class women. In New South Wales and Victoria tents and water carts selling illicit alcohol made the rounds of pastoral runs and immobilised entire station staffs, male and female, for days at a time. The low position of women selling 'sly grog' or acting as a barmaid in the 'damned whore' role is a subtext in the goldfields watercolours of that alcohol-addicted bachelor S.T. Gill and in the work of other artists.

Colonial Women and Paid Work

It was made abundantly clear to middle-class women that their only excuse for working outside the home was stark poverty. Even playing the piano could not be done by a 'lady' on a concert platform and was reserved for the drawing room in the colonial home. Work outside the home brought disgrace on the head of the family. Lucy Osburn's father turned her portrait to the wall when she announced she was going to study nursing as a career. Caroline Chisholm was an isolated example of a woman who left the home to work but hers was philanthropic unpaid work and her supportive husband was a rare example. However, business partnerships on the land did exist. For example, the husbands of Esther Johnston, Emmeline Leslie, Charlotte Bussell and Elizabeth Macarthur relied on them in time of illness or enforced absence.

Most female convicts were given a hard time when they were assigned to work as domestics in households. The harshness of the penal system did not encourage convict women to be virtuous: an assigned female convict who rejected the sexual advances of her master could, on his word alone, be returned to the Female Factory as being of 'bad character'. There women of 'bad conduct' were placed in the despised

The First Lesson, *painted 1869 by Melbourne artist, George Folingsby, who saw his wife as a typical Victorian 'Angel of the Hearth'. In colonial Australia possession of a piano represented the height of middle class respectability. From a private collection acquired recently by the Queensland Art Gallery.*

Artist unknown. This oil painting presents a stereotype of 'The Angel of the Hearth'. The artist shows a dutiful wife of the Victorian period, hard at work sewing. Private collection.

Third Grade and punished by being put in the stocks, having their heads shaved or a heavy spiked iron collar placed around their necks.[16] Should an assigned domestic become pregnant to her master, she was turned out to sleep on the streets and denied a reference, making it almost impossible for her to get another job, or she was sent back to the Female Factory as a Third Class 'incorrigible'.[17]

Women forced to work due to lack of money were widely despised and often suffered sexual harassment by male employers. This meant middle-class women were even more reluctant to abandon their closeted domestic role as the 'angel of the hearth', tending children, sewing and embroidering.

White Women and Marriage

Women were regarded as chattels in any marriage and the property of their husbands. Should they want to leave the marriage, like Georgiana McCrae or Charlotte Atkinson, they soon learned that everything they owned, including their children, belonged to their husbands and the courts automatically favoured the man. Charlotte Atkinson had been left the lease of Oldbury under her husband's will but when she remarried George Barton, the lease automatically passed to him. She had trouble obtaining maintenance for her children through the law even though Barton was violent to her and finished up insane in an asylum. Under one judgment of the period only a woman's sewing machine was her own and even children at the breast were the property of their father. Small wonder that women like Lucy Osburn decided to pursue careers rather than enter into what could turn out to be a loveless marriage.

Organised religion supported the oppression of white Christian women and kept many in violent or abusive marriages. The Book of Common Prayer stated a wife should 'obey' and 'serve' her husband. A commentary on the marriage service in the 1850s described how 'equality breeds contention . . . and one of the two must be superior or both would strive for dominion'. As relatively late as 1891 Lady Mary Windeyer, wife of William Windeyer, Chief Justice of New South Wales and a friend and supporter of Sister Lucy Osburn, complained that Australian 'women had been looked upon as chattels, men being so to speak their owners'.[18] They were unpaid housekeepers, unpaid farm managers, unpaid secretaries to their husbands and mothers of large families. Only women married to wealthy men avoided domestic drudgery. Many were illiterate (forty per cent of females in Australia up to the middle of the nineteenth century could not read or write).

Fashions and Farmwork

Fashionable clothing in the Victorian age was designed to make women look more curvaceous or 'feminine', which meant looking childlike or helpless and hence pleasing to men.

In the 1830s the height of fashion was to wear enormous 'leg of mutton' sleeves and voluminous bonnets from which peeped a glimpse of ringletted curls. The 1840s were the years of the submissive droop—droopy bonnets, droopy shoulders and droopy skirts which were, in turn, replaced by that horror of all horrors for women— the crinoline or whalebone cage supporting an enormous bell of a skirt. It would be hard to imagine an outfit less suited to domestic work in the hot summer climate of Australia than the crinoline, widely adopted by the end of the 1850s. Each hooped skirt demanded at least five metres of material and sometimes more. Bush women are said to have ridden long distances to evening entertainments with their crinolines tied in a figure of eight to their saddles.

Wearing a long, very full skirt and cooking over a camp oven on an open fire was hazardous in the extreme, as Mary Ann Friend's illustration of cooking over one on the beach at Perth demonstrates. Mary Ann camped on the beach near Perth with recently arrived middle-class migrants from Britain who had brought entire libraries and grand pianos with them. Their crops withered and died in the sandy soil so that they faced starvation.

Some squatters' wives and city women would rather have been dead than out of fashion and insisted on wearing crinolines in the kitchen. But by the 1860s so many serious accidents, resulting in death or severe disfigurement, had occurred that the fullness was swept to the back and supported on a pad of horsehair named the bustle. By the 1870s crinolines were only worn by the poor and unfashionable.[19]

Women like Annie Caldwell battling to survive on the land, probably wore the same outfits for years, although there were frequent complaints that their boots wore out quickly and were hard to replace. Georgiana McCrae's journal describes how she made and remade clothes for herself and her children when they were short of money.

The crinoline and its covering.

Contraception and Childbirth

This fashion plate of the Victorian era shows just how cumbersome was the whale-boat cage that supported the crinoline. Some women were burned to death when their crinolined skirts swung too close to open fires. Private collection.

Contraceptives such as condoms, diaphragms or Dutch caps were not supplied by the local doctor or pharmacist to help Australian colonial women limit their families, and none were available for purchase in shops or by mail order before 1873. Some women douched themselves with vinegar after sex to prevent conception or threw themselves down stairs in an effort to kill the foetus. There were other, mainly unsuccessful, folk remedies such as taking hot baths and drinking strong spirits.

Condoms were made of silk and were expensive, so few found their way to Australia. Brettena Smyth, pioneer of female contraception, caused a public outcry from church and civic authorities, when, following her husband's death in 1873, she sold imported condoms and Dutch caps from the family grocery store and advertised them in the local newspapers. 1873 was a watershed for female contraception. However advances in contraception were blocked on all sides and progress was slow. Most delicately nurtured, early colonial women had not heard of them, as such subjects were never discussed by their mothers. They married in their early twenties, bore a child every eighteen months to two years, falling pregnant once again as soon as the last child was weaned. They often lost several infants to disease, but usually managed to raise at least five or six to maturity.

Georgiana Molloy was not the only pioneering woman whose child died. Scores of babies died from cholera, typhus, typhoid, chronic dysentery or accidental drowning in creeks or waterholes. Most homesteads had one or more wooden crosses in the garden to mark the graves of infants. Lack of sanitation represented a major health hazard in colonial Australia: long, hot summers ensured that tropical diseases proliferated and plague and cholera often arrived by boat from India with army regiments. Then the causal link between sewerage and infection was not known. Today we realise that disease was often transmitted by water carts bringing drinking water from sewage-filled creeks or by settlers siting their vegetable gardens too near the cesspits. In times of drought cattle and sheep were allowed to drink at waterholes normally reserved for humans and their excreta could spread typhoid and hydatid infection. In the 1840s and 1850s, Georgiana McCrae described how the main killers of Melbourne's children were dysentery and typhoid. Cholera was prevalent in Sydney and Brisbane where Mary McConnel's little boy died, motivating her to

Mary Ann Friend arrived at the Swan River in the 1830s and with nowhere to stay had to camp on the beach. She painted a watercolour showing herself cooking over a camp oven beside her tent. Hand coloured lithograph from a private collection, England.

found Brisbane's first Children's Hospital. In the bush, settlers often used wooden benches over smelly cesspits as toilets but by the 1850s these primitive arrangements were replaced by the slightly less evil-smelling pan closet.

Women *had* to be brave to face the dangers of childbirth. In colonial Australia more women died from complications of childbirth than from any other cause. In the first decades of settlement doctors and most midwives were poorly trained in what we now regard as basic hygiene. In the cities the midwife would deliver the baby and if the woman had no family to help her, would stay for at least a week to care for mother and child. Like Dickens' Sarey Gamp, some midwives were alcoholics and, so it appears from the histories of Mary McConnel and Georgiana Molloy, were some of our early bush doctors.

Georgiana Molloy died a slow and painful death from infection of the uterus following the birth of her seventh child. Her doctor, who was probably drunk, was inept in the extreme. It was usual for doctors to protect their suits by delivering babies wearing an apron covered with blood from previous operations or from post-mortems conducted in the mortuary. They wore these germ-laden aprons with pride as a badge of competence![20] Sister Lucy Osburn tried to bring in the principles of 'hygienic nursing in medicine' but found herself ostracised by doctors who feared change or, perhaps, female challenge to their power.

In mid-century Vienna, Ignaz Semmelweis discovered that the death rate from puerperal fever, a postnatal complication caused by infection, was far higher in hospital wards attended by doctors who had come straight from post-mortem rooms or operating theatres than in births attended by midwives. By insisting on adequate use of antiseptics he lowered the death rate in women delivering babies from ten to one per cent. Semmelweis's findings provoked much controversy in the medical world and were not adopted in Australia until long after he was dead. Before this, most Australian women were encouraged by midwives to give birth wearing old clothes lying on an unwashed sheet or an old cloth. A clean sheet was only placed under the mother once the afterbirth had come away or been removed manually.[21]

Midwives attended the majority of the births, on occasion dragging the baby out and damaging it. (One husband in the bush, faced with no help and his wife's difficulties in giving birth, tied a rope to the baby's leg to pull it out like a calf. This was the only birthing practice he knew.) Doctors were usually called when desperate measures were needed such as Caesarean births, which often led to the death of the mother from haemorrhage or infection because of unsterile conditions.

Aboriginal Birthing Practices

At this time few women approached middle age without some complications of pregnancy such as prolapsed wombs or varicose veins. However, white women attended by Aboriginal women on remote properties often did better than those attended by white midwives. Unlike invasive British-trained midwives who (prior to the Florence Nightingale–Lucy Osburn era) often had dirty fingernails, the Aborigines did not touch either the woman's genitals or the baby's head and actively encouraged the mother to disrobe and give birth in a squatting position. They had the wisdom to see that in many respects this was better for the woman. The baby dropped into a shallow trench lined with a soft bed of freshly gathered silky ti-tree bark and leaves. Aboriginal women did not wash the baby for some days after delivery believing it safe to do it only then and they were horrified to find that white people cut the umbilical cord close to mother and baby.[22] They regarded it as far healthier to wait for some hours and cut the cord further away. They were also amazed that white women would even consider giving birth in a hospital among a crowd of strangers because for them the very thought of a male surgeon was repulsive. They firmly believed hospitals were contaminated by the spirits of the recently deceased which would harm mother and child. In view of Semmelweis's findings Aboriginal women certainly had a point!

Barangaroo, wife of Bennelong (after whom Bennelong Point was named), had her 'borning' ceremony described in the First Fleet Journal of Lieutenant David Collins. The new mother was 'smoked' with medicinal herbs on different parts of her body to stop bleeding and to encourage a good milk supply. Lieutenant Collins reported seeing Barangaroo heating a special tool to sterilise and then cut the umbilical cord several hours after she had given birth. Shortly after, Barangaroo walked around the gardens and grounds of the first Government House, where she had insisted on having her baby, since she regarded it as a propitious site for the baby's future.[23]

The traditional Aboriginal technique of getting the mother up and walking as soon as possible is far closer to current Western practice than the rigid nineteenth-century insistence on the mother 'lying-in', confined to her bed for two or three weeks before and after the birth. In addition, Aboriginal women understood the importance of psychological support. The mother in labour was supported by women of her group who sang ritual songs to prevent haemorrhage, to relax the mother and to make the birthing process easier.[27]

Considering that the equivalent of a civil war between black and white people over land and stock was raging, it is remarkable how often examples of peaceful cooperation between Aboriginal and white women appear in the memoirs, journals and letters. Many Aboriginal women were caring nurses to white children on remote stations. Their knowledge of remedies produced from native plants often helped white women raise children days or weeks away from any form of other medical assistance. Many Aboriginal women knew herbs that would cure most common eye ailments—especially the very prevalent one known as 'sandy blight' which

Aboriginal women treated by making an infusion from leaves to bathe the infected eyes.[24] When Truganini had become disillusioned with Protector of Aborigines George Robinson, she became a healer concerned with native remedies for her people.

The help was not all one-sided. Georgiana McCrae, for instance, sheltered Aboriginal women like Kitty who had been beaten by their husbands. The kindness of the white women was, on occasion, repaid by courageous Aboriginal women who, at considerable danger to themselves, brought news from the native camps of mischief planned against the invaders' homesteads and cattle. Their deeds are worthy of remembrance as illustrations that the bond of common womanhood did sometimes triumph over racial intolerance.

Women in the Outback

The bush, difficult as it was, brought many middle-class women freedom from the constricting and conventional social life of the cities. These women often acted as partners rather than chattels of their husbands. Writing letters, doing accounts, comparing bloodlines, supervising workers and reclaiming land gave Eliza Hodgson, all three Macarthur women and Annie Caldwell a sense of personal achievement.

However, there is a paradox in these pioneer female farmers. Although their letters often show the prescribed standards of their time—charm, gentleness, femininity and subservience to male demands—different qualities were required to confront the realities of employing convict labour (even through the medium of overseers), and to deal with tough problems such as drought, flood and fire.

Emigration to the fledgling settlement at Port Phillip was described by Georgiana McCrae as 'eating the bitter bread of banishment'. Denied the right to paint by her husband, she did have the opportunity to use her creativity to design two homes which, in conventional Britain, would probably not have happened. Georgiana McCrae drew up the architectural plans for *Mayfield* and supervised the builders; she laid out a garden, and then designed a second cottage at Arthurs Seat on the Mornington Peninsula complete with garden. Georgiana McCrae demonstrated just how practical she was by lining the walls with calico to keep out insects and cold winds; Georgiana Molloy made primitive fly screens by sewing calico over frames and fitting them into glassless windows.

The one complaint that all the women had in common was of hordes of cockroaches, mosquitoes, fleas, gigantic spiders, snakes and ants that swarmed through the larders. In *Notes and Sketches of New South Wales (1839–1844)*, Louisa Meredith described how in the pantry at Homebush

> whatever I touched seemed alive with ants and their industry was unwearied; day or night their 'runs' or paths were always black with countless millions and none of our destructive or protective measures seemed to make the least difference. If one million were scalded two more supplied their place.

Adversity also favoured culinary experiment. Mrs Beeton's recipes were of no use in the bush. At Cressbrook Station in the Brisbane Valley, Mary McConnel made her own pineapple preserve, while other women described the delights of roast flying fox and ibis. Baked bandicoot, cockatoo pie, roast bush turkey and kangaroo tail soup were prepared by other women in an effort to escape from the monotony of roast mutton, damper and black billy tea.

Running a dairy was a daily chore that never ended: cows had to be milked twice a day; cream had to be separated and then churned for butter, which took hours. Life in the bush demanded considerable fortitude and flexibility.

Colonial Women Artists

Middle-class women were allowed accomplishments like painting and music, but were not permitted by 'polite' society to become professional singers, writers or artists. They could use their talents at home, provided these activities did not conflict with the comfort of the breadwinner and the woman did not seek public recognition or payment for her work. Painting professionally would have provided talented Georgiana McCrae with a much-needed income. Instead she forfeited her home, not once but twice, and was trapped in an unhappy marriage to a man who refused to let her paint professionally even though it was he who had failed as a provider. Late in life talented Georgiana mourned the loss of the creativity denied her by her husband. 'What a happy woman I would have been, had I but been allowed to continue the practice of my profession!' she wrote to a grand-daughter.

According to the redoubtable Dr Samuel Johnston, 'Portrait painting is an improper employment for a woman. Public practice of any art and staring into men's faces is very indelicate in a female'. Not only was it considered indelicate but immoral. 'Ladies' had to be chaperoned in the presence of a gentleman so that painting men, nude or not, was out of the question. Restrictions on women painting men's portraits continued until the early twentieth century and explains why brilliant and avant-garde female artists like Mary Cassatt and Berthe Morisot had to paint mothers, children and female servants while their male Impressionist colleagues were free to paint studio nudes and prostitutes in cafes and cabarets.

Georgiana McCrae was only allowed to paint the portrait of Octavius Browne, a male family friend, because it was a wedding gift, painted for friendship rather than profit. Octavius was to marry the daughter of Georgiana's London friends, James and Lucia Cummings, and Georgiana painted his portrait in oils. The watercolour was a preliminary study and shows Octavius wearing a red shirt and white moleskin trousers and carrying a water bottle slung from his belt. It remains one of Georgiana's most vivid portraits in watercolour and its composition and technique are as professional as any colonial portraits made by male artists.

Martha Chauncey (1813–1876), a talented professional miniaturist, was honoured by having a portrait hung at the London Royal Academy's prestigious Summer Exhibition of 1835. Like Georgiana McCrae, Martha abandoned a profitable and serious career as a portrait miniaturist on her marriage to an aristocratic army officer, who dabbled in sketching. Martha, her husband, and her sister Theresa, a talented sculptress, embarked for South Australia and arrived in February 1837, a few months after its proclamation as a colony.

When aristocratic, ginger-whiskered Captain Charles Berkeley proved disastrous as a farmer, Martha saved them financially by painting. By 1847 she had exhibited fifteen works in Adelaide and sold landscapes of the growing town and its semi-rural properties. Martha and fellow professional Georgiana McCrae had totally different experiences with their failed farmer husbands. While Andrew McCrae drowned his sorrows in the Melbourne Club and refused to allow his wife to earn money out of her artistic talent, Captain Berkeley did not appear to object to his wife selling her work or taking portrait commissions.

Hand in hand with the notion that it was not ladylike to use one's talents to earn money went the myth that only men could create art or literature of any lasting value. This argument was tellingly used for centuries by men to wither women's creative urges. Charlotte Waring and her daughter Caroline Louisa Atkinson published books but could not use their own names and wrote under the pseudonym of 'A Lady' or 'An Australian Lady'. Even the Bronte sisters (Currer, Ellis and Acton Bell) and Marian Evans as 'George Eliot' had to write novels under a pseudonym.[25]

To become a professional artist or a writer, women had to fight for recognition from a society bent on frustrating their ambitions. Women, like children, were to

Merchant banker Octavius Browne dressed as a bushman. In 1841 this was painted for Octavius as a wedding present by Georgiana McCrae, whose overbearing husband did not allow her to paint for money so portraits of this size are generally of her own family. Octavius only gave Georgiana two sittings instead of her normal three. The resulting portrait measures 24 x 19 cm. Photograph courtesy Christopher Day Gallery; portrait now in the La Trobe Collection, State Library of Victoria.

GERTRUDE

THE EMIGRANT;

AN IRISH SKETCH OF COLONIAL LIFE

BY

An Australian Lady.

Title page drawn by Caroline Louisa Atkinson for her novel Gertrude the Emigrant. *Authorship of a novel was regarded as suitable only for men so the title page does not give the author's name: it simply says 'by An Australian Lady'.*

be seen and not heard. Fathers wanted to marry them off while the majority of husbands wanted them permanently pregnant and fully occupied with domestic affairs. True art or literature was a work of genius to which a woman 'by her very nature, could not hope to attain' and this attitude lasted longer in Australia than elsewhere. It is significant that the first two volumes of the *Australian Dictionary of Biography*, published in 1966, lack separate entries for many important Australian women or, grudgingly, provide one or two lines about them in the entry under their husband's name, something that does not happen in the later volumes. Esther Johnston, pastoralist; Mary Connel, Georgiana Molloy, Mary Penfold, founder of the famous winery; and prize-winning artist Mary Morton Allport rate only a couple of lines in the early volumes of the *Australian Dictionary of Biography*—under their husband's entries. Walyer and Fanny Cochrane Smith were Aborigines and ignored.

Mary Morton Chapman (Allport), born in 1806, was another British-trained artist. She was the daughter of a publican, and, like so many clever girls, she acquired an education as a teacher, and then married the son of the owner of the school. When Mr and Mrs Joseph Allport emigrated to join family members, her solicitor husband took up land in the Brighton area of Tasmania and he and Mary lived in a wooden hut little larger than a dog kennel. Like Andrew McCrae, Joseph Allport proved a better lawyer than a farmer, so clever Mary was allowed to paint landscapes, flowers and portrait miniatures for money and advertised her portrait miniatures in the *Hobart Town Courier* of 13 July 1832. She achieved distinction for her miniatures, lithographs and studies of Tasmanian flowers, shown but not sold in Hobart exhibitions between 1845 and 1863. She also exhibited a chess table with 64 painted panels showing Tasmanian native flowers (now lost) at the 1885 Paris Exhibition. Her work, which deserves to be better known, is mostly housed in Hobart's Allport Museum and still awaits an Australia-wide exhibition. She was

Maria Caroline Brownrigg has painted a typical family evening in the pre-television era. Such intimate domestic scenes are rare in Australian art. Maria has shown details like the pleated front to the piano and the cords holding the pictures. Courtesy H.P.M. Industries and Hordern House Rare Books.

one of Australia's first artists to see the decorative possibilities of bush flowers.

Financial hardship or loss of a breadwinner was the spur that led all these women to paint for money and/or fame and, in the case of Charlotte Atkinson and Louisa Meredith, also to write for money. Martha Brownrigg's[32] father served in South Africa and there in January 1830 she married naval Lieutenant Marcus Freeman Brownrigg, expecting to enjoy a life surrounded by servants. Instead Martha and her children followed her husband to New South Wales in 1852 and he was offered the job as the manager of Australia's largest pastoral and coal company, the Australian Agricultural Company, at Port Stephens. With the job went a handsome house named *Tahlee* overlooking the water.[33]

After four years Martha's husband was abruptly dismissed from his important position and Brownrigg entered some form of litigation against the company. Meanwhile Martha and her children had to live on very little, surrounded by their handsome furniture in a cottage near Port Stephens. While waiting for her husband's name to be cleared Martha painted portraits for a living. But as few people valued 'women's art' at the time and there were not art galleries or dealers to sell her paintings or find commissions for portraits, she found it difficult to make a serious living.

Martha painted her own family in their Port Stephens cottage. Some of her paintings are shown hanging from elaborate chains on the flower-patterned wall. Martha's eldest son, Marcus junior, plays the piano while a younger son watches his sisters dutifully embroidering or writing letters around a handsome Victorian circular table with a central pillar. An embroidered footstool suggests family handicrafts; a bird in a cage and a bookcase full of handsome bound editions have been brought out with the family. Martha has left us one of the most vivid souvenirs of colonial life.

Colonial Women Writers

The isolation of Australia and the fact that many women were never able to return 'home' meant that letters and journals were vital as a way of keeping parents and siblings aware of the writer's new life. These journals and memoirs have contributed to Australia's rich literary tradition and for this reason I have included extracts from the memoirs of Mary McConnel. Novelists like Caroline Louisa Atkinson suffered from the same discrimination and condescension as female artists.

Letters from home were a lifeline for women. Sailing ships took more than three months to bring them and they were eagerly awaited, providing the only link with home. Loneliness, love and a sense of obligation to ageing parents kept women writing. Paper was costly and scarce, and before the institution of the regular post to Britain in the mid-1840s, sending a letter through a ship's captain was exorbitantly expensive. Many people wrote both down and across the paper, making them hard to read. Letters reveal that female convicts who could write had rudimentary spelling and a small vocabulary. They wrote home infrequently, usually picking up a pen to detail major events like the death of a child. Their letters and journals reveal struggles for personal growth and, sometimes, for survival. They talk about death because so many children and friends died young. There are things they do not reveal due to social conventions and concepts of female modesty. There are a few hints of sexuality, sexual problems, difficulties with pregnancy and general health.

Australia has a strong tradition of excellence in white women's writing because women maintained links with family and friends through this medium.[27] Women writers gained an internal satisfaction from making sense of lives so much harsher than the ones they had known in England. Most were not writing for publication: Georgiana McCrae wrote as a means of defining herself and to resolve marital unhappiness, while Molloy wrote letters thirty and forty pages long to James Mangles, a man she had never met, when left alone on a farm with only her children for company. Mangles, an amateur botanist, became the recipient of Georgiana's botanical specimens and of her innermost thoughts and feelings.

Middle-class or aristocratic women kept journals. Georgiana McCrae, imbued with the ideals of aristocratic Georgian England and France, kept two; one was private and contained material that she either burned herself or on her deathbed demanded her son destroy. The other was for general circulation and it proves Georgiana with her French education had a wicked wit. Just like Georgiana McCrae, the Bussells and Georgiana Molloy, many British middle-class women were horrified when they saw the windowless bush hut that would be their temporary home. Many lived under canvas while their slab huts or homesteads were built: Georgiana Molloy had her first baby lying on a board in a tent. The baby soon died. Women's letters and journals provide glimpses of the difficulties of housekeeping when housework was time-consuming, back-breaking drudgery. Wooden drum washing machines were invented in the 1860s but they frequently broke down and there was no-one to mend them. Many, including one belonging to Georgiana Molloy's neighbours, the Bussell family, proved so useless they were converted to butter churns. The laundry was thus a dreaded chore: clothes were boiled, rinsed, starched, mangled and ironed. It took an entire day in the week.

Women's letters home also contained pleas to send dark dress material with a small overall pattern which did not show dirt as easily as paler fabrics and so meant less washing and ironing. In the bush wives had to sew their own as well as their children's clothes and make men's shirts. The imported Singer sewing machine did

This photograph shows how laborious the washing and ironing of clothes and bedlinen was in colonial Australia. Whenever possible, middle class families left the laundry to be done by convict staff or paid domestics. Private collection.

not appear until the 1860s. At Elizabeth Farm the Macarthur women wore their clothes until they fell apart as Elizabeth Macarthur described to her son in England when scolding him for buying cheap fabrics. These, she insisted, cost just as much to ship to her as more expensive fabrics which would give more wear.

While many educated middle-class women kept diaries or wrote memoirs, what has been hard to find are well-written memoirs by working-class women, many of whom were illiterate. So the story of pioneer selector Annie Caldwell, who travelled hundreds of weary miles with seven children and no husband, is unique in Australian colonial literature.

Women went to the outback in covered wagons, like Annie Caldwell, or on open carts piled high with their personal belongings, which often were damaged on the journey. Watercolour by George Lacey in the National Library of Australia.

Her heart-warming story, told by her daughter Martha in this book, is the story of all those nameless women who trekked across dusty plains in wagons or open carts with babies in their laps. They lived and bore children in conditions that would horrify us.

Almost every small town in Australia has a memorial to a digger in a slouch hat. Where are the memorials to all those Ann Caldwells, the careworn selectors' wives, their faces lined and aged beyond their years? Bush women or selectors' wives worked for a better life for their children. They lived in primitive huts with dirt floors, built out of split logs, rammed earth, canvas, timber and tin. Photographs show their kitchens as rickety lean-to sheds partitioned off with a piece of sacking, their sinks old kerosene cans. All money earned from farming went back to develop the property or to feed and clothe the children. There was little money to spare for frivolities or new clothes.

In none of the European countries in which I have worked and studied could I find so many resourceful, determined and talented women who wrote long interesting letters or kept so many witty and informative diaries. Australian bush women were probably born no braver than the rest but the extraordinary hardships, isolation and adversity of bush life ensured they had to be resourceful and strong if they were to survive.

However, most people can only take so much stress. Some tend to internalise their distress, turn it in on themselves and become depressed or suicidal. Not all pioneer women coped well with the death of their children, with lack of companionship, abusive male partners, drought, bushfires and floods. While some like Mary McConnel and Georgiana Molloy were sustained by faith in God, others descended from a state of clinical depression into madness, filled their pockets full of stones and drowned themselves in creeks or waterholes, or hanged themselves.

Aboriginal Women

The stories of three Aboriginal women are included in this volume not as 'token' Aborigines but because Aborigines have in the past been the silent, unnoticed ghosts in our histories.

They are Walyer, the 'Amazon', who fiercely defended her territory, urging her people to resist and kill the invaders; Truganini, who believed safety for her people lay in 'conciliation' whereby the two groups agreed to live in separate areas; and Fanny Cochrane (later Cochrane Smith), who in spite of appalling treatment by Europeans as a child was a generous, hospitable and greatly loved Aboriginal woman, a singer who recorded her people's music on wax cylinders for posterity and donated land for a church, which today her descendants are attempting to buy back now it has been deconsecrated. Each chose a different path dependent on the choices and constraints that existed for them.

The first one hundred years of European settlement, as taught for generations, consisted of discovery, convict settlement, free settlement and exploration. For Aborigines it was a time of dispossession, 'racial cleansing' and cultural annihilation. If Aboriginal men suffered at the hands of the newcomers, Aboriginal women experienced the double burden suffered by women on the losing side of a war. As has happened in present-day Bosnia, Aboriginal women suffered rape, brutalisation and enslavement. Truganini and Fanny were confined at Wybalenna, a death camp where most of their race was wiped out, on Flinders Island.

Charles Rodius, a French-born artist transported for theft, portrayed Tooban, wife of the chief of the Shoalhaven tribe (NSW), as both intelligent and highly attractive. Lithograph dated 1834. Private collection.

These years were filled with brutality to women, both white and Aboriginal. Aboriginal women were used as sexual conveniences by Tasmanian sealers, ringers and stockmen on large stations. Their services, both sexual and domestic, were often traded to white men by their husbands in return for grog, sugar and tobacco.[28]

Frequently these women would have to supply the sexual needs of two or even three men who all mistreated them. Children from such unions were disclaimed by the fathers: rape or casual sex was a common occurrence in the outback. Many white men regarded it as one of the perks of the job to raid 'the blacks' camp' for women whenever they pleased.

The history of contact between the two races is bleak. However, it is occasionally relieved by acts of kindness and humanity by individuals on both sides. Aborigines sheltered and fed explorers, saving them from dying of thirst, and caring for them in their gunyahs, not for financial reward[29] but out of simple kindness. Mary McConnel's diary records her indignation when a black woman named Kitty whom she had befriended had her front teeth knocked out in a fight with her husband, and both she and Georgiana McCrae sheltered Aboriginal women whose husbands pursued them. Georgiana's portrait of the gentle, smiling Eliza, who came every year to visit her, is one of the warmest portrayals of an Aboriginal woman in colonial art, as is the portrait of skilled Aboriginal midwife Tooban by the French convict artist Charles Rodius.

The multi-racial Campbell family ran a highly successful business on Stradbroke Island. While the husbands were away fishing for dugong, the women were in charge of extracting oil, bottling and selling it. In Aboriginal lore dugong oil was renowned for its medicinal properties. Private collection.

A group of women married to members of the Campbell family ran their own dugong oil-refining business successfully. In the photo five women appear, one white, two Aboriginal and two who may be Kanakas (one wears the same dark bodice and white scarf as the Kanakas of Melanesian origin in the photograph on the canefields). All are well dressed, one has a ruffled blouse, another a bodice with a velvet insert and gilded buttons. It is obvious that care has been expended on the choice and maintenance of their clothing. Beside the women stand three whiskery men, arms akimbo, in working clothes—the Campbell brothers, who fished for and caught the dugong, which at the time were still eaten on the island. These women look more intelligent and are better dressed than their hirsute husbands, and were a vital part of this enterprise. They boiled down the dugong flesh and then bottled the oil, which was sold for high prices in all states of Australia and in Britain. It was used to treat joint pains, catarrh, bronchitis and a variety of other ailments. Oral tradition says that the Aboriginal women acted as 'medicine women' to other women on this then-remote island where there was no doctor. But as none could read or write there are no records of the business. I sense a remarkable story of courage, cooperation and achievement.

During Australia's first century little or nothing was recorded about Aboriginal women, who lacked birth certificates and any written history. All we are left with are fascinating snippets from old photographs like one owned by the Lutheran Church Archives of South Australia. In it, handsome Rosina Pingilina wears a flowered dress with a demure white bow at the neck and stands beside her husband Johannes Pingilina, an Aborigine converted to Christianity by the Lutheran missionaries at Bethesda in the middle of the nineteenth century. Unfortunately all that is known about Rosina and her husband is that they were valued assistants in the work of the Lutheran mission in northern Queensland.

28

Non-Anglo-Saxon Immigration

Few non-Anglo-Saxon women are recorded in Australia's first century. Racist sentiments were aired in state Parliaments at the mere thought of letting in non-Anglo-Saxons. Terms like 'vermin' and 'white trash' were bandied around and there were threats that women from cultures and religions other than white Anglo-Saxon Protestant would breed like rabbits and overrun the land.

A NSW Treasurer, Thomas Holt, of the Donaldson government, described Mediterranean peoples as 'worthless, idle and vicious'. Holt insisted, 'I could hardly imagine a greater evil could happen to this Colony than that of a large scale Immigration of the scum of the population of Spain'.[30] He was referring to the starving Spanish peasants, who, in 1858, were seeking admission to Australia with the help of their government.

The unfortunate Spanish peasants were sent to Hawaii, Havana and Florida instead. Holt remained a member of the Legislative Council until 1883 and blocked all attempts at immigration by other racial groups although he was charitable enough to Anglo-Saxons and a leading benefactor to the Royal Prince Alfred Hospital and the Salvation Army.

Thanks to Holt and racist politicians like him in every state in Australia, immigration of families from Spain and other southern European countries never eventuated. America chose to accept 'the huddled masses, yearning to be free' from non-Anglo-Saxon cultures. Australia did not. By the end of the century some single Italian and Spanish men without families were allowed onto the New South Wales and Queensland canefields to replace Kanaka labour. After demonstrating they were of good character over a period of years, they were allowed to send home for brides, some of whom they knew only from photographs.

Up to the end of World War II intense racial prejudice continued against anyone with a complexion darker than fair-skinned Anglo-Saxons. Only in 1960 did the *Bulletin* finally remove the racist legend *Australia for the White Man* from its masthead[31] at the request of editor Donald Horne.

From the earliest days Australia had allowed German migration, especially in South Australia and what would become Queensland. The rationale for this was that Germans were fair-skinned and blond and could easily become true Aussies. They were hardworking and Protestant which meant smaller families than immigrants from eastern Europe, Mediterranean or Asian countries who the Australian authorities feared would breed in large numbers. Men from certain areas could only enter as indentured labour without wives or children. Esther Johnston, of Spanish-Jewish extraction, is an exception but she arrived as a convicted felon. Esther was an outstanding woman, who made her mark on colonial Australia. But before I included her portrait and her story in my book *Pioneer Women, Pioneer Land*[32] few Australians had heard of her.

I was requested by several members of state education departments to include women of non-Anglo background in this volume because no such women's diaries and letters were included in *Pioneer Women, Pioneer Land*. They asked me to find memoirs, histories, diaries and letters from outstanding Afghan and Chinese women. Unfortunately this proved impossible as Chinese and Afghan men were specifically denied the right to import women during Australia's first century of British settlement. This policy caused brothels for single Chinese and Afghan men to proliferate in the nineteenth and early twentieth century. Ironically illiterate Japanese women (then one of the poorest countries in the East) were sometimes imported as prostitutes to lead miserable lives in these brothels.

The search for diaries of Afghan and Chinese women was like looking for the Holy Grail. Should any readers have any such material I would be delighted to see it.

German wives and daughters were almost the only non-Anglo-Saxon females allowed to migrate to colonial Australia. In 1846 George French Angas depicted the German settlement of Bethany, in the Barossa Valley, where women were not as isolated as in other areas because blocks of land were small and the Germanic style houses were close together. Lithograph, private collection.

Chinese Women

Single Chinese men were tolerated on the goldfields or as owners of market gardens around our cities, and they grew nearly half the vegetables in colonial Australia. They also worked as cabinet makers or on sea cucumber boiling stations like the one run by Mary Watson's husband. Some replaced Kanakas in the canefields. Under the racist White Australia policy, up until 1900 few Chinese women were allowed into Australia or any permanent basis for fear of a rise in the Chinese population – three to six months being the visiting period allotted to wives. Cartoons of the period in the *Bulletin*, which was enormously racist as was the *Queenslander*, show the Chinese as pigtailed villains, known as 'the Yellow Peril' at that time.

In the 1850s John Dunmore Lang told a Brisbane audience at a meeting on immigration:

> We don't want the *flat faces*, the *pug noses*, the *yellow complexions*, the *small feet* and the long pigtails multiplied a thousand-fold among us as they would very soon be if the Chinese ladies came to us as well as the gentlemen. It would require only a few years of unlimited Chinese immigration to swamp the whole European population of these colonies, to obliterate every trace of British progress and civilisation. [italics are mine]

The Reverend Dunmore Lang received roars of applause for this racist speech.[33]

However the Chinese did not want their women to come to Australia any more than Australians wanted them. Chinese men considered it was the job of women to stay home, care for elderly relatives and children, maintain the land and vegetable gardens, and honour the husband's ancestors until their husbands came home; otherwise whole villages or family names could be lost. They feared that an exodus of Chinese women to Australia or America would destroy the family structure of China. A few women were granted temporary entrance permits for one or two years and then left while, later, Chinese men like distinguished Sydney businessman Quong Tart married English wives.

Any Chinese women who did manage to slip through the net and enter Cooktown during the goldrushes for any length of time would have had enormous difficulty achieving anything other than bearing and raising children. With the exception of peasant women who worked in the fields, most Chinese women's feet were bound tightly in childhood so they remained only three inches long. The unfortunate women could only totter around in slippers, often in great pain. Jung Chang's *Wild Swans* describes the life of the author's grandmother and reveals that a Chinese women's most prized asset were her bound feet, known as 'three inch golden lilies'.[34] They suffered excruciating pain from broken bones and ingrowing toenails, which grew until they pierced the balls of the women's petite curved feet.

Most Chinese girls were married off at fifteen and sixteen with no say whatsoever in their choice of husband. Husbands had to have enough money to bribe Government officials to allow their wives to enter Australia on six-month permits only. An extension was only given if the wives were pregnant but they had to leave directly after the baby was born.

Jung Chang states it was regarded as virtuous for lower-class girls to be illiterate: it was the lower-class and hence impoverished Chinese who joined the rush to the Australian goldfields. There are indications that illiterate Japanese and Chinese 'comfort women' or Pacific Island women were supplied. These women had been smuggled into Australia as prostitutes by gang leaders under such hazardous conditions that many died. Theirs is truly a hidden story as nothing was recorded.

New South Wales was as fearful of Chinese overpopulation as Queensland or Western Australia. On 23 July 1857 Henry Parkes (who had previously voted against the importation of starving Spanish migrants) stated in an editorial in the *Empire*

> . . . the number [of Chinese] in the census papers is stated to be 1806 . . . fortunately . . . out of the whole number of Chinese stated, only six are females . . . Without women the Chinese cannot **germinate**, they cannot make a nation.[35]

Faced with such difficulties, some relatively wealthy Chinese married British or Australian women including highly successful and respected Sydney businessman, Mei Quong Tart, who on 30 August 1886 married Margaret Scarlett and together they raised a large and happy family.

Afghan Women

The majority of Afghan camel drivers (most of whom came from Pakistan or northern India rather than Afghanistan) were only allowed to enter Australia as bachelors. Obviously the politicians once again feared they too might 'germinate' and create a nation. From 1860 onwards, these unfortunate Afghans with their imported camels opened up much of the interior to 'White' Australia, but have received little credit. Many became itinerant pedlars hawking tinware, household goods, ribbons and laces and trinkets around outback properties and, desperately lonely, often stole or bought Aboriginal brides. Sometimes their marriage contracts would include financial support for the bride's mother, brothers and sisters. In Australia there are still many descendants of these marriages but I have met no authorities on the subject who possess diaries or letters from grandmothers or great-grandmothers. Presumably the wives were illiterate or circumstances were such that written material did not survive.

Strict Moslem religious observances also militated against any records about bartering or stealing brides. After the wedding the women never appeared again in public, which explains why only Afghan men and girls before puberty are seen in 'Afghan' photographs. Religious beliefs ensured Muslim women only went out of the house on two occasions—once to get married and the second time to be buried.

Early immigration laws prevented Afghan (or Indian) men bringing wives with them so some married white women. This photograph shows Mr. and Mrs. Dervish outside their home at Maree. Courtesy Book Dept., James R. Lawson, Sydney.

All Afghan wives were heavily veiled and were not allowed to be photographed as this would bring shame on their husband. Descendants of 'arranged' Afghan—Aboriginal marriages can be found in Queensland and in central and southern Australia. A few Afghan men married white women and these seem the only wives allowed to be photographed.

Kanaka Women

Kanaka women did not need entry permits: they came here as slave labour, sometimes in chains. Kanaka women were 'blackbirded' to Queensland ports—a nineteenth-century euphemism for kidnapping by force. The young men and very few women (because the plantation owners did not want to have to feed and support women and their children if they became pregnant) came from various Pacific Islands, brought here for money by unscrupulous sea captains. Young attractive girls who had been captured were often appropriated by the ship's captain and then sold into prostitution on arrival.

Bounty hunters were paid a fee for each able-bodied Pacific Islander they brought to Queensland. None of the unfortunate Kanakas could read or write. No-one cared enough to record their suffering and, once again, no diaries or letters remain to provide information.

Photographs of the period reveal haggard Kanaka women forced to work in the canefields alongside the men. These early photographs communicate a striking image of the past to us.

Kanaka women, snatched from their own Pacific Island cultures were forced to toil from dawn to dusk and lived on the cheapest of starchy foods. When they fell sick or gave birth they had no medical help and a large proportion died in their first year here. Surviving to middle age was an achievement for these unfortunate women, as it was for Aboriginal women.

Suffering is etched into the faces of these unfortunate women forced to hoe beneath the blazing sun at Yeppoon, Northern Queensland, in the 1890s. By then numbers of Kanaka women had increased: some were sold into prostitution in coastal brothels and most died young from overwork or in childbirth. Private collection.

In 1888 there were about 8,000 Kanaka labourers in Queensland; however fewer than 500 were women. By 1891 there were 9,362 Kanakas under contract on the canefields but the proportion of women remained roughly the same since the blackbirders received a higher bounty for able-bodied men from plantation owners. Nominally, Kanakas were 'indentured' for a period of three years; in practice they were used as slave labour for that time. Between 1892 and 1900 about 11,000 Pacific Islanders were imported. Some plantations gave them specially built accommodation and European food which made them constipated: others left them to fend for themselves and worked them nearly to death. Many beautiful Queensland homesteads complete with ballrooms, billiard rooms and avenues of jacarandas were built out of the enforced labour of the Kanakas.

Forced recruiting of Pacific Islanders ceased in 1904 when some 3,600 were repatriated. Kanaka men and women who had lived continuously in Australia for twenty years or who had achieved the distinction of owning a small plot of land were allowed to stay. Many of the women managed to learn a little English. Once Queensland Government legislation banning them from working in private households was relaxed, those who remained were allowed to become nannies and house servants to Queensland families of planters. Brief descriptions of them appear in Queensland memoirs of the period but there is as yet no full biography of a Kanaka woman. However, a Solomon Islander, Noel Fatnowna devotes a chapter to his mother's story in his book *Fragments of a Lost Heritage*.[36] devotes a chapter to his book. Background to the blackbirding period is provided by Nancy Cato in her novel *Brown Sugar*,[37] and *Pastures of the Blue Crane* by Hesba Brinsmead.

Twenty Heroic Women

The women whose stories I have related are not placed in order of merit. All are truly remarkable. Nine of these inspiring women were included in my book *Pioneer Women, Pioneer Land*.[47] Eight years later, I have updated most of their histories in the light of new research or information from descendants, for which I am most grateful.

Wherever possible I have used the women's diaries, memoirs or letters: their words are far more important than my own and I want the readers to feel that these women are talking directly to them. Ann Caldwell's remarkable story has never been published in book form and her name is unknown to most historians or to the general public. However all Australians should know the names of Ann Caldwell and other outstanding women such as Lucy Osburn, Walyer, Mary Penfold, Mary McConnel and Fanny Cochrane Smith as well as those of Mary Reibey, Caroline Chisholm and Elizabeth Macarthur.

Australians today have benefited from the contributions of these women, who worked hard to establish civilisation in a harsh, male-dominated land, and I hope that reading about them will help present-day Australian women to achieve their own goals and ambitions.

---

[1] Friend, Robyn. *We who are not here: Aboriginal People of the Huon and Channel Today*. The Huon Municipal Association, Tasmania, 1992.

[2] Hughes, Robert. *The Fatal Shore*. Collins, Harvill, London, 1987.

[3] Dixson, Miriam. *The Real Matilda. Women and Identity in Australia 1788 to the Present*. Penguin Books, Ringwood, revised edition 1984, chapter V, The Irish.

[4] Summers, A. *Damned Whores and God's Police*. Penguin Books, Ringwood, Victoria, 1975, reprinted 1994.

[5] Summers, A. *Op cit*.

[6] Summers A. *Op cit*.

[7] For comparable experiences in Canada read the journals of Susannah Moody, a nineteenth-

century emigrant from Britain whose outstandingly well-written diaries have been published in several editions. Cited in Robinson, Jane: *Wayward Women: A Guide to Women Travellers.* Oxford University Press, London, 1990.

[8] Australia's alcoholic legacy. See Young Dr. R. McD. *Alcohol Related Expectancies and the Treatment of Problem Drinking.* Unpublished Ph.D. Thesis, University of Queenland, 1994 (p. 14) cites number of alcoholic drinks consumed by heavy drinking Australian males as *6–12 drinks per day on each drinking day although some only drink at weekends.* National Campaign Against Drug Abuse survey 1993, identifies heavy or 'binge' drinkers as 27% of Australian males.

[9] A. Summers. *Op cit.*

[10] Hollis, Patricia. Chapter on 'Separate Spheres' in *Women in Public; 1850–1900.* Allan and Unwin, Sydney, 1979, and Allan, Margaret. Women's Separate Sphere. Distance Education Centre, University of South Australia. n.d.

[11] Bible. St Paul. *Letter to the Ephesians*, verse 6. Cited frequently by Gisborne and other nineteenth-century male writers to reinforce male dominance over wives. See also 1 Corinthians.

[12] Cited in Allan, Margaret. *Op cit.*

[13] Only one Turner drawing of a nude (probably made at Petworth), which managed to escape Ruskin's bonfire when he became executor of Turner's will, is now in the Department of Prints and Drawings, British Museum.

[14] Ruskin, John. *Sesame and Lillies.* London, 1865. For details of Ruskin's obsession with younger women and subsequent attacks of mental illness in 1871, 1878 and 1881, see Whelchel, Harriet. ed. *John Ruskin and the Victorian Eye.* Harry N. Abrahams, New York, 1993. See also Gisborne, T. *An Enquiry into the Duties of the Female Sex.* Cadell, London, 1797.

[15] Ellis, Sara. *The Daughters of England.* London, 1841. Cited in Allan, Margaret. *Op cit.*

[16] Head shaving and iron collars used as punishments for 'difficult' female convicts only ceased at the Hobart Female Factory when Mrs Mary Hutchinson became Matron in the 1830s. Cited by Dixson, Miriam. *Op. cit.* p.152.

[17] Crooke, Robert. *The Convict.* Unpublished MS, written in 1886 by a former Van Diemen's Land convict chaplain, cited in Dixson, Miriam, *op. cit.* Described how married men were in many cases improperly intimate with their female servants.

[18] *Sydney Morning Herald.* 10 June 1891. Cited in Dixson, Miriam. *Op. cit.*

[19] Flower, Cedric. *Duck and Cabbage Tree.* Angus and Robertson, Sydney, 1967.

[20] Shorter, E. *A History of Women's Bodies.* Allen, Lane, London, 1982 and 1983.

[21] Gandivia, B. *Tears Often Shed. Child Health and Welfare in Australia from 1788.* Charter Books, Sydney 1977.

[22] Grimshaw, P., Quartly, M., et al. *Creating a Nation.* Chapter on Birthplaces. McPhee Gribble, Melbourne, 1994.

[23] Collins, David, (ed. B. Fletcher). *An Account of the English Colony in New South Wales.* Reprinted from the original First Fleet Journal by Reed Books, Sydney, 1975.

[24] Pownall, Eve. *Australian Pioneer Women.* Currey O'Neil, Melbourne, n.d.

[25] *Another Two Years at Sea by a Lady* is based on the journal of Mary Ann Friend (of which the Western Australian section is quoted in full in de Vries-Evans, *Pioneer Women, Pioneer Land.* Angus and Robertson, 1987). Nineteenth-century literature has many travel books published anonymously by 'A Lady' who feared to upset male members of her family by doing something as masculine as publishing a book.

[26] No mention of Martha Brownrigg in *Australian Dictionary of Biography* but Mary Morton Allport receives three lines of her husband's full-page entry in Volume One.

[27] Clark, Patricia and Spender, Dale. *Life Lines, Australian women's letters and diaries 1788–1840.* Allen and Unwin, Sydney, 1992. Heney, Helen. *Dear Fanny.* ANU Press, Canberra, 1985.

[28] McGrath, Ann. *Women, Class and History* (ed. Elizabeth Windschuttle). Chapter 10. *Aboriginal Workers—Spinifex Fairies.* Fontana, Sydney, 1980.

[29] Old Nan's bravery was recorded by author Ernestine Hill in her book *The Territory*, Angus and Robertson, Sydney, 1951.

[30] I am indebted to archaeologist Gillian Alfredson who found this quote from *Votes and Proceedings of the Legislative Assembly of New South Wales*, 1855, which contains the proposal from the Spanish Consulate dated 19 July, 1855, and the evidence of Thomas Holt to the Select Committee chaired by the Colonial Treasurer, Charles Cowper, on 6 November 1855 from which this statement is taken.

[31] The removal of the racist slogan on the *Bulletin*'s masthead as late as 1960 was cited by an Australian politician of Italian background, Franca Arena, in a program on multiculturalism on the ABC in 1994.

[32] De Vries-Evans, Susanna. *Pioneer Women, Pioneer Land*. Angus and Robertson, Sydney, 1987.

[33] Cited on page 149 of Rolls, Eric. *Sojourners: the epic story of China's Centuries of Relationship with Australia*. University of Queensland Press, Brisbane, 1992.

[34] Chang, Jung. *Wild Swans*. Harper Collins, London, 1991.

[35] Rolls, Eric. *Op cit.* p.148.

[36] Fatnowna, Noel. *Fragments of a Lost Heritage*. Angus and Robertson, Sydney, 1962, 1989.

[37] Cato, Nancy. *Brown Sugar*. William Heinemann, London, 1974. Brinsmead, Hesba. *Pastures of the Blue Crane*. Oxford University Press, Oxford, 1972.

[38] De Vries-Evans, S. *Pioneer Women, Pioneer Land*. Angus and Robertson, Sydney, 1987.

CHAPTER 1

Mary Reibey
(1777–1855)

SYDNEY'S FIRST FEMALE TYCOON

Molly Haydock, better known by her married name of Mary Reibey, stole a pedigree horse, was transported to Sydney and there went from rags to riches. Her international fame is largely due to Catherine Gaskin's bodice-ripping romance *Sarah Dane*, published in 1955, which many readers incorrectly believed was the true story of Mary's life.

Catherine Gaskin, an Australian-born popular novelist, based her fictitious account of a tenacious, intelligent and spirited girl confronting a new life in a convict colony on the few facts that were known about the life of Mary Reibey in the 1950s.

Her heroine Sarah was the orphaned daughter of an alcoholic baronet's grandson and a beautiful wayward actress. She was seduced by a lecherous aristocrat and transported for stealing money which should by rights have been hers. Sarah was fortunate to escape a nightmare voyage in the ship's hold with lice-ridden, brawling convicts by becoming a nursemaid to some children whose mother was bed-ridden. This led to a shipboard romance and a marriage proposal by Gaskin's hero, the darkly handsome Lieutenant Andrew Maclay.

Illustrations in the *Reader's Digest* edition of *Sarah Dane* showed Sarah arriving in Sydney as a blue-eyed, long-legged beauty, in a clinging skirt, her blonde hair bound with a blue ribbon. In reality Mary was petite with deep brown eyes, and on arrival in Sydney her dark hair was growing, having previously been cropped as short as any boy's; Mary wore men's trousers rather than a skirt and had not bathed for months. Unlike the sexually experienced Sarah Dane, Mary did not have a broken romance in England with a parson's son, and probably wore boy's clothes to protect herself against sexual assault. Neither did she steal money—she stole an expensive bay mare, a childish prank that went sadly wrong.

Now, four decades after *Sarah Dane*, the discovery of the Mary Reibey letters in England has proved that Mary's life was totally different, but just as fascinating, as that of Sarah Dane. The discovery by the Australian historian Nance Irvine of many of Mary's letters to her aunt and her cousin David Hope[1] in an English baronet's country house helped to unravel the complicated story of Mary's transportation to Sydney in 1792.

Mary's parents had died shortly after she was born. She was reared by an elderly nanny (to whom she later sent money on a regular basis) and by her maternal grandmother. Her father's family were middle class, staunch Catholics and landowners. Mary's maternal grandmother, Mrs Law, a Quaker, had given her a good education at Blackburn Grammar School, but religious differences had brought estrangement between Mary's mother, Jane Law, and her father's people, the Haydocks.

Mary was strong-willed and headstrong. In that respect Catherine Gaskin's character Sarah Dane, with her determination, tenacity and occasional touch of temper did resemble Mary Reibey.

Mary loved her grandmother, who unfortunately died just as she was about to enter her teens. Lack of love and security turned an intelligent girl and a good student into a rebellious tomboy. None of her Catholic relatives fancied dealing with the teenage problems of a difficult girl brought up in a different religion.

For lack of a guardian, Mary was consigned to a bleak Dickensian orphanage or School of Female Industry. Public welfare institutions in the Georgian and Victorian period treated the inmates harshly, fed them on stale bread, porridge and gristly meat, as described so vividly by Charles Dickens in *Oliver Twist*. Wherever possible the orphans were sent out to earn money as day labour. It was likely that Mary was put into domestic service.

Only one of her aunts, Mrs Penelope Hope (nee Law), cared about Mary. But Mary's aunt could not legally adopt her; it was necessary for her husband to offer the financial guarantees necessary for guardianship and he would not do so.

Mary had been well grounded in writing and mathematics but unfortunately no diary or letters from this critical period of her life have come to light. In June 1791 she ran away from the orphanage and adopted the name and clothing of James Burrow, a recently deceased boy she had known from the orphanage. Lacking money, she would have had to sleep in doorways, barns and hedgerows.

In the eyes of the law Mary was just another teenage runaway living rough. With her slim figure disguised in male clothing and calling herself James Burrow, Mary stole an expensive bay thoroughbred mare from a field near Chester. Thoroughbred horses were her passion and for the rest of her life she would delight in owning, driving and riding them. In August 1791, two months after leaving the orphanage she rode the horse to the neighbouring town of Salford and offered it for sale, claiming it was her uncle's. Her extreme youth made the buyers suspicious that she could be entrusted with such a valuable animal, so they summoned the constables. On suspicion of stealing the horse she was arrested and put in jail. The plucky thirteen-year-old girl with her undeveloped boyish figure and cropped dark hair continued to insist for months that she was James Burrow, which probably protected her from the dangers of rape and sexual harassment in the brutal conditions of Stafford County Gaol, where male and female prisoners were not separated from each other and females were routinely abused.

Mary's trial and subsequent appeal took almost two years out of her life. The days must have dragged by for the young free-spirited girl, masquerading as a boy.

Before Mary appeared in court she had to submit to a delousing by her gaolers. When her cap, trousers and loose peasant smock were removed, her disguise was blown once and for all.

In July 1791 Mary was found guilty, sentenced to hang and led from the dock back to the stinking goal, awaiting death on the gallows. There, lonely and friendless, she 'celebrated' her fourteenth birthday.

Had a responsible male member of Mary's family been willing to act as her guarantor and guardian until she attained her majority, she would have walked out of the court free and gone on to live a normal middle-class life. But probably not wanting a gaolbird in a 'respectable' family not one single male relative came forward to help her. This seems to have been Mary's problem, that after the death of her grandmother, no-one cared about her. Only the threat of hanging made independent-minded Mary write to wealthy family members for help. And only then was an appeal lodged by Blackburn residents including her uncle, Adam Hope, married to a sister of her mother, to save her from the gallows and asking that she should be transported instead of being hanged. Reticent as ever, Mary wrote nothing down about her own feelings even in later life.

The appeal to the court described her as 'a poor helpless orphan prevailed upon by another girl to leave her situation in the month of June last [1791] drawn in by the wicked contrivance of some evil-minded person'.

The judge was impressed by the fact that Mary's parents were educated, had owned farming land and that Mary could read and write (a privilege enjoyed by less than half the population prior to the introduction of compulsory and free education).

From gaol Mary learned that due to her relative's appeal her death sentence had been commuted to transportation for seven years. Today she would have been put on probation or sent to a children's home and given counselling. Mary's theft of a pedigree horse in the eighteenth century is equivalent to a 'street kid' stealing a Mercedes, but whereas today it would be unthinkable for any child convicted of theft to be sentenced to be hanged, in the lawless eighteenth century, horse-stealing was punishable by death.

By the time the *Royal Admiral* sailed for the Antipodes with its cargo of human misery, Mary had just turned fifteen.

Reports by Captain Bond of the *Royal Admiral* also reveal that Mary, along with the other eighty-seven female convicts, spent the entire voyage in the overcrowded hold of the ship, which was about the size of a large ferry, among the stench of unwashed bodies, rancid food and human excreta. Along with its cargo of brawling human beings, the hold was also infested with rats and cockroaches.

To guard her virginity amid scenes of depravity, Mary kept her hair cropped short and wore the same trousers and smock she had worn in prison.

Mary's harrowing voyage meant she crossed the equator in the sweltering heat of the hold. There, among murderers, pickpockets and whores, she witnessed birth, lovemaking, fist-fights, and the deaths of some convicts. Such events must have speeded the transition of rebellious tomboy into strong-minded young woman, determined to survive, come what may, in a new land.

By the time she arrived at Sydney, Mary had seen more of life than most women double her age in England. Eighty-eight convicts were still sick when the ship docked at Sydney and disembarking the female prisoners took a long time.

From the deck of the ship Mary penned a letter to her aunt Penelope in England. It may have been that aunt, filled with concern, or more probably guilt, who had given Mary two guineas before her deportation (the purchasing power of two guineas would be approximately one thousand dollars today). Mary had managed to guard the money from the many thieves and pickpockets during the entire voyage.

Mary's first Australian letter to her aunt is the most poignant of all her correspondence, although she may have posted an earlier letter from Rio. Headed *Bottany* (sic) *Bay*, the letter reveals that no-one had explained to Mary that because Botany Bay lacked adequate water, the convicts had been shipped to Port Jackson, as Sydney Harbour was then known. Mary wrote her letter on the deck of the convict ship on a warm spring day in October 1792. From there she gazed across Port Jackson at unfamiliar trees, the rustic bridge across the Tank Stream which led down to smelly mudflats around the harbour and at bark-roofed slab huts straggling along the main thoroughfare named George Street.

This letter shows that she had decided to put a brave face on her deportation. Her writing was clear and strong with the occasional spelling mistake and some hasty ink blots on the paper.

> My dear aunt
> We arrived on the 7th [October 1792] and hope it will answer better than we expected for I write this on board of [the] ship but it looks a pleasant place enough. We shall have a four pair of trousers to make a week and we shall have a pound of rice a week and four pound of meat besides greens and other vegetables. The[y] tell me I am for life which the Governor told me was but seven years which grieves me very much to think of but I will watch every opportunity to get away in too [sic] or three years. But I will make myself as happy as I can in my present and unhappy situation. I will give you further satisfaction when I get there and is [sic]

settled. I am well and hearty as ever I was in my life. I desire you will answer me by some ship that is coming and lett [sic] me know how the children is and all inquireing [sic] friends.

At that stage the authorities must have arrived to claim the convict women, most of whom were to go upriver by boat to the infamous Female Factory at Parramatta. Mary finishes, 'I must conclude because we are in a hurry to go ashore'. She signed off with a wry sense of humour as, 'Your undutifull niece, Mary Haydock'. Later she added a sad little postscript describing how a Mr Scott took her two guineas from her under the pretext that he could procure her freedom. This confidence trick taught Mary a lesson. It was probably the last time that any man pulled the wool over her eyes concerning money.

Mary's first letter was found at Cadhay, ancestral home of her descendant Sir Peveril William-Powlett. It was bought by a private collector for $40,000 at a Sotheby's auction in 1987. Sotheby's had a facsimile printed in their catalogue.

When Mary wrote that letter to her aunt she had not yet met her future husband, Thomas Reibey. His ship was also in the harbour at the time and he may well have spotted Mary already. She could have met him later that day, but she never recorded their first meeting in writing. Tour guides, romantic novelists and the first volume of *Australian Dictionary of Biography* are all wrong. Now we know Mary did *not* meet her husband aboard the convict ship.

Tom Reibey, or Raby as he often wrote his name, was employed as first mate by the powerful and wealthy East India Company, who had also chartered Mary's convict transport the *Royal Admiral* to the British government. Records of the East India Company show that Tom arrived in Sydney the day before Mary, aboard the company's store ship *Britannia*.

In later life Mary Reibey was considerably embarrassed by the fact she had been transported for what was, in effect, a premeditated theft. To protect her children and grandchildren, she insisted she had been a madcap farmer's daughter who went for a joyride on a neighbour's horse, returned it sweating badly and got herself arrested by mistake.

Mary's ability to read and write (most other female convicts who could only sign their names with a cross) and her educated speech had been duly noted by the authorities. She could do complicated arithmetic, write letters and answer for herself so she escaped the mind-numbing sewing and laundry of uniforms at the Female Factory, a grim institution at Parramatta, which combined the role of not-so-sheltered workshop, brothel for the officers and a marriage market. Its bedraggled, brawling, swearing, alcoholic inmates had a fearful reputation in Sydney. Instead of going to the Female Factory, Mary was assigned to Lieutenant-Governor Major Francis Grose as nursemaid–cum–housekeeper. Doubtless Mrs Grose was happy to have the educated Miss Haydock in her employ.

Her future husband, Tom Reibey, may have been allowed to visit her at Major Grose's residence. It is known that during Mary's first two years in the colony Tom Reibey was granted permission to marry her. The young couple (he was twenty-five while she was seventeen) married at the first St Philip's Church, a simple building with mud brick walls lined with wood, which was later replaced by a stone church with a dome.

Their wedding was on a spring morning in September 1794 and, like the fictional Sarah Dane, Mary may have worn a long white dress and carried a posy of bush flowers. How happy she must have been after so many years of rejection to have finally found someone she could trust and love. Their marriage was a perfect partnership: they supported each other in their endeavours until Tom's premature death at 42 years in 1811.

It is significant that none of Tom Reibey's relatives came from India to act as

Detail from a lithographed panorama of Sydney made by Major James Taylor. The stone house in the foreground is that of Major Grose where Mary worked as a nursemaid. Courtesy Tim McCormick Rare Books and Paintings, Sydney.

witness at the wedding. It is now believed that Tom's mother was Indian. His father, an educated Englishman in the employ of the East India Company, had abandoned Tom's mother, in favour of marriage to a British girl with a handsome dowry and a place in the class-conscious British community. A relationship with an Indian mistress was quite common with the bachelors in the East India Company and many paid off their mistresses and then married English girls with dowries. This could explain why Mary made no effort to seek out anyone from the Reibey family when she eventually took her children to see her own relatives. To the eighteenth-century colonial mind, being of mixed race was as shameful as being an emancipist or former convict. Possibly these secrets formed a bond between this young couple who were determined to succeed in the new colony.

After their marriage Tom Reibey applied for a free settler's grant of land along the Hawkesbury River. But he was a better sailor than farmer. Clearing, ploughing and sowing land along the Hawkesbury with its floods and droughts soon palled. Subsequently Tom Reibey acquired a second land grant in Sydney and began transporting Hawkesbury grain and cedar to Sydney by water, while Mary ran their farm. They bought up leases from farmers who had failed and increased their landholdings. The hardworking Reibeys gave assistance to other settlers during the great Hawkesbury floods of 1806 and Tom's knowledge of boats helped him to save the lives of several people.

Their first-born son was called by his full name of Thomas to distinguish him from his father. Their second son was named James. The four of them returned to Sydney where Mary opened a general store in The Rocks area. Stocking the store would have been easy due to Tom's contacts with the East India Company.

At that time The Rocks was far different from the present-day 'picturesque' sanitised tourist area. It was Sydney's first commercial and working-class residential district, filled with taverns, sly grog shops, gambling dens and brothels, its seamy waterfront lined with warehouses and counting houses.

In Governor Macquarie's Sydney, with a population of just over 10,000 people, more than 100 grog licences were issued annually by the government, while the illegal grog shops advertised their presence by a striped red and white pole placed discreetly outside. Every night men flocked to these areas for rum and women. For many ex-convicts and convicts, living without their families, rum was the only diversion. The clientele of the pubs was swelled by the wealthy crews from the whaling ships, who arrived with several months' wages in their pockets to spend.

Seafarers from all over the Pacific had heard of the notorious Rocks with its tangle of hilly lanes and steps and tumbledown cottages. The noise of revelry and snatches of drunken song was supposed to be heard at sea for a mile on a calm night. There were others who said that the smell from its insanitary back-street hovels carried nearly as far!

There was no running water in George Street or at The Rocks. Horse-drawn watercarts supplied water to the whole area, unless the householder was lucky enough to own a well in his or her yard.

Tom soon went back to sea, leaving capable, hard-working Mary in charge of their thriving store. At sea he could easily make money, using years of experience with the East India Company, dealing in commodities such as timber, wheat and sealskins. Profits of as much as five hundred per cent on money invested could be made if the ship owner or charterer was as lucky or as smart as Tom Reibey. From then Tom was frequently away from his wife and children, busy sealing, carrying coal and timber to Newcastle and, after he built his own ship, trading with Fiji and other South Pacific islands.[2]

At first Mary accompanied her husband on the shorter trading trips. But as more children arrived, she stayed at home and concentrated on bringing up the children and looking after their business affairs and doing the accounts.

Eventually the Reibeys were able to move out of their first small house and general store in George Street, which they probably let out, and move into much larger premises in what would later be named Macquarie Place. The Reibeys named the large stone house with its adjacent grainstores Entally House, after a mansion Tom had much admired in India. The business grew and took on Edward Wills, who soon became Tom's business partner.

Nine years after their marriage Mary and Tom had five children and were asset-rich. Mary had prodigious energy and taught the younger children to read and write and had some assigned convict women to help with the household chores.

The young couple ploughed their money back into investments to secure their children's future. The value of their land on the Hawkesbury and in Sydney had greatly increased and their ships carried goods as far as China and India. In Tom's frequent absences on voyages Mary did the accounts, managed the store and hired additional staff. The business thrived as more and more whaling and sealing ships came to Sydney to buy their provisions. Mary's workload increased even further. To help her with their growing family of lively boys and girls, Thomas brought back a Fijian girl named Fee-Foo, who acted as nursemaid to the children while Mary ran their business enterprises. They imported, warehoused and then sold everything from tea, sugar, rice and coffee to cashmere shawls, velvet waistcoats, ivory tea-chests, china dinner sets, calico by the roll, ready-made shirts and even chamber pots.

By 1810 Mary and Tom had been happily married for sixteen years. She was now thirty-three and one of the busiest and most prosperous women in the colony, known for her thrifty ways and her business acumen. She had great ability to spot a sound business prospect and then negotiate a bargain as capably as any man.

In the intervening years Sydney had changed for the better. The bark-roofed slab huts that had once housed convicts were now white-painted cottages with flowers outside them and parrots hanging in cages from hooks by the doors. *Entally House* in Macquarie Place with its handsome stone frontage and triangular pediment, was a house they could both be proud of. Mary must have felt that she had redeemed her past and that years of happiness and prosperity awaited the pair of them.

In October Tom Reibey returned from India with an undulant fever he had picked up following a severe bout of sunstroke. He failed to rid himself of the fever and six months later, in May 1811, he died.

Mary was left a widow with commercial loans outstanding to wharf and warehouse

Mary Reibey's home and general store in George Street (facing today's Regent Hotel) are on the left of this watercolour by S.T. Gill, painted in 1860. Private collection, courtesy Christies, London.

42

owner Robert Campbell. She had to administer three ships, several farms, some shops, a hotel, a general store and warehouse. And there were seven children to support. Throughout the funeral preparations Mary comforted the bewildered children and under enormous stress she remained dignified and capable.

'Bad news never comes singly' is an old English proverb that Mary would have known. Tom's partner Edward Wills, the only man she could depend on for sound commercial advice, died only a month after Mary's much-loved husband.

Their eldest son, young Thomas, was fifteen. He had previously made trading voyages with his father and dreamed of becoming a ship's captain, as did their second son, James. Mary still had to educate bookish eleven-year-old George, ten-year-old Celia, quiet demure Eliza, lively and beautiful Jane Penelope and baby Elizabeth Anne.

With a large family clamouring for her attention and numerous business problems to solve there was little time for tears. Mary simply carried on doing what she was good at—managing the family business—until her sons Thomas and James left school and were able to run the shipping and carry on trading in the Pacific.

After Governor Macquarie arrived in Sydney, life became easier for former convicts, or emancipists as they were known. Both Mary Reibey and Esther Johnston were invited to Government House, an honour previously denied to anyone with the 'convict taint'. However, even then most free settlers and ex-Army officers refused to meet socially with former convicts, although they were prepared to do business with them provided there was money to be made.

Governor and Mrs Macquarie recognised that Mary Reibey had made valuable contributions to the economy of New South Wales. In 1812 Mary applied for her first land grant and was given 812 acres of fertile land near that of John and Elizabeth Macarthur at Camden. Mary moved her family from their combined home and business premises at Macquarie Place back to smaller premises at 12 George Street. Entally House with its offices and warehousing facilities was leased to the Bank of New South Wales (now Westpac) in whose foundation Mary played a part and in which she would later become a major shareholder. It was a wise decision on her part: this move into smaller premises cost less in maintenance and was easier for a woman on her own to run, and freed up capital to pay off outstanding loans.

But as her beautiful, dark-eyed daughters grew older Mary realised that her social ostracism would create severe problems for her daughters in spite of her wealth. The limited higher education that was available in Sydney was restricted to boys. There were far too many depraved drunken men searching for wives and mistresses for Mary's taste. She wished for something better for her daughters and she wanted them to have everything she had been denied—piano, dancing and deportment lessons—all the graces of young ladies. She even had their portraits painted. Watercolour miniatures on ivory show Mary's daughters as sloe-eyed beauties with swanlike necks and magnolia complexions. These miniatures, possibly by Richard Reade, suggest the daughters with their striking resemblance to each other may have taken after mother in her younger days but we have no picture of Mary at that time.

She made certain the two eldest boys went to England to finish their education before entering the business world. Girls from 'good' families could then do little that was not chaperoned. They were kept out of sight in the schoolroom until they 'came out' at seventeen or eighteen, at a summer ball at Government House, at which they wore white dresses, smiled demurely and waltzed with young men among whom a suitable marriage partner for life might appear.

Marriage was an economic contract among the wealthy in Britain as well as in the colonies. Loving parents took account of the feelings of their daughters but others did not. Good dowries and marriage contracts played an important part in choice of wives by middle-class men. The Reibey girls had large dowries but lacked social acceptability among the 'Exclusives' or 'Pure Merinos' who ran the colony. Most governors' wives, other than Mrs Macquarie, would not invite the likes of Mary Reibey, ex-convict, and her daughters over the threshold of Government House, however wealthy they had become.

To understand the hostile climate in which Mary lived and worked, it is necessary to know that in colonial Sydney the 'convict taint' haunted the children of even the most successful emancipists. It did not abate for decades and it was only in the second half of the twentieth century that it became socially acceptable if not desirable to have convict forebears. Mary's letters are mute on this subject. Reticent as ever, she swallowed her pride and continued working to achieve security and a good future for her children.

Comparison between the lives of Mary Reibey and Sarah Cox (Wentworth) is interesting. Both of these intelligent, hardworking women faced similar problems caused by the 'convict taint' as their attractive daughters grew to womanhood. They wanted them to find husbands among the more educated settlers rather than among former convicts, but for years the phrase 'damned convict whore' would haunt Sarah Cox, who was born in Sydney in 1805 to convicted blacksmith Francis Cox.

Francis Cox had left a wife and children behind in England, and together with Fanny Morton, his mistress, had been transported for life. Sarah, their daughter, was intelligent, good at figures and quick to learn, but she was a working-class girl expected to marry an uneducated working man from her own class. Strong-minded Sarah—neat, clean and pretty—had other ideas. She left the grime of the blacksmith's shop and became a milliner's apprentice, sitting in a workroom making hats for the wealthy ladies of Sydney. But while Mary was educated enough to read and do accounts, Sarah, according to her biographer Carol Liston, 'was barely literate'.[3]

After a brief engagement to a ship's captain, Sarah formed a relationship with her lawyer, William Charles Wentworth, son of Dr D'Arcy Wentworth, one of the colony's leading medical men. William Wentworth had returned from London, where he had shepherded the constitution through the British Parliament, as a hero and started the *Australian* newspaper in Sydney in 1824.

Ironically William Wentworth had been ignorant of his own convict roots until he was made forcibly aware of them by an attack in the House of Commons in 1819, shortly before he took up with Sarah Cox. In front of all the members of the British House of Commons he learned from a political opponent that his father had been transported for highway robbery and that he was called the 'son of an Irish highwayman by a convict whore'. He reacted to the shock and shame of learning he had convict ancestry by going on a series of drunken sprees and behaving outrageously before his peers.

The affair Sarah Cox had with Wentworth was passionate but his intentions, at that time, certainly did not include marriage. Sarah was deemed unmarriageable in the eyes of 'polite' society—uneducated, without a dowry, with the dubious social distinction of being the daughter of a convict woman, 'living in sin' with another convict. Wentworth had defended Sarah in a breach-of-promise suit against the sea captain who had refused to marry her.

Wentworth's contribution to Sarah's well-being was to make her pregnant and move her from her father's home in Sydney to a love nest in Petersham, where she gave birth to Thomasine. Wentworth acknowledged his paternity on Thomasine's birth certificate, but Sarah's boisterous, boozy lover had a law degree from an English university and was expected to make a 'good' marriage. Wentworth became a skilful barrister, a brilliant public speaker and politician and, on far too many occasions, an aggressive, abusive, brawling drunk.

In 1827 Wentworth bought 105 acres (42 hectares) at Vaucluse including a 'genteel dwelling house of eight rooms, stables, detached kitchen, dairy, gardens and orchards' where he installed Sarah and their children. It says much for Sarah's skills in managing a difficult and sometimes disturbed personality that she was able

to persuade Wentworth to move her to *Vaucluse House*, where she and her children lived, totally apart from his working life and public appearances, and Sydney society's scorn as 'the convict whore'.

In October 1829, William Wentworth defied Sydney society and married Sarah 'the damned whore', at the church where Mary Haydock had married Tom Reibey—St Philip's. Sarah's calm in the face of her husband's drunken rages and public outbursts, her native shrewdness, practical commonsense and tactful handling of this difficult man had finally convinced him to marry her and legitimise their two children and a third as yet unborn. Wentworth became the public champion of the convict classes and favoured the creation of a 'bunyip aristocracy' to which emancipists could be admitted. The Wentworths became exceedingly rich because gold in large quantities was found on one of Wentworth's pastoral leases.

Wentworth loved Sarah in his fashion but was unfaithful to her on many occasions. In spite of the ring on her finger, Sarah would always occupy an invidious position in the snobbish, cliquey colony which despised anyone with the 'convict taint'.

For Sarah, marriage was the beginning rather than the end of her social problems. Even as the lady of well-run, handsome Vaucluse House, polite Sydney society steadfastly refused to invite Mrs Sarah Wentworth or her ten children to functions. Sarah responded by limiting invitations to members of her own family. She realised there would be no young men of good family beating a path to her door to marry her beautiful but headstrong daughters, despite all their accomplishments in music, dancing, painting, needlework, some French.

In Sydney Town, Sarah was unable even to chaperone her own daughters at social events because she was not officially invited to them. She was also excluded from Wentworth's political functions as both wife and hostess, because, to the

Government House 'set' (once Governor Macquarie had left), those 'damned convict whores' did not exist.

In 1853, the refusal of snobbish Sydney society to mix socially or marry with emancipists would eventually persuade Sarah to move to England. Sarah, who in her own quiet way was a remarkable and determined woman, sailed to Britain in charge of her 20-year-old son, the six youngest children and their governess. Wentworth joined them all fifteen months later. They and their stunning daughters could now mix with the offspring of their social peers amongst whom 'suitable' husbands would be found and, in turn, their sons would receive a broader education at Oxford or Cambridge.

Sarah Cox's biographer, historian Carol Liston, has suggested that the tragedy of Wentworth's marriage to Sarah was the couple's self-enforced lengthy separation from their homeland for the sake of their children. This constant moving around England and Europe destabilised a family already predisposed to arguments and quarrels.

The psychological effects on the Wentworth children of enforced isolation from the country of their birth was profound. Of their six daughters, only Thomasine and Fanny had stable marriages. One son had a marriage that was never consummated and lived a life clouded by racing debts and illegitimate children. One daughter, Diddy, remained unmarried while three other daughters, as beautiful as they were headstrong, married a year after their father's death and most of their marriages failed sensationally.

From all contemporary accounts, Wentworth suffered from severe and temperamental changes of mood. He may have had manic-depressive tendencies but it is difficult to know how much was due to insecurity over his illegitimacy and convict origins and how much was due to an imbalance in brain chemistry.

Sarah suffered badly from Wentworth's mood swings and from homesickness. Her life seemed to consist of moving house, taking inventories and moving again as Wentworth became increasingly restless. He did not want to be an expatriate but knew how ambivalent the inhabitants of Sydney were towards him should he return with his wife. But he did keep Vaucluse House as a refuge for Sarah in case things should change because she loved it and had such happy memories of the house.

But in the end, both Sarah and William died in a foreign land. Liston's biography records that Sarah died aged seventy-three in Eastbourne, a town she scarcely knew, far from Vaucluse.

The same prejudices that Sarah Wentworth experienced had been applied to Mary Reibey more than a generation earlier.

The Reibey girls were beauties and Mary wanted the best for them. How to let her daughters meet suitable young men was a daunting problem for her. The doors of Sydney's upper-crust homes were barred to her and her daughters. Mary would have negotiated business deals with the major shipowners like the Campbells of Campbell's Wharf, but it is unlikely that their wives would have received her.

Mary's letters to her cousin David in England, who looked after her business affairs, contain no hint of the pain of social rejection. However, Sarah Wentworth's life of exile for the sake of her children's future illustrates the sort of snubs and discrimination Mary and her children would also have suffered among the free settlers. Mary had no husband to defend her or to formulate strategies for marrying her daughters into the strata of educated society she wished them to join.

So, in 1816, Mary advertised her eleven Hawkesbury farms, the house in Cockle Bay, Darling Harbour and the George Street store for sale. Apparently, she had had enough of prejudice and intended to leave the colony and settle in England, where she must have felt that her daughters had a better chance of finding suitable husbands. But selling up was not as easy as she had thought. Business confidence had fallen away due to the recession of 1811–1812. Mary's properties failed to sell for anything like the prices she believed they were worth.

Mary demonstrated flexibility and entrepreneurial flair by turning a setback into an advantage and changed her plans. Thomas and his younger brother James now took over as resident directors of Thomas Reibey and Company of Tasmania. They needed a Tasmanian residence suitable to their position and she hoped they would both marry landowners' daughters. Accordingly Mary purchased for them two thousand acres of fertile land at Hadspen on the South Esk River.

Thomas Reibey built handsome *Entally House* at Hadspen in Tasmania and became one of Tasmania's wealthiest settlers. With her knowledge of property, Mary was able to give him excellent advice on the design and building of *Entally* with its long verandah and substantial farm buildings, coach-house and farm cottages. The house was ready just before she departed.[4] She must have been delighted that in Tasmania her sons had all the advantages of gentlemen. But the 'convict taint' still dogged Thomas and his family.

Mary took advantage of the drop in prices to add still more ships to the Reibey fleet. It is important to understand that, shrewd as she was to see a business advantage, Mary was never a wild speculator like so many men of her period. Instead she always thought her plans through very carefully before acting and then carried them out with determination. Her philosophy towards work and investment was summed up in her maxim 'no-one will do well who is not thrifty, correct and sober'.

Unable to realise her assets to set herself and her daughter up in style in England and introduce them to suitable marriage partners, Mary decided to become a tourist in the land of her birth.

Leaving Thomas and Richard at *Entally* in charge of the two youngest girls, Jane Penelope and Elizabeth Anne, Mary sailed away to spend the second half of 1820 and 1821 in England taking her eldest daughters, Celia and Eliza on a voyage of a lifetime.

It was a business trip as well as a holiday. The day after Mary arrived in London she wrote in her diary[5] that she had been to the city, visited her shipping agent and arranged for purchase and shipment of goods back to Sydney and Hobart.

She found the cold of the British winter bothered her and was frequently ill with coughs, colds and attacks of asthma. The climate of Sydney seemed infinitely more desirable. But the delights of London, a place she had probably never visited, beckoned. With her excited daughters in tow, she went sightseeing and shopping in Regent Street and central London, buying history books and a 'fowling piece' or gun for George. They attended the theatre. Then Mary bought more goods for her stores and supervised their shipment at the wharves.

On 13 April 1821 she paid a visit to young Mr William Charles Wentworth in his chambers at The Temple and according to one of her letters 'staid with him too long till 'twas too late to go'. The purpose of her visit was to place a friend's son in a paid position in Wentworth's office. By now Wentworth had realised that his parents were convicts. Did this make him all the keener to talk over the situation for emancipists in Sydney, to which he was already thinking of returning? Unfortunately nothing else is known about this fascinating meeting. But her letters home record that Mary paid a second visit to Wentworth the following day.

Shopping and business completed, Mary and her daughters went north to visit Mary's relatives—she was playing to the hilt the role of the wealthy widow returned from the colonies with two fine daughters. She had their portraits painted on ivory in miniature to take home with her as well as her own, in which she looks prematurely aged, steel-rimmed glasses perched on her nose, a strong, determined chin—in all a picture of respectability.

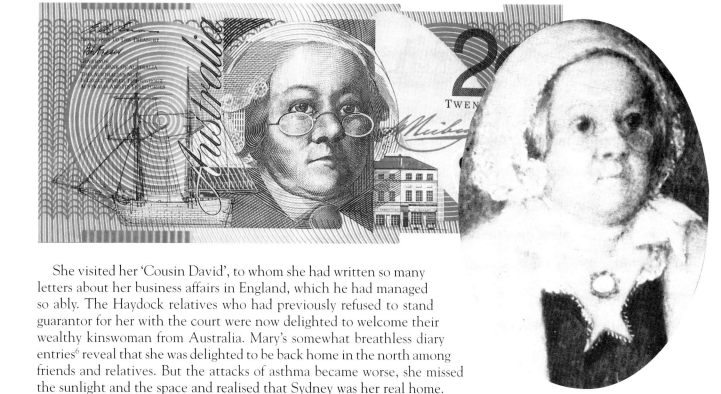

She visited her 'Cousin David', to whom she had written so many letters about her business affairs in England, which he had managed so ably. The Haydock relatives who had previously refused to stand guarantor for her with the court were now delighted to welcome their wealthy kinswoman from Australia. Mary's somewhat breathless diary entries[6] reveal that she was delighted to be back home in the north among friends and relatives. But the attacks of asthma became worse, she missed the sunlight and the space and realised that Sydney was her real home.

Mary's daughter Eliza briefly attended Mrs Duncan's finishing school in Scotland to obtain some ladylike accomplishments. But Eliza soon missed Sydney also and begged to be allowed to return to New South Wales with her mother and sister. Could it have been that she already had a romantic attachment? The three of them made the long voyage 'home'. A few month's later, Eliza, with her newly found 'finishing school polish', announced her engagement to the British-born Lieutenant Thomas Thomson.

Mary found Sydney changed. Sir Thomas Brisbane had succeeded Governor Macquarie, who had always supported the ex-convict emancipists in their business endeavours. But Brisbane was determined not to become embroiled in the bitter quarrels between Emancipists and free settlers or 'Exclusives'. Mary was now a prominent figure among ships' captains, merchants and traders. She frequently made the fifteen-day trip to Tasmania aboard one of her own ships while sons Thomas and James ran the Tasmanian side of Thomas Reibey and Company efficiently and branched out into the trade of the more socially respectable field of banking.

Back in Sydney Eliza married her lieutenant at fashionable St James's Church and all those bonnets and ballgowns purchased in Bond Street were shown off to the guests.

Eighteen-year-old Celia married Thomas Wills, son of her father's long-deceased partner. Jane Penelope, the daughter who most resembled Mary, had no need of a ball at Government House to find a husband; she married wealthy James Atkinson, who she met when he bought the family home and store in George Street. There was no longer such a need to keep on working and Mary sold off or leased most of her properties.

When her youngest daughter Elizabeth Anne married aristocratic Adjutant Joseph Long Innes in 1829 she brought to the marriage a valuable block of land in George Street—a gift from her mother—on which the Sydney General Post Office now stands.[7]

The years rolled on. By 1846 Mary was fifty-nine, rich and respected in business. But her hard-won sense of security was shattered when *The History of Margaret*

Mary Reibey is one of the few Australian women accorded the distinction of having her portrait on the currency. No extant portrait of Mary is known when young and it seems none was ever made. Her likeness on the Australian $20 note is taken from a portrait made in old age. From the Mitchell Library, State Library of New South Wales.

Catchpole, a novel by the Reverend Richard Cobbold, went on sale in Sydney. This account, just as romanticised as Catherine Gaskin's *Sarah Dane*, claimed to be the 'true story' of a woman transported for stealing a horse, who married well, owned properties and whose children were sent 'home' to be educated at England's finest schools and meet suitable marriage partners. In the novel the heroine's children are remarkably good-looking. She wishes to forget her past. In England they marry well and live rich, distinguished lives, totally unaware of their mother's convict past. In some respects the book sounds more like a blending of the life of Sarah Wentworth coupled with some of Mary Reibey's business achievements.

The Reverend Cobbold is unlikely to have known anything about Mary and drew on his vivid imagination. But he claimed his book was based on events in the life of Margaret Catchpole, an illiterate cook–housemaid who had once worked for his mother. Margaret Catchpole, like Mary, had stolen a horse, been caught and sentenced. But she had done this twice and been double Mary's age when transported.

In 1800 Margaret Catchpole had escaped from prison to join John Cook, a man who had asked her to marry him but whom she claimed she had refused. When captured she had been heading for a smuggler's boat to escape. She had been disguised as a sailor, but put up quite a fight, was sentenced to die for the second time but finally had been transported to Sydney in December 1801 (Mary had arrived in October, almost a decade earlier). The real Margaret Catchpole was assigned to work as a cook in the house of Commissary John Palmer. Margaret refused to marry and chose instead to work as a midwife and was granted an absolute pardon in 1819.

Although both women resided in the Sydney area, it is unlikely they ever met. Mary was small, slim in build, sloe-eyed and active as quicksilver. A portrait in old age shows Margaret Catchpole as a coarse-featured woman with lank hair, a pasty complexion and a long bulbous nose.[8] In a letter to England Margaret described how 'my eyes are not as good as they were and I have lorst (sic) all my frunt (sic) teeff'. She and Mary Reibey were poles apart, their only bond being that they were both hardworking women.

The Reverend Cobbold wrote his *History of Margaret Catchpole* without knowing of Mary's existence but his book caused her considerable pain and embarrassment when it became a best-seller in Britain and Sydney. A piece of street theatre resulted titled, *Catchpole, the Female Horse Thief*, where the main character was shown as crude, rude and violent, attacking her captors and screaming oaths. Poor Mary! People tittered and pointed whenever she drove out in her carriage or entered a shop.

Because the real Margaret Catchpole had died in 1819, nearly seventeen years previously, Mary Reibey could not produce her and so silence all the rumours, which were worse than her own dark secret. Sydney and Hobart people whispered behind their hands and pointed at Mary, obviously considering her to be the model for both the book and the play.

By now Mary was grey-haired, had rich and powerful friends and felt reasonably secure about her long-established Sydney business affairs. Her main worry was for her children and grandchildren in Tasmania. Van Diemen's Land, as it was known, sounded from Lady Jane Franklin's acid comments on Richarda Allan's marriage to Mary's son, Thomas, as if it were even more snobbish and prejudiced than Sydney.

The Catchpole scandal had unjustly made Mary's sons and daughters-in-law scapegoats for one wrong action in her past. Most of all she worried about Thomas, now head of the family business, hardworking, devout and a leading shareholder in several banks. According to Lady Jane Franklin, Thomas sought a knighthood. In all events he was never awarded one, although his son, young Thomas, would eventually become Premier of Tasmania.

On 22 February 1838, Lady Franklin once more reflected the prejudice of her times. In a letter to a sister in London she wrote scandalous tittle-tattle about Mary Reibey, recalling the fact Mary had been transported for horse-stealing, even though the offence had occurred forty-eight years previously. In that letter Lady Franklin described Mary's eldest grandaughter as

> . . . very pretty young woman with a quiet and modest demeanour but in spite of her beauty and her father's riches I cannot conceive that the Arthur family would have been happy with the match . . . the mother is said to have been transported to Sydney for horse-stealing and now lives in affluence, driving a phaeton drawn by two white ponies through the streets.[9]

One might have expected this much prejudice from a stupid woman, but Lady Franklin was well educated, something of a bluestocking and an intelligent freethinker. Nevertheless even she could not forget Mary's convict origins.

But by that time Mary had long succeeded in marrying off her daughters in 'good' society. Even her eldest grandaughter, Mary Ellen, the daughter of Mary's eldest son Thomas, had just married the son of wealthy free settlers in Tasmania and was off to London on honeymoon.

Mary had not read Lady Jane's letter. But she must have learned that the cliquey Tasmanian 'society' was once again abuzz with gossip about her convict past. It had to be stopped for the sake of the Tasmanian branch of Thomas Reibey and Company.[10] James Reibey was now a director of the Derwent and Cornwall Banks. The scandal could affect her children and her grandchildren. Mary acted swiftly.

Mary sailed to Tasmania in one of the Reibey ships and stayed at Entally with Thomas and Richarda, daughter of the 'Exclusive' Allan family, about whose marriage to Thomas Lady Franklin had been so scathing. At the gracious Georgian homestead Entally, which Mary had carefully entailed so that it would pass to her grandchildren, she quietly asked her friend the Bishop of Tasmania to help her. The Bishop, mindful of the money that members of the Reibey family had donated to the work of the church, was keen to oblige Mrs Reibey. The fact he had recently made Mary's grandson, Oxford-educated, horse-loving Thomas Reibey, rector at Holy Trinity Church in Launceston, also played an important part in his decision to help her clear her name.

The second edition of Cobbold's book carried a foreword containing a letter from the Bishop, explaining that the book was roughly based on the story of the late Margaret Catchpole *and no one else*. Gradually the pointing accusatory fingers ceased.

With the whole family married except George, Mary now occupied a cottage close beside the Tank Stream and, retired from business, did charity work for churches and schools. However, she still took a keen interest in the development and planning of Castlereagh Street, where she owned several shops.

In her final years Mary lived off rents from her remaining shops, houses and commercial properties. She felt the need for country air and space for her beloved horses and moved to a property at Newtown where she built herself a new house. By now her wealth and the scandal surrounding her had turned her into a Sydney legend. Mary insisted on driving her own carriage with its thoroughbred white horses into town to supervise her remaining properties.[11]

With so many children and grandchildren, there were sorrows as well as joys. A year after the family had danced at Celia's wedding, at the age of twenty-one, Celia died of puerperal fever, one of the results of unhygienic childbirth practices that killed so many young women. Another family tragedy was George, the scholarly son, for whom Mary had bought the books and the gun in London. George died in Tasmania aged twenty-three, killed in an accident while out shooting—probably with the 'fowling piece' Mary had bought him. Mary buried herself in work and grandchildren, desperately trying to forget.

One son-in-law ran up debts which had to be paid by Mary, another was quietly pensioned off. Mary ensured that, contrary to popular custom, he signed over the guardianship of the family home and the children of the marriage to his wife.[12] Mary's shrewd advice ensured her daughter retained her children when divorce was a scandal and a woman automatically lost custody of children and property if she left her husband.

It was over half a century since Mary had arrived in Sydney as a teenage convict, determined to make the best out of life in a new land. On 30 May 1855 she died at Newtown, surrounded by children and grandchildren, and was buried beside her husband in the Devonshire Street Cemetery, with only the simplest of inscriptions '*Mary, widow of the above Tom Reibey*'.

---

[1] Mary Reibey's letters are published in full in Nance Irvine's *Dear Cousin—The Reibey Letters*, Janet Press, Glebe, Sydney, 1989 and the originals of all but Mary's first letter have been donated to the Mitchell Library by Mary's descendants. At the time of writing Mary's first letter is held in England where it was bought at a Sotheby's book sale and is reproduced by courtesy of its current owners, arranged through Tim McCormick of Rare Books, Sydney. Her complete biography was written by Nance Irvine, *Mary Reibey—Molly Incognita*, Library of Australian History, Sydney 1982.

[2] For several incidents in Mary's life I am indebted to the account by Dymphna Cusack in *The Peaceful Army* originally published in 1938. Unfortunately many facts about Mary were not known at the time Cusack wrote her lively essay. (A second edition of *The Peaceful Army* was edited by Dale Spender and republished by Penguin Books, Ringwood in 1988.)

[3] Liston, Carol. *Sarah Wentworth, Mistress of Vaucluse*. Historic Houses Trust, Sydney, 1988. This is the definitive biography. Transcripts of the original materials are held in the Trust's library at Lyndhurst, Glebe, Sydney. Sarah's complex relationship with her husband is dealt with by Liston in *For Richer, For Poorer*, a compilation of essays on early colonial marriages edited by Penny Russell, published by Melbourne University Press in 1994.

[4] Entally House has been restored by the Tasmanian Scenery Preservation Board. It is now open to the public and run by the Tasmanian Parks and Wildlife Service.

[5] *Diary and Journal of Mary Reibey 1820–21*. Mitchell Library.

[6] *Diary and Journal of Mary Reibey 1820–21*. Mitchell Library.

[7] Donkin, Nance. *The Women were There*. Collins Dove, Melbourne, 1988.

[8] Margaret Catchpole's idealised portrait when young in Reverend Richard Cobbold's *History of Margaret Catchpole*, published London, 1845 and 1847 by Henry Colburn. Reprinted, Ipswich, England 1971. Like Mary Reibey, Catchpole had dark eyes and hair. An unflattering portrait of Catchpole in old age showing far coarser features than those of Reibey, appears on page 49 of Donkin, Nance, *And the Women Were There*, Collins Dove, 1988 (source unnamed). Catchpole's letters are in the Mitchell Library (Mss 1116 and 4211).

[9] Lady Jane Franklin to her sister Mary Simpkinson, 22 February 1838.

[10] Walsh, G.P. Entry on Mary Reibey in Volume One of *Australian Dictionary of Biography*, Melbourne University Press, 1967. Mary is one of the few colonial women to receive an entry under her own name rather than that of her husband in this volume.

[11] Irvine, Nance. *Molly Incognita*. Library of Australian History. Sydney, 1982. This biography states Mary Reibey did *not* meet her husband on a convict ship.

[12] Irvine, Nance. *Ibid*.

CHAPTER 2

Esther Johnston
(1771–1846)

FROM CONVICT RAGS TO RESPECTABILITY

Esther Johnston's life was one of the strangest in Australian colonial history. Caught shoplifting two pieces of black lace in July 1786 she was sentenced to transportation to New South Wales aboard a vessel of the First Fleet. At the time she was a pregnant 15-year-old apprentice milliner. Today she would have been let off with a caution by a local magistrate, but in August 1786 she received her seven-year sentence because it was government policy to send young convict women capable of child-bearing to the new colony to redress the sex ratio of one female to seven male convicts.

In spite of three excellent character references and the fact she was a first offender, well educated, and well spoken, unlike most female convicts, Esther's petition for clemency was ignored by the Home Secretary. She was kept locked up in the infamous Newgate Gaol awaiting transportation. Her pregnancy saved her from serving one year in the convict hulks which were even worse than Newgate. On the hulks female convicts were treated as unpaid whores, bullied, raped, starved and abused by male gaolers. Some women went mad at the horror, others committed suicide. Fortunately for Esther, the women prisoners in Newgate were housed four or five to a cell, which provided some protection from sexual harassment by their gaolers.

Esther's baby was born in Newgate on 18 March 1787. Esther gave her maiden name as Abrahams, but said that the baby's father was named Julian and was a Marrano or exiled Spanish Jew whom she had married in a private ceremony. A search through synagogue records of the period has failed to find a marriage entry, but some entries were destroyed by fire in World War II, which makes it difficult to research her statement further. The name 'Juliano' occurred fairly frequently among Jews resident in Spain in the sixteenth and seventeenth centuries, and many of these did flee to England due to religious persecution.

Esther gave her age as 20 when she arrived in chains aboard the *Lady Penrhyn* with her baby and 36 other women from Newgate Gaol. She probably thought that since she was only 17, raising her age would afford the two of them some slight protection against the lecherous crew and soldiers. The *Lady Penrhyn* was a small ship to undertake such a long voyage and was comparable in size with the 'Lady' series of ferries which operate on Sydney Harbour (averaging 400 tons). These small barques were skilfully guided by navigators on their uncomfortable voyage, across the Atlantic to Rio de Janeiro, then back around the Cape of Good Hope, over the stormy southern reaches of the Indian Ocean, around Van Diemen's Land, finally anchoring at Sydney Cove, New South Wales where they discharged their cargoes of human misery. The length of the voyage ranged from six to twelve months, depending on storms and the amount of time allowed for recuperation in the ports en route.

In the filthy, airless hold of the *Lady Penrhyn*, Esther and the other women from

Newgate Gaol were joined by 66 female convicts from the hulks and from county gaols. Many women held in the county gaols were half-naked, their clothing ripped and worn threadbare in places. Most female convicts were covered in lice and reeking with body odour since washing facilities had been withheld from them for months. There was no privacy in the ship's hold. Convict women were herded together in darkness and conditions hardly suited to animals, with minimal sanitation, a meagre and monotonous diet, and no candles permitted due to the high danger of fire. Some convict women from the hulks suffered from dysentery, others from venereal disease and typhoid. Five died even before the ship sailed. The offences of these women ranged from pickpocketing, shoplifting and fraud, to prostitution, but unlike the men, none were murderers.

Naturally the women from Newgate Gaol were more eagerly sought after as mistresses by the soldiers and sailors on board since they thought there was less risk of contracting venereal disease from them as it was believed that many women held on the hulks had been raped or seduced by disease-ridden soldiers.

Aboard the *Lady Penrhyn*, half-naked women who had been brutalised by the system traded sexual favours for extra food or deck privileges and it was hard to enforce discipline. According to Lieutenant Arthur Bowes, the ship's surgeon,[1] the female convicts were punished for thieving and fighting by having thumbscrews or iron fetters placed on their wrists. A horrified Captain Arthur Phillip requested the authorities to send more clothes. He had written to Under Secretary Nepean on 17 March 1787 concerning the ships lying at anchor at Portsmouth:

> The giving of cloaths to those convicts who have been embarked at Plymouth is so very necessary. I have ordered it to be done . . . but . . . unless orders are being given for their being washed and cloathed on their leaving prison or the hulks, all that we may do will be to no purpose.

Phillip feared that an outbreak of disease on board would prevent the ships being allowed to call in at foreign ports for fresh water, greens and meat. He continued:

> The situation in which the magistrate sent the women on board the *Lady Penrhyn* stamps them [the magistrates] with infamy—tho' almost naked and so very filthy, that nothing but cloathing them could have prevented them [the women convicts] from perishing, prevent a fever which is still on board that ship, and where there are many venereal complaints.

The Government was not as brutal as many previous historians have stated. They did eventually send spare clothes and shoes for the women. Unfortunately these arrived too late to be brought on board and had to be given by Phillip to those of the convict women who needed them desperately at their next port of call, Cape Town.

Among this motley crowd how must young Esther have felt, nursing her baby, the only thing precious in the world left to her, surrounded by women who were fearful and angry at their uncertain fate and cursing or brawling much of the time? Esther must have worried long and hard as the days dragged on over their fate in an unknown land where life would be difficult and dangerous for both her and her child.

Esther's long black hair, dark almond-shaped eyes and composed manner attracted the attention of Lieutenant George Johnston, who had the difficult task of keeping discipline among the unruly convict women. A soldier's son from a prominent Scottish family, he had already served with distinction against the French in the West Indies and it was predicted that he would have a brilliant military career. He was brave and forthright, but, as events were to prove, naive and easily influenced. George's portrait, painted shortly after his arrival in Australia, shows a tall, handsome young man with piercing blue eyes and fair hair. Probably it was an immediate attraction of opposites between the blonde young lieutenant and the raven-haired convict girl. Their shipboard liaison was to last for the rest of their lives and survive long periods of separation. It must have started before they reached Cape Town, because there George Johnston purchased a nanny-goat, presumably to provide milk for Esther and her baby Rosanna.

The First Fleet sailed into Sydney Harbour on 26 January 1788 and on 6 February the women convicts were allowed to disembark. George Johnston and Esther Abrahams-Julian lived together from that time and she became his de facto wife. Possibly they did not marry because she thought her Spanish husband was still alive, but this remains a mystery, like so much of her life.

On 4 March 1790 their first child was baptised at St Philip's Church, Sydney, and given the name of George, like his father. Two days later George Johnston left Sydney in the *Supply* with a detachment of marines and 190 of the most hardened male and female convicts, bound for Norfolk Island where a new penal settlement had been founded two years previously. He was accompanied by Esther and his baby son, but Rosanna , Esther's first child, appears to have been left behind in Sydney.

Norfolk Island had a grim reputation as one of the worst penal settlements in the world, second only to Devil's Island.[2] Convict women were bought and sold like cattle, the going rate being about ten pounds, and when their masters were tired of them they flogged them nearly to death or sold them off to the highest bidder. In *The Fatal Shore*, Robert Hughes recounted how the island's beadle acted as auctioneer in the grain store where women were forced to parade around the room stark naked, with a number painted on their backs like sides of beef. By the end of their stay in Norfolk Island some of the women were so badly battered that their price had dropped to the cost of a couple of gallons of rum.[3]

Esther must have shuddered when she saw the fate of some of the convict women who had accompanied her to Sydney on the First Fleet.

The following year George was posted back to Sydney on health grounds and Esther followed him three months later aboard the *Supply*. There was a reunion between the lovers and on 9 March 1792 their second son Robert was born. Captain Arthur Phillip stood as godfather to the child, giving normally reticent Esther a certain social standing in the infant colony. In January 1796, George was sent to Norfolk Island again, to take charge of a detachment of soldiers, and he took his sons with him. From a letter in the National Library from convict John Grant it appears that the wife of Judge Advocate Richard Atkins looked after the Johnston children during this period, along with her own.

Governor Phillip recommended the recall of the marines to England, but George, as the governor's aide, decided that his future lay in Sydney with Esther and his sons to care for and he accepted a commission as a Captain in the New South Wales Corps. This ensured him a land grant of 1200 acres (45.4 ha), covering most of present-day Petersham and Annandale up to Glebe, which at that period was mainly bush. George christened the whole property Annandale in memory of his birthplace near Dumfries, in the lowlands of Scotland.

Together George and Esther supervised the clearing of the dense scrub, using the sixteen convict servants assigned to him as captain. In 1799 they designed and built Annandale House, one of the first large brick buildings in New South Wales, where today's Parramatta Road crosses the end of Johnston Street. *Annandale House* was the centre of its own village built by the Johnstons. They owned a butchery, a bakery, a blacksmith's forge, a general store, and in the grounds were an orangery and a vineyard.[4] Their large, single-storey homestead with its ten rooms, long hall and wide verandahs remained a Sydney showplace for over a century until it was demolished in 1905. The wide driveway to *Annandale House* was lined with imposing Norfolk pines, brought back as saplings from Norfolk Island by George Johnston.

George and Esther became some of the wealthiest settlers in New South Wales through hard work on their property and through obtaining extensive land grants around Sydney and on the Georges River (named after George Johnston). Esther also received two large grants in her own name of Esther Julian making her financially independent.[5] In 1804 George Johnston quelled the rebellion of some 200 Irish rebel convicts at Rouse Hill, near Toongabbie, with only two dozen soldiers to help him, by tricking the convicts into believing he possessed larger forces. As a result he was promoted to the rank of major and appointed commander of the New South Wales Corps. As aide-de-camp to the governor George often had to spend long periods at Government House in either Sydney or Parramatta. Doubtless he knew that he could trust Esther to run the property efficiently in his absence, for she had a good head for figures and a far better business brain than he had.

By this time Esther, still unmarried and officially using the name of Esther Julian, had a large family—Rosanna, George, Robert, David born in 1800, Maria born the following year, Julia born in 1803 and the sickly baby Isabella who died.[6] George spent Christmas 1807 with his family at Annandale. He returned to Sydney as commander of the Rum Corps leaving Esther in charge of the homestead and the farm only to find that the Corps Paymaster, John Macarthur, had been imprisoned by Governor William Bligh and was due to be tried by one of his debtors, the alcoholic Judge Advocate Richard Atkins. The Rum Corps was in an uproar, claiming Macarthur had been jailed unjustly, and that Atkins, as a crony of the governor, was unfit to serve as head of the judiciary and should be dismissed.

John Macarthur easily managed to convince George that Sydney should be placed under military law to prevent an uprising. He produced a petition to this effect, calling upon the somewhat naive George to take responsibility and to act as senior officer in the colony in the absence of Lieutenant Governor William Paterson. Urged on by Macarthur, the only person who stood to gain by the whole Rum Rebellion, George Johnston took command. Unfortunately for him the whole affair blew up before he was able to seek Esther's prudent opinion; she was more cautious and with

Handsome Annandale House with its stables and outhouses, home of Esther and George Johnston, was demolished in 1905. Esther brought back the Norfolk pines as seedlings from Norfolk Island. Painting by B. Hoyte, Mitchell Library, State Library of NSW.

the fate of her children to consider, would probably have counselled restraint. George was to regret his impulsive decision for the rest of his life, since it cost him his army salary and six thousand pounds in legal fees.

On 26 January 1808, with the band playing, colours flying and swords drawn, George Johnston led his troops to the Bridge Street Government House and handed Bligh a letter calling on him to resign. Contrary to popular legend Bligh was not hiding under the bed although an illustrated handbill or broadsheet circulated at the time shows this. Major George Johnston assumed the title of Lieutenant Governor and kept Bligh under close arrest in Government House until June 1808. In that month Lieutenant Colonel Joseph Foveaux arrived from England to take over the governorship of the colony; George had been promoted to Lieutenant Colonel before news of the rebellion reached London.

Little has been written about Esther's role in the affair. From the days of the Roman empresses and Napoleon's Josephine, desirable women have played a powerful political role behind the scenes. George was still entranced by Esther's intelligence and good looks. She could have been as effective a governor's wife as any of her predecessors. It may have been her natural reluctance to expose herself and her past to public scrutiny that prevented George from incriminating himself still further and moving her into Government House to fill a social role while deposed Governor Bligh was under military arrest. It is entirely in keeping with Esther's character that she would have deliberately chosen to play a discreet role. At that period emancipists were not welcome at Government House. It must have been a curious sensation for Esther, the socially unacceptable part-Jewish convict, to realise that she was now a real power behind the scenes during the entire six months of Johnston's governorship, and could, had she wished, preside at official events. Unfortunately Esther did not keep a diary and George's diary is now missing so there is no record of her movements or thoughts[7] in this unusual period in colonial history.

On 23 March 1809 George sailed for England to attend the inquiry into Bligh's deposition and the Sydney *Gazette* recorded that he received full military honours at his departure. Two years later he was found guilty of mutiny, but his only punishment was to be cashiered from the army, since the general opinion was that he had acted in good faith and been used as a stooge by John Macarthur in Macarthur's devious struggle for power.

Not unnaturally George was very bitter that his military career as the most senior officer in the colony had been destroyed, causing him loss of both income and social prestige. He never received any compensation for administrative work he had undertaken, or official entertaining expenses at *Annandale House* during his provisional governorship.

The Johnstons had, in 1802, brought out from England the first thoroughbred stallion from the Duke of Northumberland's own stud and had sown the first clover in Australia on their Illawarra land, obtaining seeds from the Duke. This made them pioneers of Australia's agriculture and stock breeding.

To Esther's relief, George finally returned to New South Wales in April 1813, after an absence of four years, with his large land grants still intact. He found that under Esther's careful management Annandale had become one of the finest commercial beef properties and thoroughbred stud farms in New South Wales. She must have had a hard life without him: numerous advertisements she placed warning of the penalties of cattle duffing and trespassing on Annandale land show that unscrupulous men tried to take advantage of her husband's absence, and she had difficulties, as a former convict herself, disciplining convict labour. However, she was able to administer the estate, educate her children, and come to terms with the death of her young daughter, Isabella, in George's absence.

Esther had always been used to handling large sums of money and property of

Esther Julian Johnston. Portrait attributed to Richard Read, Sr. Esther, who had been transported for shoplifting lace, with a fine sense of irony is wearing an ornate lace cap. The portrait shows her when widowed and her strength of character is evident. Private collection, courtesy Sotheby's Sydney.

Portrait miniature on ivory of Rosanna Julian, Esther's daughter by an unknown Spaniard, possibly painted on her marriage to Isaac Nicholls. The likeness of mother and daughter is striking.

Opposite: *Esther's daughter, Julia Johnston, painted by Richard Reade, Sr. in 1824. To the rear on the right can be seen the tomb of her dead brother. Julia is portrayed as an elegant young lady with a parasol and pearls. Private collection courtesy Sotherby's, Sydney.*

her own, partly because, unlike most colonial women (whose money and land automatically became the property of their husbands on marriage), she had been encouraged by George to manage her own financial affairs. Therefore in his absence she was able to negotiate large government contracts always in her own name of Esther Julian for the purchase of Annandale beef, pork and corn. She received a substantial land grant of 570 acres (259 ha) of land on the Georges River, near Bankstown, in the name of Esther Julian.[5]

In Sydney, now governed by the Scottish Presbyterian Lachlan Macquarie, marriage certificates had become important for the first time. Many liaisons between officers and their convict de facto wives had been solemnised at his insistence. In 1810 the governor revoked Esther's large land grant possibly due to her irregular relationship with George and his role in the mutiny. Three years later, after Macquarie and his wife had met Esther he revised his previous decision and reconfirmed the grant.

In 1814, the year which would have marked their silver wedding and 12 months after his return from Britain, George Johnston finally married Esther and legitimised their children. They had lived together for 25 years. The marriage licence was granted to George Johnston and Mrs Esther Julian, indicating that she was previously married to Rosanna's father. Possibly it was Esther who had delayed this marriage believing that Rosanna's father was still alive. Perhaps she received word that Rosanna's father was dead, and so she finally consented to the marriage for the sake of the inheritance of her other children.

The real facts will probably never be known. George Johnston's three leatherbound diaries which would have revealed the full truth about Esther and Rosanna were stolen from the English home of his great-grandson, Mr Douglas Hope-Johnston, in the 1930s, an era when convict ancestry was still considered shameful. Mr Douglas Hope-Johnston had intended to write a biography of his ancestor, George Johnston, but was bound by his father's will to 'erase a number of purely private family references and comments'.[8]

There is a family legend that certain members of the Johnston family did not wish this biography to be published because of the references to illegitimacy and transportation and that the disappearance of the diaries, which is of incalculable loss to Australian history, was connected to the proposed biography, which was never published.

Macquarie and his wife soon realised that George had no further political ambitions and after their marriage George and Esther became frequent visitors to Government House. George, the Johnstons' eldest son, was appointed to an important government post but tragically was killed in a riding accident in 1820. The governor and his wife attended the funeral. His parents never fully recovered from the shock of young George's death, and three years later, in January 1823, when Esther was probably 52 years old, George died and was buried beside his eldest son in the family vault at Annandale. In a portrait, probably of her engagement, Julia Johnston poses in fashionable costume beside the family vault. The portrait of a proud, aloof-looking girl in her finery seems determined to lay to rest the 'convict taint' of her mother.

George's will provided that Esther would administer the Annandale property plus her own land at Bankstown and near Lake Illawarra which amounted to about 2460 acres (1118 ha). This would pass to Robert on her death; their youngest son, David, would inherit the main land grant at Georges Hall, Bankstown, immediately. The will caused a deep rift between Esther and her second son, Robert, who believed that it was unfair and that he should have had the management of Annandale following his father's death.

Violent family scenes took place in which the girls sided with their brother Robert. Not surprisingly, in 1829 Esther announced that since so much trouble was caused

by the will she planned to leave the colony, mortgage Annandale to the bank and live off the interest in England. She placed an advertisement in the *Australian* to that effect. Robert instituted proceedings to declare his mother insane so that he could gain control over the estate. An official enquiry into her mental state was held in 1829, when several of her children again sided with Robert to prevent Esther mortgaging the property to the bank. One witness, Jacob Isaacs, actually testified that the Johnston fortunes had been accumulated by Esther Julian trading under her own name rather than by George Johnston. However male power prevailed. Robert Johnston contested his father's will successfully, and control of Esther's property passed to the crown. The outcome of the case proved unsatisfactory to both parties and the old taunts of 'damned convict whore'[9] and 'convicted for theft' were raised once again against Esther. It was a disturbing and difficult time for a woman who had achieved so much and who had sought to redeem herself in the eyes of society.

A deeply troubled Esther finally left Annandale and went to live on David's property at Georges Hall, on what was then the outskirts of the city. Here she lived for many years, a formidable old lady who may have consoled herself with alcohol and eventually died, probably aged 75. Towards the end of her life she probably suffered from Alzheimer's disease. She had days of complete lucidity but often her mind wandered. Sometimes her memory failed and she was back in the past, reliving scenes like the past, riding her favourite thoroughbred horse across the lush paddocks of Annandale or in Newgate Gaol awaiting transportation.

Hers was a life that had turned full circle. From a convict girl who appeared to have nothing to live for, she had become the wife of one of the richest members of the colony and a substantial landowner in her own right. The sad outcome, that Esther should later lose everything she had worked for through family property feuds due to the provisions of the will of her husband, who had sought only to ensure her financial security, was one of life's ironies. Destiny had allowed her to climb from the depths of public degradation as a 'damned whore' to the heights of respectability. In spite of the absence of any documentation in the way of letters or diaries concerning Esther's own feelings, her story is intriguing. She remains one of Australia's most determined, financially successful yet vulnerable colonial women.

---

[1] Bowes, Arthur. *A Journal of a voyage from Portsmouth to New South Wales in the Lady Penrhyn.* MS collection, Mitchell Library, Sydney.

[2] Hughes, Robert. *The Fatal Shore.* Collins, Harvill. London, 1987.

[3] *Ibid.*

[4] Bergman, George G. J. *The Lieutenant-Governor's Wife. The Amazing Story of a Jewish Convict Girl.* Australian Jewish Historical Society. Sydney, 1970. Also Bergman, G. & Levi, J. S, *Australian Genesis: Jewish Convicts and Settlers.* Adelaide, Rigby, 1974.

[5] Johnston Papers. Dixson Library, Sydney. Reg Gen Dept Grant Books, Series II p.261, Series III p.169, p.363, Series VI p.94. Grants recorded at Cabramatta, Georges River, Lake Illawarra.

[6] Memorial No 167A to Macquarie cited in Bergman and Levi, *op. cit.*

[7] George Johnston did keep a diary but this was either lost or stolen from the home of his descendants in London earlier this century, in a move to obliterate all record of Esther's convict background.

[8] Johnston Papers, *op. cit.*

[9] *Ibid.*

CHAPTER 3

Charlotte Waring Atkinson (Barton) (1795–1867)
Caroline Louisa Atkinson (Calvert) (1834–1872)

AUTHOR OF AUSTRALIA'S FIRST CHILDREN'S BOOK, AUSTRALIA'S FIRST FEMALE NOVELIST AND AN IMPORTANT BOTANIST

The distinguished botanist and artist Caroline Louisa Atkinson was the first Australian-born woman to have a novel published in her own land. Like her contemporaries Louisa Meredith and Georgiana McCrae, she had the artistic ability and enterprise to illustrate her own writing. She was one of the first local writers to find topics in the Australian bush suitable for a novel, and the remarkable achievements of her short life made her an outstanding woman of the period in which she was one of Australia's first female journalists.

A large collection of Caroline Louisa's watercolours and pen and wash drawings has been donated to the Mitchell Library by her granddaughter, Miss Janet Cosh. Caroline Louisa Atkinson was famous as an artist although she never exhibited or sold her works in her own lifetime, preferring to concentrate on her botanical studies, her novels and newspaper columns. In an era when most upper-class colonial women were educated to think that catching a husband and bearing his children was a career in itself, Caroline Louisa stood out as a creative and interesting woman.

Like the Brontë sisters, Caroline Louisa's life was very productive but spanned a tragically short period. Also like the Brontës, she loved and wrote about the beauty of wild places, far from civilisation. She had a fertile imagination but she lacked their fierce passion which produced heroes in the mould of Heathcliff and Mr Rochester. Unlike the novels of Charlotte or Emily Brontë, those of Caroline Louisa Atkinson have no unforgettable dominating male characters in the central roles.

Charles, the upper-class, handsome but unprincipled 'colonial experiencer' who courts the heroine in *Gertrude the Immigrant*, and the gentle caring Edward of the same novel, are no match for the Brontë heroes. Her heroine, Gertrude Gonthler, has more in common with the self-effacing, highly moral Jane Eyre created by Charlotte Brontë than with the wild passionate Catherine Earnshaw of Emily's romantic masterpiece, *Wuthering.Heights*.

Caroline Louisa suffered from a heart complaint, possibly caused by rheumatic fever as a child. However, she never let periods of ill-health stand in the way of documenting rare species of Australian native plants and she filled her adult years with a wealth of activity as an artist and writer. In these respects she resembled her namesake Louisa Meredith. She came from an educated background and in some ways her life was easier than Louisa's, with less time devoted to housekeeping and the demands of child-rearing. Circumstances moulded her as a gentler and more feminine character, but she too possessed a fierce determination to research and record the Australian flora and fauna that surrounded her and to write distinctively Australian novels, at a time when few such works were published.

As the child of two creative parents, it is hardly surprising that Caroline Louisa showed talent as an artist and writer from an early age. Her father, James Atkinson, was the author of a highly successful book and her mother was also a writer and amateur artist.

Caroline Louisa was born at Oldbury, in the southern tablelands south of Sydney. Assisted by assigned convicts, her father, James Atkinson had started breeding cattle and sheep on a large land grant. He was fortunate with the weather and with his choice of hundreds of acres of excellent farming country in the Sutton Forest area. James Atkinson seems to have been kind and considerate. Unlike many other members of the squattocracy, he went to great pains to make friends with the local Aborigines, giving them tea and tobacco, and they never harmed or killed his stock. James was young, hardworking and intelligent and his farm prospered. He had good practical experience of farming in southern England and was fascinated by current scientific theories of animal breeding and husbandry and realised that, as yet, no textbook had been written about Australian farming conditions.

After five years, James decided to return to Europe and look at farming practice in other countries and may have hoped to find a wife. Accompanied by Charles Macarthur, son of the wealthy banker and pastoralist Hannibal Hayes Macarthur, James and Charlie toured around examining farms in England, Germany and Holland while James gathered material for his projected book on farming under Australian conditions. However, he did not find a suitable bride willing to live in an isolated farmhouse in a convict colony.

The two young men returned to Australia on the *Cumberland*, the same ship as Charles's Aunt Harriet (wife of Admiral Phillip Parker King) who was returning home from a visit to England with her four sons. James and Charlie Macarthur joined the ship at the London docks, as did petite, dark-haired Miss Charlotte Waring, who was sailing to Australia to act as governess to Charlie's younger sisters. The young people were all travelling first-class and were to be joined at Southampton by the Kings and Mrs King's brother, pastoralist Robert Lethbridge and his wife, who had been visiting relations in the west of England.

Charlotte Waring had been interviewed in London and employed by Mrs King to act as governess to her four nieces. Charlie Macarthur must have confirmed what Mrs King would already have explained when she interviewed Charlotte for the post—that his mother was often confined to her bed with a lingering illness that left her very weak. She had been unable to spend much time with her children or supervise their education. Charlotte was being paid an exceptionally high salary because she was required not only as a governess but as a mother substitute for little Emmeline, then only five years old. Although most governesses travelled steerage, Charlotte Waring was travelling with the Kings in first-class. Mrs King had been impressed by Charlotte's ladylike manners and accomplishments and by the fact that, unlike many other candidates, she was not afraid to sail ten thousand miles to live in a convict colony. It had been agreed that at *Vineyard* Charlotte was to eat with the Macarthur family (rather than below stairs in the servants' hall) as the children's mother was so often confined to her bed.

On board ship the good-natured Charlie Macarthur introduced her to James

Atkinson and the three of them ate meals in the cuddy or main cabin. The normally shy James had plenty of opportunity to talk to Charlotte, whose enthusiasm for books delighted him. They were the same age, both born in 1795 and both past thirty, though Charlotte did not look her years. (Women of thirty with no dowries were widely regarded as past the marriageable age in the nineteenth century.)

Charlotte Waring had received an exceptionally good education for a young woman of that period. She had studied music, drawing (under John Glover), Italian

Caroline Louisa Atkinson's watercolour of the flour mill on the Oldbury property. George Barton, her stepfather, was initially employed to manage this mill. Courtesy the late Miss Janet Cosh, now in Mitchell Library, State Library of New South Wales.

and French. James soon realised that Charlotte, with her love of books and learning, would make an excellent wife and a stimulating companion.

Charlotte's early life had not been happy. Her father had remarried and now had a second family and her stepmother appears to have rejected her. She had learned to read and write at a very young age and had strong opinions of her own. Charlotte had been sent away to be brought up by an aunt, had no private income or dowry, which was why she had had to support herself as a governess from an early age. In the economic depression and social upheaval following the Napoleonic Wars many young middle-class women of good families were working as governesses but their social position presented ambiguities in the rigid hierarchies of Georgian and Victorian society. Should they be asked to change for dinner and eat with the family or should they be sent to the servants' hall where the conversation was considerably more ribald? Governesses were meant to be meek and demure and were certainly not intended to marry into the landed gentry.

When Mrs King and the Lethbridges joined the ship at Southampton, Mrs Harriet King was annoyed to find that James Atkinson was obviously much 'taken' with the governess she had engaged for the children of her invalid niece. James Atkinson was personable, well educated and relatively wealthy, in land and sheep if not in money. Life as a governess, even on a relatively high salary, was not a desirable future for a penniless but intelligent thirty-year-old woman who dreamed of having her home of her own and children.[1]

Harriet King was less than amused by the shipboard romance between the young squatter and the governess. She blamed Charlotte rather than the infatuated James Atkinson and wrote to her husband:

> I am much disappointed in Miss Waring, the Governess, she is very different from what she ought to be, or we expected. We had not been two hours on board before I saw she was flirting with Mr Atkinson and ere ten days were over she was engaged to him. She came around in the ship from London but altogether it was only about three weeks' acquaintance . . . I have spoken to her and represented how vexed Hannibal and Maria will be, but she told me she must be mistress of her own actions.

Charlotte had been supporting herself by teaching children since her late teens at a time when most middle-class women were loath to go out to work for money. Mrs King thought she had made a good choice, and thinking Charlotte would remain a spinster had chosen her among scores of applicants. Now she was annoyed. Governesses were expected to mind their manners, be seen and not heard and accept cast-off clothing with thanks—not, like Miss Waring, become engaged to one of the colony's largest landowners before they had even started work for her relations. She decided to have a word with Charlotte but found she had met her match.

Spirited Charlotte refused to be browbeaten into giving up a chance of marriage to such an eligible man as James Atkinson. Firmly she stood her ground when reprimanded by Mrs King. But as the Macarthurs had paid her fare and as Maria Macarthur was ill, it was agreed she would still go to *Vineyard* for six months and then marry. This would give the Hannibal Macarthurs time to find another governess.

Early in 1827 the *Cumberland* reached Sydney. Charlotte bade James a sad farewell and was rowed up the Parramatta River where she landed at the Macarthurs' private jetty. She was shown over their handsome stone mansion known as *Vineyard*, a household fit for a prince, run by an Indian butler and flocks of maids specially imported from Scotland. Only the outdoor servants and the maintenance staff were convicts.[2]

As governess, Charlotte's duties consisted of educating Elizabeth, aged eleven, who would in her teens marry Harriet King's son, Philip Gidley, and Elizabeth's younger sisters—gentle Annie, who loved gardens and would eventually marry Lieutenant John Wickham and move to Brisbane's *Newstead House*; temperamental Kate, who would marry Patrick Leslie, first squatter on the Darling Downs; little Emmeline, the baby of the family was doubtless too young for lessons. Charlotte taught the girls the accomplishments of young ladies of the period. They studied literature, French, music as well as dressmaking and embroidery. The Macarthur girls who missed their mother as illness had deprived them of her company for long periods,[3] became very fond of Charlotte. Confronted by the ambiguous social position of a governess, Charlotte wished to prove that she was just as good as the *Vineyard* Macarthurs, who, at that time, had money to burn but who were in trade rather than in a profession like her own father.

Charlotte's father is believed to have been a widowed barrister who had retired early from work due to ill-health, remarried and did not have a great deal of money to support his new family.[4] Charlotte was an unusually brilliant child and related how her father had a passion for natural history.[5] Certainly both Charlotte and her youngest daughter Caroline Louisa inherited a passion for botany and wildlife.

Charlotte was given a few days off so she and James could spend a brief holiday together at *Crows Nest Cottage* on Sydney's north shore. There they were chaperoned by Miss Elizabeth Wollstonecraft, sister of one of James' friends, who was engaged to marry Alexander Berry. Berry was a wealthy shipowner who as an absentee landlord ruled over thousands of acres at Shoalhaven and hundreds of convict labourers like some medieval prince. He did not take to educated, strong-minded Miss Waring at all and prophesied disaster for the marriage, so it seems unfortunate that James Atkinson appointed Alexander Berry as executor of his will.

In September 1827 Charlotte left the Macarthurs' employment, married James Atkinson at Cobbity. She and her new husband lived in a one-storey wooden dwelling named Mereworth while a much larger English-style country house named *Oldbury* was being built for them on the slopes of Mount Gingenbullen at Sutton Forest.[6] Atkinson's book, *An Account of the State of Agriculture and Grazing in New South Wales* had just been published in London and aroused great interest in New South Wales.

The 1830s were prosperous times for those on the land. There was a boom in wool prices and James Atkinson increased his holdings until he leased or owned some 324 hectares around Sutton Forest and other areas. Atkinson loved the bush. He also enjoyed exploring the remote gorges of the Shoalhaven area and had set up a second cattle station at Budgong on a tributary of the Shoalhaven River.[7] The couple had three children, Jane Emily, who is believed to have died in infancy, James and Caroline Louisa, (often known as Louisa) who was born at Oldbury in February 1834.

Unfortunately James Atkinson contracted an illness, which his daughter Louisa believed 'was caused by drinking from a spring on a mountain named Razorback on the Sydney road which James climbed when overheated'. His fatal illness may well have been typhus or typhoid, caught from water polluted by animal excrement and the 'overheating' a result of fever.

James Atkinson died aged thirty-nine in the prime of his life—baby Caroline Louisa was only two months old. On the one occasion she was taken into her father's sickbed, her crying disturbed her dying father who requested that his daughter be removed from the sickroom.[8] This did not prevent Caroline Louisa from admiring his achievements when she grew up. Her independence of spirit, her way with words and her keenness for studying flora and fauna was derived from her father as well as her mother. The local Aborigines, with whom the Atkinsons had been on friendly terms, came to offer condolences.

James Atkinson's will named his wife, and two friends, Alexander Berry from Berry's Bay, Sydney and Shoalhaven, and John Coghill of Kirkham, as executors.

Detail of a botanical watercolour with identification notes in pencil by Caroline Louisa Atkinson. Reproduced courtesy the late Miss Janet Cosh and now in the Mitchell Library, State Library of New South Wales.

This choice was to prove a thorn in the side of Charlotte and her family and Caroline Louisa's first years were passed in an atmosphere of financial stress and family crisis. Running cattle and sheep properties on the edge of the brooding, isolated Belanglo forest was hazardous.[9] Many escaped convicts who had turned to bushranging sheltered there and killed travellers and attacked homesteads in the area to obtain money. Such robberies occurred at least ten times at Charlotte's cattle stations.

On 30 January 1836 Charlotte was threatened with physical harm by a bushranger when out riding with her new farm manager or superintendent, George Barton.[10]

The clash of the bushranger and the lady property owner was reported in the *Sydney Herald*. At this time 'ladies' were meant to be chaperoned in drawing rooms if men who were not related to them were present, and it aroused considerable comment that a lady like Charlotte had been travelling unchaperoned with her male farm manager and this may have made her decide to marry Barton.

A month later Charlotte and George Barton were married at the chapel at Sutton Forest and Barton left the mill and moved into the big home. Marriage changed the balance of power between them. No longer was Charlotte the employer of George Barton in sole control of her property and her life. Wives could not own property in the nineteenth century, so by law Barton took control of her money and her farm. Charlotte became merely the wife and chattel of the lessee of Oldbury. Following her marriage the two male executors leased the farm to her husband, granting him an annual sum from the property on which to maintain her new stepchildren.

Charlotte's life soon turned into a nightmare. She discovered her husband was totally unconcerned with the care of the stock on the property and spent most of his time drinking. When she questioned the amount of money he spent on alcohol, he erupted into bouts of manic rage in which he destroyed furniture and had to be restrained by servants. She began to fear for the safety of her children and found that she now had to do most of the farm management. She was mortified to watch her second husband taking large sums of money from the farm account to spend on drink.

As she was now virtually running the property single-handed Charlotte had to make visits of inspection on horseback to Budgong through deep gorges and over mountain tracks. Having been threatened by a bushranger on that same route, she took a convict labourer named James Barnet with her. It showed considerable courage to make the hazardous journey at all but left Charlotte vulnerable in court to Barton's claims that she was sleeping with Barnet and other convicts on her overnight journeys of inspection.

Had the executors of the estate backed Charlotte against her husband's fevered claims it would have been different. But Alexander Berry had never liked Charlotte and did not support her now that the property was declining. The mill was sold to Charles Throsby and many of the Oldbury sheep, once famous for the quality of their wool, were sold off cheaply. By now Charlotte and her husband were living in a state of open warfare. Barton threatened to sell off the furniture and Charlotte took fright. She was worried that as his wife she had no redress in law against his unreasonable claims, so she sent some of her best pieces of furniture to be cared for by friends in Sydney. She could no longer tolerate his wild bouts of rage and feared for the children's safety. There was no possibility of divorce at this period. Charlotte decided the only course of action open to her was to run away and live in the small bush hut at Budgong and try and obtain a separation by legal means with enough income to maintain her and her children.

She realised she must leave her beloved Oldbury to her violent husband, who she now regarded as a 'raving lunatic'. Charlotte took advantage of the fact that a 'friend from England' was staying at Oldbury and travelling around looking at rural property to purchase. Charlotte decided to accompany the young man some of the way, continue on to the slab hut at Budgong and not return.

She packed the necessary household items and clothes onto a dray and slung her precious writing desk from the saddle of one of the packhorses. The children begged to take their pet koala, who was placed in a pannier, slung from the other side of the saddle of a packhorse. When Barton was sleeping off a drunken spree, the adults, a couple of convict servants, an Aboriginal boy named Charley and the three children set out across the rugged Belanglo forest and down the steep Meryla Pass.[11]

Five-year-old Caroline Louisa always remembered that harrowing journey on horseback down the steepest of isolated and thickly forested gorges. Many years later she would use this as the basis for a short story which was published in the *Sydney Morning Herald* of 22 October 1861. Caroline Louisa disguised the fact that her fiction was based on her mother's moonlight flit from Oldbury by calling the story *A Night Adventure in the Bush*. It is an interesting piece of descriptive prose with a sting in the tail: the short story form amply demonstrates her verbal fluency and command of language. Under the name of Louisa Atkinson, she became one of Sydney's first and widely read professional female journalists as well as a published novelist, although in the Victorian age her novels often had to be published anonymously as by 'A Lady'.

And this is the short story she wrote based on her journey to Budgong with the family pet.

Detail of a botanical watercolour with identification notes in pencil by Caroline Louisa Atkinson. Reproduced courtesy the late Miss Janet Cosh and now in the Mitchell Library, State Library of New South Wales.

A lady, her family, a friend, and several servants, including an Aboriginal boy, performed a journey which, though not long, was rendered difficult by the nature of the ground traversed. So steep were the mountains and so lacking in bridges were the streams that no vehicle could cross them. Goods were conveyed on packsaddles placed on the back of bullocks. The party, with the exception of the drivers, were mounted on horseback. The first fifteen miles accomplished, with great fatigue, danger and delay, the cavalcade reached the descent from the mountain. The horses groaned audibly, trembled and even sank powerless on the dangerous declivity, hardly encouraged by the sight of the yawning gully at the side of the narrow road. Coaxing, shouting and other exertions of will surmounted this difficulty. The party proceeded briskly, leading their horses; the pack bullocks and their drivers soon falling into the rear.

Onward trudged the travellers to the foot of the mountain where they were to camp for the night in a deep narrow vale where mountains rose abruptly on either side of the creek.

Persons who travelled these parts with their stock had erected a yard near the stream to secure their cattle during the night. Near this the party sat down, after lighting a fire, to await the arrival of the tents, provisions and their servants, for only Charley, the black boy, had accompanied them. But, as total darkness closed above them and the absentees came not, all ears strained to catch the first sound of them. Conversation flagged and then ceased. During this anxious hush the fire died down . . . when suddenly appeared a small light, scarcely larger than a spark.

'Charley, what is that?' inquired several tremulous voices.

'Debel, debel, I believe,' returned the lad, whose teeth were chattering. On came the light, about two feet from the ground.

'Nonsense, Charley. What can it be?' Charley again hinted at the possibility of the presence of His Satanic Majesty, while the little luminous speck crept onward towards the horror-struck group.

'Can it be a bushranger?' whispered the lady.

'I believe so, Miss,' returned the little Aboriginal.

Imaginations presented a picture of a bushranger with a lighted pipe in his mouth, about to fire upon the helpless victims, who were rendered visible by the flickering of a tongue of flame in the fire while darkness concealed him, and goodness knows how many more!

The lady fainted. The young people were panic-struck, Charley equally so. The gentleman from England was entirely unused to the bush. He entered into the general alarm but he surmounted it by throwing some dead branches on the almost-expiring fire. The bright blaze shot up, illuminating the surrounding scene—not revealing a band of brigands, but setting the light flickering in a way that bore evidence of its insect origin. Inspired by new courage, active exertions were made and a small brown beetle captured. The light appeared to be emitted from a pale yellow spot on the underpart of the body.

Still the men and the pack bullocks did not arrive. The dews of evening were falling and there were no tents erected, no supper to refresh and invigorate the weary travellers. There is nothing like sitting in the dark, watching and listening to evoke fear. In spite of the bushranger turning out to be just a little beetle, fear held possession of all hearts when the tramping of heavy feet was heard. One of the pack bullocks was running wildly down the mountain, dragging behind him a heavy body.

Again the black boy was applied to, as being better provided with bush lore, but he was overpowered by cowardice and superstition. In reply to a volley of questions, he expressed an opinion that the bullock had killed his driver, and was dragging his lifeless body behind him. This ghastly suggestion was received as fact, everyone being too horror-struck to reflect that, as the driver was in no way attached to the bullock's harness, he would not be dragged [by the animal].

On rushed the animal, concealed by the darkness, plunged into the creek and hurried to the stockyard, where it was in the habit of being released from its load. There was a pause, as of death. Once again hurried feet were heard. The three pack bullocks had assembled at the stockyard, each dragging something behind them—their loads, suggested someone; and so it proved. Now came the drovers and related the cause of their detention to the family around the fire.

As the family were intending to make a lengthy stay they had brought with them a very important member of their household, no less than their pet bear. This portly gentleman had been accommodated in a pannier basket, swung on one side of the packsaddle, while to give balance, a hamper of earthenware and a writing desk were suspended on the other side.

Whatever were the bear's thoughts on this occasion, he had given no expression to them until he found the ox his bearer descending the steep mountain side. This was too much for any gentleman, so the bear became angry and stuck his long claws through the wickerwork deep into the bullock's back . . . The ox began to run. The shaking caused the bear to roar, much to the horror of the bovine trio, who ran away, scattering their insecure load along the road, breaking the fragile earthenware, scattering the pieces and releasing the bear, who speedily climbed up a tree. The drovers, being unable to coax him down, set about felling the tree to get to the bear, trusting the bullocks would keep to the right road. By this time night had closed down.

The bear, it must be understood, was neither the great Polar, the Californian brown or the American grizzly, but only a *Phascolarctus*, of gumleaf-eating habits (better known as a koala), not given to hugging its prey to death!

Charlotte and her children spent seven months at Budgong—from December 1839 to June 1840. Their living accommodation was extremely basic. Budgong only had a wooden slab hut with its dirt floor. It was so remote and difficult to reach even on horseback it was difficult to bring groceries and other supplies down the steep path into the ravine where cattle were corralled beside the hut. Everything had to be reached by dray or packhorse over great distance. However, at last Charlotte was free from George Barton's drinking, his mood swings, and violence towards her and her children and was free to devote most of her time to their lessons.

In front of the children Charlotte put a brave face on things and turned their stay into an adventure. She read to them and took them on long nature rambles in the bush, either on foot or on horseback, even going as far away as the coast at Jervis Bay. This appreciation of nature and naming of species of plants and animals would have a deep effect on her youngest daughter and motivate her to become a botanist and writer.

Caroline Louisa turned six at Budgong. She was old enough to absorb her mother's fascination with native birds, animals, insects and plants, a passion which would stay with her all her short life. George Barton did not waste time searching for them. He stayed at Oldbury, drinking heavily and sleeping off his drinking bouts with the Oldbury sheep and cattle uncared for and the farm sliding into chaos.

Eventually Barton also fell out with Alexander Berry and with the other executor, John Coghill, a former sea captain-turned-amateur farmer, who found being Atkinson's executor time-consuming and frustrating and wanted only to relinquish his responsibility for running the estate. Coghill left most of the management of James Atkinson's will to Alexander Berry and his clerks, who after a series of legal battles managed to invoke the law and have George Barton turned out of Oldbury.

By now much of the money from the estate had been exhausted by litigation and management fees but Charlotte and the children returned home. They were warmly welcomed by the local Aborigines, who had been attached to James Atkinson, whose memory they had not forgotten. When Charlotte mentioned his name and showed the Aboriginal women a locket she wore around her neck containing a piece of her late husband's hair they became visibly upset. Probably Charlotte did not know this, but it went against local Aboriginal custom to name the dead. Charlotte would write about this event which remained in her memory for many years.

Charlotte was worried about the older children's schooling and wished them to attend school in Sydney so the executors leased Oldbury (from which most of the good stock had now been sold) to a farmer named T.B. Humphrey, who ran his

Caroline Louisa Atkinson. A drawing made to illustrate her novel Gertrude the Emigrant, *showing her heroine Gertrude and the ex-convict Mrs Doherty returning to the homestead watched by Aborigines.*

own cattle there. But the tenant's rent was only enough to provide a small income which made life hard for Charlotte. George Barton's sworn statement that his wife had cohabited with convicts had seriously damaged her reputation in certain circles. Berry chose to believe her husband's accusations and tried to delay paying the sum of one thousand pounds owing to Charlotte from her late husband's will. He also sought to have the children removed from her by claiming she was not a fit parent, which caused enormous distress both to Charlotte and her children.

But like many other courageous women, Charlotte turned adversity into a challenge. To make some money for herself and her family she wrote the first book specially designed for Australian children. It was called *A Mother's Offering to her Children* and was published in 1841. It was based on simple tales of bush life and the author's previous encounters with local Aborigines and was written in the form of a dialogue between a mother and her children. Charlotte managed to persuade a Sydney bookseller, George William Evans of Bridge Street, to publish her book.

Writing was not seen as a suitable occupation for nineteenth-century ladies so the book had to be published under the pseudonym 'A Lady Long Resident in New South Wales.[12] It was favourably reviewed by the *Sydney Gazette* who praised the writer as 'a person of taste', and advertised for sale by the publisher in the *Australian* of 18 and 30 December 1841. But like most Australian books it did not sell in large numbers as there were few bookshops and it certainly did not make her rich.

In an attempt to remove the children from Charlotte's care, both executors appointed Edward Corry, a young solicitor recently arrived from England, as the children's guardian. Charlotte found this an affront to her educational skills and her rights as a parent. She was accused of leaving the children alone in their remote home at Sydney's Rose Bay, when, ironically, it was the executors who were causing her to travel by coach down the pot-holed South Head Road to the city to consult lawyers so she might fight her battles in court.

The whole affair dragged on and on. Finally, in July 1841, Charlotte's case came to court as *Atkinson versus Barton and others*. Justice Dowling was a fair and honourable man and appointed Charlotte guardian of her own children. He ordered she be paid three hundred and fifty pounds a year for their maintenance.[13]

However, the price of wool crashed overseas and that and a prolonged drought caused a depression on the land. The tenant at Oldbury went bankrupt and during the next couple of years failed to pay any rent at all so Charlotte still had difficulty in receiving her child maintenance from Alexander Berry. Strong letters were exchanged between them. By this time Berry loathed her and called her 'a notable she-dragon'. Charlotte was powerless against the wealthy and well-connected Berry and was forced into the expense of returning to court once again to obtain the maintenance previously granted by Justice Dowling.[14]

The case of Charlotte and George Barton and her protracted quest for child maintenance is indicative of the low status of women seeking justice against violent husbands in colonial New South Wales. It illustrates very vividly the fact that women in the Victorian period had no rights to their own money after they married.

Why did someone as intelligent as Charlotte marry George Barton in the first place? She does not seem to fit into the category of victim or 'women who love too much'. She had already demonstrated sufficient judgment to make one secure and loving marriage, which was only terminated by the premature death of her husband. Unfortunately, like most women in colonial Australia, Charlotte wrote nothing down about her feelings. Undoubtedly one of the factors which propelled Charlotte headlong into a disastrous marriage with Barton was her isolation at Oldbury and the difficulties she faced as a woman employing convict male labourers. The final blow must have been the attack by the bushranger on Barton and herself on the way to her cattle station at Budgong. At the time Charlotte married Barton, there was an almost total breakdown of law and order in the Berrima and Sutton Forest areas, partly due to shepherds working in the enormous and (at that time) unmapped Belanglo forest area where there were many former convicts only too happy to shelter bushrangers and fugitives from the law.

In hindsight Barton seems to have suffered from alcoholism and a psychosis of late onset, for which, at the time, there was no drug treatment. But even when Barton's behaviour was floridly disturbed, Berry, who owned vast estates in the Shoalhaven Region and knew of the lawless state of affairs there, continued to believe Barton's claims against Charlotte. It was only when Barton requested enormous sums of money from the estate that Berry finally turned against him.

The powerful and autocratic Alexander Berry and his fellow executor John Coghill were finally exonerated by the court from all suggestions by Charlotte and her lawyers of misappropriation of the Oldbury funds.

For the next six years Charlotte's life was never free of stress and legal wrangles as she struggled against Berry and Coghill in order to gain access to money which was rightfully hers. Clearly at this period the New South Wales judicial system was heavily weighted against Charlotte, both as a woman and a lone parent. The child maintenance allowance of three hundred and fifty pounds per annum awarded to her by Justice Dowling was later reduced by a hundred pounds on appeal by the executors, which seems punitive in the extreme.

Only after a second appeal by Charlotte was the children's maintenance raised again and then only by fifty pounds, less than Dowling's original judgment. By this time Charlotte was living at Rose Bay, then an isolated and inexpensive country area reached by the Old South Head Road. Later she moved closer to the city, renting a terrace house in Darlinghurst, in order that the children could receive a good secondary education in central Sydney. She now needed more money rather than less.[15]

In spite of her educational qualifications and her previous good character, male judges other than Justice Dowling preferred to believe the unreliable evidence of the proven alcoholic Barton that Charlotte was not fit to be custodian of her own children. The end of this sorry saga of injustice was that Barton became so violent that he was forcibly taken away to an asylum and certified as a 'raving lunatic'. He never recovered his faculties and died insane in a padded cell.[16]

For some years they stayed on in Sydney, where young Charlotte and James John attended Sydney College. Oldbury had been left in trust for James John until he was 21 and, since the house was let once again, Charlotte decided to remove her young family to live at Fernhurst, Kurrajong Heights a particularly beautiful rural area. As Caroline Louisa was a delicate child it was decided not to send her to school in Sydney, and Charlotte undertook her daughter's education herself. She was an artist and a keen naturalist and she passed on this love of the native flora and fauna to her daughter, together with her artistic aptitude. Charlotte naturally encouraged her daughter to write articles and novels.

Caroline Louisa's first novel, *Gertrude the Immigrant: A Tale of Colonial Life*, was published by an 'Australian Lady' in 1857, when she was only 23 in Sydney. Its anonymous author was the first Australian-born woman to write a book and have it published in her own land. The book tells the story of Gertrude, a young German girl who emigrates to Australia and becomes a housekeeper to a Mrs Doherty, a former convict who has become the owner of a property in the bush. Mrs Doherty is quite an emancipated woman and runs the farm herself, assisted by Edward, the overseer. It is a classic Victorian romance. Edward falls in love with Gertrude but is too shy to speak his heart. She falls for the handsome Charles, but he turns out to be a former bushranger with a criminal record. After some violent action scenes in which Mrs Doherty meets a dreadful end at the hands of Charles, Gertrude and the trustworthy Edward are united.

Although Gertrude is portrayed as a pious Bronte-style heroine, always rushing off to consult her Bible, she is nevertheless a woman of great strength of purpose

Illustration by Caroline Louisa Atkinson made for her novel Gertrude the Emigrant *shows a dance in the wool-shed, lit by candles in bottles. A chalk line was drawn across the floor to separate the colonial 'gentry' from the workers.*

and determination and is not afraid to speak her mind. This is surprising in a book written in an era when women were meant to be meek and subservient and their husbands were the autocratic heads of the households.[17]

Caroline Louisa illustrated the book herself, having been taught to draw by her mother, who had also given her a thorough grounding in English literature and syntax, the arts and the sciences. Caroline Louisa had been encouraged by Charlotte and became an ardent collector of botanical specimens and an illustrator of plants and native animals. The widowed Charlotte had a very close relationship with her youngest daughter and although Caroline Louisa never had any formal schooling, she received an excellent education.

Writing as Louisa Atkinson, she published three more novels, which were also serialised in the *Sydney Morning Herald* and the *Sydney Mail*. They were *The Ground of the Carlillawara Claimaints*, *Tressa's Resolve* and *Myra*. These were all written for Australian readers. Caroline Louisa believed fiercely in the value of education for women and their duty to reform the often cruel alcoholic and male-dominated society which she had seen at Oldbury through George Barton. She was a deeply spiritual girl, totally uninterested in material wealth, and with a 'simple, unaffected and sincere faith', according to her friend, Dr William Woolls, the renowned teacher and amateur botanist. She expressed her religion in practical ways through care for the sick and needy.

After the success of *Gertrude the Immigrant* and the serialised books, she had another book published by a Sydney firm, *Cowanda*, or *The Veteran's Grant*, a tale of life in the Australian bush which includes a vivid account of life on the Turon goldfields. Caroline Louisa also contributed articles on a regular basis to the *Horticultural Magazine*. In January 1865 she amazed her readers by providing a free pot of cranberry jam with each copy of the magazine, to encourage them to eat the native cranberry or *Lissanthe sapida*. Caroline Louisa was considerably in advance of her time in her belief that Australians should learn to eat their own native fruits.

Until her death 14 year later, this hardworking young woman wrote a steady flow of articles and novels which were published, often in serial form, in the *Sydney Morning Herald* and the *Sydney Mail*.[18] Her stories, studded with delightful descriptions of animals, birds and native plants, are still very readable today. *A Night in the Bush*, reproduced above, shows a delightful sense of humour and a fine eye for detail. She wrote simply and with feeling about the countryside she had explored herself—the land between Windsor and Wisemans Ferry, and the then remote bush around Kurrajong, Springwood, Mount Tomah, Berrima and Illawarra.

Caroline Louisa's novel *Tom Hellicar's Children* was also serialised by the *Sydney Mail* in 1871, when it received wide acclaim as an Australian novel, written for Australians. The story is about the three children of Tom Hellicar, left in an uncle's guardianship on their father's death. The plot details the sad treatment that they and their mother receive at this man's hands after being left helpless and at the mercy of a trustee who turned out to be only interested in his own selfish ends. Some of the plot would certainly have been suggested by the Atkinson family's difficulties with their father's trustees over Oldbury, and the small amount of money the trustees allowed them for living expenses out of this large estate.

In her novel Caroline Louisa clearly understands her characters. The villain is not all vile, as in a classic Victorian melodrama; he has powerful motivations for his mercenary conduct, and these are revealed by the author.

Tom Hellicar's Children was set in New South Wales during the gold rush period. It can be enjoyed today, even though the moral of the story that good eventually triumphs over evil may be no longer fashionable in novels. The book contains some vivid descriptions; particularly remarkable is a passage dealing with the rounding-up of wild horses or brumbies. One of Tom's children rides down a rocky hillside after a wild horse in an incident which could have served as a model for Banjo Paterson's *The Man from Snowy River*, published nearly quarter of a century later.

She had the ability to create a convincing character and situation in a few sentences:

> There was an awful mystery about Mrs Heland's illness. The doctor did not know, and nobody knew. She used to say, If dear Doctor Peel was alive, she was sure he would know, to which everybody answered, 'Very Likely.' Some people thought she had been married previously and was the widow of Dr Peel, others thought he was her brother or her uncle . . . However he was dead and Mrs Heland's sufferings continued unalleviated. Whatever they were, they occasioned obesity. She was always found either reclining on her couch or seated in an armchair, covered with greasy chintz, with her large puffy feet on a high footstool and cased in slippers run down on one side . . . At night she had to take a strong glass of hot gin and water, about which she uttered every night little shrieks and shudders, but said that she must not be so naughty as to disobey the doctor, and so drank it.

As a keen observer of the social nuances that existed in the colony of New South Wales at the time and an Australian-born woman, she was without the snobbishness and pretensions of writers from England, such as Louisa Meredith. She ridiculed class distinctions as being unimportant in a pioneer land where men and women must create their own opportunities. However, she saw with the writer's eye what happened to British immigrants and tellingly recorded her observations in passages such as the following:

> Among the group around the table was a young man, perhaps four-and-twenty years of age, with long heavily oiled hair curling inwards on his neck and a brilliant satin waistcoat, much worn and soiled, and with a large brassy ring on his finger.

A man who had aspired to be a gentleman and had gone down, and down to tawdry ruin.

Atkinson's characters are not fired with the desire to make a fortune in the colony and then return to England to enjoy their wealth. Her heroines were Australian. They want to remain in Australia and settle on their own properties and enjoy the beauties of the Australian bush. Her books are important in Australian literature because they herald the emergence of a truly indigenous approach to fiction writing.

In Australian literature Caroline Louisa can be regarded as perhaps standing midway between Ada Cambridge and Rosa Campbell-Praed. Like Ada Cambridge, she had an excellent sense of humour and this is communicated in her writing. However, Ada Cambridge merely wrote 'to buy pretty things for my babies' while Caroline Louisa was a compulsive writer, diligently recording the changing patterns of Australian society during the gold rush period and its effect on the lives of the women of that era.

Caroline Louisa's love of her own country is revealed in this account of a camping trip in the bush:

> There is a charm in this nomadic life, which they who have not tried can form no idea of. They who have tried it grow so attached [to it] as to be quite averse to a settled mode of existence . . . When night comes the bush traveller unladens his horses, puts on their hobbles and then attends to his own comforts. Probably he has no tent to erect, perhaps he builds a screen of branches, in any case a good fire is a matter of course in summer, as in winter. A few coals are raked out and the tin quart-pot set to boil. As the bubbles rise around the rim, a generous handful of tea is cast in . . . Tea is now ready. With the aid of a tomahawk or small axe one rapidly strips a little sheet of bark from the nearest tree, and, turning the inner side uppermost, mixes on it a dough of flour and water. This is pressed out very thin and divided into circular cakes. A glowing mass of embers is laid on it. They require turning in a few minutes and the bread supply is complete. These 'leather jackets' [damper] make an acceptable addition to the salt beef or bacon which comprises the meal. Repose follows and what a sound sleep it is, with the light blue smoke curling above . . . and driving away the mosquitoes which sound their little war trumpets most annoyingly . . . with a saddle for a downy pillow. The cries of flying foxes and opossums and other nocturnal animals do not break the traveller's repose.

This extract was taken from Caroline Louisa's Nature Guide newspaper column. However, her most enduring work was undoubtedly her botanical research. Caroline Louisa was still young when her family moved to Kurrajong (some 60 km from Sydney) and it was there that she learned to go out, often on horseback, sometimes for days at a time, collecting plant specimens, writing descriptions and making drawings of them. She was often accompanied by Mrs Emma Selkirk, the wife of a Richmond medical practitioner. Her mother encouraged her on these expeditions, criticised her drawings and her writing, and no doubt hoped that the long days in the open air would improve her daughter's delicate health. Together, the doctor's wife and the eager young girl clambered over rocks and down gullies to collect plants. The two created a minor scandal in the district by wearing trousers on their collecting trips, rather than conventional but restricting long skirts.

The stern disapproval of the wowsers and the gossip of frustrated old maids was of little consequence to Caroline Louisa. She continued to collect plants, roots and seeds in a large leather satchel which she wore schoolboy fashion across her chest. She also kept up a regular correspondence with William Woolls, the noted amateur botanist who was in constant contact with experts at Kew Gardens, and with Baron

Ferdinand von Mueller, the founder of the Melbourne Botanical Gardens, who was a fanatical writer of letters to his devoted team of plant collectors around Australia. The Baron was supplied with specimens by many dedicated amateur collectors. Caroline Louisa's specimens were by far the best documented and packaged. Most of the flowers and seeds she pressed and dried herself.

Both men were enthusiastic about Caroline Louisa's work and Woolls went so far as to describe her as 'the most interesting of Australia's daughters', praising her numerous talents and the sincerity of her character. In March 1871 Woolls wrote her a letter of congratulation, full of excitement because she had just rediscovered a particularly rare orchid, the *Rimacola elliptica*, which had eluded all other specimen hunters for nearly 70 years. Baron von Mueller, whom many of his colleagues found a most difficult and critical man, praised her work for its meticulous accuracy and attention to scientific detail and named two plants in her honour. One was a species of mistletoe she had discovered.

Caroline Louisa continued to write a series of nature articles under the title *A Voice from the Country*. These described the flora and fauna of Kurrajong and Berrima, as seen at different times of the year. They were published in the *Sydney Morning Herald* for some 12 years as part of a Nature Calendar to guide fellow naturalists on their rambles in different seasons. It was through the publication of these articles that her work attracted the attention of such renowned botanists as Woolls, von Mueller and the Reverend William Branwell Clarke, the distinguished naturalist and geologist who first discovered gold in New South Wales. By March 1861 she had provided Woolls and von Mueller with over 300 plant specimens, many of which were exceptionally rare.

Caroline Louisa's newspaper articles were written for the Australian rather than the English market and commanded a wide audience. One of her readers was her future husband, a courageous Englishman named James Snowden Calvert. He had come to Australia aboard the same ship as the explorer Dr Ludwig Leichhardt.[19] While at sea, Calvert was so enthralled by Leichhardt's account of the bush that he asked permission to accompany the explorer on his planned expedition to Port Essington. By 1844 Leichhardt was ready to leave and James Calvert joined him as the second youngest in the party. Although Calvert played only a minor role on the expedition, he emerges from Leichhardt's journal as reliable and dependable and was the only one of the whole party to escape criticism from the explorer in his letters. Leichhardt described him as a good talker, a man with a sense of humour who enlivened the party and made 'a good companion'. He was severely wounded on one expedition by native spears.

On his return from the trip Calvert became manager of Cavan Station, near Yass, and developed his interests in native plants and botany. Possibly he and Caroline Louisa were introduced by William Woolls or through William Sharpe Macleay. It was a case of instant attraction and strong mutual interests. The wedding was at Oldbury in 1869 and it was certainly 'a marriage of true minds' in the Shakespearian sense.

Caroline Louisa's mother was now dead and her brother, James John Atkinson, was living at Oldbury. The Calverts moved to Sutton Forest to be near him. She wrote a glowing account of her new home to her friend Mrs Woolls, saying that it had 'wonderful gullies at the back with unknown treasures in them'. Together Caroline Louisa and her new husband continued to collect, sketch, write and press specimens. Baron von Mueller corresponded with the couple, requesting specimens of grasses and rushes from 'your thus far unknown locality' and asking for seeds to send to the noted English naturalist Joseph Hooker.

The Mitchell Library in Sydney contains a large collection of Caroline Louisa's drawings of Australian native ferns, which she drew and painted and attempted to classify, as well as birds and animals. Baron von Mueller arranged that she should

*Caroline Louisa Atkinson.
Photograph taken around the
time of her marriage. Courtesy
the late Miss Janet Cosh.*

contribute some of these drawings as illustrations to a book which was to be published by the University of Kiel in Germany, but the university department was unable to obtain sufficient funding and the work was never published. However, the English botanist George Bentham acknowledged Caroline Louisa's detailed original botanical research on Blue Mountains and Berrima specimens nearly 120 times in his great book entitled *Flora Australiensis* and her work was praised by her botanist contemporaries in Australia, both amateur and professional. She was also preparing to write her own illustrated book on Australian flora and fauna.

Her contributions to Australian science are all the more remarkable when it is realised how poor was her health. Towards the end of her life she was forced to slow down because of heart disease. After Oldbury was sold, many of the albums of flowers that she and her husband had pressed were burnt, along with numerous drawings and manuscripts by Caroline Louisa and her mother, in the fire at their former home.

Caroline Louisa's death was tragic in the extreme. The Calverts had a small daughter, also named Louisa. Still weak after the birth of this baby only eighteen days previously, had stayed at home while her husband went out on horseback to collect specimens for their research. The horse shied and James Calvert was thrown off and suffered a sprained ankle. Frightened, the horse then galloped home to *Swanton Cottage* on Oldbury where they lived. Hearing the galloping of a horse's hooves, Caroline Louisa ran to the window, her little girl in her arms. She is believed to have seen the riderless horse and feared her husband had suffered an accident. She had a fatal heart attack.[20] Her husband found her dead when he limped home several hours later. She was only thirty-eight and had been married for just three years and was deeply involved with the book which might well have made her famous in botanical circles overseas.

For several years James Calvert was so desolate that he scarcely ventured out, devoting himself to bringing up his baby daughter. Dr Woolls wrote an article about Caroline Louisa's life to act as her obituary. In addition to her artistic and literary work he described her kind and generous nature, her love of the small children she taught in her Sunday School classes and the help that she had always given to friends, neighbours, the sick and those in need.

Few women of the colonial era have so many monuments. There are commemorative plaques in Caroline Louisa's honour at Sutton Forest and in Richmond churches, and more recently a memorial to her was placed in Powell Park, Kurrajong Heights. Various scientific seminars have been held on her botanical discoveries and the *Epacris calvertiana* was named after her by Baron von Mueller. *Tom Hellicar's Children*, *A Voice from the Country* and *Excursions from Berrima* have been republished in commemorative editions.

[1]   King Papers, Vol. 1, Mitchell Library, Sydney. Mrs King's letter about Charlotte Waring is quoted in Dorothy Walsh (ed.), *The Admiral's Wife*. Melbourne, Hawthorn Press, 1967.

[2]   For an account of life at Vineyard and the Macarthur girls see de Vries-Evans, Susanna, *Conrad Martens on the Beagle and in Australia*. Pandanus Pres, Brisbane, 1995.

[3]   Clarke, Patricia. *Pioneer Writer*. Allen and Unwin, 1990. A biography of Caroline Louisa Atkinson mentions Charlotte teaching the Macarthur girls. Emmeline Macarthur's memoirs are in my book *Pioneer Women, Pioneer Land*. Angus and Robertson, Sydney, 1987.

[4]   Clarke, Patricia. *Pioneer Writer*. *Op. cit.* This book contains a full listing of all Caroline Louisa Atkinson's books and articles and with the paper by Margaret Swann published in the *Journal of the Royal Australian Historical Society*, Vol. 15, 1929, pp. 1–29; MS by Janet Cosh, Mitchell Library and Maiden, J.H., *Records Australian Botanists*, Royal Society of New South Wales, are the main sources of information on the lives of Caroline Louisa and her mother Charlotte Atkinson, see *Mrs Meredith and Miss Atkinson*. See also *Our First Woman Novelist—Caroline Atkinson* (sic) Melbourne *Age*, 25 October 1947.

[5]   According to Caroline Louisa, Charlotte Waring was a gifted child who could read at a very early age. Caroline Louisa says Charlotte could 'read fluently' at two years (which is hard to believe)

and that she possessed 'great clearness of mind. Charlotte was too marked a character not to meet with persons to whom her uprightness and courage made her obnoxious'. In present-day language this could be translated as Charlotte was a brilliant and strong-minded woman who did not suffer fools gladly and who some men (such as the executors of her husband's will), loathed because she refused to be browbeaten. Related in 1987 by the late Miss Janet Cosh whose notes on her distinguished ancestors are in the Mitchell Library MS collection catalogued under Calvert.

6   Oldbury is at the time of writing privately owned and has been classified by the National Trust. It is built of a honey-coloured stone which gives it the air of a manor house in the Cotswolds and is built in a plain, unadorned Georgian style with a handsome portico.

7   The late Miss Janet Cosh provided details about her ancestor's early life and permission to reproduce some of Caroline Louisa's paintings.

8   Clarke, Patricia. *Op. cit.*

9   Scene of the notorious Belanglo Forest backpacker murders of the 1990s.

10 Clarke, Patricia. *Op. cit.*

11 There are conflicting accounts in the sources as to whether Emily died in infancy or took part in the flight from Oldbury and died later.

12 Charlotte Barton's book, published anonymously, was for many years believed to have been written by Lady Gordon Bremer and it was only in 1980 that Marcie Muir, in *Charlotte Barton, Australia's First Children's Author*, revealed that this important book in the history of children's literature was by Barton.

13 Archives of New South Wales.

14 Madrell Papers, Letter Berry to Coghill January 1842, and Berry Papers, both in Mitchell Library.

15 Additional details of Charlotte's fight against the executors of her husband's estate, Alexander Berry and John Coghill, and the subsequent court proceedings, taken from Courts of Petty Sessions at Berrima and Sutton Forest and the Supreme Court, are contained in Clarke, Patricia. *Op. cit.*

16 I am indebted to psychiatrist Dr Marion Tyrer for discussions about George Barton's illness and alcoholism.

17 Novels by Louisa Atkinson. Some were published anonymously according to the conventions governing women's writing in the nineteenth century:
Gertrude the Emigrant: A Tale of Colonial Life by An Australian Lady. J.R. Clarke, Sydney. 1857. (This is her best fictional work.)
Cowanda, the Veteran's Grant. J.R. Clarke, Sydney. 1859.
Debatable Ground or the Carlillawarra Claimants. Serialised in the *Sydney Mail*, 1861.
Myra. Serialised in the *Sydney Mail*, 1864, and finally published by Mulini Press of Canberra in 1983.
Tom Hellicar's Children was serialised by the *Sydney Mail* in 1871 and published by Mulini Press in 1983.
Tressa's Resolve was serialised in the *Sydney Mail* of 1872 and, to the best of my knowledge, has not been published in book form. Mulini Press have paid tribute to Caroline Louisa Atkinson's importance in early Australian women's writing and the fact she was one of Australia's first women journalists. They have republished two collections of Caroline Louisa's articles from *The Illustrated Sydney News*, *Sydney Morning Herald* and *Sydney Mail* under the titles *A Voice from the Country*, 1978, *Excursions from Berrima*, and *A Trip to Manaro and Molonglo in the 1870s*.

18 Caroline Louisa Atkinson's manuscript material is stored in the Mitchell Library, Sydney; MSS catalogued under her married name of Calvert (although she wrote most of her work under the name of Atkinson). Their holdings comprise correspondence, drafts of articles and press clippings, almost four dozen watercolours of ferns for the book which was never published, sketches of Oldbury, birds, plants and butterflies plus uncatalogued material. Additional notes have been donated to the Berrima Historical Society by the late Miss Janet Cosh.

19 *Dr Ludwig Leichhardt's Letters from Australia during the years 1842–1848*, Melbourne, 1944. Claiming that her daughter was delicate in health, Charlotte Barton was reluctant to give her consent to the marriage. Louisa cared for her invalid mother until her death and, like her mother before her, also married in her thirties but, interestingly enough, continued to write many of her articles under her single name of Atkinson.

20 Caroline Louisa's death certificate gives the cause of death as 'heart disease'. Other sources have said that she also suffered from tuberculosis or, as it was then known, 'consumption'.

CHAPTER 4

Frances (Fanny) Leonora Macleay (1793–1836)

WRITER, ARTIST AND SCIENTIFIC RESEARCHER

Fanny Macleay has become well known through letters she wrote to her elder brother describing Sydney over the period from 1826 to 1836. But Fanny was not just a good letter writer. She had a wider education and a greater interest in colonial politics and scientific research than most colonial women. It is this factor plus her wicked sense of humour which adds sparkle to Fanny's letters. Unfortunately for Fanny, who was fascinated by scientific research, she lived at a time when doctors, scientists and clergymen wanted women confined to domestic routines and argued against their right to receive higher education claiming that education would undermine women's health and fertility and hinder them from fulfilling their family obligations.

From childhood Fanny had this strong interest in science. She became an accomplished artist and natural history painter and made highly accurate scientific drawings of flowers, insects and fossilised bones for her father, who was a scientist of repute. In addition she helped her father write exact descriptions of new acquisitions to add to his vast collections of insects and other specimens.[1]

She became deeply involved with two great collections and made a series of scientific drawings of entomological, botanical and zoological specimens for her favourite brother, William Sharp Macleay, who was just as dedicated to science as her father. Fanny provided practical assistance by packing Australian specimens in brine in sealed containers to send by sea to other collectors; they responded by sending specimens of their own to add to the Macleay Collection. Like Georgiana Molloy, Fanny dried seeds, labelled them and placed them in special albums to send to her brother William and other collectors overseas.

She adored and admired William, who had attended boarding school and Cambridge University where he performed brilliantly. Fanny longed for the benefits of higher education and her letters reveal that she felt an intellectual chasm existed between her and her adored older brother. She makes self-disparaging remarks in her letters to William, such as 'I am only *une simple femelle*' (a simple female). Occasionally she loads her letters so thickly with these comments the reader wonders if she is being ironic.

Instead of going to university, Fanny and her sister spent much of their time on 'lady-like accomplishments' like needlework. William Sharp Macleay's expensive private education was intended to let him take an important place in the world. It did and eventually he became a judge in colonial Cuba. However, Fanny's home-based education was designed to enable her to assist her father, render her more marriageable and to make her a good mother. Ironically, she, who underneath her complaints, loved children, never had any of her own; instead she was forced by her mother and a strong sense of 'family obligation' to spend

No portrait of Fanny Macleay
is known. However Victorian
artist W.H. Hunt's watercolour
represents all those women who
kept families close through letter
writing as did Fanny with her
favourite brother William.

years caring for her younger sisters as though they were her own children.[2]

A succession of governesses taught all six Macleay girls to speak French and Italian, to read, draw and to dance and play the piano. But this was not enough for Fanny. For the rest of her life she tried to improve herself through extensive reading of scientific books and novels from her father's library. In Britain she talked to the eminent scientists who visited their London home or their country residence, *Tilbuster Lodge* in Surrey, situated near Selbourne, the collecting ground of the great naturalist, Gilbert White. Her father, Alexander Macleay, realised his eldest daughter was exceptionally intelligent and could help him with his research. He ensured she was taught the rudiments of botany, entomology, zoology, ornithology, marine biology, conchology, astronomy, horticulture and landscape gardening from the books in his library.

To understand Fanny's life and the forces that shaped it, it is necessary to know something of her family history. The Macleays were an ancient Highland family who had lost their ancestral lands in the Jacobite rebellion by siding with Bonnie Prince Charlie against the House of Hanover.

Alexander Macleay was born in the isolated fishing village of Wick in Caithness. He had gone south as a young man to work for a wine merchant named William Sharp before entering the public service. His temperamental but beautiful wife, Eliza, had borne him seventeen children several of whom died in childhood and adolescence.

Alexander named his eldest son William Sharp out of gratitude to his employer. Other children followed at yearly intervals with a regularity that weakened Eliza's constitution and made her depend on her clever eldest daughter, Fanny, to act as a surrogate mother. Constant childbearing coupled with epidemics of the usual infant illnesses and the harrowing deaths of four children made Fanny's mother nervy and temperamental: domestic staff rarely stayed long in the Macleay household.

Alexander Macleay remains an enigma to many historians and has never been the subject of a major biography. He was a dour, sandy-haired Scot. Yet dour Alexander had a wild spendthrift streak, borrowing constantly and spending money he did not possess on buying the largest insect collection in the world and later, in Australia, on land and sheep and cattle in the Australian wool boom. In New South Wales he extended the homestead at Brownlow Hill, laid out five acres of magnificent gardens at Elizabeth Bay and nearly bankrupted himself building elegant Elizabeth Bay House.

He probably shared the old romantic Highland dream of the days when his ancestors had hundreds of clansmen who fought for them and lived in tenanted crofts. This burning desire to own vast acres motivated many educated but *nouveau poor* Scots, who were forced to leave their homeland for Australia and north America.

But Alexander Macleay was also, throughout his career as a public servant, a model of probity, thrift and rectitude. Hampered by so many children to feed and clothe, Macleay steadily worked his way up in the public service to become Secretary to the British Transport Board. But through no fault of Macleay's the Transport Board was abolished at the end of the Napoleonic Wars and Macleay found himself in the prime of life out of a job. He also had to support an enormous family (by today's standards) on a relatively small government pension.

Fanny was Alexander Macleay's favourite daughter. To act as artist to her father's scientific collection , she was sent for lessons in 'accurate' scientific drawing and painting by a Mr Bell and by a M Pelletier, a French natural history artist[3] who could not speak English. This gave Fanny a chance to practise her French and improve her drawing. Her major formal paintings were elaborate watercolours of flower arrangements in classical urns in the Dutch still-life style. These were exhibited at London's Royal Academy in 1816, 1819 and 1824[4] and later, in Sydney, she did a large watercolour of waratahs.

Most of all during her time in London, Fanny adored accompanying her father to the British Museum. 'I could spend my whole life there,' she wrote to William, who was by now working as an attaché at the British Embassy in Paris.

But the demands of home often interfered with her interests. In 1814 when Fanny was twenty-one and longed for time to draw, write, study botany and help her father with his collection, she found herself working long hours as 'nurse, cook and housemaid' to six younger brothers and sisters forced to spend many weeks in bed with whooping cough. Fanny nursed the children devotedly even though she told William 'their coughs are enough to worry me out of my senses'. In the pre-antibiotic era, children frequently died of whooping cough. Caring for six demanding and fretful patients was an enormous responsibility for a young unmarried girl. In private to William, Fanny complained, 'I am sick, very sick of Children'.

Fanny mixed socially with many of the leading naturalists and scientists of her day, and when her brother William was working abroad, wrote to tell him how she had sent the eminent naturalist Robert Brown 'Twelve drawings or daubs as you would call them . . . in case one or two things may be worth copying into the *Bot. Mag.* Fanny referred here to *Curtis's Botanical Magazine*, whose brilliant editor Robert Brown was William's friend, and who had fallen in love with Fanny.[5] Her flustered, nervous mother who depended totally on Fanny to look after her young brothers and sisters, actively fuelled Fanny's fears that Robert Brown was too old to be a suitable husband for her. Had her mother only encouraged the relationship, Robert Brown might have made an excellent husband for Fanny, who loved scholarship, science and writing and was so little interested in the frivolous pastimes of her younger sisters.

After Fanny's premature death her mother would bitterly reproach herself for interfering. Fanny had no other suitors until the Macleay girls eventually found popularity as potential brides among Sydney's many bachelors.

On his retirement from British Government service Alexander Macleay had hoped to devote himself to scientific research. But bank failures in Britain left him deep in debt, he now had two young sons to educate and a third son, Alexander Rose (Alec), who was often unemployed and prone to acquire large gambling debts and six daughters to marry off. Fanny's father was now fifty-eight. He had no inherited money to look forward to so there was nothing for it but to apply for a job in the colonies, put the two youngest boys into an English boarding school and leave spendthrift young Alec to find paid employment as a clerk in the Scottish Customs Service and hope he would at last stick at something.

Once Fanny realised the amount of her father's debts could never be paid off by his meagre pension from the British Government, she encouraged him to move to Sydney. This was something that her flighty younger sister Christiana Susan, who enjoyed London's social round and was mooning over a young man there, found hard to forgive.

However, Fanny also made sacrifices to emigrate. The one that hurt her most was that moving to New South Wales took her even further away from her brother William, who was expected to return to London on long service leave within a year or so. Far away in the West Indies and working in the British Colonial Service, William greatly missed London and its intellectual and cultural life. Despite Fanny's pleadings he resolutely refused to spend his long leave visiting his family in New South Wales, yet another sub-tropical colony. William kept busy serving as British Commissioner in Havana and overseeing measures for the abolition of the slave trade. He remained single and devoted all his spare time to his career, his collections and his scientific research. His hard work paid off. At a relatively young age, William

Sharp Macleay was rewarded when he was made a judge and became as distinguished as his father.

In 1825 Alexander Macleay accepted an appointment as Colonial Secretary in New South Wales. He arrived in Sydney in January 1826 along with his wife and six unmarried daughters.

Arriving in the midsummer heat and humidity of Sydney after a long tiring sea voyage, Fanny and her sisters were dismayed to find the Colonial Secretary's house in Macquarie Place cramped and gloomy. The family keenly missed the spacious flower-filled garden they had enjoyed at *Tilbuster Lodge*. In her first letter from the convict colony Fanny moaned to William the house was 'the worst and ugliest in Sydney', and the only official residence in Sydney without a verandah (possibly an exaggeration). She described the official residence as having small dark bedrooms with no outside windows, 'unfit for a cat to sleep in they are so small and close'.[6] The Colonial Secretary's house had only two large airy bedrooms. Her parents took one and all six girls were forced to share the other, until such time as more bedrooms could be built.[8]

The Macleay girls may have grumbled about the size of the house but they found it large enough to cheer themselves up by hosting an elegant dance and supper party for ninety people. Doors were taken off their hinges, window sashes removed and the empty spaces garlanded with long loops of Australian native flowers. Fanny informed William gleefully that theirs was the prettiest ballroom ever seen in Sydney.

Initially Fanny told William their new garden was only a 'neglected rubbish hole'[7] but with her usual determination she and her father set about choosing fruit trees and flowers to fill it. But her mother suffered from migraines and a host of other ailments so Fanny had to fulfil her mother's social role and play hostess to her father. The novelty soon wore off and Fanny discovered to her dismay that she found colonial life intellectually and artistically stultifying. Care of so many younger children gave her little time to read, draw and paint or help her father write up his scientific notes.

Fanny loved the beauty of the flora and fauna she found in Sydney but deplored the fact that, during the wool boom everyone in the colony (including her own father) was hell-bent on making money out of land and sheep and boasting about their investments. 'They do not know the value of money and are inclined to squander it away to please any idle fancy which may arise in their pates,' she told William scathingly.

In Britain Alexander Macleay had been a close friend of relations of Governor Darling's wife. So the Macleays were frequently invited to dinner at Government House where they soon met 'everyone who was anyone' in the colony. They rapidly became one of the most powerful families in New South Wales and envious tongues wagged about favouritism by Governor Darling when Alexander Macleay was given a large grant of land at Brownlow Hill, (near his friends the Macarthurs at Camden). Alexander promptly borrowed to stock his land with sheep during the heady days of the wool boom in New South Wales. Then he unwisely borrowed even more money to purchase more acres as the sheep started breeding and his flocks increased.

The Macleay girls were not as attractive as their blonde-haired mother, Elizabeth (Eliza) Macleay. Contemporary observers described them as 'accomplished and intelligent,' vivacious in personality, good conversationalists, accomplished in piano playing, singing, needlework, at a time when lady-like accomplishments were what was required of girls who were intended to marry into middle-class and professional society. The girls aroused considerable jealousy among other unmarried daughters because it was felt Lady Eliza Darling favoured them too much.

However, Sydney's numerous bachelors pursued them vigorously at parties and

Detail from a watercolour of a specimen of verticordia *made by Fanny Macleay held in the Botany Library, British Museum of Natural History.*

imagined fondly that each daughter would receive a handsome dowry. But the local bachelors did not know that Alexander Macleay was still paying off his English debts and had other ideas for his colonial salary rather than bestowing it on sons-in-law. He borrowed even more money against his salary to develop wonderful gardens on his grant of 54 acres at Elizabeth Bay and built what would be known as 'the most beautiful house in the colony' where he planned to retire for the second time. Fanny was worried about the amount of the borrowings. 'I shall feel pleasure if we ever get comfortably settled there,' she wrote to William, 'because we may then venture out to walk, without being teased by idlers joining us as they do at present.'⁸ Possibly the 'idlers' were also after the affections of the charming Misses Macleay.

Fanny was pleased because she thought that laying out the gardens and grounds at Elizabeth Bay would force her father to take much-needed exercise and 'it will give Mama something to interest her and something to talk and think of.' Doubtless Fanny hoped it would take her mother's mind off matchmaking. Eliza Macleay realised six unmarried daughters were a great drain on the family finances which she felt would be better employed setting up her two younger sons as pastoralists. However she was delighted over the unexpected burst of popularity her unmarried daughters now enjoyed among Sydney's bachelors.

Fanny told William that most men in New South Wales were 'Monsters of Vulgarity'. She was particularly horrified by the attentions fat gout-ridden Sir John Jamison, one of the colony's wealthiest men, showered on her. Her mother, sensing a potentially wealthy bridegroom, insisted Fanny accept an invitation to visit Sir John's elegant mansion at Regentville.⁹

Clever Fanny quizzed the Macleay's convict servants about the wheezing blubbery baronet. They told her that Sir John had kept a series of convict mistresses who had borne him three children. Even as he courted her, the old rascal was living with the mother of four more of his illegitimate children. His current mistress was yet another young convict, who posed as his housekeeper and who he kept tucked away from 'polite society' out at Regentville. Fanny told William that 'I really detest Sir John, but am obliged to go to Regentville tomorrow'. Obviously the housekeeper and her children were kept out of the way when the Macleays visited Regentville. Sir John cornered Fanny and popped the question but quick-witted Fanny told the portly baronet that she found her own name too pretty to consider changing it.

Amazingly enough Fanny's stinging rejection of Sir John's advances did not prevent the aging baronet from attempting to woo her younger sister Susan, who moaned to Fanny how 'my mother wishes me to sell myself and marry Sir John' and who plucked up courage to refuse the baronet also. (Not surprisingly Sir John became one of Macleay's worst enemies and years later would join with other enemies to have Macleay dismissed from his post as Colonial Secretary.) Mrs Macleay's ambitious marriage schemes frequently misfired. Red-headed Kennethina coolly rejected a proposal from wealthy widower Thomas Iceley and remained single all her life. It took Mrs Macleay ten years to marry off her remaining daughters and not all of the husbands were as wealthy as she would have wished. Some, like extravagant Archie Clunes Innes who married Margaret Macleay, kept having financial problems and returning to stay with the Macleays. Archie along with his brood of children ate them out of house and home and exhausted Mrs Macleay still further. Another of Fanny's suitors was razor-slim Colonel Dumaresq, brother of the Governor's wife, Eliza Darling. Fanny did not like him at all and wrote how, 'she (Lady Darling) makes believe she would like a connexion be delighted if I should become [sic] of hers.'¹⁰ Fanny was quick to make it plain that marriage to elderly Colonel Dumaresq was far from her mind and after years of paying polite social calls, Fanny's younger sister Christiana Susan, who was still mooning over a young

Pencil drawing by Fanny Macleay showing the Colonial Secretary's House in Macquarie Place, Sydney after extra bedrooms had been built to house the Macleay family. Private collection through Historic Houses Trust of New South Wales.

Englishman named Guthrie who had returned to England,[11] finally accepted the persistent Colonel and, to Fanny's surprise, made an enduringly happy marriage.

Fanny had no intention of marrying a man she did not love and admire as she loved and admired her eldest brother and her father. Fanny was detached enough to look at the life of her own mother. Eliza Macleay was exhausted and her nerves on edge through bearing seventeen children and losing some of them. She was constantly preoccupied over the career prospects of her sons and the lack of dowries and marriage opportunities for her six daughters. Fanny's mother was plagued by stress and tension headaches, and worried over the lack of money to run a busy household and feed and clothe so many offspring in a manner suited to her husband's social position. At that time there were no proven contraceptive methods to limit families so Eliza Macleay's stressful life could not have seemed enviable to her eldest daughter. For many years Fanny, the champion childminder, must have thought that freedom and happiness lay in *not* having children and a husband and envied her brother William his freedom as a single man.[12]

It seems that Fanny attracted men by the warmth of her personality and her keen sense of humour rather than by her good looks. No portrait of her remains but in letters to William she refers to her petite figure and her 'pug' or snub nose. She always compared herself unfavourably to her elder brother although her sense of inferiority may well have been induced by William's superior education at university and subsequent successful career in Paris and Cuba. In letters to her adored brother she would often disparage her own looks and her considerable achievements in drawing and painting (she called her drawings 'daubs' but praised his scientific research extravagantly. On one occasion she refers to herself as 'your insignificant *petite soeur*' when in achievement and personality she was far from insignificant.

Meanwhile, undeterred by his wife's constant matchmaking schemes, Alexander Macleay set about what became his passion—creating magnificently terraced and landscaped gardens at Elizabeth Bay. But the urgent need to finish the mansion to accompany them had disappeared. Governor Darling had now kindly authorised expensive renovations to the Colonial Secretary's house including four additional bedrooms and a verandah. Elizabeth Bay House took second place to its acres of pleasure gardens until Alexander Macleay would finally retire for the second time from public life.

Finding good cooks and domestic staff for the now-enlarged Colonial Secretary's residence was a constant problem. Fanny ironically informed William 'Have I mentioned we are in danger of starvation? We cannot find a cook'. Eliza and Alexander Macleay were loathe to employ convicts and money was short so the Macleay girls were now forced to be their own housemaids, fetching and cleaning and constantly carrying jugs of hot water from the kitchen to the bedrooms. Worn out with housework and longing to get on with her own scientific and painting work, Fanny complained to William, 'this is the very worst sort of slavery. Very often I wish myself in a bark hut where at least I should not be striving to keep up an appearance of respectability.' Soon there were even more responsibilities. Governor Darling's wife, Lady Eliza Darling had a strong social conscience. She planned to establish what became known as the Female School of Industry for twenty young orphaned or fatherless girls and asked the Macleay girls to help raise money to start the proposed school by sewing baby clothes for a fund-raising bazaar. With their father dependent on the Darlings' goodwill, how could his daughters refuse?

So Fanny was given the unpaid post of Treasurer-Secretary of the School of Industry and carried out the job with her usual efficiency.[13] She assured William that the post gave her nothing but trouble with 'wretches' of matrons who frequently embezzled money. Fanny was unusual for her times in that, although she believed in God and the power of the Bible, she was broadminded and tolerant about the religious opinions of others. Lady Darling intended 'her' school to combat the growth of Catholicism and refused to admit Catholics, however deserving, as pupils. Privately Fanny did not agree. 'Better a good Catholic than a careless Protestant,' she observed. She was equally tolerant of Quakers and other dissenters in an age when religious bigotry was rampant. The boarders at the school were mainly orphans, illegitimate or homeless. The aim of the school was somewhat similar to the school established by Caroline Chisholm in India so that they would not be drawn into prostitution which was then rampant in Sydney. Fanny gradually became more and more involved with the school. She and her sister Kennethina (who was eighteen years younger than herself) gave selected pupil-teachers instruction in reading, writing, arithmetic and needlework so that monitors could, in turn, instruct the other girls. Of course teaching, and raising money for the school all conspired to prevent Fanny painting or starting her novel. But it was valuable work and saved many orphaned working-class girls from a life of poverty and degradation.

While Fanny toiled away unrewarded financially or academically, William published scientific papers and books incorporating Fanny's drawings and notes. He received wide acclaim for his scientific papers, was elected a Fellow of the Royal Society and a member of the Linnean and Zoological Societies. Fanny's contributions to the family achievements in the area of natural history never achieved recognition as at that time scientific societies did not admit women to full membership. The papers they had written might be read out for them by a male member, but women, however brilliant, remained isolated from the rich world of scientific meetings and conferences where men acquired their reputations.

The Macleays' scholarly work on the classification of plants and insects provided a basis for a more rational and historical approach to nature. Their link with Charles Darwin lay in Alexander's long friendship with Conrad Martens who drew and painted Elizabeth Bay House and who had also been with Darwin[14] on the *Beagle* during the ship's South American voyage.

Whenever Fanny had time to spare from the demands of family and the School of Industry, she helped her father with his collections and with the complex and time-consuming task of writing them up and sending information to other amateur scientists. Fanny's botanical drawings formed a part of the great Macleay Collection.

Long before the advent of the camera, talented women artists specialising in carefully detailed botanical drawings like Fanny Macleay, Caroline Louisa Atkinson, the Scott sisters in New South Wales, Fanny Charsley and Ellis Rowan in Victoria (see Volume 2) and Eliza Buckland and Mary Morton Allport in Tasmania, would work long hours without pay and with scant chance of exhibiting their work. Of them all, Allport and Rowan were the only ones to secure exhibitions. These dedicated talented women, provided the only means of recording visually the remarkable diversity, colour and richness of Antipodean flora and sometimes of the fauna.

Fanny was happiest when drawing. But just as she settled down to work domestic chores or child care would intervene and she had to break off.

She also loved books and writing. Fanny had written to her brother regularly describing her life and that of her family in London and she continued writing regularly from Sydney. She described in Jane Austen tones the 'Perfect Monsters' of suitors the Macleay girls met; and gives William a good indication of the political machinations of the colony. Fanny's letters sparkle with wit and occasional malice and reveal her as a born writer and an exceptionally good judge of character.

But writers need to read widely. Fanny devoured novels whenever she had the time, including those of Sir Walter Scott[15] then at the height of his popularity as a historical novelist. She had a secret ambition which she dared reveal to no-one. When she was twenty-five, an age at which a young women was deemed to be 'on the shelf' in Victorian England, Fanny had plucked up her courage and revealed to William that she hoped to write a novel. Touchingly she wrote how she trusted William would not be 'offended' by this disclosure because writing novels was something middle- and upper-class girls did not do. Men were novelists, not women. (She was telling the truth. Jane Austen wrote under the pseudonym 'A Lady' and the Brontë sisters published under male names like Currer, Ellis and Acton Bell while the pseudonym 'George Eliot' was taken by another talented female novelist, Marian Evans.)

Fanny's letters to William, although erratically spelled, reveal that with a good editor to help her, she might have been capable of writing a sparkling satirical novel. Drawing on her mother's frantic and sometimes ludicrous efforts to marry off so many daughters without dowries she immediately spotted the greed of the Sydney bachelors for dowries. They mistakenly supposed that the six rather homely Macleay girls would be given a small fortune on marriage to match their elevated social position and their accomplishments. Fanny's novel could well have been an Antipodean *Pride and Prejudice*, with Fanny playing the central role of Elizabeth Bennett.

Making their trousseau and wedding gowns appears to have occupied much of the Macleay sisters' free time. The flighty and free-spending Margaret Macleay caused Eliza and Fanny much worry when she married young, handsome Archie Innes, who was well-connected but poorly endowed with worldly goods. Fanny related to William how she and her sisters gathered together around a table in an upstairs bedroom and sewed 'with our own poor paws', Margaret's trousseau as well as their own outfits for the wedding. 'Poor darling Papa's constant shortage of cash prevented them or the bride from visiting a dressmaker. It was a case of 'all silk hats and no breakfast' for these weddings. Deep in debt, but concerned that no-one would find out, the Macleay girls sought to keep up appearances and maintain the outward appearance of an elegant lifestyle while working as hard as any domestic servant.

Another trousseau had to be hand-stitched when the vivacious Rosa Roberta, described by Fanny to William as 'poor unmonied Roppy' finally was allowed to marry Arthur Pooley Onslow, once he had paid off all his outstanding debts. (Rosa's eldest son would eventually marry Elizabeth Macarthur (q.v.) who would then become Elizabeth Macarthur Onslow. Their first child, James, would inherit Elizabeth Bay House as well as the broad acres of Camden Park and a handsome fortune, a fact that would have delighted Eliza Macleay had she lived long enough to see it.)

However, in the mid-1830s, the Macleay girls struggled to save every penny. Meanwhile their father was blithely ignoring their increasing protests over mountains of domestic work and spending everything he earned and more, designing and laying out acres of Sydney's most exquisite private gardens at Elizabeth Bay. Fanny noted with dismay that her father was also borrowing to continue stocking his farm at Brownlow Hill, now farmed by her younger brothers George and James. She notes sadly how the sheep and cattle died of disease and drought that ravaged New South Wales that summer and how they started to decline in value as the golden days of the wool boom ended.

Fanny wrote almost every month, often annoyed with William because he failed to reply. She kept him up to date on family news, gave details of Christiana Susan's wedding, titbits about Margaret's and Rosa's numerous pregnancies and the bonny babies that resulted and how 'poor darling Papa' was working. She described how Kennethina and herself gradually assumed more responsibility for teaching and supervision of meals at the Female School of Industry.

Fanny had enough political sense to warn William that Chief Justice Frances Forbes loathed her father and was plotting his removal as Colonial Secretary. Fanny described the magnificent mansion John Verge had designed for her father at Elizabeth Bay, where they would move as soon as he retired and the laying of the foundation stone there in March, 1835.

Although she never lived at *Elizabeth Bay House* Fanny was a frequent visitor at the building site. She wrote numerous letters to China, Mauritius, the West and East Indies, North and South America, South Africa, New Zealand and England to obtain exotic trees, shrubs and bulbs to fill the acres of terraced gardens that sloped down to the harbour. Twenty gardeners were employed in laying out and maintaining the magnificent gardens that Alexander Macleay, in the grip of a dream, intended to be the showpiece of the colony.

In 1836 the Macleays held a large garden party at Elizabeth Bay, possibly to celebrate Fanny's engagement. At the age of forty-three, and after refusing many other rich and powerful suitors, Fanny finally married the man who had won her heart as well as her quick and clever mind. Her intended husband was dark-haired Thomas Harrington. He was of Anglo-Indian parentage and several years younger than her and worked for her father. Like Mary Reibey's Anglo-Indian husband, also named Thomas, little was known in New South Wales about Harrington's parentage. Thomas Harrington's father was probably an officer with a British regiment, the Indian Army or the East India Company. For social reasons young men working for these organisations were never permitted to marry their Indian or Anglo-Indian mistresses. Children born of these liaisons were numerous. Some, like Thomas Harrington, were lucky enough to receive a good education but suffered from intense racial prejudice from both Europeans and Indians. No records remain as to how Thomas escaped from the rigid world of colonial India and entered the colonial public service in New South Wales where he was promoted to Assistant Colonial Secretary under Alexander Macleay. One thing is certain, Mrs Macleay and her sons did not regard Harrington as a good match for Fanny. He did not own a house and like Alexander Macleay (who may have urged his assistant to emulate him, borrow from the bank and invest in sheep and land), Harrington had outstanding debts.

Thomas Harrington was highly intelligent and probably deeply sensitive about his background. Possibly he dealt with racial prejudice by making ironic and witty comments about social events and customs in the former convict colony, where he found that he was still an outsider due to his Indian blood.

Initially Harrington was attracted by the vivacious Susan Macleay but after her marriage he realised that Fanny was much cleverer and more amusing than Susan and switched his interest to Fanny who had a wit as sharp as his own. Initially the sparks flew between them and Fanny told William, 'this person is much admired by my sisters but I am much afraid of him for he is very clever and I think satirical, so that I avoid his company'.

An Antipodean Elizabeth Bennett had finally met her Mr Darcy, but unlike Jane Austen's fictitious and wealthy Mr Darcy with his handsome Georgian mansion, Mr Harrington lacked those financial attributes which would have made him a desirable son-in-law to Eliza Macleay. Fanny's brother George did not approve of the match either. It seems as though Harrington had high principles in a colony where many with a total lack of principles became wealthy. George's letter to William stated that Harrington was in his opinion, 'too scrupulous . . . to be any other than a poor man'.

But the die was cast. Fanny had fallen in love at last. She kept the very first note Thomas had penned her on the evening of 16 December, 1830 in which he politely informed Miss Macleay that the visiting cards she had ordered would be ready for her at Carmichael's the engravers very soon. Harrington had exchanged small gifts with other members of the family and had asked if he could have one of her botanical drawings. Fanny scrawled a little note in the margin saying she had sent him not one but *three* drawings.

Another letter to William makes it obvious that George Macleay was not only a racist but as snobbish as most of the colonials Fanny despised for their narrow-mindedness. In a letter to William about the wedding, George scathingly described the ultra-polite Harrington as 'a half-caste Indian' and observed wryly, (possibly echoing his mother) that 'the marriage could not be helped'.

But this time Fanny was older than when Robert Brown had proposed and far more determined. She wrote very little to William about her feelings, obviously fearing he would be instructed to talk her out of her marriage by letter. This was her last chance at escaping the role of eternal maiden aunt and marrying someone she found attractive and intellectually compatible. She would marry Thomas Harrington come what may and refused to listen to any of her family.

Fanny was now in her forties and had been previously courted without success by Sir John Jamison, Henry Dumaresq and Captain John Rouse. Like all the best romantic novels, Fanny's love affair started off with misunderstandings and even downright hostility and ended in a wedding. Although no portrait of Fanny exists, from a watercolour of fair-skinned Rosa and another portrait of their blonde fair-skinned mother, Eliza Macleay, it is easy to imagine Fanny was as fair-skinned as Harrington was dark—an attraction of opposites. Eventually she decided to tell William of her admiration for 'her husband to be'—a man who attracted her in mind and body.

A few months before their wedding, Fanny suffered vomiting and palpitations of the heart. But in the bustle and excitement of wedding preparations, she probably did not wish to cast a cloud over the ceremony by insisting on seeing a doctor.

On 26 June, 1836 Fanny finally walked up the aisle on her father's arm. It was a simple wedding with the gown probably sewn by herself and Kennethina. Eliza Macleay was not happy with the groom's financial position and later wished she had never objected to Fanny's proposal from Robert Brown in London.

The newlyweds spent their honeymoon on the family property at Brownlow Hill and then returned to live in Sydney. Fanny enjoyed two months of married happiness before disaster struck.

William had scarcely read the account of the wedding before he received the news that Fanny was ill with palpitations of the heart and had gone into a coma. She recovered, spent three days wretching violently and then, at the point of death, received the sacrament and, according to George, 'bade farewell to my Father, Mother, Harrington and Kennethina.'[16]

Alexander Macleay was devastated. He was now sixty-seven but the shock of Fanny's death aged him so that within a short space of time the Colonial Secretary looked far older than his years. He became depressed and probably his work suffered in consequence.

It was at this critical juncture that Chief Justice Forbes (who Fanny had always detested) and her rejected suitor Sir John Jamison plotted his downfall and subtly influenced the new Governor against Alexander Macleay and his work.

In 1837, Macleay's enemies succeeding in having him ousted from office by Governor Bourke, who had replaced the Macleay's good friend Governor Darling. Alexander was appointed a member of the Legislative Council, but by now, although few realised the extent of his debts, Alexander Macleay, the prudent public servant, was nearly bankrupt due to the enormous costs of building and furnishing Elizabeth Bay House. The handsome colonnade designed by John Verge to adorn the house (painted at Macleay's request by professional artist Conrad Martens to show how the house should have looked, had there been enough money to finish it according to Verge's specifications) was never completed due to lack of money. Today magnificent Elizabeth Bay House remains, just as Fanny had predicted, 'quite the finest house in the colony' and a memorial to the entire Macleay family.

In March 1839 William retired from foreign service and came to Sydney, (ironically doing the very thing Fanny had been urging him to do all these years). By now Alexander Macleay was in danger of having his loans called in by the bank and being declared bankrupt. Successful bachelor William now had far more money than his father, having retired young from the bench. So Alexander's eldest son dutifully loaned his father money to tide him over what was regarded as merely a temporary recession in the economy. But the days of the wool boom were over, never to return in Alexander's lifetime, and during the great depression of the 1840s that bankrupted so many of his friends, Macleay was unable to pay back the loan, or even the interest payments, to his son.

Accordingly they agreed that Alexander Macleay would subdivide and sell off most of his gardens and land at Elizabeth Bay (which explains why today the gardens have disappeared and *Elizabeth Bay House* is now entirely surrounded by buildings.) Alexander assigned the title deeds of his beloved house to William. It was agreed William's parents would stay on in the mansion they had built as guests of their son. But constant bickering and fights over money ensued. It soon became apparent William and Alexander had totally different philosophies and could no longer live under the same roof. So William rattled around alone in the lonely splendour of *Elizabeth Bay House* while Alexander and Eliza Macleay and their unmarried daughter Kennethina, went to live with their married daughter, Christiana Susan Dumaresq at *Tivoli*, Rose Bay (now Convent of the Sacred Heart).

Premature death ensured Fanny was spared the sight of the family rift. It would have distressed her beyond words to see her beloved brother and father each hating the other so much they refused to speak. William Macleay never married. He extended his scientific collections, helped in the development of Sydney's Australian Museum and played host to those interested in science at *Elizabeth Bay House*. Helena Scott, unmarried daughter of Alexander Walker Scott, carried on some of Fanny's role of scientific artist to William's collection in a paid capacity. Helena's father had gone bankrupt so Helena Scott badly needed money to support herself. William Sharp remained unmarried and died in 1865.

Unfortunately the plants that Fanny had helped collect and import to Australia and the handsome gravelled promenades, the shady trees and little stone grottoes she loved, are now buried under bricks and mortar at Elizabeth Bay.

A stone memorial tablet in St. James's Church, Sydney describes how 'Frances Leonora Harrington was endowed with superior talents and eminent in graceful accomplishments' and honours her philanthropic work on behalf of the orphans' school. After her death her mother wrote to William acknowledging what a gap her death had left in their lives and confessing that she 'did not sufficiently appreciate the blessings bestowed on us in Fanny'.

Clever, capable, witty Fanny captured the hearts of all who have read her entertaining letters to William. But her scientific and artistic work remains as underrated in death as during her life.[17]

---

[1] The famous Macleay Collections now form part of the Macleay Museum, together with Annabel Swainston's notes on the family and other collections in the University of Sydney and the Australian Museum, Sydney.

[2] Windschuttle, Elizabeth. *The Women of the Macleay Family 1790–1850*. Historic Houses Trust of NSW, Sydney, 1988. This is, at the time of writing, the definitive biography of the family and provides an excellent description of Fanny's scientific work as well as of other aspects of her life. See also *Fanny to William, The Letters of Frances Leonora Macleay*, Beverley ed. Earnshaw and Joy Hughes, Historic Houses Trust of NSW, Sydney, 1993.

[3] Fanny Macleay to William Macleay, 22 September 1815. Mitchell Library, State Library of New South Wales.

[4] Graves, Algernon. *The Royal Academy of Arts. Complete Dictionary of Contributors from 1769–1904*. London, Henry Graves, 1905. This is the definitive reference work on contributors to the Royal Academy, which also keeps handwritten listings of contributors.

[5] Kerr, Joan (ed.). *Dictionary of Australian Artists*. Oxford University Press, 1992. Entry by Elizabeth Windschuttle on Frances Leonora Macleay.

[6] Fanny to William Macleay, 8 October 1836.

[7] *Ibid.*, 10 April 1826.

[8] *Ibid.*, 12 September 1826.

[9] *Regentville* appears in two paintings by Conrad Martens (formerly in the Consolidated Press Collection) as a handsome building with neoclassical columns set among broad acres. It was greatly admired for its elegance.

[10] Fanny to William Macleay, 21 April 1826.

[11] *Ibid.* 8 October 1826.

[12] Windschuttle, Elizabeth. *Women of the Macleay Family. Op. cit.*

[13] Windschuttle, Elizabeth, and Deakin, N. *The Women Were There*. Collins Dove, Melbourne, 1988.

[14] De Vries-Evans, Susanna. *Conrad Martens on the Beagle, and in Australia*. Pandanus Press, Brisbane, 1993.

[15] A full set of novels by Sir Walter Scott was found in the Macleay Library.

[16] Fanny's final illness is described in letters by George Macleay to William Sharp Macleay, 18 August 1836 and Mrs Eliza Macleay to William S. Macleay, 20 August 1836.

[17] Fanny's remaining correspondence is contained in the Macleay family papers, held in the Mitchell Library, State Library of New South Wales, presented by the Macarthur-Onslow family. They eventually inherited *Elizabeth Bay House* through Fanny's sister Rosa who married Arthur Pooley Onslow and whose son married Elizabeth Macarthur-Onslow (q.v.). The letters are held in three volumes of William Sharp Macleay's papers, A4300 (1812–1826); A4301 (1827–1831); A402 (1832–1836). Fanny's weekly letters to the brother she idolised have been transcribed by Beverley Earnshaw and Joy Hughes, who, aided by Susan Hunt, turned them into an illustrated book *Fanny to William, the Letters of Frances Leonora Macleay*, Historic Houses Trust of NSW, 1993.

Note: All unreferenced quotes are taken from Fanny Macleay's letters, held in the Macleay and Macarthur Papers in the Mitchell Library, State Library of New South Wales, Sydney.

CHAPTER 5

Caroline Chisholm
(1808–1877)

THE IMMIGRANT'S FRIEND

Caroline Chisholm is one of the world's great social reformers—a heroine on the grand scale. To appreciate her remarkable achievements in changing emigration policy and providing refuges and employment for women, it is necessary to understand the dreadful situation Caroline encountered when, in 1838, she first arrived in Sydney. She found a penal colony where men outnumbered women by four to one while in the surrounding country areas men outnumbered women by as many as twenty to one.[1] To correct the imbalance and lower the high incidence of rape of white and Aboriginal women the British Goverment established a 'bounty' system which actively recruited young, single, working-class girls from the poorer parts of Britain. The scheme was funded by using money raised from selling land to wealthier immigrants to pay the fares of women from workhouses, teenage girls from orphanages or widows evicted from their homes.

The 'bounty' system was intended to reduce the numbers of destitute and unemployed in Britain. 'Bounty' agents received a commission for each person they persuaded to emigrate and ships were specially chartered for that purpose by the government. Victorian workhouses were harsh places where the poor were often regarded as little better than criminals.[2] Evicted or destitute families were torn apart, the women sent to one workhouse, their husbands to another, and the children incarcerated in orphanages.

Workhouses inmates ate stale bread and a bowl of thin soup or gruel and were given work scrubbing floors and sewing mailbags. 'Bounty' agents told them that New South Wales had a sunny climate and plenty of cheap mutton so destitute women signed up by the boatload. Once they arrived, however, they found there were few jobs and no hostel accommodation for them.

One of Caroline Chisholm's achievements was to save over a thousand of these women from living on the streets, where the only work available to them was prostitution. She achieved this at a time when respectable women were not meant to know about sordid aspects of colonial life (like unwanted pregnancies and sexually transmitted diseases). However Caroline had been brought up by her mother to work for the poor and disadvantaged and to provide practical forms of help.

Caroline's marriage was unusual for the times in which she lived: it was a partnership rather than the ordinary Victorian marriage where the husband expected to be obeyed at all times. Part of this was due to the fact that Caroline had the intelligence and foresight to make her husband promise, before she agreed to marry him, that he would support her in whatever form of philanthropic work she chose. This 'equal marriage partnership' took place at a time when wives were seen merely as chattels and props to their husband's careers and most middle-class wives were taught to regard their husbands as a cross between God and Sir Galahad.

The Chisholms first met at a regimental ball held near Caroline's family farm in Northamptonshire. Like many other Scottish migrants to Australia, Archibald

Chisholm's grandparents were educated land-owning Highlanders, who had lost their money and lands supporting the Jacobite cause. Archy had grown up in a large family who had found themselves nouveau poor rather than nouveau riche. He joined the Indian Army instead of a kilted Highland Regiment, because he lacked sufficient money to buy a commission and the Indian Army demanded no up-front payment for young officers as did the more prestigious British regiments.

Archibald's playmates had all been the children of crofters or tenant farmers. For centuries they had worked their small farms but now were being evicted, their roofs burned over their heads to force them to make room for sheep belonging to absentee landlords. Demand for wool by the mills in the new industrial towns made sheep more profitable than the penniless clansmen farming the crofts had ever been. These proud folk, many of whom spoke only Gaelic,[3] found themselves homeless through no fault of their own, forced to leave the Highlands and emigrate to North America or Australia. This explains why Archy Chisholm would loyally support his wife's work on behalf of penniless migrants.

A contemporary portrait shows Lieutenant Archy Chisholm in uniform as the ideal romantic hero—tall, dark and slim. Caroline Jones, as she was then, was thirteen years younger than Lieutenant Chisholm The daughter of a wealthy farmer who had died when she was a child, Caroline was nearly as tall as Archy, with a curvaceous figure, clear grey eyes, and a peaches-and-cream complexion. She had a sweet smile which lit up her face and made women like her as well as men. Her natural charm, coupled with determination and a strong and outgoing personality, was to be of great help to her in raising funds for her charitable causes. An engraved portrait by Michaelangelo Hayes presents us with an image of a pop-eyed woman with a huge shelf-like bosom and a prim smile. The portrait obviously fails to do Caroline justice because in reality most contemporary writers described her as very attractive. (After her husband left Sydney, she was besieged by an admirer and had to discourage him by insisting she was happily married.)

Archibald and Caroline soon discovered they shared a common bond. Both had lost one parent when young and both came from backgrounds familiar with rural poverty.[4] Caroline's father had always encouraged her to think for herself, to care for others, and unusually for those times to take an active part in any discussions.

Blandford Fletcher painted the tragic plight of widows and children evicted from their homes. Sent to the workhouse many emigrated to Sydney and slept in the streets which moved Caroline Chisholm to found a hostel to shelter them. Queensland Art Gallery.

Her mother had impressed on Caroline the obligation to care for those less fortunate than herself. Mrs Jones had kept on the family farm after her husband's death, and although not luxurious, life was comfortable. The family were evangelical Christians and meals were often shared with those less fortunate.

Archibald Chisholm was, like many of Scotland's oldest Highlanders, a Catholic; Caroline was a Protestant, but soon after her engagement she converted to Catholicism. Her faith in a non-denominational God was her inspiration: for the rest of her life she would help those in need whether they were Catholic or Protestant.

Archy was deeply attracted to Caroline but his time for courtship was brief as he was soon due to return to his regiment in India. After several meetings, Lieutenant Chisholm formally asked her mother for Caroline's hand in marriage. He was smitten; it was Caroline who had reservations. As well as her stipulations about her philanthropic work, she made it absolutely clear she had no intention of entering the social merry-go-round of dinner parties, race meetings and balls, which were considered part of the duties of an officer's wife stationed in India. Of course Caroline realised that her request was unusual for the times. She gave Archibald a month to make up his mind.

Archy Chisholm thought it over and accepted. He kept his word and remained a devoted worker for her philanthropic endeavours at a time when most men saw women as handmaidens ministering to their comfort, and intellectual inferiors rather than partners. She did, however, make one important concession to her husband and converted to Catholicism. Having been brought up a Protestant, her decision, in an intolerant age, took great courage. But courage would become Caroline's trademark.

At her wedding Caroline wore a white dress and orange blossom in her shining auburn hair, which set off her magnolia complexion. Archibald was recalled to India, just as he had expected, and Caroline later joined him in Madras. Officers' wives welcomed her and introduced her to the busy social round of tea parties, polo and regimental balls. For a farmer's daughter, life in the garrison town of Madras was a different world. Social life among officers stationed in India during the 1830s (when servants cost only a few rupees a month) was ironically described by Lady Julia Maitland,[5] who wrote that each horse:

> . . . had a man and a maid to himself—the maid cuts grass for him—and every dog has a boy. I enquired whether the cat had any servants, but found she was allowed to wait upon herself, and as she seemed the only person in the establishment capable of so doing, I respected her accordingly.

India was even then one of the world's poorest countries. Everywhere Caroline went, begging children thrust out hands to her, deliberately maimed by their parents to attract sympathy. Indian and Anglo-Indian child prostitutes swarmed everywhere in this garrison town. Indian men, women and children often slept in the streets on a piece of cardboard, too poor even to afford a modest shack.

The contrast between the idle, gossipy life of pleasure, devoted to dinner parties and regimental balls, and the grinding poverty she saw around her deeply disturbed Caroline's conscience although the other officers' wives accepted it as the natural order of things. Caroline prayed to God for guidance that she might be shown something she could do for the hordes of children who surrounded her whenever she went to the bazaar. With a shock she realised that some of them were the illegitimate offspring of British soldiers, who were strictly forbidden to marry Indian girls. She learned the Army authorities did not care that British soldiers' children were begging in the streets.

Caroline decided God wanted her to start a school for the daughters of the soldiers.

Caroline Chisholm. Engraved portrait after A.C. Hayter which does not do the subject justice. Caroline Chisholm was a strikingly attractive young woman with a magnolia complexion and titian hair who is shown at work with a map of Australia behind her. Private collection.

At that time the British Army did not provide education for other ranks' children; the common soldiers were meant to remain bachelors while officers' sons were sent back to British boarding schools like Eton and Rugby. Officers' daughters were either educated by their mothers, had a governess imported from Britain, or were sent home to school. Children fathered by soldiers (and by sergeants and officers) ran wild—the girls, with their gipsy looks, huge dark eyes and delicate limbs, were often sold as sex slaves to the rich or would slide into prostitution.

By now she was convinced that, as a Christian, saving children from prostitution or degrading marriages was God's plan for her life. When she announced her proposed school for the children of the 'other ranks' the officers' wives were horrified. Archibald was warned that this plan was 'unbecoming' for an officer's wife and that the Chisholms would be social outcasts should they move out of Army married quarters into the smelly, overcrowded Indian district to run Caroline's school.

However Archibald remembered the promise he had made when he married her and stood firm. He agreed to finance part of the expenses of setting up a school from his pay, while Caroline raised the rest from donations. She realised that young girls without a dowry needed education in budgeting, bookkeeping, cookery, cleaning and ironing. Her aim was to secure 'her girls' paid employment, better marriage opportunities, and help them live happier and more productive lives. It was in many ways quite a modern and progressive school as the girls governed themselves by a series of committees, the elder girls acting as 'Assistant Housekeepers', ordering and cooking food for the rest. In addition Caroline taught them reading and writing and nursing.

In May 1836 Caroline gave birth to a son, christened Archibald after his father. The following year she bore a second son, named William after her own father. In subsequent years she had several other children, all stillborn. (At the end of her life she referred to three dead and six living babies.)

The rigours of army life and the hot and humid climate of Madras adversely affected the health of both Caroline and Archy. He applied for long leave in the colony of New South Wales, where the climate was milder and there were servants to look after their children.

The couple arrived in Sydney in September 1838 and settled into a comfortable house in Windsor, where they employed a housekeeper. Ten months later Caroline gave birth to their third son, who was named Henry. After years in the humid heat of Madras, she loved Sydney with its mild climate and beautiful harbour.

In 1840, Archibald was recalled to active service with his regiment. He was sent to fight in China, in what became known as the Opium Wars. They both knew he could be away for years. Staying on in their home at Windsor seemed the best thing for their children. Secure in her conviction that God had a plan for her life, Caroline was certain she would find philanthropic work in the penal colony. She had initially thought of setting up another school and prayed for guidance. But her husband's insistence that the miseries of unemployed immigrants who slept in streets and doorways around The Rocks area of Sydney should be her special field made her channel her energy into caring for orphaned girls and penniless widows.

From talks with immigrant girls recently arrived from Britain, she learned many were from orphanages or workhouses. Sheer misery had made many decide to take the Government bounty and leave for New South Wales.

By now the wool boom was over but immigrants still flooded into a reduced labour market. The Government closed the Immigration Barracks and the new arrivals were required to leave their ships within ten days. Sydney had no cheap hostels. Penniless girls with few possessions were camping in two large Government-owned tents in the Domain or sleeping in doorways, while they tried to find work. Most were tousled and bedraggled after a three-month voyage without washing or laundry facilities in one of the overcrowded emigrant hell-ships. Some had been sexually abused by the ships' crews, because discipline was lax and most captains simply ignored what was happening, only concerned to deliver the immigrants and collect the price of their passage from the Government.

Caroline soon discovered that girls who dressed and spoke well could find jobs as housemaids in the city. Others were forced to beg or enter a life of prostitution.

None of the upper-class Government officials' wives or the squatters' wives on charity committees seemed to care about these girls, who they saw as 'fallen' or 'disgraced'. Caroline found some girls positions as domestic servants and took others home with her to Windsor where she gave them exactly the same practical education in cookery, thrifty housekeeping and accounts as she had given her pupils in India.

The catalyst that turned Caroline from a teacher of domestic science into a fiery activist urging reform of the entire system of emigration was her meeting with penniless flaxen-haired Highland lass who was seduced with gifts by a wealthy man. Flora and her widowed mother had been evicted from their home; arrived penniless in Sydney as migrants under the 'bounty' scheme and had camped in a large tent in the Domain, the sole welfare measure provided by the government. Flora's fresh beauty and obvious innocence drew the attention of a wealthy male admirer who, Caroline noted, had bought the pretty young girl many expensive clothes and 'trinkets'. Flora was flattered and fancied herself in love with her seducer. She did not heed Caroline's warnings that he was married, and trustingly believed her lover would soon propose marriage.

Caroline continued visiting the immigrants' tent and observed Flora and her wealthy lover. 'Each time I visited I observed a little more finery on her,' she commented. But Flora turned a deaf ear to all Caroline's advice and continued her romance with her married admirer.

Poster advertising single British women could emigrate to Australia for five pounds. These were displayed in orphanages and workhouses to try and balance the overwhelmingly male population of New South Wales and Tasmania. Private collection.

Months later, Caroline spotted Flora standing on cliffs near the harbour, pregnant and contemplating suicide. Caroline talked her out of suicide. She realised she must set up a properly administered women's refuge so that unemployed homeless girls did not have to camp out in the Domain or live from hand to mouth on the streets.

Caroline knew that men in the bush were desperate for wives. Some went to the Female Factory and asked the matron for a suitable wife, who was then free to depart with him. Caroline decided to initiate a scheme whereby girls could go out to the country and meet single men in need of a wife. She asked the governor's wife to intercede with her husband, Sir George Gipps, for the use of a large disused wooden shed previously used as an Immigration Barracks.

In seeking help from the Governor's wife, obviously Caroline was a realist. She knew that being a convert to Catholicism would automatically put Protestant clergy against her scheme, although she intended that women from all denominations would use her hostel. She was horrified to find one group of sixty-four orphaned girls had only fourteen shillings and one penny between them, which was not enough to pay for hotel accommodation. They were sleeping in doorways, constantly propositioned by men, because the government tents in the Domain were already overflowing with migrants.

When Caroline was finally granted an audience with the reluctant Governor Gipps, Caroline knew that this was not the time to play the coy Victorian wife. She must be as businesslike as a man, speak out clearly and concisely about the dangers to women and children of living in the streets, and produce facts and figures to back up her plans for opening her Immigration Home or hostel for women. Sir George described how he

> expected to have seen an old lady in white cap and spectacles, who would have talked to me about my soul. I was amazed when my aide introduced a handsome, stately young woman, who proceeded to reason the question as if she thought her experience worth as much as mine.[6]

So 'handsome, stately' Caroline won round one of her battle. Although Governor Gipps did not believe she would succeed he decided to let her use the deserted Immigration Barracks in Bent Street which, according to the memoirs of Judge Thierry, was nothing more than a 45-foot long, draughty shed.[7] It was built from wooden slabs with a dirt floor and partitioned into several small rooms. In the Barracks the old storeroom served as Caroline's bedroom, pantry and office but such was the need for accommodation that soon more than 100 women were housed there.

Caroline's first night there was a dreadful one. She described how

> I retired weary to rest. Scarce was the light out than I fancied dogs were in the room and in some terror I got a light. My first act was to throw on my cloak and get out the door . . . my second thoughts were, if I did so, my desertion would cause much amusement and ruin all my plans. [Bravely she] lighted a second candle and seating myself on my bed, kept there until three rats descending from the roof alighted on my shoulder. I feared that I would catch a fever . . . but to be out-generalled by rats was too bad. I got . . . up, cut bread into slices, placed the whole in the middle of the room, put a dish of water convenient and . . . sat on my bed reading . . . and watching the rats till four in the morning. At one time I counted thirteen . . . The following night I gave them a similar treat, with the addition of arsenic.[8]

Worse than the rats were the males on the make who prowled around the girls' hostel by night and by day. Caroline described how

When I first opened the Home, the greater part of my duty was of a very unpleasant nature—sailors, soldiers, draymen and gentlemen would visit the Home; and, as there were several doors, I had no sooner turned one party out, than it reported that another was in. I was almost weary of telling them—These are the single women's quarters, you cannot stay here.[9]

Life in India had taught her that the best way to protect girls from an unfortunate marriage or becoming a single mother was to provide them with paid work. To find work for 'her' girls, Caroline decided to activate a network of contacts in the bush and see if jobs as maids, cooks or nursemaids could be obtained. Once working there she thought most of them would find husbands.

Caroline continued to protest against the system whereby young, innocent girls who arrived in Sydney Harbour were visited aboard the ships by the madams of brothels in all their jewellery and finery. The madams would impress these poverty-stricken girls with talk of an easy life, but omit details such as the dangers of disease. At a time when 'ladies' did not mention such matters, Caroline outraged some delicate sensibilities by relating the full facts in her report to the Land Immigration Commissioners.[10]

To forestall the brothel madams, Caroline met every ship that arrived, taking the friendless girls back to the Barracks. Soon the value of her work was recognised by the public. She was offered the loan of a bullock dray returning to the bush after delivering wool, so that the girls could ride on this. But she had not reckoned on the girls' fear of the unknown. A bushranger named Jackey-Jackey had robbed and then murdered an elderly woman returning to Sydney from Bathurst. It was not an isolated incident and the Sydney newspapers had been full of such stories. Faced with the open dray and one lone drover to protect them, the girls' fears—of rape

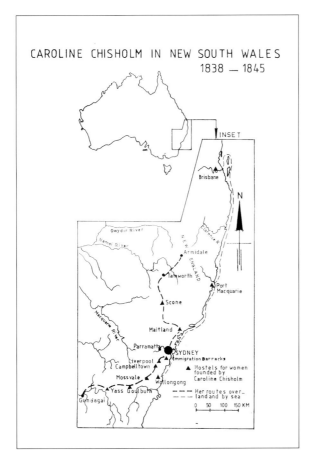

Map drawn by Jake de Vries showing sites where the committees set up by Caroline Chisholm placed hostels for immigrant women and routes taken by her in search of jobs for women. Copyright Jake de Vries.

and murder by armed bushrangers, of venomous snakes that dropped from trees, and of dingoes that hunted like wolves—overcame them. Caroline described how 'their fears overcame their good resolutions, and I had to send the dray away empty'.[11]

She was keen that no word of this should leak out or Governor Gipps would find out and withdraw his grudging permission for her plans to find employment for these girls. So she sat them down and gently explained that dingoes did not hunt and kill humans like wolves, and that most bushrangers had been captured. There were good men out in the bush and perhaps they would be lucky enough to find one before long. With a flash of her old humour, Caroline noted that the thought of finding husbands so soon seemed miraculously to cheer the group.

The next day she ordered two drays instead of one, which meant another bullock drover to protect the girls from marauding bushrangers and outlaws. The girls rode on the slow, lumbering bullock carts from one homestead to another, and were placed in homes where there was a wife who needed domestic help. Caroline was nobody's fool. She recorded on several occasions how she refused to leave pretty teenage girls with single men when she thought they might abuse her trust.

Caroline's enormous workload increased still further because of drought and the depression caused by the fall in the price of wool. The Immigration Commissioners still did almost nothing to help migrants. Although the number of immigrant ships coming to the colony decreased in the depression, Caroline's journeys to the interior now became longer and her parties larger, with a total of 147 men and women on one journey. Caroline's farming background meant she was a good horsewoman. She bought herself a large white horse named Captain and from then onwards rode into the bush with her parties of women, like some medieval Crusader, wrapped in a cloak.

Back in Sydney, to put her case to the people of New South Wales and to Government officials, Caroline wrote letters and pamphlets in clear, concise language. Convinced of the rightness of her cause, she developed a talent for working the media—not to publicise herself but to advance the humanitarian causes in which she was involved. The *Sydney Morning Herald* published her emotive appeal for better conditions and paid work for immigrant women and asked for drays to help transport them to the interior. The following day she received offers of help and gifts of food and money from farmers and settlers, shamed to realise just how bad the situation was for female immigrants. At last people began to realise that most homeless 'bounty' immigrants were decent girls looking for work rather than prostitutes looking for clients. Gifts of money, tins of biscuits, tea and coffee poured in (tea was vital, as the water supply was often contaminated and boiling the water for tea sterilised it).

Over the years Caroline received and answered by hand mountains of letters from intending immigrants, five thousand alone from famine-ridden Ireland. Letters from parents, distraught with worry and grief at separation from their children, went straight to Caroline's heart and received her immediate attention. She was an excellent organiser and enlisted others to her cause through her public speeches. Caroline had that elusive quality known as charisma and a wonderful sense of humour: she was warm-hearted, loyal and supportive of those in need, at whatever cost to herself. She persuaded women in the country towns to form Ladies' Committees to find jobs for the girls and because the trips on the drays could last several days established a system of shelters along the way.

Caroline's aim of finding her girls employment spread. Soon voluntary committees were set up to act as employment agencies and place girls in country towns ranging from Port Macquarie, Moreton Bay Settlement (Brisbane), Wollongong, Maitland, Scone, Liverpool, Campbell Town, Goulburn, Yass and Mittagong (see map). Even though roads were bad Caroline visited these towns herself by road or by boat.

Several branch hostels were set up under the supervision of clergymen. Initially the Protestant churches had reservations because she was a Catholic but when they realised that Caroline was trying to help migrants of all denominations they joined in what they realised was valuable work. However, she did encounter resistance among Anglo-Saxon Protestant 'ladies' against employing Irish Catholics because they were believed to be by far least educated of all the migrants.

As her workload increased, Caroline was caught between love for her own young family of boys and her duty to a hundred girls and young women—daughters of Irish peasants or dispossessed Highland crofters. She soon realised it was hard to fulfil the duties of manager and matron of a large Immigrants Home (as the old barracks was now called) and to supervise her own lively boys. After she had found the two eldest playing in the street, strictly against her orders, she sent them back to her housekeeper at Windsor, but could not bear to part with Henry her youngest, now a sturdy toddler who was still living with her at the Home.

The final straw that broke the camel's back came when Caroline found a distraught woman in her office asking for a white gown in which to bury her dead child. Sydney was rife with cholera, dysentery and infant fevers. She described how 'A lady whose esteem I value told me I could not, should not, risk my child's life, that I must either give up the Home or my selfish feelings for my child'.

Fearing the woman's child had died from an infectious disease such as cholera or typhus—acquired from the lice that swarmed throughout the old building—or even bubonic plague or dysentery, Caroline packed up her little son's clothes and sent Henry to live with his brothers under the care of her housekeeper at Windsor.[12] We can guess what pangs of distress and guilt Caroline suffered at sending her child away, even though it was to save his life. She continued her work which gave hope to women, drawing comfort from the belief it was what God intended her to do.

The fact that Caroline and Archibald were separated by his military duties had certain benefits for her work as an unpaid social worker and reformer. In the period when contraception consisted of coitus interruptus or a douche with a solution of vinegar and water, it is easy to see how most married women bore a child every eighteen months or two years.[13] Free from the pains and dangers of childbirth (which killed so many women in colonial Australia), and released from the time-consuming breastfeeding and caring of infants, Caroline devoted her time, energies and organisational skills to do what no-one else was prepared to do—improve the lot of working-class women.

Caroline Chisholm riding her white horse soon became a familiar sight in the bush. She made frequent trips with the girls to place them in homes which she herself had usually investigated and if there was a wealthy bachelor or widower with a farm she would try and place a girl on a neighbouring farm and many marriages ensued. Caroline Chisholm was good at managing people and persuaded rough tough ex-convicts to help with the yoking and unyoking of the bullocks. The journeys were tiring and in the wet season the drays struggled over rutted bush tracks or roads, deep in mud. When the going was particularly rough the girls climbed down and walked beside the drays, setting out from Sydney at five in the morning. When fording a stream, to lighten the load on the bullocks she would put a toddler in each of Captain's enormous leather saddlebags and carry them across, comforting the frightened children beside her.

Her determination and endurance on these gruelling trips into the bush was phenomenal. Before refrigeration, they could not take fresh meat with them. Salads were thought to be harmful to the digestion so the parties lived on the traditional stockman's diet of roast mutton, salt beef and damper, washed down by black billy tea and cases of biscuits donated by the public. Eventually the stress and responsibility of organising the lives of others, coupled with a diet without vegetables or fresh milk, would take its toll. Unknown to her or to her doctors, slowly Caroline was developing kidney disease.

By December 1841 she added a school to the Immigrants Home. Between 1839 and 1842, 23,705 Irish immigrants arrived in Australia compared with 5,986 Scots and 12,227 English and Welsh.[14] In 1843 the potato blight had started to ravage Ireland whose peasant population had traditionally lived off potatoes. Starvation soon followed in the country areas and emigration seemed the only escape from the misery in Ireland. The numbers of Irish unemployed and destitute arriving at Australian ports soared. One migrant Irish family were so short of money they were reduced to eating potato parings their children had found in dustbins.[15]

Through her work, Caroline became convinced that the greatest force for good were the ties of family love and that convict men could be redeemed by wives and families. She understood a great deal about human nature and realised that it was necessary for a child to experience love and security so they, in their turn, could give love and security, and by this means break the vicious cycle of child abuse and exploitation. She realised that the penal system separated men from their families as a punishment but this punishment would not rehabilitate them.

Caroline began to work hard to achieve family reunions for convicts and became involved with a scheme to send entire families of emancipists or free settlers to settle on small farms in the bush near Wollongong.

By 1844 the unemployment situation was so bad that the Committee on Distressed Labourers asked Mrs Chisholm to give evidence. This in itself was remarkable, as previously women had never been asked to provide figures to Government committees.

Caroline, practical as ever, collected statistics on the numbers of unemployed through placing notices in the *Herald* inviting them to register with her. In her report she told the Committee there were 2,034 unemployed men and women and dependent children, all needing support. She urged that many of them be resettled by the government on small blocks of vacant Crown land. It was a brave and ambitious plan that would later be incorporated into the Selection Acts of 1860–61, but, like the Selection Acts, her proposal aroused hostility among the wealthy squatters who wanted to lock up all the land for themselves.

When her proposal was rejected by the Government, Caroline demonstrated determination, intelligence and flexibility by opening an employment agency in Bent Street, Sydney, right beside the Immigrants Home, and staffed by volunteer workers from various churches.

To protect 'her girls' she drew up employment contracts in triplicate which were revolutionary for the time in providing good conditions for workers. Over the years the agency she started found jobs in the country for some 14,000 young women, some of whom showed their appreciation of Caroline's help in starting a new life by sending her a piece of their wedding cake.

Archibald Chisholm returned to Sydney in March 1845. By this time he was retired from the army and had been promoted to the rank of Major. Together they formed a plan to open their own Colonization Society since Caroline was convinced that the corrupt Government 'bounty' system, if restarted, would only take advantage of the migrants. The Chisholms decided to take a brave step, returning to Britain to start their own Colonization Society. Caroline eagerly looked forward to seeing her mother and showing her the youngest boys for the very first time.

Again Archy stuck to his promise made before their wedding. He would help Caroline mount a campaign for better conditions for immigrants on board the transport ships, and try to stop the sexual abuse of the unfortunate 'bounty' girls, who had no means of redress against the captains and crews who saw them as fair game. The Chisholms decided they would lobby the British Government for a better deal for migrants.

Several months after Archy's return, Caroline discovered she was pregnant again, but this did not deter her. Their fourth son was born on board ship and christened Sydney after the city Caroline had grown to love.

In London they found a small house in the then-inexpensive north London suburb of Islington. Caroline's mother, Mrs Jones, came to live with them to look after the boys, leaving Caroline free to lobby the Government through her pamphlets, reports to powerful people like Lord Shaftesbury[16] and interviews she gave to the London press.

Caroline believed passionately that their Family Colonization Loan Society would help families living below the poverty line to migrate to Australia. She hoped that if the Society paid the ships' captains and chartered the ships they could dictate far better conditions than existed under the present bounty scheme. Someone responsible to the Society would meet the migrants on arrival, have suitable accommodation waiting for them and help them find work.

Caroline spoke about the new society and their loans at meetings, answered mountains of letters, wrote pamphlets giving advice to migrants on everything from footwear and clothing as well as how to survive on a bush diet of salt beef, damper and billy tea. She also interviewed all those intending migrants who swarmed to her home seeking information. During all this bustle, she had another daughter, named Caroline after her mother, and then two years later, when she was 43, little Monica, her last child was born. In pregnancy and after confinement Caroline occupied any free time she had left by writing books and pamphlets.[17]

Ironically Caroline Chisholm herself was not the 'angel of hearth and home' that stern moralists advocated. She had little free time left for housework and childminding . . . When Dickens visited her he commented on Caroline's poor housekeeping. Her strength was that of a fearless, honest crusader. This, coupled with her charm of manner and frank approach, persuaded wealthy merchants and landowners to donate money to send children from poor families on a specially

Engraving showing a rival Sydney employment agency where a male employer ogles a young female emigrant applying for a job. Private collection.

Engraving showing the cramped space below decks on an emigrant ship. There was no privacy, no space to wash or dry clothes and bounty emigrants were expected to prepare all their own meals. Private collection.

chartered ship to rejoin their parents in Australia as, due to the recession, the Government had ceased sponsoring migration to New South Wales and many families had been torn apart. She was convinced of the good influence of family life and that wives ('God's police' as she so emotionally named them—a phrase that has passed into the language[18]) were desperately needed to civilise Australian men; the unwritten agenda being that this would also lower the rate of sexual abuse of white and Aboriginal women.

Mrs Chisholm did everything in her power to encourage family reunions. From 1854 her efforts increasingly turned to land reform so that emigrating families could farm their own small blocks, purchased on easy repayment terms.

Fearlessly she tackled another subject that 'nice' women were not meant to speak about—the abuse, sexual and otherwise, of defenceless women by officers and crews of immigrant ships. In Sydney she had been so angered by the cruel treatment meted out to a young orphan named Margaret Bolton that she had helped the girl bring a law suit against the ship's captain and the ship's doctor. Caroline's involvement and a wave of publicity ensured that Dr Richard Nelson and Captain Robert Richardson were convicted and fined by the court.[19] Such abuse had been going on for decades on board ship and this was a landmark case. Caroline lobbied the Government for protection of female migrants against what we would now term harassment.

Caroline was determined that the outrageous treatment of immigrant 'paupers' must end. Next she agitated for and won the right for inspectors to check each government migrant ship, which would change the spartan living conditions bounty migrants had endured for a decade. These included no proper washing or cooking facilities and bunks in which women were forced to sleep two at a time. In a pamphlet the Chisholms published at their own expense, entitled *The ABC of Colonization*, Caroline explained how emigration should operate for those without sufficient means. Practical as ever Caroline told her readers exactly what sort of clothes and footwear they should bring with them and even included recipes for staple fare like mutton, salt beef and damper once they had arrived.

The poor and needy flocked to Caroline's London home for information about emigrating to Australia through the Chisholms' society. She interviewed them, gave them practical advice on the price of food and tools in the colony, discussed jobs available to them—and if she thought they were employable and were sufficiently stable to withstand the stresses of migration, would help them to emigrate through the Colonization Society.

All over Britain Caroline held a series of public meetings demanding better food and a proper dining room for the immigrants on board government ships. The shipowners—greedy for profit under the bounty system packed the maximum number of passengers on each emigrant ship—making women and children share bunks on the long passage. While one shift was sleeping the other shift would cook their food in a makeshift galley or huddle together on the swaying deck to keep warm. Sanitation on board ship was rudimentary to say the least, giving rise to sickness and death.

Together Caroline and Archibald Chisholm were responsible for changing the harsh government-run emigration system for the poor and destitute into one that was far more humane. Her pamphlets insisted the government allocate each woman or child over twelve a bunk to themselves on board, that bedding and cutlery and 'sufficient privies be provided; with separate ones for women and children'. The Chisholms' Colonization Society raised money through loans and public subscriptions, they chartered their own ships, funded by the generosity of benefactors including Dickens' friend, the philanthropic Miss Burdett-Coutts.

Caroline's work for immigrants was praised by Charles Dickens, who was fascinated by tales of convicts, transportation and emigration. Dickens had suffered

grinding poverty, working long hours as a child in a blacking factory, described so vividly in *David Copperfield* in which two families, the Micawbers and the Peggottys, emigrate to Australia. In *Great Expectations* Dickens created the most famous convict in fiction—Magwich, who terrified little Pip on the marshes, was brought food by Pip, was recaptured by the police and transported to Australia again. Pip is the hero of Dickens' great novel in which Magwich finally leaves the fortune he has made in Australia, the 'great expectations' of the title.

Dickens gained knowledge of convict transportation and emigration from Caroline Chisholm In Dickens' magazine *Household Words*, in March 1850, an

Detail from an oil painting by an unknown nineteenth century artist showing the rigours of life as a migrant aboard ship during a storm. Private collection.

anonymous article written by the famous author entitled *A Bundle of Emigrants' Letters* begins with an enthusiastic description of 'Mrs Chisholm's work' and describes the founding of the Family Colonization Society. Caroline had obviously loaned Dickens some of her letters from intending or past migrants and he quoted some emotional passages from them.

A week later Dickens published an article influenced by another letter Caroline had sent him, titled *An Australian Ploughman's Story*. The hero, Big Jem, a ploughman sent out to Australia as a convict, pleads for a wife to share his simple home in the bush and declares: 'It is virtuous wives who rule us most and in a lonely land make the difference between happiness and misery'.[20] Through Dickens and through Caroline's own writings and speeches, public support for better conditions for government-assisted migrants was aroused. Many of the points Caroline Chisholm suggested in her report to the Committee [21] were eventually incorporated into the Passenger Acts of 1852 and 1855.[22]

Before the days of telegraphic transfer of money, Caroline talked with bankers and arranged a means of money transfers whereby emigrants working in New South Wales could send relatively small sums (which banks had previously not wanted to handle) home to parents or relatives in England.

Caroline and her husband worked extremely hard for their Family Colonization Loan Society (set up in 1850) and all their work was on a purely voluntary basis. They received no salary at all: Archy supported his wife and children on his meagre army pension and every penny they raised went towards providing better conditions for those who emigrated. As applications from working-class migrants and their families continued to pour into the Islington house, Caroline drew up plans to charter two twin-screw steamships, which were to be named the *Caroline Chisholm* and the *Robert Lowe*, to take migrants to the new colony of Port Phillip [soon to become Melbourne] under far better conditions than the old Government 'hell-ships'. But they needed someone really reliable to run the Melbourne side of the society.

After long discussion it was decided Archy should go back to Australia and run this important side of their joint operation and she would join him later. Between 1851 and 1854 Caroline and Archibald were separated in body, though not in spirit, through their deep commitment to the society. She stayed on in Islington and interviewed the women who wanted to emigrate, still using the Islington house as an office.

During its first four years under her direction, the Chisholms' Colonization Society sent seven ships to Australia, containing 1,288 adults, 475 children and 68 infants.[23] Caroline ensured the society's chartered ships had a matron on board for every 50 females to 'instruct them in housewifery and were provided with bathrooms, wash houses, irons and stoves'.

Funds raised were used to help the migrants rather than employ staff, and it was left to Archibald to run the Australian side of the organisation free of charge. He welcomed the new migrants on arrival and collected repayments on their loans when they found work. The fact that both Chisholms shared a common aim provided one of the bonds which cemented their loving partnership even when they were forced to spend four years apart.

When England declared war on Russia in March 1854, the Society's ship that was to be renamed for Caroline and in which she was to sail, accompanied by a second ship, was no longer available for charter. The mighty Turkish empire was disintegrating and the Crimea would be the next seat of war. Both Caroline's planned emigrant ships were requisitioned by the Government in order to carry British soldiers to the Crimea.[24] Caroline's travel plans had already been delayed once by a visit to Rome to collect young William, who was boarding in a seminary there studying for the priesthood. The head of the seminary feared William's health was not robust enough to enter the priesthood. So they decided William should terminate his studies and accompany his family back to Australia and hoped the long sea voyage would improve his health.

Caroline travelled to France and then on to Rome. Her parish priest had previously written to the Vatican telling them about Caroline's hard work with the poor and dispossessed and requesting the honour of an audience with the Pope. His request was granted. On arrival at the Vatican, she was overcome when Pope Pius IX gave her a gold medallion and a white marble bust of herself, which he had commissioned from an Italian sculptor. It showed her in profile, her hair swept up into a knot on top of her head. She was elated when His Holiness took her by the arm and praised her and although Caroline only spoke a little Italian,[25] she understood the words *excellentissima, perseveranza* and *brava*.

The Crimean war meant that Caroline and the boys had a long wait for a ship; eventually they were given passages on the *Ballarat*, sailing in the late spring. One of the conditions of sailing at a reduced fare was that Caroline was to act as matron to the young women on board.

Parting from her mother was terrible: both women realised it was unlikely they would ever meet again in this life. The evening before the ship sailed Caroline was asked to make a speech to the assembled migrants. Caroline intended to refer to the difficulties they all faced when leaving elderly parents behind in Britain. She started by saying 'I have an aged mother . . .' but tears filled her eyes and she could not continue.[26] Only too well she understood the anguish of women, torn between loyalties to parents, husbands and children.

But at least she knew that their Colonization Society was in capable hands. Secretary Samuel Cogden now had a committee composed of well-known and influential people such as the explorer Count Strzelecki and the future Premier of New South Wales, Sir Stuart Donaldson.

In July 1854, Caroline, Archy and all their children were finally reunited in Melbourne. But she found that the discovery of gold had totally changed Australian society as she knew it.

Governor La Trobe chronicled the impact of the gold discoveries:

> Cottages were deserted, houses to let, business is at a standstill, and even schools are closed. In some suburbs there is not a man left . . . The ships in the harbour are, in a great measure, deserted . . . Both here and at Geelong all building and contract works, public and private, almost without exception, are at a standstill .
> . . The price of provisions in the towns is naturally on the increase, for although there may be an abundant supply within reach, there are not sufficient hands to turn it to account.[27]

The population of Victoria tripled as daily bulletins appeared on billboards and in newspapers about the latest gold strikes. Shepherds in the bush, unskilled men and tradesmen in Sydney and Melbourne left work and wives to cope alone with woodchopping and drawing water and livestock and headed off to the diggings to live in tents. Some women followed men onto the gold fields and put up with the difficult conditions of camp life. But

> . . . for every respectable woman on the goldfields there were two of the other kind, temporary brides and . . . housekeepers who went when the money went. Diggers' weddings were an uproarious feature of life in Melbourne as men back from the goldfields, flourishing champagne bottles, lolled in carriages with brightly dressed brides as they raced along Collins Street. Some lodging houses in the town would supply a young lady who, for a 'consideration' would act the role of a bride. Carriage and footmen would also be provided for the bridegrooms, who lit cigars with banknotes, waved flags, dressed ostentatiously and behaved outrageously.[28]

Archibald was gazetted to the rank of Major but his health had been badly affected by the years in India, making him unfit for heavy work. His army pension now had to support them all including six-year-old Caroline and three-year-old Monica. The Chisholms still refused to take any payment from the society which was their beloved brainchild, but they soon discovered war in the Crimea and the gold rush had changed the previous patterns of emigration. Now it was single men in search of gold who poured into Victoria rather than single women.

Caroline employed a widowed migrant named Mrs Ann Clinton to act as governess to her daughters, freeing her to continue working, as she felt personally responsible for all the girls and married couples she had previously helped to emigrate. In spite of the gold rush, some had not found work and others were having difficulty repaying their loans. Caroline could understand their problems. She and Archibald had their own money worries. For years they had been renting houses and now they lacked sufficient capital to buy a house to secure their old age. But Caroline was always certain of the power of prayer and trusted God would provide an answer.

She and one of her sons set off in a pony and trap to the goldfields over terrible roads thick with mud, where overturned wagons were everyday occurrences and there was little overnight accommodation. Caroline wanted to see life on the diggings for herself. Women had told her how they wanted to rejoin their husbands but feared the journey was too expensive and dangerous. Caroline felt she must not let these women down. In a bumpy horse-drawn cart with horsehair seats and worn-out springs, Caroline was carted over rough roads to Bendigo, Kyneton and Castlemaine. Here a collection was organised to build overnight accommodation for working-class women and children travelling out to see their menfolk.

Each time she spoke in public, a man would tell her that the sight of her acted as a spur to send for his wife and children but others complained there were no cheap inns on the way and the price of family reunion was too high. Caroline became convinced that she must do something to help reunite miners with their families. So she poured her time and energies into raising funds to build Shelter Sheds to lodge women and children cheaply on the way to the goldfields. (Today this part of Caroline Chisholm's work is commemorated by a park bench in Kyneton and a plaque on the Essendon Nurses Home showing where the Caroline Chisholm Shelter Shed for diggers' families once stood.)

At the diggings Caroline saw slatternly drunken women selling their bodies or dealing in sly grog at the back of refreshment tents, which made her keener to reunite families. She was one of the very few women who braved bad roads, infected drinking water, bushrangers and lack of sanitation to visit the goldfields.

On her return to Melbourne she was asked to talk at public meetings about her visit. She started one speech by saying, 'I am not one of those who like to ask "What will the Government do for us?" I do not think that is the question. For us the question of the day is, "What shall we do for ourselves?" '[28]

She explained how landlords were taking advantage of the influx of new diggers to raise prices of food, rooms and water to extortionate levels. At the diggings men lived in tents, ate cold food, and had no washing or toilet facilities. She wrote to the Governor, Sir Charles Hotham, and urged the establishment of inexpensive shelter sheds to act as staging posts at Essendon, Keilor, Sunbury, Gisborne, Wood End, Carlsruhe, Malmsbury and Elphinstone. Other areas at which she had stopped also volunteered to raise funds for Mrs Chisholm's sheds.

But by now Archy was ill and worn-out and wanted to retire from public life so they rented a house in Melbourne's Elizabeth Street North. It soon became apparent to charitable bodies that although they never complained the Chisholms were very short of money: they had been working for many years for the good of others without thought of any payment for themselves, confident God would provide.

A sum of money was subscribed in Melbourne to establish Major Chisholm and his sons in a general store. With the money subscribed, Archy and two of their sons bought a general store in Kyneton, hoping to benefit from the gold rush trade. Meanwhile Mrs Chisholm's Shelter Shed Committee was busy raising funds for the shelters.

Caroline and the girls stayed on in Melbourne to oversee and equip the Shelter Shed project, intending to rejoin Archy at Kyneton once the sheds were fitted out. Each had a paid keeper who charged overnight guests a very small fee. The sheds were extremely basic but widely used. Caroline Chisholm's Shelter Sheds became known as Chisholm Shakedowns and travellers slept on bunks and straw mattresses.

During this busy time Caroline made frequently visits to her husband at Kyneton. Their delicate son, William, married an Irish girl, found work and stayed behind in Melbourne.

Caroline wanted to change the laws to help the many innocent girls who were drawn into a life of prostitution in Melbourne's brothels and was frustrated that women had no voice in Parliament. (Not that Melbourne was exceptional, London was estimated to have had 80,000 prostitutes at this time and Paris even more.[29]) The gold rush meant organised brothels boomed to accommodate lucky diggers, and many hired or 'married' prostitutes for a day or a week before returning home. Caroline wrote an angry letter to the press when a girl of thirteen was found dead in a house of ill-repute in Little Bourke Street. The girl had died of a heart attack, a one-pound note still on the bed beside her. Once again she demanded homes or subsidised lodging houses for 'females and distressed families on landing'. But her health was failing and she realised she could no longer run an immigrants hostel in Melbourne as she had all those years ago in Sydney.[30]

In December 1857 she gave up their rented home and joined Archibald at Kyneton, in accommodation behind the family's general store. The following March she and Archibald were delighted to find themselves grandparents when William's wife had a son. But their store at Kyneton was doing badly due to competition from other businesses. Caroline was often in pain and the doctor believed that harsh winters at Kyneton had adversely affected her health.

Leaving the boys in charge of the store, Caroline and Archibald returned to Sydney, where they rented a shabby, inexpensive house in Redfern. Archibald, gaunt and pale but still distinguished, with an upright carriage and silver hair, managed to find work in a draper's shop. It was not what he envisaged but they needed the money. Their small capital was still tied up in the Kyneton store which, due to low turnover, proved unexpectedly hard to sell.

The family settled into a routine but were soon jolted out of it by the shock of receiving the news of William's death. He had never been strong since Rome, and to make matters worse William's baby died the following day. The unfortunate Chisholms were too short of money to return to Melbourne for the joint funeral of their son and grandson.

However, Sydney's milder climate improved Caroline's health. As soon as she was well enough, she accepted invitations to speak at public meetings on topics of concern to her—like the free selection of unsurveyed blocks of Crown land for immigrants, who would receive extended credit terms to pay for their land. Caroline spoke on a platform with John Robertson, Premier of New South Wales, who was attempting to pass the Land Selection Act that allowed settlers without capital to take up relatively small blocks of land on favourable mortgage terms. She also crusaded for the right of unmarried mothers (meaning those who had been raped or seduced) to receive government assistance, and spoke out in favour of early closing of shops and stores, as at this period employers made their staff work ten- and eleven-hour shifts on the shopfloor for low wages.

Eventually the younger boys sold the Kyneton store for far less than they had paid for it and joined their parents in Sydney. The Redfern house was too cramped for them all so they rented a larger home in Stanley Street. By now everything had changed. The old barracks on the corner of Bent Street where Caroline's Immigrants Home had once stood, was now pulled down. In its place was the handsome new Subscription Library. Migrant ships were powered by steam and had far better sleeping conditions including separate cabins for all migrants.

In July 1862 Caroline started a girls' school in Stanmore, where her daughters Caroline and Monica did their lessons along with the daughters of paying clients. Later the school moved to larger premises at Tempe but Caroline's failing health meant she rarely taught pupils now.

However she still received appreciative letters from women whose lives she had changed for the better. By now her fame had spread as far as France. In 1862 the French historian Jules Michelet devoted a chapter to 'la glorieuse Madame Chisholm' in a book titled *La Femme*. Michelet described 'Madame Chisholm' as a 'living legend' and as a suitable candidate for canonisation.

Such praise was gratifying. But by now she was in great pain from what would eventually be diagnosed as kidney disease.[31] Alarmed by the swift deterioration in her condition, Archy and her doctor decided she must return to London to consult a specialist. They decided that as Caroline and Monica could not be left behind and should finish their education in Britain. They would all return to Sydney once Caroline was better. In 1866 the family arrived in London without their son Harry, who had married and stayed on in Sydney. But instead of improving, Caroline's health worsened. 'Dropsy' or severe swelling in her legs caused by kidney failure made walking very difficult.

Major Archibald Chisholm was now over seventy, still erect but too frail to work. Caroline was forced to rest in bed for long periods but, as always, she detested being idle. When she felt well enough, she took up her pen and earned a little money from journalism. But it was obvious to visitors that their funds were low and Caroline lacked many comforts. Friends lobbied for government support, stressing that Caroline had dedicated her entire life to the needs of others.

Eventually the British Government awarded Caroline a small pension in recognition of her outstanding service to Australian emigration. She was not totally bedridden and spent the next few years in a small back bedroom in a dingy little house at Highgate Hill, north London, where she was delighted to received visits from her children and adored grandchildren.

In spite of pain and discomfort from her illness, Caroline never became depressed. She was consoled by her religious faith and the fact that she had fulfilled God's plan for her life. She trusted totally in God and, as she had done all her life, was convinced something would turn up to improve their living conditions.

Caroline was right. Something did. In the last year of her life her daughter Caroline (by now married to editor Charles Gray) paid for her parents to move to a larger and more comfortable home at 43a Barclay Road, Fulham. Caroline's bed was placed in a bay window so that she could look out over the quiet street lined with beautiful trees, which gave her enormous pleasure. She died of bronchitis aged sixty-eight on a Sunday—the Feast of the Annunciation—as the church bells rang out over London. Her last words were 'Take me home'. Her body was taken to the Roman Catholic Cathedral of St Felix in Northampton, near the farm where she was born. Archibald was distraught by her death but was too frail to attend the funeral. Without her his life had little purpose and he died a few months later. Their shared tombstone in Northampton's Billingham Road Cemetery carried the message

> Pray for the Souls of Caroline Chisholm, the Emigrants' Friend, who died 25 March 1877 and of Archibald Chisholm, Major, Madras Native Infantry, who died 17 August, 1877, aged 81.

That inscription, under a simple white cross, marks the grave of this talented, determined woman, who sought only to help others.

Caroline Chisholm seems a very modern woman in many respects. Certainly her religious faith was typical of the period but her tolerance was highly unusual in a period when religious intolerance and sectarianism was rife. She converted to Roman Catholicism in a country which had the Church of England as the established religion and laws which actively discriminated against Catholics. She was unconventional in other ways: in her prenuptial contract which gave her freedom to pursue her interests and her work; in her concern for the well-being of 'fallen women', their children and the 'undeserving poor'. All her life she campaigned through the press and Parliament for causes when women were intended to have a modest demeanour, reticence and circumspection. Caroline Chisholm was aware of the social conventions of her time; her intelligence and social conscience caused her to break out of the barriers than confined most women of her period and change Australia for the better.

The French Catholic historian Jules Michelet summarised it well:

> Australia has a Saint, an English woman without wealth and without assistance who has done more for the new world than all the emigration societies and the British Government together—a simple woman who succeeded in her aims by force of character and vigour of soul.[32]

[1] Caldwell, J. C. *Australians—Historical Statistics*, p. 23. Fairfax, Syme, Weldon Associates, Sydney, 1987. Gives a rate of 80 per cent of male population in rural areas.

[2] Pool, Dennis. *What Jane Austen Ate and Charles Dickens Knew, the Facts of Life in Nineteenth Century England.* Simon and Schuster, London and New York, 1994.

[3] Hellier, Donna. *Families in Colonial Australia*, edited by Patricia Grimshaw. Allen and Unwin, Sydney, 1985.

[4] A perceptive article on the Chisholms' marriage by academic Patricia Grimshaw appears in *For Richer, For Poorer, Early Colonial Marriages*, edited by Penny Russell, Melbourne University Press, Melbourne, 1994. The standard biographies of Caroline Chisholm are by Margaret Kiddle, *Caroline Chisholm*, Melbourne University Press, Melbourne, 1950, and Mary Hoban, *Fifty-One Pieces of Wedding Cake*, Lodden Press, Kilmore, Victoria, 1976 and Bogley, Joanna, *The Immigrant's Friend*, Moorhouse Publishing, U.S., 1994.

[5] Maitland, Lady Julia (writing as 'A Lady'). *Letters from Madras During the Years 1836–1839*, London. Cited Hoban, *Fifty-One Pieces of Wedding Cake*, Lodden Press, Kilmore, 1976 and Polding Press, Melbourne 1984.

[6] *Sydney Emigrants Journal*, 1850, cited Kiddle, *Caroline Chisholm, Op. cit.* p.14.

[7] Thierry, Judge Roger. *Reminiscences of Thirty Years Residence in New South Wales*, London, 1833. Provides a description of the Immigration Barracks.

[8] Chisholm, C. *Female Immigration Considered in a Brief Account of the Sydney Immigrants' Home.* James Tegg, London, 1842 cited in Kiddle, Margaret, *Op. cit.*

[9] *Ibid.*

[10] *Ibid.*

[11] *Ibid.*

[12] *Ibid.*

[13] Gandivia, E. *Tears Often Shed. Child Health and Welfare in Australia from 1788.* Charter Books, Sydney, 1977.

[14] Madgewick, R. B. *Immigration into Eastern Australia.* 1937. Cited in Kiddle.

[15] Cited Kiddle, p. 63.

[16] Lord Shaftesbury, English philanthropist and reformer who succeeded in banning children under nine from working in mills, women and children from working underground in mines and the use of small boys as chimney sweeps. He was active in several other good causes including the 'Ragged Schools' movement, legislation to provide lodgings for the poor and support for the work of Florence Nightingale.

[17] While in London Caroline Chisholm wrote and published *Emigration and Transportation Considered*, published John Oliver, London, 1847. Dedicated with permission to Earl Grey. *Comfort for the Poor! Meat Three Times a Day!* A pamphlet urging the poor to emigrate to NSW but advising them of the realities. In 1849 she published *Family Colonization Loan Society by the Grant of Loans for Two Years or More Without Interest . . . to the Colonies of New South Wales, Port Phillip and South Australia by Mrs Chisholm: The ABC of Colonization having appended . . . the rules of the Family Colonization Society*, 1850. The advice aroused such interest that in 1853 her articles were reprinted under the title *Mrs Chisholm's Advice to Immigrants*.

[18] Summers, Anne. *Damned Whores and God's Police*. Penguin Books, Melbourne, 1974 and 1994. This is the book that burst the conventions of our predominantly male political history.

[19] *Australian*. 19 May 1842. Cited in Kiddle.

[20] *Household Words*. Charles Dickens vol i, (1850) page 43. Cited in Kiddle.

[21] Chisholm, C. *The ABC of Colonization. A series of letters addressed to the Gentlemen forming the Committee of the Family Colonization Society viz Lord Ashley, MP, the Rt. Hon. Sydney Herbert, MP, the Hon. Vernon Smith, MP, etc.* published John Olivier, London 1850.

[22] *Argus*, 2 September 1855. Cited in Kiddle.

[23] Dark, Eleanor. *Caroline Chisholm and her Times*, in Flora Eldershaw's *The Peaceful Army*. WEC Publishing, Sydney, 1938.

[24] Hoban, M. *Fifty-One pieces of Wedding Cake*, p. 317.

[25] From a report in the *Times*, London, dated 8 August 1854.

[26] *Illustrated London News*, 7 October 1854.

[27] La Trobe Papers, La Trobe Collection, State Library of Victoria.

[28] *Argus*, Melbourne, 11 November 1854.

[29] Pool, Dennis. *What Charles Dickens Ate and Jane Austen Knew*. Simon and Schuster, 1994. This figure is quoted in a number of sources. The figure for Paris was even higher per head of population according to the report of Dr Parent-Duchâtelet on prostitution in the 1880s and Dr Hollis Clayson, *Painted Love, Prostitution in French Art*. Yale University Press, Boston, 1992.

[30] *Argus*, Melbourne, 13 June 1857.

[31] Kiddle and other biographers mention Chisholm's kidney disease while Hoban suggests Caroline Chisholm only returned to London to 'finish off' the education of her daughters.

[32] Michelet, Jules praised Caroline's work in a chapter 'Femme Protectrice des Femmes' in his book, *La Femme*, Paris, 1862, p. 468.

CHAPTER 6

Walyer
(?–1831)
Truganini
(1812–1876) and
Fanny Cochrane Smith
(1834–1905)

THREE REMARKABLE ABORIGINAL WOMEN

The lives of the three women Walyer, Truganini and Fanny Cochrane Smith span the period from 1803, the start of European settlement at Risdon Cove in Van Diemen's Land (renamed Tasmania in 1855), through the terrible 'black wars' when Aborigines were hunted down and killed like wild animals by the military and 'all able bodied volunteers', to 1905 the year of Fanny Cochrane Smith's death. In the opinion of European settlers the problem of the indigenous people had been solved. By 1824, the estimated population of 5,000 in 1803 had shrunk to less than 500. In contrast four years later the white population totalled 16,924—made up of 13,143 males and 3,781 females.[1] It was a society based largely on self-interest, greed, cruelty and indifference to the human rights of the Aborigines.

Each woman's experience mirrors what was happening to her people at that time. The choice each made reflects the pressures that constrained them. Walyer chose armed resistance, Truganini assessed the odds and chose exile, and Fanny Cochrane Smith chose accommodation.

Walyer (?–1831)

Walyer was born near St Valentine's Peak, in the north-west of Tasmania. There were no birth, marriage or death certificates so it is difficult to find documentary evidence about individual Aboriginal women. Our documentary evidence is based on the occasional reference to them in official reports, personal letters and diaries. What is known of Walyer brings to mind the story of Boadicea, the warrior queen of the Iceni.

Walyer was of Tommeginne descent[2] and her people were under pressure on several fronts: white sealers and rival Aboriginal groups preyed on Aboriginal women, and white settlers with their herds and crops were moving onto Aboriginal land, hunting and driving out the kangaroo, the staple Aboriginal food.[3] Sealers were a serious problem and notorious for their brutal treatment of Aboriginal women. Relationships between the indigenous people and the newcomers were further strained by the acute shortage of women among the whites. The women

Map of Tasmania including site of Walyer's birth, Oyster Bay (where Truganini, Fanny Cochrane and other Aborigines were exiled) and Cambria (where Louisa Meredith lived). Copyright Jake de Vries.

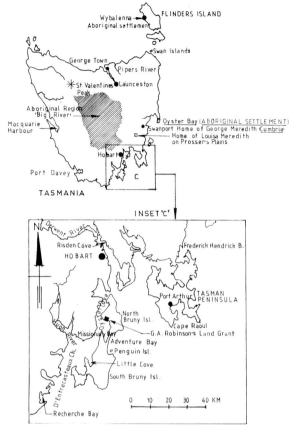

FOUR 19TH CENTURY TASMANIAN WOMEN

were excellent swimmers and hunters of seals, and when seals became scarce, of game such as kangaroos and muttonbirds. Finally Aboriginal groups displaced from their land by white settlement were forced into traditional territory of other groups; this provoked fighting among Aborigines and further disrupted their traditional life.

Walyer's date of birth is not known, but as a teenager she was abducted by Aboriginal men and traded to white sealers living on the Bass Strait islands[4] for dogs and flour. After living with the sealers for some years she escaped in 1828. She returned to lead the Emu Bay people against the invaders and taught them how to use firearms.

She came to the notice of the authorities in Van Diemen's Land in June 1830, and was described as the leader of a small group of Aborigines (consisting of eight men, a boy and another woman), who were feared by Aborigines and whites alike.

The missionary George Augustus Robinson called her 'the Amazon'. She had taken over the leadership of a tribe known for its aggressiveness.[5] He described how she would stand on a hill and give orders to her men to attack the whites, taunting them to come out of their huts and fight.

In September 1830, Robinson reported his first contact with Walyer's group, by which time it had grown. According to Vivienne Rae Ellis:

> . . . Robinson persuaded Trucanini . . . and two other Aboriginals . . . to go and talk to the warriors while he remained a short distance behind pleading that the sight of his white skin would cause alarm. Walyer and her warriors sprang forward, brandishing their spears. Trucanini and the others abandoned all show of bravery and fled back to the leader who, unarmed, waited in a sweat of nerves to learn what had happened.[6]

Robinson blamed Walyer's 'mob' for the trouble west of the Tamar River. Walyer was reported to have a fowling piece which she fired at the huts of whites, calling to them to come out as well as a dog which would sniff out white settlers.[7]

By December 1830 Walyer was reported in the Bass Strait area on tiny Penguin Island[8] where she attempted to persuade the five Aboriginal women working for the white man to murder him and steal his boat.[9] They refused. Walyer was unable to get off the island and was caught. She was taken to the Swan Island Aboriginal Station by Robinson's expedition. She kept her identity secret, presenting herself under the name of Mary Anne. But she gave herself away when she was reunited with her beloved dog and unwisely called to him by name—'Whiskey!' Robinson already knew that 'Whiskey' was the name of Walyer's dog and so her real identity was revealed.

Walyer's hostility to white men was well known and her influence on other Aborigines was feared by Robinson who kept her isolated from the rest of the Aborigines. She was regarded as 'desperate—and possessing a deal of cunning'.[10] In spite of Robinson's efforts to isolate her, Walyer managed to warn the Aborigines of an impending massacre by soldiers coming from Launceston. The Aborigines were terrified by this information but Walyer remained cool. She boasted about the numbers of whites she and her group had killed.

Walyer's warning of an impending massacre is fascinating as two months earlier, on 7 October 1830, a military operation called the 'Black Line' or the 'round-up' had been ordered by Lieutenant-Governor Arthur. All able-bodied men had joined forces to drive the Aborigines remaining at large across the island onto the Tasman Peninsula, where they were to be captured. Rumour also had it that all the Mission Aborigines, including Truganini, were to be killed.

Walyer's fears for Aborigines were well founded and her intense distrust of the white man's intentions towards the Aborigines was vindicated by events. The removal of nearly all Aborigines to Wybalenna Aboriginal Station on Flinders Island in Bass Strait (there were a number of small isolated groups who were brought in during the 'thirties) seemed to put the seal on the extinction of the race—they died at an appalling rate. Walyer seemed clearly aware of what the future held in store.

From the little we know about Walyer, she emerges as a powerful and intriguing figure. There were reports of fierce warrior tribes in Tasmanian Aboriginal culture, but no tradition of female leadership. Many of the Aboriginal women who had lived with the sealers as captives or free associates were of strong character who resisted attempts to 'Christianise' or civilise them, but no other Aboriginal woman translated her experience with European culture into a fierce resolve to fight it in an organised way. To what extent this was fuelled by an awareness of the toll European settlement had taken on the population of the original inhabitants is conjecture. But the Aboriginal population dropped from the 1803 broad estimate of between 2,000 to 8,000 to the pitiful band of 120 'rescued' Aborigines on Wybalenna Station, Flinders Island in 1835.[11] To the great relief of Robinson and other authorities, Walyer survived only a few months in captivity. She died on 5 June, 1831. Did she will herself to die?

Truganini (1812–1876)

Truganini, also spelt Trucanini and Trugernanner, was a Tasmanian Aborigine born on the D'Entrecasteaux Channel side of Bruny Island in Recherche Bay in 1812. The island had been visited by most explorers including Cook, Bligh and D'Entrecasteaux in order to take aboard water and timber. The local Aborigines were described by the explorers as friendly, confident and not at all surprised at the appearance of men so unlike themselves. The explorers could not know that the Aborigines believed their own dead returned as white men, their colour drained by

the rigours of their journey.[12] The Nuenonne people remained unconcerned about any threat posed by the 'white men' until the appearance of whalers and sealers and the abduction, rape and enslavement of Aboriginal women.

Mangerner (or Mangana), Truganini's father, was an elder of the Lyluequony extended family group. By the time she was seventeen several members of her family had been killed by marauding bands of whalers and sealers and convicts—her mother had been killed by whalers, an uncle was shot by a soldier, two tribal sisters were kidnapped and a blood sister, Moorinna, was abducted and shot by sealers.[13] Truganini experienced at first-hand the brutality of white men when she and two friends, including Paraweena, her betrothed, were taken across the channel by timber sawyers. Without warning the sawyers threw Paraweena and the other Aborigine overboard, chopping off their hands at the wrist as they clung to the side of the boat. They took the helpless girl ashore and raped her repeatedly.[14]

Truganini's experience with Europeans had been a harrowing one by the time she and her father met George Augustus Robinson in March 1829 on Bruny Island and decided that he was different from the white sealers and sawyers she had met previously and could be trusted. This was her tragedy that she believed in Robinson and his 'Friendly Mission' to her people.

Robinson was a curious product of his time. He was self-educated and self-opinionated, a lover of nature who enjoyed being out in 'the bush'. He was devoutly religious and, unusually, sympathetic to the plight of the Aborigines, he believed that religion and civilisation would save the Aborigines: Christianity would save them from spiritual darkness while 'enlightenment' would equip them to take their place in the new world.[15] Robinson started his career as a builder in Van Diemen's

Opposite: *Tasmanian Aborigines encamped around a fire painted by John Glover, who would later visit Oyster Bay and see Truganini and Fanny. Tasmanian Museum and Art Gallery.*

An isolated Tasmanian farming and fishing settlement in the 1840s by John Skinner Prout. Walyer and other guerilla leaders fought isolated white settlers, like those on the farm in the centre of the painting. Watercolour from a private collection, courtesy Christie's, London.

land. He abandoned that profitable occupation to become a 'secular missionary'[16] to 'bring in' the Aborigines before they were exterminated.

Lieutenant-Governor Arthur of Van Diemen's Land appointed Robinson guardian of Aborigines on Bruny Island. Robinson learned their language and won their confidence. He advocated a policy of reconciliation, whereby Aborigines would be encouraged to 'come in' to safe depots where they would be issued with food and clothing and would be safe. He persuaded a number of Aborigines from Bruny Island to accompany him on his expedition of conciliation which became known as the 'Friendly Mission'. Robinson met the lively and intelligent Truganini within a week of his arrival on Bruny Island and recruited her as an interpreter and guide.

The group settled on the north shore of Missionary Bay, on the western side of North Bruny Island. Robinson planned to establish a native village, based on the European model with houses and vegetable gardens.

Truganini married a Nuenonne man of Bruny Island called Woorrady, who was 20 years older than her, in July 1829.[17] She was extremely petite in build—only 1.3m (four foot three inches) tall. The portrait of Truganini painted by Thomas Bock in 1837 when she was 25 years old shows a young woman with an attractive face with pleasing features, intelligent lively eyes and full sensual lips—justifying various contemporary descriptions of her as a very attractive young woman.

In August 1829 Truganini's father, stepmother and brother crossed the channel to visit the Recherche Bay area, leaving Truganini behind. Bad weather had forced the brig *Cyprus* carrying convicts to Macquarie Harbour Penal Settlement to shelter in the bay. The ship was overpowered by the convicts on board who put ashore on an isolated spot the master, officers, commanding officer's wife and baby, surgeon, crew, and the colonial painter William Buelow Gould. While ashore the convicts kidnapped Truganini's stepmother and took her on board the *Cyprus* which eventually reached China. Truganini's stepmother was never heard of again.[18] Truganini's brother Robert was also killed leaving their father, Mangana, devastated. He died of grief within months. Truganini's whole family had vanished. Perhaps this personal experience of loss and vulnerability influenced Truganini to choose the course that she would follow for the next decade.

In January 1830 Truganini and her new husband, Woorrady, joined Robinson's expedition as guides and instructors in Aboriginal languages and customs. Woorrady was a renowned hunter and storyteller, knowledgeable in ritual and healing. After the death of Truganini's father he was the only surviving adult male of the Nuenonne tribe. The 'Friendly Mission' left Bruny Island 3 February 1830 on the *Swallow* and sailed the short distance to Recherche Bay where Robinson, believing that the ship was too small, abandoned it and the party continued the journey on foot.

This expedition lasted nine months and was a test not only of physical endurance but also of Robinson's 'conciliation policy'. What he learned filled him with shame at the barbaric behaviour of his own people. In the north-west at *Woolnorth*, the 250,000-acre sheep run granted to the Van Diemen's Land Company, Robinson learned of the massacre in 1827 of 30 unarmed Aborigines on a muttonbird-collecting expedition. A Van Diemen's Land Company shepherd told Robinson that the Aborigines were massacred and their bodies thrown over the cliffs because 100 sheep had been killed. Six Aboriginal women in a sealers camp confirmed the story, telling Truganini and her friend Pagerly that tension existed between the shepherds and the Aborigines over women. The sheep had been killed by Aborigines in retaliation for the death of an Aborigine, who had killed a shepherd intent on rape. The dead Aborigine belonged to another extended family group altogether.

Robinson's attempt to persuade each group of Aborigines he encountered to return with him to the safety of Bruny Island, where they would be safe and could live in peace with plenty of food, shelter and clothing, met with very limited success. During this nine-month period locating the scattered and elusive groups, Robinson compiled a record of the different languages and customs of those with whom he made contact.[19]

The party travelled up the rugged south-west coast eventually cutting across to Launceston, following the trail of camp fires and grass fires that Aboriginal groups would light deliberately to flush out game or to encourage new growth for game.

Having located a group, the Mission Aborigines would strip off any clothing they were wearing and would call out with assurances of friendship, while Robinson and the European members of the group kept well out of sight. It was on this first expedition that contact was made with Walyer, the feared woman warrior and her group. Truganini and the Aborigines in her party must have been very conscious of Walyer's fearsome reputation and the fact that they were in hostile territory.

Truganini's biographer, Vivienne Rae Ellis, in her book *Trucanini: Queen or Traitor?* claims that because of Truganini's fondness for Robinson, she willingly allowed herself to be used as a lure to bring her people to the mission settlements and their destruction. Rae Ellis also notes that the Aborigines with Robinson were disparagingly referred to as 'the decoy blacks'. She deals with contemporary allegations that Truganini was promiscuous and that she became Robinson's mistress on the expeditions. In assessing accounts of Truganini's sexuality we have to be wary of judging from a late 20th century, Judaeo–Christian perspective. She was a member of another culture which had its own customs and taboos. The stereotype of Aboriginal women created by white society—accessible, exploitable and disposable—is neither appropriate nor valid.

More serious is the accusation that Truganini betrayed her own people, that she allied herself with Robinson and the newcomers, encouraging her own people to leave the land which was essential to their spiritual and physical well-being. What motives could she have had for luring her own countrymen and women away from their territory?

Her relationship with Robinson and desire to please him is suggested, but the information Rae Ellis provides is not entirely convincing. Truganini certainly does not emerge as enslaved by her passion for Robinson and proceeds to have other relationships (to the indignation of the authorities). Truganini did not benefit financially from bringing in Aborigines, unlike Robinson whose decisions became increasingly influenced by financial considerations, receiving large land grants for his work.

All those who met Truganini formed the opinion that she had a lively intelligence. It seems highly likely that with her bitter experiences of white men she would have concluded that the struggle for Van Diemen's Land lay between totally unequally matched opponents. She and her close friend and fellow negotiator for the Friendly Mission, Drayduric, (usually known as Dray), who spoke far better English than Truganini, had visited Hobart. Both young women had seen ships arriving there filled with even more armed soldiers and settlers. Truganini's experience of the murder of her parents by armed whites and her pack-rape by timber sawyers, (who were never prosecuted for killing her Aboriginal lover or raping her) would have made her believe white men would always use force to obtain their demands whether for Aboriginal women or for land. But instead of choosing Walyer's solution and joining her band of guerilla fighters, Truganini must have decided it was better for her people to accept Robinson's terms, remain a free undefeated people and go of their own accord rather than as prisoners to a safe haven on Flinders Island, where they would receive shelter and food, regroup and recover. She must have believed that when things were safer, they would be allowed to return to their own native lands.

Robinson later denied that he had ever promised the Aborigines would return to their own lands. But Henry Reynolds in his 1995 book *Fate of a Free People* cites an Aborigine named Walter George Arthur stating in 1846 'we were not taken

prisoners but freely gave up our country to . . . the Governor after defending ourselves . . . Mr Robinson made for us with Colonel Arthur [the then Governor and no relation to Walter George Arthur] an agreement which we have not lost from our minds since . . . and we have made our part of it good'.[20]

Did Truganini believe that Robinson had promised an agreement whereby they would return to the mainland. This could well explain why she had a long-lasting affair with Robinson, hoping to bind him closer to her with ties of kinship and then, disillusioned by what happened, refused to speak to him because she believed he had broken the unwritten treaty? Certainly Robinson, false hair piece and all, was a big improvement on the whalers and sealers she had previously associated with. Truganini told Tasmanian settler and historian James Erskine Calder that 'Mr Robinson was a good man and could speak our language and I said I would go with him and help him. I knew it was no use my people trying to kill all the white people now; there were so many of them always coming in big boats'.[21] It is important to give Truganini recognition for a considered decision. She was certainly not the promiscuous bimbo portrayed in some accounts of early Tasmanian settlement but an intelligent woman who realised clearly that the most important thing was to ensure the survival of her people.

Robinson's expedition arrived in Launceston on 2 October 1830, just as the infamous Black Line was about to get under way, and it met a hostile reception from the townspeople. One month earlier, on 9 September, while Robinson and his party were attempting through conciliation to persuade Aborigines to go to safe 'depots', Lieutenant-Governor Arthur had issued a proclamation calling on all settlers to voluntarily join the police and military for one determined effort to capture or drive all Aborigines out of the settled parts. Van Diemen's Land was to be divided into six districts under the command of a military officer. On 25 September further details of the round-up were published with the date of commencement set for

7 October 1830. Over 3,000 volunteers took to the field armed with rifles, muskets and hunting knives.

There were demands that the mission Aborigines be put in prison with others caught by the Black Line dragnet, but George Whitcomb, a Customs Department employee and a most exceptional man, offered to put up the 'Peace Mission' in his own house. A week later Robinson's expedition sailed out of Launceston past George Town and headed east to continue their task.

In the north-east corner of Van Diemen's Land, 'large ferocious tribes' were reputed to live. As in previous encounters the numbers of these extended family groups were wildly exaggerated by the Europeans. Robinson's party met only small groups, the remnants of much larger populations which had been decimated by the activities of sealers and whalers. The Pipers River tribe was reputed to number 700 ferocious people. Robinson's report listed 72 males, six women and no children.[21] He explained the Black Line situation to them, urging them to go to the safety of Swan Island, three kilometres off the north-east coast, where a mission station was to be established.

The expedition made its way eastward along the north coast making contact with other tribes with the assistance of Truganini, Woorrady and other members of the group. A number of local people were persuaded to leave their territory and relocate on cold and windy Swan Island where Truganini and Woorrady also lived for a time. In all, twenty-three Aborigines were settled on Swan Island by Robinson.[22]

Early January 1831, Truganini, Woorrady, two other Aborigines, Robinson and another European left Swan Island and returned on foot to Hobart Town, following the east coast, where they stayed with Robinson's family for two months.

The Black Line united the settlers against the perceived common enemy. At the same time it showed how ineffective the mobilisation of thousands of able-bodied men had been in capturing Aborigines—their tally was two captives and two woundings. Hostilities declined markedly from this time as by 1835 all but one family group of Aborigines had been removed from the mainland. However, the impact

Benjamin Duterrau's reconstruction of George Augustus Robinson's Friendly Mission intended to persuade Tasmanian Aborigines to surrender. Truganini is the petite figure on the right. Oil 121 x 170 cm. Tasmanian Museum and Art Gallery.

Insert: Detail from portrait of George Augustus Robinson by Benjamin Duterrau. Private collection, courtesy Christie's, Australia.

119

on the Aboriginal population was to bring home to them just how hopeless their situation was.

Robinson was well rewarded for his efforts with a grant of 2,560 acres (approx 1040 ha) of land, a salary increase to £250 per annum backdated to his initial appointment to the Mission, and a gratuity of £100 in recognition of his zeal, courage and ingenuity.[23] The Aboriginal members of the expedition received a boat which was let out to hire on the Derwent River and the proceeds used to pay for 'luxuries' for its owners.[24] Truganini received nothing personally for her work, which included saving Robinson from drowning when crossing a river (he could not swim) and saving two other white men from drowning.

From 1830 to 1835 Truganini and Woorrady remained members of Robinson's expeditions into the Tasmanian interior attempting to persuade remaining Aborigines to join the mission Aborigines and thereby avoid extermination. Robinson, who was genuinely interested in Aboriginal language and customs, continued to record the language and traditions of various groups with which he made contact, leaving to posterity an important ethnographic record of precontact Tasmanian Aboriginal society.

Lieutenant-Governor Arthur agreed to Robinson's proposal that all Aborigines should be removed from the mainland to Gun Carriage Island (today known as Vansittart) off the east coast of Van Diemen's Land, so that they would not be able to interfere with the settlers. The island was chosen for its remoteness and because escape would be difficult. It was in effect banishment rather than preservation. The *Charlotte* sailed out of Hobart Town with its human cargo of misery on 3 March 1831.

There was a problem with the choice of Gun Carriage Island: sealers were well entrenched there at a settlement of ten or eleven cottages with established gardens, pigs, goats, fowl etc. These sealers had captured and bought for flour, sugar, tea and tobacco Aboriginal 'wives' who formed an essential part of their workforce. The sealers were now ordered by Robinson to leave and give up their Aboriginal women. In the often-heated confrontations that ensued Robinson was not supported by the lieutenant-governor, but was successful in persuading Arthur to agree to several points: to protect 'his' Aborigines from sealers; the establishment of an asylum on an island for Aborigines; and the removal there of all tribes captured elsewhere. Governor Arthur also agreed that roving parties of whites hunting down Aborigines should be halted. The governor felt Robinson's conciliatory 'persuasive' approach had been far more successful and should be the only method used, with force resorted to only in case of attack on whites by Aborigines.

Successful forays onto the mainland followed in which Truganini, Woorrady and other 'Mission Aborigines' were essential to find and persuade scattered remnants of various tribes such as the Oyster Bay and the Big River 'tribes' to come in. It was significant that in each group women formed a small minority, while children were even more rare. Only the west coast Aborigines, who were more isolated and whose women had not been subject to frequent abductions, had a good balance between the sexes and children of all ages in their midst. The remnant of the Big River group, which surrendered peacefully at the end of 1831, consisted of 16 men, 9 women and one child.[25] Robinson received £100 and the Mission Aborigines received 50 sheep between them for this work.[26] Robinson was promised £1,000 for the capture of the remaining west coast tribes and was appointed Superintendent of the Aboriginal settlement to be established on Flinders Island. Plomley believed[27] that Robinson's success depended substantially on the support of the Aborigines of the Friendly Mission. Other factors in persuading the remaining groups to come in were: the expansion of settlement into the interior; aggressiveness of sealers, stock-keepers and settlers in fighting Aborigines; and finally the devastating drop in birthrates and jump in deaths because of disease. Aborigines were particularly prone to respiratory infections.

On one of the expeditions to the west coast Truganini saved Robinson's life when a group of Aborigines attacked the expedition. On 1 September 1832, after crossing the Arthur River, Robinson made contact with the local Aborigines. From the beginning it was clear something was amiss and it was assumed that the group had no intention of joining the Friendly Mission Aborigines and were intending to 'abscond'. A display of spear sharpening made it apparent that something more serious was being planned. The Mission Aborigines were not armed except for the spears used for hunting kangaroos, but they were not sufficient for defence in case of attack. Robinson attributed his escape to Truganini who saved his life by staying with him and helping him across the Arthur River as he could not swim.

There were a number of west coast groups who were reluctant to leave their homes for exile and they resisted. Shamefully Robinson used force. It seems fair to assume that the £1,000 which Robinson had been offered for removing the remainder of the west coast tribes from the mainland motivated his actions.[28]

A serious problem developed with the very high death rate of Aborigines who had surrendered and were at Macquarie Harbour awaiting transport to Flinders Island. In a mass tragedy Aboriginal groups from the west coast died like flies— within 17 days nine members out of a group of 11 died. The unsanitary and inhumane conditions they were kept in while waiting transport to Flinders Island must surely have contributed to their deaths. They were initially housed on the ground floor. The white prisoners on the level above set out deliberately to make a nuisance of themselves: they taunted the Aborigines, poured water between the floorboards and urinated over them. The Aborigines were moved to the hospital building but they refused to stay there as they feared the surgeon was after their bodies for dissection.

The death rate of the Aborigines on Flinders Island was also alarmingly high. By comparison, the Aborigines who were off the island and on the 'peaceful' expeditions with Robinson suffered no losses. Truganini and her friends were deeply affected by the deaths of the people they had brought in and their commitment to 'saving' their fellow Aborigines gradually evaporated. The last time that Truganini took part in a 'capture' was in December 1834. In February 1835 Robinson reported to the Colonial Secretary that the entire Aboriginal population had been removed from the mainland. Unknown to him one family remained at large.[29]

Truganini spent most of the next twelve months at Robinson's home in Hobart Town and left on 1 October 1835 on the *Tamar* for Flinders Island with a party consisting of Robinson, his sons Charles and William and a group of Aborigines. They were heading for the new settlement on Flinders Island named Wybalenna, Aboriginal for 'native houses'. Robinson, the new commandant, was horrified at the conditions there. Clothing was inadequate, game had been depleted by sealers and the mortality rate among Aborigines was high. He immediately set about making changes. Aboriginal housing was improved and additional houses were built, totally disregarding the Aborigines' avowed preference for communal quarters, and two larger huts were converted into a school and a chapel. There were Sunday School classes, cooking, sewing and literacy lessons, planting of corn, collecting of firewood and improvements to various buildings. All contact between the soldiers stationed on the island and the Aborigines was forbidden. But this was ignored as Robinson, to his great fury, found shell necklaces and other Aboriginal artefacts in the soldiers' and officers' quarters.[30]

In a letter to the Colonial Secretary's office dated 31 July, 1837 Robinson admitted that the Aborigines had been misled into believing that he would return them to their homeland after a period of exile. He was quick to excuse himself of all blame for this but by then his attitude to the Aborigines in his care was changing and hardening. In hindsight it seems logical that Robinson must have put this idea in their minds to make surrendering to the Friendly Mission more attractive: of course 'bringing Aborigines in' secured Robinson financial and other rewards. [31]

Soon after joining the supposed 'asylum' at the Wybalenna Aboriginal Settlement on Flinders Island, Truganini realised that the future proposed for them was be domestic servants to the British 'masters', with the total loss of their Aboriginal identity and culture. As part of the transformation process, Robinson insensitively renamed Truganini 'Lallah Rookh'—after the last princess of a tribe in a popular poem of the time by the Irish poet Thomas Moore. Perhaps in protest, Truganini never learnt to read or write and neither did the other adults. Only the younger Aborigines acquired some literacy skills and they were fairly rudimentary in spite of Robinson's glowing accounts. Truganini clung to traditional Aboriginal lore, becoming angry when an Aborigine repudiated the Aboriginal creation myth in preference for the Bible version. She turned on him demanding 'Where you come from? White woman?'[31]

In March 1836, Truganini returned to the Tasmanian mainland ostensibly to bring in the remaining Aboriginal groups still at large. Instead she defied Robinson, and warned them 'not to come in'.[32] This group consisted of parents and their four children. They refused to go with the mission Aborigines and remained free until 1842. This was the mission's last expedition. In the period since 1829 there had been no deaths among the expedition members in contrast with the situation of the Aboriginal people at the settlement.

By July 1837 so many Aborigines had died on Flinders Island that Truganini warned Robinson that there would be no-one left to move into the houses under construction. The destruction of Aboriginal culture and the organised efforts to replace it with Christian studies, subsistence agriculture, stone houses, a chapel and clothing were in place. After three years, the Wybalenna Aboriginal settlement on Flinders Island was in the process of extinction. In February 1839 an influenza epidemic swept through Wybalenna reducing the number of Aboriginal survivors to sixty-nine.

Robinson's achievements in removing Aboriginals from the Tasmanian mainland were hailed a great success by the authorities and resulted in his receiving the promised financial reward and in being appointed Protector of Aborigines in New South Wales with his principal headquarters at Port Phillip then part of New South Wales.

In 1839 Truganini, her husband and fourteen other Aborigines left Flinders Island to go to Melbourne with Robinson. His appointment reflected the British Government's concern that after fifty years of contact with Europeans, the condition of Aborigines was more wretched and debased than prior to the arrival of European 'civilisation'. Their population had dwindled alarmingly and they were demoralised 'losing the better aspects of their own character in exchange for the most objectionable qualities of the Europeans'.[33]

The duty of the Chief Protector of Aborigines, with the help of four Assistant Protectors was to watch over the rights and interests of the natives, protect them from any encroachment on their property and from acts of cruelty, oppression or injustice, and represent their wants, wishes and grievances to the government of the colony. To facilitate this the Chief Protector and each Assistant Protector was commissioned as a magistrate. The natives were to be persuaded to locate to a settlement where they were to be taught to read and write, and encouraged to cultivate the soil, build suitable houses for themselves and be guided towards European civilisation and social improvement. The education of the children was of primary importance. Each Protector was to learn the language of the natives, take charge of and account for provisions, clothing given to him for distribution to the natives, and to obtain accurate information as to their numbers in his district— and all other important particulars with regard to them.[34]

Sir George Gipps, Governor of New South Wales, was faced with an intractable problem: how to reconcile the rights of the indigenous people with the growth of the European population and the expansion of European settlement into the interior. Official government policy was to protect and assimilate them—the reality was their continued displacement, decimation and cultural impoverishment.

The Port Phillip settlement was experiencing all the problems of a rapidly growing, materialistic settlement intent on becoming rich quickly. Conflict was inevitable. The Government's aim was 'to do justice and shew kindness to the Natives' wrote Lord John Russell to Gipps.[35] London hoped that as soon as the natives understood the value of civilisation, that is, a settled existence, private ownership of property, monogamous marital relationships and Christianity—they would abandon 'their barbaric ways and learn to fit into white man's society'. Missionaries believed the Gospel would lead the natives out of darkness and into an understanding of God's purpose. The Gospel would replace the corroboree, and subsistence agriculture, the hunt. The settlers saw the Aborigines as wild animals who broke the legs of their sheep and then danced a corroboree round the sheep as they writhed in agony, leaving their dogs to finish off the work they had begun. Stories of worse atrocities abounded. 'Murderous savages' so terrorised country districts that men were forced to sell off their stock and walk off their properties. When settlers asked for adequate protection they received lectures from city philanthropists.[36] But there were two sides to the story and considerable evidence exists as to the brutality of some white men. A pattern of revenge and escalation of violence was established.

As in New South Wales, so in Van Diemen's Land and again in Port Phillip, few people appreciated the impact of the 'invaders' on the Aborigines. The squatters and selectors with their herds of cattle and sheep had inflicted a serious loss on the indigenous people with no compensation for the land, game and traditional hunting rights they had forgone. Game had been shot or driven off and sheep and cattle now grazed on the native grasses and roots. The Aborigine killed kangaroo for food, the white man killed kangaroo for sport. The 'indolent but hungry natives' took to stealing and begging for food, and to revenge and violence in retaliation for humiliation and repression. Aborigines believed that the death of an extended family member must be avenged by the death of a member of the murderer's extended family. Therefore killing any white man at all, even if indirectly unconnected with the death of an Aborigine, was the revenge the dead Aborigine's kinsmen were obliged to take under their law. Relations between the settlers and Aborigines in Port Phillip reached flashpoint with fears of a repetition of the slaughter and bloodshed in Van Diemen's Land in 1830.

At Port Phillip Truganini was left to her own devices and made contact with the local Aborigines and according to Vivienne Rae Ellis[37] reverted to her 'promiscuous ways' with the sealers. The close working relationship and bond established in the previous years between Robinson and the Tasmanian Aborigines came to an end as Robinson worked to establish himself in Port Phillip and found that he no longer needed the Mission Aborigines.

In April 1840 when Robinson went off on an eight-week journey inland, the Mission Aborigines 'absconded'. Most were brought back but Truganini ran away again. Robinson on his return asked that the Tasmanian Aborigines be returned to Flinders Island.[38]

By 1841, totally disenchanted with the conditions that prevailed, Truganini, together with two female and two male Tasmanian Aborigines escaped to Western Port. While on the run they terrorised shepherds and in a fight shot two whalers, one of whom had reputedly abducted and shot Truganini's sister, Moorinna, in 1828.[39] During their six-week rampage they stole food, firearms, ammunition, clothing and a little money. They had no compunction about shooting men but when they encountered two women and a child on a station the women were assured that they would not be harmed.[40]

The escapees were captured; the men were hanged and the three women returned to Flinders Island with Woorrady who died on the journey. According to a police statement published on 26 November 1841, immediately after her capture Truganini freely admitted to being an active participant in at least one of the attacks.[41] During the trial Truganini testified, and her statement was supported by an Aboriginal policeman present at her capture, that she had been with the other women and had hidden behind a (sand) bank while the attack took place. Robinson testified that Aboriginal women were completely dominated by Aboriginal men, to Truganini's excellent character and that she had saved his life. It was Robinson's evidence that now saved Truganini's life.

Is it possible that Truganini and her companions, the 'mission Aborigines', having put their trust in the policy of 'conciliation', had been disillusioned by their experience of the safe asylum at Wybalenna? Certainly they had seen it lead to the Aboriginal people's virtual extinction through disease and cultural annihilation. On meeting the indigenous people of the Port Phillip region, with whom Truganini had formed friendships, the Tasmanian Aborigines realised they were confronted with exactly the same situation in Port Phillip as had existed in Van Diemen's Land thirty years earlier. Was this the reason they absconded and ruthlessly killed any white men they met (as Walyer had boasted she had done eleven years earlier as retribution for the death of her kinsmen[42])?

At the age of thirty Truganini was a widow. She found only fifty-four Aborigines left alive on Wybalenna, members of different tribes who spoke their own languages. The new superintendent, Dr Henry Jeanneret, believed his task was to instil Christian morals and stamp out Aboriginal customs. Jeanneret was particularly critical of the Aborigines. He sneered at their local patois, developed as the lingua franca to overcome the language problems, as ' . . . barbarous English . . . replete with native words . . .'[43] He was particularly outraged by their sexual practices such as polygamy, their initiation ceremonies and corroborees, and the hunting/gathering expeditions for food—all of which the Aborigines made clear they wished to continue. In addition the Aborigines had not adapted to European ways: they intensely disliked gardening and other forms of work and had to be bribed by tobacco, sugar and tea; their huts were untidy and they allowed their dogs to live inside with them; and the literacy classes held by the catechist or instructor were not achieving results. In spite of her demonstrated high intelligence, Truganini was classified as ' . . . an indifferent student' who refused to learn to read and write. With most of the Aboriginal women this perceived lack of success extended to domestic crafts such as sewing and knitting.

Jeanneret was a hard and difficult man and rigid disciplinarian.[44] He separated children from their parents because he believed the parents provided a bad example, and sent the children off to Van Diemen's Land to the Queen's Orphan School, which had an appalling mortality rate.

Truganini wanted to live as an Aborigine, according to her traditions, and this drew down Jeanneret's wrath upon her. He complained about her shamefully immoral conduct and her constant absconding with Mathilda. He 'married' Truganini to Alphonso (Mannapackename was his Aboriginal name) whom he regarded as the steadiest of the Aboriginal men. Truganini's 'husband', also known as Big Jemmy, was a widower, six years older than her.[45]

In spite of Jeanneret's Christianising program the Aborigines clung to their traditions. Truganini acquired a reputation as a medicine woman healing through traditional methods. She used bone from the arm of a deceased relative, charred in the fire, placed over the source of pain and firmly bound in place, to ward off sickness and premature death. She treated headache and lumbago by bleeding—cutting the skin with sharp fragments of glass and when sufficient blood had been let, applying moist clay to the wound to stop the bleeding. She also extracted teeth.[46]

Rae Ellis describes how at this time Truganini was unpopular with her own people who reproached her for her close association with Robinson and her role in bringing them there. She was taunted by fellow Aborigines with the prediction she would live to be the last of them as a punishment for her actions.[47] Her exploits in Victoria must have been known to them but this did not redeem her in the eyes of the surviving Aborigines at Wybalenna.

The unremitting efforts of the superintendent notwithstanding, several traditions survived including the Aborigines' intense need to return to the bush and live a wandering life in the traditional manner with only windbreaks for shelter. Sick Aborigines would often ask to move into the bush and their last wish was to be allowed to die there. Another custom was never to pronounce the name of a dead friend or relative. Such references when made by white visitors were greeted with horror and indignation.[48]

If the Aborigines were unhappy at Wybalenna, so too were the authorities. Dissatisfaction with the brutal way in which Jeanneret administered the settlement resulted in his dismissal in 1843, reinstatement on appeal to the Colonial Office in 1846 and his second dismissal. Soldiers garrisoned at Flinders Island regarded it as a punitive posting. In April 1847 Wybalenna was closed down.

Dr Milligan, the settlement's medical officer, was reappointed superintendent and supervised the departure of forty-six Aborigines including fourteen adult males, twenty-two adult females, five boys and five girls who left for the mainland in October 1847. No record of their identity was made. Of the 120 Aborigines who had been at Wybalenna when Truganini had arrived in February 1835 seventy-four had died there. Of the thirteen Aborigines who had gone to Port Phillip only five had returned: the three women: Truganini, Fanny and Mathilda, and two men.

Oyster Cove, their new home, was 40 km south of Hobart across the channel from Bruny Island, Truganini's birthplace. The reserve was bounded by steep hills on three sides and was lightly timbered with only part of the reserve cleared. There was some initial interest from the residents and authorities of Hobart Town in the newcomers, but in time these sightseeing visits petered out and the settlement became increasingly dilapidated and the residents apathetic.

The Aborigines' dislike of domestic work and gardening was noted by the superintendent with the laconic observation that 'They are intelligent enough to perceive that they have a fair claim to support and good treatment without any exertion on their part'.[49] In fact, they were a free people who disdained slave labour.

However, they continued to die in great numbers and by now alcohol began to play an increasing part in their decline as a supply system for 'grog' developed through the local woodcutters and sawyers. In April 1851 when Robinson made a visit to Oyster Cove, a list of the thirty Aborigines living at the reserve was handed to him. Their numbers had been reduced by a third from the forty-six who had arrived four years earlier. Robinson's journal of this visit does not mention Truganini except to list her name as a resident. He received gifts of shell necklaces from Mary Ann and Fanny. It is highly significant that Truganini did not give him a parting gift nor was she a member of the party of Aborigines who saw him off. Her disillusionment had overcome any previous regard she had held for him.

The physical decline of the Aboriginal Reserve at Oyster Cove was arrested with the appointment of a new superintendent, John Strange Dandridge, in 1855. In a report a year later Dandridge commented favourably on the condition of the Aboriginal huts and the general tidiness.[50] But two years later only five men and ten women were alive.[51] The 1861 census records only two men and six women as being alive.

No children had been born for many years to Aboriginal members of the community. In 1851 there were only four children left belonging to the community at Oyster Cove and they were sent to the Queen's Orphan School.[52] In January 1853 after anxious requests from the Aborigines these children were returned to the station. There is no record of Truganini having children and it is likely that she was infertile—a common condition among Aboriginal women who had had contact with white men.

Truganini's husband Alphonso died in 1851. In the 1860s William Lanne, 23 years younger than Truganini, became her third husband. His story is interesting in that it was his family which avoided both the Black Line of the settlers and refused Robinson's offer of 'safe asylum'. The family was reputedly the last to leave Van Diemen's Land (in 1842) for Wybalenna. In 1847 when the Aborigines were moved to Oyster Cove, Lanne was about 12 years old. He was sent to the Queen's Orphanage for five years and returned briefly to Oyster Cove. Here he met up with some sailors, and discovered a liking for sea life and went whaling. In February 1864, after the death of Tillarlbunner, William Lanne was assumed to be the last surviving full-blood Tasmanian male.

Details of early deaths at Oyster Cove are few but later ones are better documented. Dysentery swept through the station in July 1867 and left Truganini as the sole surviving full-blood Tasmanian woman. She remained at Oyster Cove with William Lanne and Mary Ann, a part-Aborigine and Fanny Cochrane Smith's half-sister.

In February 1869 William Lanne completed his last whaling voyage. He had been ashore a week when he became ill with choleraic diarrhoea, was hospitalised and died. His health had not been good—he was overweight and like many sailors drank too much. His body was placed in the hospital morgue where steps were taken to ensure its security.[53] The Royal Society of Tasmania and the Royal College of Surgeons in London fought for possession of the body. One of the honorary doctors, W. L. Crowther, assisted by his son, secretly removed Lanne's skull, substituting the skull of another corpse, having promised it to the Royal College of Surgeons.[54]

To prevent Crowther getting possession of the rest of the body, Dr Stockell, the Resident Medical Officer of the General Hospital, contacted a Dr Agnew, Honorary Secretary of the Royal Society of Tasmania, informed him about Lanne's skull and decided to get possession of the hands and feet, which were cut off.[55] William Lanne's mutilated body, with a possum skin rug, spears and waddies, and a Union Jack draped over the coffin, was borne by four of his shipmates to St David's Cathedral. The procession was watched by a large crowd lining the streets to pay their respects to the last male of the Tasmanian race. Lanne's body was buried but snatched the following night, while under police guard, by Stockell, two assistants, and, according to Crowther, the superintendent of the police.[56] Stockell was determined to retain the body for the Royal Society of Tasmania. Crowther had organised a similar expedition but he and his men were too late. When they dug up the coffin it was empty with the unwanted replacement skull lying nearby.[57]

News of the disappearance and mutilation of Lanne's body caused a furore. The grave was officially reopened the following Monday, Dr Crowther was suspended from his position as honorary medical officer, his son was suspended as a pupil at the Tasmanian General Hospital, and a police hearing was called to examine allegations that Stockell had cut off Lanne's head. Stockell was cleared of this charge but suspicion then centred on Crowther, who refused to answer any questions in relation to the skull. Crowther was never reinstated as honorary medical officer. Stockell appears to have received some official sanction for his actions for he was never required to account publicly for what happened to the body after its removal from the grave.[58] The actions of several responsible citizens of Hobart are incomprehensible. Today the mutilations appear to be the work of ghouls and savages rather than the actions of civilised people. The only mitigating factor is that in the second half of the nineteenth century there was a widespread post-Darwinian belief that the interest of science was paramount and medical men were encouraged to extend their knowledge by dissection. Body-snatching was widespread. It only ceased when medical men were given legal access to corpses.

Truganini was reputed to have had a passionate and jealous relationship with Lanne in spite of their age difference.[59] She was grief-stricken and horrified at the daily lurid chronicling of the treatment of his corpse. She asked Reverend A. D. Atkinson, who was stationed at Oyster Cove, to take her out in the boat to a channel named 'The Shepherds', the deepest part of the D'Entrecasteaux Channel, and cried out, ' . . . all were now dead . . . and that the people in Hobart had got all their skulls . . .' She then exclaimed, ' . . . Oh, father, father . . . bury me here. It is the deepest place. Promise me'.[60]

Oyster Cove was closed down a few months after Lanne's death as only Truganini and Mary Ann, a part-Aborigine, remained. Truganini was fifty-seven years old and had been prone to acute bronchitis and other respiratory infections.[61] She liked going to North Bruny, her own country, particularly to the Adventure Bay area, spending time on the beach gathering shellfish and seaweed. She would camp out for three or four days and sometimes visit Fanny Cochrane Smith. After Lanne died Dandridge would take her on these expeditions and although he wrote of feeling ' . . . a certain amount of discomfort . . . the occasional escape from the malaria of this station improves my own health as well'.[62]

Truganini had come to like the Dandridge family and was promised that she would always have a home with them. When Mary Ann died in July 1871 serious consideration began to be given to Truganini's position. She had a fairly robust constitution and apart from a broken arm in 1859 at Oyster Cove she had survived the epidemics of influenza and dysentery that had taken their toll on the settlements at both Wybalenna and Oyster Cove. By 1873, after a severe bout with bronchitis it was decided to move her away from the dampness of Oyster Cove.[63] Lyndall Ryan attributes Truganini's move from Oyster Cove to the 1874 floods.[64]

Truganini had lived at Oyster Cove for 25 years, fishing and hunting, when she finally moved to Hobart with her guardians, the Dandridge family. It was during this short period of her residence in Hobart that various stories about Truganini gained currency and the belief that she was a 'Queen', a heroine and saviour of her race, became widespread.

According to Rae Ellis, Truganini was dubbed 'Queen' of her race by white people at a time when she was the sole living subject. She became a celebrity in Hobart Town and was invited to meet various important visitors to the city. But during her stay at Wybalenna and at Oyster Cove, Truganini was never a leader of her people and in fact was despised and taunted by the Aborigines at Wybalenna for her role in their banishment there. Her fame is attributed to her powers of survival.

Truganini died on 8 May 1876 in the Dandridge family home. At the very end she was fearful that her body would be mutilated as Lanne's had been and she asked to be buried behind the mountains.[65] Her corpse was immediately taken to the hospital and Mrs Dandridge wrote to the Colonial Secretary informing him of the death of 'the last Tasmanian Aborigine'.[66] The authorities were determined that there would be no scandal associated with the disposal of Truganini's body. The people of Tasmania expected a solemn ceremonial burial and compliance with Truganini's expressed wishes, but scientists wanted to retain the skeleton. The Royal Society of Tasmania lodged a formal request for her remains. Truganini was secretly buried just in front of the little Protestant chapel at the Cascades Reformatory at 11.00 pm with a Church of England service read by Reverend Canon Parsons. Truganini had been baptised by Bishop Nixon at Oyster Cove[67] but to the end of her life retained her belief in traditional tribal spirits.[68]

Photograph showing Truganini in old age wearing a shell necklace. Tasmanian Museum and Art Gallery.

As the 'last full-blood Tasmanian Aborigine', Truganini after her death continued to arouse a morbid curiosity in the general European community. Her body was exhumed in 1878 by the Royal Society of Tasmania which was authorised to keep her skeleton on condition it was 'decently deposited in a secure resting place accessible by special permission to scientific men for scientific purposes'. In 1888 Truganini's bones were exhibited in a box at the Centenary Exhibition in Melbourne. In 1904 the skeleton was articulated and placed on public display in the Tasmanian Museum, Hobart. As a result of public pressure Truganini's skeleton was stored in a museum vault from 1947, accessible to scientists only. Finally, to mark the centenary of Truganini's death, the skeleton was cremated on 30 April 1976. On 1 May 1976 the Aboriginal community scattered the ashes in the D'Entrecasteaux Channel. Rae Ellis suggests that only the skull was Truganini's and that the skeleton was unlikely to be hers because of its size.

After her death Truganini's fame spread beyond Tasmania and continued to arouse controversy: Aborigines see her as a symbol of their continuing struggle; the European community have cast her as a scapegoat—making her responsible for enticing her own people to Flinders Island and causing their premature deaths. What was Truganini's reason for joining Robinson in his attempts at reconciliation and his efforts to move surviving Aborigines to various mission stations? Were Robinson's actions motivated by compassion and a genuine desire to save the Tasmanian race from destruction or by financial reward? Tasmanian author Cassandra Pybus[69] sums up Robinson's motivation: 'One of the most intriguing contradictions of this complex man was that his genuine humane impulses continually fuelled his baser drives for personal and economic gratification'.

Truganini witnessed a conflict fought to the death between Aborigines and Europeans for land and women. There is no way she could have foreseen the appalling death rate in the Aboriginal settlements at Wybalenna and Oyster Cove which resulted from the Aborigines' vulnerability to European diseases and epidemics. The Aborigines' despair and loss of will to live when transplanted to the closed settlements, where they were housed in huts and restricted in their freedom to carry out their spiritual and cultural traditions, is another factor. It is important to remember that Truganini never abandoned her Aboriginality and adhered to Aboriginal customs. In spite of the close contact over fifty years with Christianity, at the moment of death her last words were a cry of fear that Rowra, the evil tribal spirit, had come for her.[70]

Fanny Cochrane Smith 1834–1905

Born in December 1834 at Wybalenna, the Aboriginal settlement on Flinders Island, Fanny was the daughter of Tanganuturra (known as Sarah).

At the age of seven Fanny was taken from her family to live in various European homes and institutions. She spent some time in the Queen's Orphan School, Hobart, where the discipline was as strict and rigid as in any Dickensian workhouse. At the Queen's Orphan School, Fanny learnt the skills necessary for domestic service. Most of her childhood was spent living and working as a maid for the Clark household on Flinders Island under appalling conditions. Robert Clark was a catechist, a minimally qualified teacher of religion, without a secondary eduction, employed on Flinders Island. Contemporary accounts describe Clark as 'dirty, dissolute and brutal'. It is terrible to think of the treatment a young child would have received from this man. From the age of twelve Fanny worked the long hours of a domestic servant for which she was paid an annual wage of £2.10 (the equivalent of about $5.00), a fraction of the wage then paid to white servants.

Wybalenna was closed down in 1847 by a government finally disturbed out of its complacency about conditions prevailing there. The surviving Aboriginal people were moved to Oyster Cove on the D'Entrecasteaux Channel, within reach of Hobart Town. Fanny went briefly into domestic service in Hobart but returned to Oyster Cove in the same year, where she lived with her mother Sarah, and her sister Mary Ann.

In 1851, after an absence of twelve years as 'Protector of Aborigines' in Victoria and New South Wales, George Robinson paid a brief visit prior to his return to Europe. He was given a list of the names of the thirty remaining Aborigines living at Oyster Cove including Truganini—listed as Lalla Rhook–Sarah, mother of Mary Ann Arthur and Fanny Cochrane, with the notation describing Fanny as the 'half caste daughter of the above', referring to Sarah. Sarah had had four children including Mary Ann, while living with a white sealer. At Wybalenna she formed a lifelong relationship with Nicermenic from Robbins Island off the north-west coast of Tasmania.[71] He had been driven from his land. The children of this relationship, Fanny and Adam, accompanied their parents to Oyster Cove. Vivienne Rae Ellis nominates a sealer called John Smith as Fanny's father, dismissing Fanny as that half-caste who 'was wrongfully granted a government pension in recognition of her status as a full-blood Tasmanian Aborigine and it was not until sometime later that the mistake was discovered'. Cassandra Pybus, writing in 1991, categorically states that Fanny was the daughter of Nicermenic on the basis of official records, contemporary witnesses, Fanny's own testimony and her parents' claims.

The deaths continued at Oyster Cove. In 1857, ten years after resettlement, there were only fifteen Aborigines left alive—five men and ten women.[72] Fanny had left Oyster Cove three years earlier and had married William Smith, a relatively educated ex-convict, and received an annuity of £24 from the Government. Fanny and her husband lived on a 100-acre land grant she had received from the Government in lieu of her maintenance at the Aboriginal settlement. Initially the couple worked as fencers and shingle splitters, then from 1856 they ran a boarding house in Hobart. Clearly Fanny must have been a very competent housekeeper and good at managing money.

Fanny maintained close ties with her people and received regular visits from them, and from Truganini. Together they would fish, hunt and collect roots, nuts, fruits, berries and medicinal herbs. Adam, her brother, lived with the couple until his death in 1857. They then moved to Nicholls Rivulet (near Oyster Cove) and took up a land grant where the first of their eleven children was born; they had six sons and five daughters in all. Fanny's grant of land, which she took great care in choosing, became the basis of a thriving timber business and market garden. Located 40 km from Hobart, the fertile land supported the large family and they lived comfortably in a five-roomed wooden house.

Contrary to the stereotype of Aborigines as indolent and unadaptable, Fanny was a successful businesswoman and a pillar of the Huon Valley community. She was noted for her hospitality and generosity—hosting annual fundraising picnics, dinners and concerts at her home.

On the death of Truganini in 1876, Fanny Cochrane Smith claimed to be the last Tasmanian Aborigine. In 1884 the Tasmanian Parliament increased her pension to £50 and granted her full title to 300 acres of land—possibly as some form of recognition and compensation for the loss of Aboriginal land. However, this grant aroused a storm of protest and Fanny was forced to defend her claim to Aboriginality. Several Fellows of the Royal Society examined her hair and her facial features and confirmed her Aboriginality. Ethnologist H. Ling Roth disputed this. The Tasmanian Parliament confirmed her title to the land in 1889, but for years Ling Roth's evidence was generally accepted. The concern about Fanny's Aboriginality sprang from certain assumptions—that the grant was made on the basis of biology and not on identity and merit and that Ling Roth was correct in identifying Fanny as part-Aborigine and that other authorities were wrong.

Fanny Cochrane Smith is seen as a dignified woman wearing a feathered hat and a traditional Aboriginal girdle of possum skins over her elegant black dress. A copy of this photograph was in the church built on land Fanny donated to the Methodist Church and was torn in half by vandals who broke into the church. Private collection.

Why shouldn't Fanny have been given land? White settlers received far larger grants. Fanny's mother had been enslaved by sealers for half of her life and then penned up in a prison camp for the remainder. Surely she deserved some compensation. But many colonial Tasmanians preferred the reassuring assumption that the Tasmanian Aboriginal race had disappeared without a trace, and that no heirs survived to claim their inheritance.

One of Fanny's formal portraits shows a handsome self-assured woman, well groomed and dressed in the Edwardian fashion. But in addition to her fashionable dress she wears a traditional girdle of possum skins around her waist, necklaces of shells, and native flowers in her curly hair. Fanny Cochrane Smith moved with confidence in European circles while proudly acknowledging her Aboriginality.

Fanny and her husband converted to Methodism (now the Uniting Church), her intelligent and generous approach to life and spiritual matters reconciling the differences between her traditional culture and beliefs and those of her husband's people. Religious services were held in her kitchen until a small weatherboard church was built on land she donated—surely a singular example of land being gifted by an Aborigine rather than its being simply expropriated. She was active in fundraising and the annual church picnic was held on her farm. A son became a lay preacher. Fanny Cochrane Smith was renowned in her district for her singing, generosity, hospitality and good humour. She became famous for her wax cylinder recordings of Tasmanian Aboriginal speech and song.

Fanny died in 1905, two years after her husband. She was greatly loved and admired, and over 400 people followed her funeral cortege. She is believed to be buried in the old Methodist cemetery but some family descendants maintain that she was buried in an unmarked grave on the hill at Wattle Grove to avoid the risk that her corpse would be dug up and her head and hands chopped off as happened to William Lanne,[73] Truganini's husband.

Fanny bridged the gap between two cultures—Aboriginal and European. She

Fanny Cochrane Smith recording traditional Aboriginal songs on wax cylinders for a member of the Royal Society of Tasmania in 1903, at Sandy Bay, Hobart. Photograph Hobart Mercury.

retained a strong sense of her Aboriginal identity and spirituality while being an active member of the Methodist Church. She combined the traditional Aboriginal skills of hunting and food gathering with planting and harvesting the produce on which her family depended for income and food. She continued to hunt and dive for shellfish, gathered bush foods and medicines, wove baskets and carried out Aboriginal religious rituals. How was this dignity and accommodation achieved? Regarded as a 'half-caste' by many, she did not fall between both worlds, rejected by each. As wife of William Smith, a European, she must have been very aware of the problems faced by her eleven children. Larissa Behrend, an Aboriginal Sydney lawyer explains: ' . . . Anyone who spends any time with Aboriginal communities knows we have no notion of half or quarter-caste. You're either Aboriginal or you're not; it depends on how you identify yourself, not on the amount of blood'.[74]

Fanny Cochrane Smith was fully accepted by her people and spent her childhood up to the age of seven with them and then returned to them at the age of thirteen. The intervening period was spent in 'conditions of squalor, neglect and brutality in Flinders Island'.[75] It says a great deal for Fanny's generosity of spirit and good sense that the harsh experiences of a vulnerable childhood did not destroy her faith in God or her acceptance of Europeans.

Her importance in the story of the Tasmanian Aboriginal people is immense but often overlooked. She was a woman of stature, intelligence and charm, and a pillar of the community, black and white—a landowner, businesswoman, and matriarch who founded a new dynasty.

[1] Martin, R. M. *History of Austral-Asia; Comprising New South Wales, Van Diemen's Land, Swan River, South Australia.* London, 1836. However, Henry Reynolds believes an estimate of 7,000 is too high.

[2] *Encyclopedia of Aboriginal Australia*, Vol. 2, M-Z, Sydney, 1994.

[3] Clark, J. 'Walyer', *200 Australian Women*, ed. H. Radi. Women's Redress Press, Sydney, 1987.

[4] *Encyclopedia of Aboriginal Australia. Op. cit.*

[5] Few historical sources document much about the lives of Tasmanian Aboriginal women. Main primary sources for material on these women are Plomley, N. J. B. [ed.] *Weep in Silence*, Blubber Head Press, Hobart, 1987 based on the papers of G. A. Robinson at Wybalena and Plomley's edited collection of Robinson's earlier papers, *Friendly Mission*, THRA, Hobart, 1966. Other sources are Bonwick, J. *Daily Life and Origins of the Tasmanians*, London, 1870, Bonwick's *Last of the Tasmanians*, London, 1870 and Calder, James Erskine, *Account of Wars, Extirpation of the Native Tribes of Tasmania*, 1875, facsimile ed. Hobart, 1972.

[6] Evidence of G. A. Robinson to the Aborigines Committee, 20 Jan, 1831, Colonial Board of Enquiry.

[7] *200 Australian Women. Op. cit.*

[8] Rae Ellis, *Trucanini: Queen or Traitor?* OBM, Hobart, 1976.

[9] Ryan, Lyndall. *The Aboriginal Tasmanians*, University of Queensland Press, St Lucia, 1981.

[10] *200 Australian Women. Op. cit.*

[11] Lord, C. E. 'The Tasmanian Aborigines' in: *Handbook to Tasmania*. Hobart, Australian Association for the Advancement of Science, 1928.

[12] Pybus, C. *Community of Thieves*. William Heinemann Australia, Melbourne, 1991.

[13] Ryan, L. 'Truganini', *200 Australian Women*. Women's Redress Press, Sydney, 1987.

[14] *Community of Thieves. Op. cit.*

[15] Plomley, N.J.B. *Friendly Mission: The Tasmanian Journals and Papers of George Augustus Robinson 1829–34. Op. cit.*

[16] *200 Australian Women. Op. cit.*

[17] Robinson, G. A. *Journal*, 3 April 1829, Mitchell Library, Sydney.

[18] Plomley, N. J. B. *Friendly Mission. Op. cit.*

[19] *Ibid.*

[20] Reynolds, Henry. *Fate of a Free People*, Penguin Books, Ringwood, 1995 pp 1–2 quotes the petition of W. G. Arthur and seven other Aborigines to Queen Victoria to prevent the return of the unpleasant Dr. Henry Jeanneret to take charge at Flinders Island and stresses the

importance of the phrase '*an agreement which we have not lost from our minds since*'. It is confusing that William George Arthur, Head of Ben Lomond tribe and the Governor of the Tasmania were surnamed Arthur, but were in no way related.

21 Plomley, N. J. B. *Friendly Mission. Op. cit.*
22 *Ibid.*
23 *Hobart Town Gazette*, 19 February 1831.
24 Plomley, N. J. B. *Friendly Mission. Op. cit.*
25 *Ibid.*
26 *Launceston Examiner*, 11 January 1832.
27 Plomley, N. J. B. *Friendly Mission. Op. cit.*
28 Colonial Secretary to George Augustus Robinson, 10 February 1832, State Archives of Tasmania.
29 Plomley, N. J. B. *Friendly Mission, Op. cit.*
30 Robinson to Montagu, 31 July 1837. Colonial Secretary Papers, State Archives of Tasmania 1/807/17237, cited by Reynolds, Henry, *Fate of a Free People, Op. cit.*
31 Plomley, N. J. B. *Friendly Mission, Op. cit.*
32 *200 Australian Women. Op. cit.*
33 Report from Select Committee on Aborigines (British Settlements), Parliamentary Proceedings 1837, vii, 425.
34 Glenelg to Gipps, 31 January 1838, *Historical Records of Australia*, Vol. I, p. xix.
35 Russell to Gipps, *Historical Records of Australia.* Vol I, p. xx.
36 *Sydney Herald*, 5 July 1839, 14 February, 2 March, 24 May 1840.
37 Rae Ellis, *Trucanini: Queen or Traitor? Op. cit.*
38 Letter to La Trobe, cited in George Augustus Robinson *Journal*, 19 June 1840.
39 Ryan, L. *The Aboriginal Tasmanians*, 1981.
40 *Port Phillip Herald*, 26 November 1841.
41 *Port Phillip Herald*, 26 November 1841.
42 *The Aboriginal Tasmanians. Op. cit.*
43 Jeanneret, H. Report on Flinders Island Establishment, 15 September, 1842, State Archives of Tasmania.
44 Walker, G. W. to Jeanneret, H. 16 September 1842, State Archives of Tasmania.
45 Jeanneret, H. to Colonial Secretary. 30 August 1842 and 31 March 1843, State Archives of Tasmania.
46 Agnew, J. W. *The Last of the Tasmanians.* Proceedings of the Society for the Advancement of Science, Sydney, 1888.
47 *Launceston Examiner*, 11 May 1976.
48 Dove, Rev T. Moral and Social Characteristics of the Aborigine of Tasmania. *Tasmanian Journal of Natural Science*, 1842, pp. 247–54.
49 Milligan, J. to Colonial Secretary, 17 June 1847, State Archives of Tasmania.
50 J. S. Dandridge's Diary of visits to the Oyster Cove Aboriginal Reserve, 27 June 1855–24 June 1869, State Archives of Tasmania.
51 Return of Aboriginal Inhabitants Residing at the Station, Oyster Cove, on 31 December 1857 and 1858. Public Records Office, London.
52 Milligan, J. to Colonial Secretary, 1 January 1853; Colonial Secretary to Milligan, J. 5 January 1853, State Archives of Tasmania.
53 *Mercury*, 4 & 8 March 1869.
54 *Mercury* 13 March 1869, Report of the Board of Enquiry held 12 March 1869.
55 *Ibid.*
56 Advertisement inserted by Dr W. L. Crowther, *Mercury*, 13 March 1869.
57 *Mercury*, 9 March 1869.
58 Stockell, G. to Editor, *Mercury*, 12 March 1869.
59 Agnew, *The Last of the Tasmanians. Op. cit.*
60 Archdeacon Atkinson, H. B. to Tasmanian Museum, 16 December 1950; quoted by Lyndall Ryan in unpublished report to Australian Institute of Aboriginal Studies, 1974 [MS 1436, Australian Institute of Aboriginal Studies, Canberra].
61 Dandridge, J. S., to Colonial Secretary, 9 October 1869.
62 *Ibid.*
63 Dandridge, J. S., to Colonial Secretary, 31 July 1873.

[64] *The Aboriginal Tasmanians*, 1981. *Op. cit.*
[65] *Mercury*, 11 May 1876.
[66] Mrs Dandridge to Colonial Secretary, 8 May 1876.
[67] *Mercury*, 12 May 1876.
[68] Agnew, *The Last of the Tasmanians*. *Op. cit.*
[69] *A Community of Thieves*. *Op. cit.*
[70] Agnew, *The Last of the Tasmanians*. *Op. cit.*
[71] *Ibid.*
[72] Return of Aboriginal Inhabitants Residing at the Station, Oyster Cove, on 31 December 1857, and 1858, Public Records Office, London.
[73] Friend, R. *We Who Are Not Here*. The Huon Municipal Association, 1992.
[74] *Sydney Morning Herald*, 15 October 1994.
[75] Clark, J. 'Fanny Cochrane Smith', *200 Australian Women*. Women's Redress Press, Sydney, 1987.

CHAPTER 7

Georgiana Molloy
(1805–1843)

PIONEER BOTANIST OF WESTERN AUSTRALIA

In a totally male-dominated society like colonial Australia it is surprising to find a woman excelling in scientific research which was then deemed a male preserve. In spite of frequent pregnancies, an overwhelming amount of domestic work, caring for a husband and young children and running a dairy, Georgiana Molloy became Western Australia's leading botanist, documenting many of the state's superb native wildflowers. She contributed substantially to world scientific research into new plant species and their curative properties.

When Georgiana Kennedy was born in 1805, her affluent, upper-middle-class family, at Crosby Lodge near Carlisle, close to England's Lake District, never dreamed that the plants she would eventually discover and send back to England would be prized by botanical gardens around the world. They would have been amazed had they known she was to exchange life in a large country house surrounded by servants for one of struggle, isolation, and poverty in a wooden hut at the tip of south-west Australia—the further corner of the colonial empire. Georgiana made this remarkable transition for one reason: she married 'Handsome Jack' Molloy, who was, in certain circles, believed to have been the illegitimate son of the sexually over-indulgent Frederick, Duke of York (1763–1827), second and favourite son of King George III, after whom Molloy named many streets on his property.

Georgiana was highly intelligent and had received an excellent education for a girl growing up in Georgian England. She studied English literature, history, music, geography, needlework, French, drawing, painting and dancing. She could play both the harp and the piano. Her favourite subject was botany, a discipline made popular by Queen Charlotte of England, the wife of George III. It involved the identification of plant species and a description of their flowers, seeds, pods and habitat, including recognition of their botanical families, and application of the correct scientific nomenclature. The specimens were drawn from life in pencil and watercolour or described in prose, then they were dried and pressed between the pages of heavy albums.

From her earliest childhood Georgiana had been serious and diligent in her approach to botany: in fact she was serious in her attitude to life in general. Her fervent desire to convert her family to evangelical Christianity meant that she was often in conflict with her more frivolous sisters, Elizabeth and Mary. Quarrels between the teenage girls and their recently widowed mother were frequent enough for the sensitive Georgiana to seek refuge at the home of her best friend Helen, the eldest Dunlop girl. When Helen married Robert Story, a young evangelical clergyman, Georgiana left home and went to live with them. She helped the Reverend Robert Story with the work of the parish and taught at Sunday School. Georgiana would have made an excellent wife for a clergyman, and her choice of husband, a rakishly handsome army officer with a trail of sexual conquests behind him, was a strange one for such a serious dedicated girl.

Where Georgiana met 'Handsome Jack' is not recorded. His portrait shows an extremely good-looking man in the dark green braided jacket of the Rifle Brigade. 'Handsome Jack' had dark wavy hair, heavy-lidded sensual eyes and an aristocratic Roman nose—a face not easily forgotten. In fact, Captain Molloy looked every inch the hero of Waterloo. The gallant captain had won several medals for bravery on the battlefield and his men were devoted to him. He was well educated having attended Harrow, one of the most exclusive schools in England, and studied at Oxford University. He had great personal charm and wit and was popular both with his soldiers and his brother officers, and had a reputation for enormous success with women. The element of mystery about his background probably contributed to his attraction.

Perhaps the tall, blonde, slender Georgiana, with her earnest sense of duty and purpose in life, attracted Captain Molloy precisely because she was so different from the society women he had danced with, flirted with and loved before. In that he was right because her determination and strength of character made her an excellent wife for a pioneer.

Georgiana was twenty-four when they married; Captain John Molloy was forty-eight, twice her age, but looked ten years younger. Tall and broadshouldered, he was a strikingly handsome man and remained so until his death. Physically 'Handsome' Jack bore a resemblance to the Duke of York. Like the Duke of Gordon, father of Georgiana McCrae, and other British aristocrats, the Duke of York paid for his son's education. Harrow, his old school secured a place at the Military College, and he was given the funds to buy a commission in a good regiment. John Molloy's mother was rumoured to have been a pretty young girl in service at the palace. There was no question of marriage between the Duke and the servant girl as there was always a faint chance that he might succeed to the throne, since he was second in the line of succession. To avoid a royal scandal the young Duke was sent away to Germany. Jack was farmed out to an Irish couple by the name of Molloy, who looked after him during his childhood and gave him their family name, for which they were probably well rewarded. Although no firm documentary proof exists, farming out a bastard child to a family in need of money who would give the child their name was standard practice for illegitimate children of royalty at that time. It was vital that royal bastards did not bear the royal name in case it should damage the succession.[2]

Georgiana and John Molloy were married from the stone manse at Roseneath and Helen's husband, the Reverend Robert Story, officiated at the wedding. After the ceremony the newlyweds travelled by carriage to London prior to sailing to Western Australia.

Georgiana realised her clothes would have to last for many years and her trousseau was a practical one. Among the plain dark gowns, bonnets, ribbons, haberdashery and other prerequisites necessary in a pioneer land Georgiana packed assorted seeds, her gardening tools and some Mexican yucca lily bulbs given her by her mother. It was her first visit to London. John Molloy enjoyed showing off his beautiful young bride. He took her to the opera at Covent Garden and to the theatre at Drury Lane but the poverty and vice of London's streets dismayed her and troubled her social conscience. Georgiana was horrified to see prostitutes, some only in their teens, hanging around outside theatres and the opera. She was told that Britain, after the Napoleonic Wars, offered little work for uneducated men and women. For many women prostitution offered the only prospect of lodgings or a square meal. She may have realised that this shortage of work applied to her own husband, who, had they not emigrated, would have had trouble finding a good position in civilian life.

Captain Molloy commissioned a portrait of his new wife from which her clear, candid blue-grey eyes look at the viewer confidently. She is dressed in the height of fashion, as though going to the opera, her shoulders fashionably bare and her long

blonde hair dressed in ringlets. The occasion of her wedding portrait was to be the last time Georgiana visited a dressmaker or had her hair professionally dressed. At this time she had little understanding of the rigours and loneliness of the pioneering life that awaited her.

Captain Molloy's reasons for emigrating were similar to those of John Macarthur because the life of a retired army officer on half pay, with no private income, presented poor prospects in Britain, with its exploding population. John Molloy could expect no inheritance of land from his adoptive parents. The idea of emigrating to the new Swan River settlement with a pretty young wife to run his household and to give him children to inherit the broad acres he could claim as a retired army officer seemed an attractive proposition.

Captain James Stirling, the first governor of Western Australia, was already known to John Molloy through a mutual friend. The Swan River settlement had been widely advertised as having 'no beasts of prey or loathsome reptiles'. No convicts were allowed and, the developers' advertisements falsely claimed, 'the emigrants will not have to wage hopeless and ruinous war with interminable forests'. They were promised good pasture land for 'the courageous ad the industrious'.

The Molloys intended to take sixteen servants with them, but during the long wait for the ship, their servants gradually dwindled to five. They selected some cattle and fine lambs, two horses, twelve ducks, fourteen hens and twelve pigs, ploughs, horseshoes, tools, guns, milk pails, saddlery, grindstones, furniture, medicines and pewterware for the kitchen. They also took additional provisions for the journey: Georgiana's listed quantities of salt beef and pork, rice and split peas, 25 gallons of vinegar, 600 bottles of wine and 233 gallons of brandy (over 2 thousand litres).

Their ship was delayed in sailing so the Molloys moved from expensive London to Gosport in Hampshire because it was cheaper to live there, and they had purchased wheat, oats, barley, potatoes, fruit trees as well as the livestock to take to Western Australia and needed barns to store them. Georgiana greatly enjoyed the excitement of purchasing household goods for her new home. John Molloy was delighted by the ease with which his young wife planned her domestic and farm purchases, saying, 'She has accomplished the whole of our purchases in as quiet and easy manner as if she had been a wife of two years standing'.

Georgiana instituted morning and evening prayers both for them and their servants. The gallant captain seems to have accepted it without comment as part

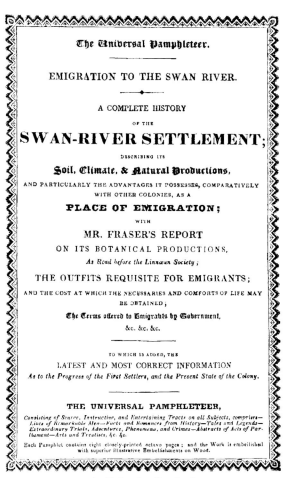

An Emigration Handbook

of married life. They were deeply in love and excited by the prospect of a new life when their ship, the *Warrior* eventually set sail. On board ship Georgiana made friends with the high-spirited Bussell brothers who were travelling steerage while the Molloys travelled first-class. They also made the acquaintance of a builder and amateur artist named Thomas Turner and his family. (John Bussell was twenty-six and the three younger brothers were nineteen, sixteen and fourteen). While they were closer to Georgiana in education and class, there were enormous differences in outlook between them. The Bussells were children of a deceased clergyman; unlike Georgiana they were accustomed to living in genteel poverty with little money and few servants. They were a penniless but devoted family who supported each other in their ambitions to make their fortune on the land. But childhood deprivations and loss had made them uninterested in helping anyone else . They saw the Molloys as richer than themselves and possibly they envied the Molloys' patrician looks and background. The Bussell brothers were athletic, intelligent rather than intellectual. They loved the idea of the open-air life and freedom of Australia. They positively glowed with health, while Georgiana was introverted, sensitive, musical, a romantic at heart and physically delicate.

Charles Bussell described Georgiana as having

the air of a lady well-born and well-bred without having mixed much in the world . . . she is rather inclined to the romantic and is delighted to have anyone with whom she can contemplate the sublimity of a night scene or . . . this or that piece of poetry.

The Bussells brought this portrait of themselves to Australia along with the dog and the sofa. From left to right: delicate Lennox, romantic Mary, practical Fanny, William the medic, their mother Mrs Bussell, John the leader, tomboy Bessie, and teenagers Alfred and Vernon. Courtesy C.H. Vines, Cattle Chosen, Busselton.

John, the eldest of the Bussell brothers, was a classical scholar who, while at Oxford, had studied for admission to the Anglican Church. Georgiana was a Presbyterian and far more keen on converting others to Christianity than the prospective clergyman John Bussell. Despite these differences, thousands of miles away from civilisation, the Bussells and Molloys would become friends and neighbours, allies in the battle for survival when pioneering in Western Australia.

At Cape Town, the Molloys replaced livestock which had died. They were warned that the Swan River Colony had failed and the settlers faced starvation. Captain Molloy questioned the reliability of this information and was determined to continue with the voyage, although replacing their livestock had depleted their funds. Georgiana was now five months pregnant and suffered agonies from morning sickness. From Cape Town Georgiana wrote to Helen Story telling her friends that she was pregnant, asking for news of other newlywed friends and saying that if they were as happy 'as Jack and I, they cannot wish for more conjugal affection. Molloy is a dear creature and I would not exchange him for ten thousand pounds per annum and a mansion in a civilised country.'[3] She was warned again that the Swan River Colony was in difficulties and it might be wiser to have her baby in Cape Town, but Georgiana felt it was her duty, as a good Christian wife, to follow her husband to Australia.

On 30 March 1830, five months after sailing, the *Warrior* anchored off Rottnest Island. A small tender ferried the passengers upriver to Perth where Captain Stirling and some disgruntled settlers were already encamped. An apprehensive Georgiana stepped ashore, realising now that their informant had been correct at Cape Town and that the new settlement was in deep trouble. The Molloys chose to pitch their tents on the sand at Fremantle rather than at flea-infested Perth.

Mary Ann Friend, wife of Captain Mathew Friend, who had arrived at the Swan River a month before the Molloys, described the failed crops, the leaky tents of the settlers who had piled their furniture up on the beach around them and the 'dread that is felt lest there should be a scarcity of provisions . . . I never slept in such a miserable place; everything so dirty and such quantities of mosquitoes and fleas!'[4]

The Molloys went upriver to Perth to visit Governor and Lady Stirling, who were both impressed with Georgiana's poise and charm; they attended a government function hosted by the Stirlings, where there were only eight ladies to fifty-eight men. Captain Stirling explained to all of them that the best land grants in the area had already been apportioned. He urged them to go south in search of better country for their crops and livestock, since many of the original settlers at the Swan River had been unable to grow crops in the sandy soil and were facing starvation. Some, like the Hentys, had realised the difficulties and sailed away for Tasmania.

Trusting the somewhat unreliable advice of Captain Stirling, the Molloys, the Bussells and the Turners chose to settle further south at Augusta on the Blackwood River. A month later they sailed there down the coast, as there were no roads at all at that time. At Augusta the Molloys and the Turners became the first white settlers in the area, surrounded on all sides by magnificent stands of jarrah, one of the hardest timbers in the world. While her husband and the few servants who remained faithful to their contracts struggled to chop down trees and clear the land, Georgiana set up home in a canvas tent with an umbrella over her bed to catch the rain. In that leaky tent without the aid of a doctor or midwife, lying on a plank of wood, Georgiana's first child was finally born, following twelve hours of agonising labour. Their baby girl was very weak, had difficulty in feeding and died nine days later. She and Jack Molloy buried their baby in a tiny grave sown with English clover.

The horror of this experience scarred Georgiana so deeply that it was three years before she could write about the tragedy. She explained what had happened in a letter of condolence to Helen Story, who had just lost a child herself. She told Helen how

> language refuses to utter what I experienced when mine died in my arms in this dreary land with no one but Molloy near me . . . I thought I might have had one little bright object left to solace all the hardships and privations I endured and have still to go through.[5]

Georgiana threw herself into homemaking to overcome her grief over the loss of her baby. Four months after the death of her first-born, Elizabeth Jane, she suffered a miscarriage and haemorrhaged severely. She felt 'faint as death and in agony and did not know what was happening'.[6]

The loss of Georgiana's first child and the miscarriage affected her deeply. There was only her husband to mourn with her and he was facing difficulties trying to decide where it was best to take up the rest of his promised land grant, as their land at Augusta was not proving as good as Captain Stirling had promised. It took half a dozen men two or three days to cut down the jarrah trees and dig up their roots and the same amount of time to cut them up into logs. This had to be done before their primitive ploughs could work the land and they could plant the grain and vegetables which would enable them to survive. The newcomers made a terrible mistake. They believed they were facing farming conditions similar to those in Britain and that such magnificent trees must mean the soil was fertile. But conditions were entirely different, although it took them several years to realise this. As soon as she had time Georgiana planted the yucca lilies her mother had given her and sewed the seeds she had bought at the Cape. Slowly the Molloys' small house took shape, with a separate kitchen and scullery to avoid the risk of fire, and private living quarters for the Dawsons, the only servants who had remained with them. At the end of August some troops arrived by ship with a doctor, and a barracks and temporary hospital were built. Inevitably Georgiana must have wondered if a doctor's presence at an earlier time would have saved her baby daughter.

Gradually the small settlement developed and Sunday services were held on the Molloys' verandah. Georgiana wrote to Helen Story complaining that the soldiers' wives, who were compelled to attend the service or forfeit their rations, often left halfway through to go to a drunken party. Rather than joining in with the heavy drinking in the settlement, the Molloys spent their evenings reading by candlelight. Their tastes varied. He read military history, she read religious books.

John Molloy received the appointment of Colonial Magistrate which carried a

Augusta Hardys Inlet W *Australia. 1838.*

Augusta, Hardy' Inlet. Thomas Turner arrived at Augusta on the same boat as the Molloys and drew the first homes they built near the beach using the hard jarrah timber, which would eventually ensure they moved away from Augusta to the Vasse River. Art Gallery of Western Australia.

small salary but gave much work in an isolated community with no other form of authority. The Government gave all working people half a gill of rum a day in rations. This meant some sold their rum rations for goods and ensured a constant supply of drunkards, who had to be put into the stocks, and much paperwork for Captain Molloy and Georgiana, who acted as her husband's unpaid secretary.

Fish were plentiful and ducks, herons and swans provided meat. Swan pie and cockatoo pie became delicacies, as did kangaroo tail soup. The settlers did not go hungry but they begrudged the time spent hunting when there was so much land-clearing and building still to be done.

The Bussells' transfer of money from England went astray and for a time they were practically penniless. There were differences of opinion between the two families over a cow belonging to John Bussell which had strayed onto the Molloys' land and over their attitude to the local Aborigines. The Bussells were merciless in killing the Nyungar if they stole their sheep; they saw the land as theirs for the taking. The increasing materialism and self-interest of the Bussells distressed Georgiana, who tried to make friends with the Nyungar, keen that they would teach her about native plants and their medicinal use.

Once their wooden house was built, Georgiana decided to concentrate on making a garden. The beauty of the native flowers provided some comfort. Her husband was busy morning, noon and night, either administering his area or visiting the government in Perth to make some official request.

The Governor and Lady Stirling visited the Molloys in November. By then Georgiana was nine months pregnant and tiring easily. She prepared a dinner which they enjoyed by candlelight, rather than in the gloom of the evil-smelling slush lamps which they normally used. She was delighted at long last to have a woman from her own background with whom to converse. Other settlers were considered 'artisans' or 'in trade' rather than 'landed gentry'. Even in the bush, the old class barriers of England took a long time to die away.

Georgiana's second daughter, Sabina, was born shortly after the vice-regal party departed, on 7 November 1831. Sabina was a strong, healthy baby but the extra work made problems for Georgiana due to shortage of domestic and farm help. Anne

Dawson worked sullenly and dreamed only of the day when they would take up their own land and she would be free of her commitment to work for the Molloys. With a child to breastfeed and care for, Georgiana now found herself doing heavy cleaning, cooking, boiling water for washing and scrubbing—work that she had never imagined herself doing, let alone under such primitive conditions. 'I never thought that I should have to take in washing and Jack carry home the clean clothes,' she wrote to her friend Maggie Dunlop. 'The last of this has not yet happened but between ourselves, the first is no uncommon occurrence.' Georgiana worked from early morning until far into the night to mend clothes, iron them and keep the house clean and run the dairy.

But for all Georgiana's hard work, it became obvious that the land was poor and unsuitable for farming. Things became so bad that two of the Bussell brothers decided to move upstream on the Blackwood River to a new area they named Adelphi. Charles Bussell remained in Augusta after taking over the job of storekeeper to the settlement on the recommendation of Captain Molloy.

The Molloys' first wheat crop was ruined by the fungal disease known as rust. Before the next crop was sown, Georgiana soaked all their seeds in saltwater and dried them to help fight the fungus and through her hard work, they were eventually able to harvest their first wheat crop. She wrote to Helen Story how 'Dearest Molloy' was often away on Government business or searching with the Bussells for better land, and for days she heard nothing more than the gurgles or cries of baby Sabina.

Eventually the Bussells and Captain Molloy found better land at the Vasse River and Molloy went there to supervise building their new home, although they would not move from Augusta for some years. Georgiana oversaw the running of the farm and the work of their reluctant worker, Elijah Dawson, who handled the plough pulled by their two oxen. Dawson now preferred to use his time to develop his own land rather than theirs. Their diet was monotonous when their flour ran out; vegetables were short and to avoid the dangers of scurvy Georgiana learned to find and cook native rock spinach and pigweed.

The relationship between the Molloys and the Nyungar people had been friendly but then the Bussells had fired on the men of the tribe when they came stealing potatoes. In her husband's absence Georgiana was forced to confront a group of thirty naked warriors who came to steal their crop. She realised that if she displayed any fear, both she and Sabina would be in mortal danger. She had learned a little of the Nyungar dialect and summoning her courage, said firmly, 'Ben-o-wai' or 'Begone', and the Nyungar withdrew, shaking their spears menacingly. She wrote how 'I was afraid to show fear, although one cut the air so close to my head with his wallabee [a thick stick] and threw a piece of broken bottle [which landed] close to my face'.

Hard physical labour was literally wearing Georgiana's slight frame away to skin and bone. A young, crippled, epileptic girl named Kitty provided baby-sitting assistance and companionship while Jack Molloy was away. On one occasion little Sabina was nearly killed when a mud-brick wall collapsed beside the child, following a prolonged rainstorm.

In 1834, four years after Georgiana's arrival at Augusta, her sister Elizabeth died. Her death was a great shock to Georgiana who wrote to Helen Story[7] that she hoped Mary, her second sister, and her mother would now settle their differences before her mother died. Georgiana related how she and her husband worked 'much harder than their servants so that their children would have more than a competency'. By now Georgiana had given birth to another girl, named Mary Dorothea, and found that carrying the

An illustration from The Emigrants Handbook, *published in 1828. Georgiana Molloy and her husband bought a tent like this to take with them to the Swan River. By the time Georgiana gave birth to her first child in it, the tent was leaking badly. Private collection.*

Tents for Travellers & Emigrants

BENJAMIN EDGINGTON,
Marquee, Tent, Rickcloth & Flag Manufacturer

baby around made her back ache. Domestic drudgery and sleepless nights with Mary Dorothea, who was having teething problems, made Georgiana tired, anxious and very thin, but she retained a sense of humour about her predicament. She wrote of her rapid weight loss that 'I have every day expected to see some bone poking through the epidermis'.

Mrs Bussell and her daughters arrived from England but Georgiana was not greatly drawn to them. They were practical people who grew vegetables, while Georgiana grew flowers. Two Bussell daughters, Bessie and Mary, went upriver to a new land grant of the family (see map p. 143) together with an elderly maid named Phoebe, who was to housekeep for their brothers. Fanny Bussell, a sweet and rather boisterous girl, stayed behind with a young servant named Emma Mould to look after Charles at Alberta. But Fanny was far too preoccupied with housekeeping and family problems to have time for Georgiana. Charles Bussell made Emma Mould pregnant, Mrs Bussell threw her out of the house while Georgiana showed a more Christian approach by taking Emma in until she had the baby, which the Bussells then appropriated, caring nothing for the mother. Disillusioned, Georgiana wrote that the Bussells 'accepted everything, and you will hardly believe they have made no return, nor have Molloy or myself ever broken their bread'.[8] Outraged by their treatment of Emma Mould, Georgiana described the Bussells 'as perfectly selfish and inconsiderate as any people I ever knew'.

To their dismay Sabina developed convulsions and fever. Georgiana nursed the child devotedly day and night until she recovered, but lost faith in the settlement's doctor who had initially diagnosed a simple case of sunstroke. Georgiana felt a sense of guilt and self-reproach over her own lack of medical knowledge.

Their maid Kitty suffered epileptic fits which grew worse. There was no known medical treatment for epilepsy at that time. The girl's plight distressed Georgiana, who nursed poor Kitty through fits until she died. As Captain Molloy was still away, it fell to Georgiana to organise the girl's burial at night in the presence of the farm servants.[9] Burning torches on sticks illuminated the pathetic scene as Georgiana read the burial service in her clear, steady voice. The torchlight in the darkness of the surrounding bush accentuated the isolation of their tiny settlement and the silence that surrounded them.

For Georgiana the intellectual isolation was also overwhelming. The few visitors who arrived at Augusta by ship were usually poorly educated and talked about nothing more stimulating than grubbing out stumps, beef, pork, potatoes, onions, whaling and harpooning, she lamented. Life became a ceaseless round of cooking, cleaning, washing and 'the odious drudgery of cheese and butter making'. Her days were occupied from dawn to dusk, and now she had to give reading and writing lessons to Sabina. If she took time off to write letters, the sewing and mending piled up beside the basket. She described how 'I must either leave writing alone or some needlework undone . . . I never open a book and if I read a chapter on Sunday, it is quite a treat to have so much leisure'. When she was pregnant again she complained that she had 'not a cap to put on the child's head' and no time to make one.

Each pregnancy further sapped her strength and gave her still more work.

> This life is too much both for dear Molloy and myself. My head aches. I have all the clothes to put away from the wash, a baby to put to bed, make tea and drink it without milk as they [the Bussells] shot our cow for trespass; read prayers and go to bed besides sending off this tableful of letters. We have drunk many dregs since we embarked on this fatal Swan River expedition, fraught with continued care and deprivations,

she wrote to Helen Story. Georgiana's chief comfort was her flower garden, from which she sent seeds home to her mother.

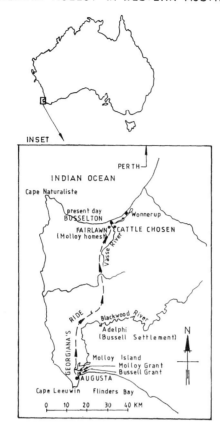

GEORGIANA MOLLOY IN WESTERN AUSTRALIA.

Map drawn by Jake de Vries showing route taken by Georgiana and her children on horseback between Augusta and the Vasse River.

They were delighted by the birth of their first (and only) son John who, they dreamed, would one day farm their acres of land. It made their hard work seem worthwhile. Sometimes in the evening, Georgiana took her children to the beach and while they played she sat and dreamed of the Storys' stone manse at Roseneath, while the waves of the great southern ocean pounded over the sandbar.

Unlike pioneer women in Canada and America, who complained bitterly of the cold, Georgiana loved the Western Australian climate and told Helen Story 'while you are burning the front . . . of your frock and your shoes at an excellent fire . . . I am sitting on the verandah surrounded by my little flower garden . . . Many of the shrubs are powerfully sweet'. The English seeds and the yucca lilies she had brought with her flowered abundantly, giving the effect of midsummer in an English cottage garden, and creepers climbed in profusion over walls and verandahs. She grew vines and peach trees from stones she had brought from Cape Town, and the success of her green fingers must have been some consolation for all her hard work and isolation from the pleasant world which she had known before. Gardening and botanising provided Georgiana's only relaxation from the constant burden of household chores, frequent bouts of sickness, and the loss of her indentured servants, who not unnaturally, as their contract ran out developed 'land hunger' in their turn. Captain Molloy was away at the time their second wheat crop was due for harvest: it was left to Georgiana to organise labourers to cut and stack the crop and to negotiate payment with them.

By September 1835 Bessie Bussell could stand the despair of farming in desperately poor soil at Augusta no longer. She pined to join her brothers on the new rich grasslands at the Vasse River and eventually she persuaded John Bussell to take her over to the new settlement. In mid-November, Bessie, John Vernon and Alfred Bussell and the Molloys' former servant Dawson rode for two days on the long bush track from Augusta to the Vasse River.[10] Bessie was saddle-sore and sunburned but delighted by their new land and 'our beautiful cattle as they lay ruminating beneath the trees'. The Vasse was now open pasture on land originally burned off by the Nyungar people, whose food sources the Bussells would soon remove from them. In retaliation they would spear the settlers' cattle, leading to death and disaster for the Nyungar.

John Molloy had not taken up his full land grant at Augusta and had received a large area of land at the Vasse. It was only a matter of time before he would transfer his stock to the Vasse but as Police Magistrate he did not want settlers like the Turners, whose financial commitments prevented them leaving Augusta, becoming downhearted. So he fixed no immediate date for leaving, preferring to wait until a home could be built for them all at the Vasse.

In December 1836, the schooner *Champion* arrived at the Vasse with Governor Stirling aboard. Georgiana received a box of gifts from her mother and an unexpected letter, together with a box of English seeds, from Captain John Mangles, a retired English naval captain and a cousin of Lady Stirling. His letter contained a special request. Could she find him seeds of native plants?

Captain Mangles' hobby was botany. He had inherited a vast annual income from his father, a director of the gigantic East India Company. He never needed to work again and spent his time writing books on the plants of the Far East and other exotic locations. Mangles owned a large and beautiful house and garden, and was a keen horticulturist and botanist.

John Mangles' hobby kept him constantly in touch with botanical gardens around Britain, but he craved academic recognition for his scientific research. Before his voyage to Australia, he had offered to obtain new exotic specimens for the collections of the Royal Horticultural Society, and various botanical gardens around England. Captain Mangles had visited the home of Lady Stirling when in Perth on his world voyage. But as his ship was departing within a few days, he had no time to explore the rest of the west Australian coastline or the interior and yearned for plants and seeds from this area.

Lady Stirling must have mentioned the young woman who was so knowledgeable about flowers and plants, marooned in her bush home in Augusta. Safely back in England, Mangles sent Georgiana a *hortus siccus* or herbarium in which to press specimens and asked her to fill it with the weeds of Western Australian to grow in his own garden and for scientific research.

Georgiana took Captain Mangles' request seriously. It represented a challenge. Although her free time was limited she collected, packaged and labelled up the seeds with leaves of the plants and, whenever possible, descriptions of the flowers and as much data as she could obtain on them from the Nyungar people. She had, at long last, found an outlet for her intelligence and enthusiasm. She had made no real friends at Alberta and found no-one who shared her religious preoccupations: now she had a colleague as interested as herself in the botany of the area.

Throughout the winter the Bussells waged warfare on the Nyungar at the Vasse, while Georgiana was thinking of her collecting work. For her the encircling bush was now a comfort and a challenge rather than an enemy. She sewed muslin bags to collect seeds, found and marked plants whose seeds she and her children would later collect. She wrote how, 'their eyes being so much nearer the ground, they have been able to detect many minute samples I cannot observe'. In the eleven months since Captain Mangles' letter had first arrived, she had spent more time in the bush than during the whole of her previous seven years at Augusta. He had become her lifeline to the outside world and a chance of a newer, wider outlook on life.

But, without warning, came the greatest tragedy of her entire life. One morning after breakfast the family and their servant Charlotte had dispersed to their various household duties; Georgiana went into the outside kitchen to bake and to churn the cream into butter. Suddenly she noticed that little John, then aged nineteen months, was nowhere to be seen. Worried that he might wander into the bush and get lost she had fastened a little bell to the toddler's belt but she could not hear it. Desperate with fear she checked if baby John was with Charlotte the maid or with her husband. But they had not seen him. Desperate she and her husband raced over to check the well, a stone's throw from the house. Her husband tried to reassure her, saying, 'Do not frighten yourself, he never goes there'. But her only son had fallen down the well and all their attempts at life-saving could not revive the little blonde-haired boy.

The shock of her son's death brought on a deep depression: Georgiana was already thin and debilitated from the effects of her last pregnancy. Now she became unable to eat, unable to sleep, riddled with guilt, constantly blaming herself for her baby son's death. Only the fact that she knew her husband and children could not cope in the bush without her and her religious faith prevented Georgiana from taking her own life. She now became obsessed with death and talked of rejoining her baby son in Heaven. There was no clergyman or counsellor to absolve her from the burden of guilt and grief she took upon herself. Her guilt was so intense she could not even write about the tragedy to her family.

The big collecting boxes stood empty for months but eventually she was able to write to Captain Mangles apologising for lack of communication and describing the painful details of little John's death, explaining how 'We tried every means of restoration but to no effect and that lovely, healthy child, who had never known pain or sickness and who had been all mirth and joyousness . . . was now a stiff corpse but beautiful even in death'.[11]

Perhaps this recounting of her own tragedy helped Georgiana psychologically by acting as a catharsis. Shortly after writing to Mangles she began her 'botanising' again. It was as though subconsciously she had rejected death in favour of life, which was represented by the flowers and seeds she once again began collecting.

From this time onwards Georgiana's thoughts veered away from spiritual questions about death and the hereafter and she concentrated all her attention on her botanical studies. She visited the collecting grounds with her children up to a dozen times in a single week, waiting for the ripening seedpods to burst, so that she could harvest them at their peak. Mangles had told her that in the past shipments of seeds from Australia had been so poorly packed that they had been useless for propagation. Georgiana was determined that hers would arrive in perfect condition.

She enlisted the aid of her husband to bring back new plant specimens from his trips to their new land at the Vasse. She even persuaded soldiers from the garrison marching through the forest with packs on their backs to collect for her. She tackled her collecting and research with precision, dedication and professionalism. Mindful of all the children who had been lost in the bush and starved to death, Georgiana never let her children go collecting without her although she found their sharp eyes ideal for collecting specimens.

The Nyungar brought her medicinal plants which she documented along with their healing properties realising that her work could be used to benefit mankind in the future. (Today cures for disease derived from plants and berries known to indigenous peoples are eagerly sought out by drug companies).

The garden Georgiana had planted with English seeds and her beloved white yucca lilies which formed a hedge were now at their best. To provide much-needed diversions for her husband and children on summer evenings they moved her piano-organ out onto the grass. There Georgiana would play to her family in the moonlight with the beautiful broad sweep of the Blackwood River gliding past, the music occasionally punctuated by the harsh call of black swans overhead and the still night air heavy with the scent of English stocks, pinks and mignonette.[12]

Winter came and another pregnancy. In June 1838 Georgiana gave birth to her fifth child (her third living child). They named the baby Amelia. The birth was difficult and doubtless mismanaged. Georgiana haemorrhaged badly, grew weaker in bed without exercise and was slow to recover. She breast-fed Amelia and by the beginning of August had taught four-year-old Mary Dorothea to read and rejoiced that by now Sabina could read for herself. But she worried over the absence of whaling ships coming into Flinders Bay to take back the specimens she had packed so carefully for Captain Mangles. She was unsure of her own abilities and was eager to hear his opinion of her work.

As spring advanced she grew stronger and could not resist taking the children collecting once more in the bush where they 'ran like butterflies from flower to flower'. Captain Molloy was once again away at the Vasse where he had finally taken up a 12,000-acre (5,455 hectare) grant. He brought some flowers new to her back with him to Augusta. Georgiana pressed them and put them into one of the collecting boxes. When she checked their contents she found a small insect among the specimens. Practical and methodical as ever she sprinkled pepper on the specimens as an insect repellent and preservative,[13] and hoped the insect had not had time to breed.

On 16 November a British schooner called at Augusta. Georgiana consigned Captain Mangles' precious collecting boxes and specimens for shipment to London.

Months later Mangles wrote back thanking Georgiana and congratulating her on the excellence of her research. He told her how pleased the Royal Botanical Gardens at Kew had been with her carefully packed seeds and notes and added that he had sent some to Sir Joseph Paxton at Chatsworth House and other horticulturalists around Britain. With his reply to Georgiana Mangles included toys for the children and presents for her. At last she had found a kindred spirit with her own interests. She wrote and thanked him and promised to send more seeds by the next whaling ship to call at Augusta.

While Captain Molloy made several more trips to the Vasse to see how their new house was progressing, Georgiana stayed at Augusta in charge of household, children and farm. Even though she knew they were leaving for the Vasse she still tended her garden and the hedge of yucca lilies. A few days before their departure she planted a red rose on her son's grave, uprooted favourite plants and bulbs of the yucca lilies and placed them in a basket to take with her. She was very sad to leave the area she had come to love—the magnificent Blackwood River with its white pelicans and tall trees overhanging the dark water, her first real home and garden. Instead, for the sake of her children's future, she did not complain but followed her husband into the small boat which would take them thirty miles up the Blackwood River where they set up camp and cooked their dinner over the camp fire.

The next day, as previously arranged, they were met by an escort of mounted soldiers to accompany them the sixty miles to their new home. But progress had to be slow with two young children and a baby. Georgiana carried her baby in a pannier basket attached to the saddle, while Sabina and Mary Dorothea rode on donkeys. They spent two more nights camping in the bush and reached the Vasse River on 10 May 1839.

Georgiana's new home was a terrible disappointment. John Molloy was a better soldier and magistrate than architect. The surrounding countryside she found flat and uninteresting and although her family was now larger than when they had arrived at Augusta, their home at the Vasse was the same size as before but less attractive and lacked glass in the windows. It seemed that there was to be little improvement in their living conditions and in many ways she felt they had gone backwards. Mosquitoes and flies were everywhere.

Where the Bussells had admired the Vasse for its acres of rolling pastures and saw future wealth through fattening sleek cattle, Georgiana saw the Vasse River as a semi-stagnant stream and no substitute for the broad expanse of the Blackwood with its magnificent stands of jarrah. Her first thought was to find some moist soil where she could bed in the plants she had taken from her previous garden.

At first she complained of the temperature being hotter during the day and colder at night than Augusta. But slowly she became enchanted by the profusion of wild-flowers, which she found lovelier than those of Augusta. Aided by a Nyungar man named Calgood, she began to collect new species.

Almost the only advantage of life at the Vasse, from Georgiana's point of view, was that the hostility between the Molloys and the Bussells now evaporated under the stress of pioneering. Georgiana gained a true friend in Charlotte Bussell, recently arrived from England.

Charlotte was a widow who had recently married John Bussell, the eldest of the Bussell brothers. She had arrived at the Vasse in 1839, a few months before the Molloys moved there. She was an intelligent, industrious and well-educated young woman with three children. Charlotte was more generous by nature than the Bussells and having experienced sorrow herself could empathise with Georgiana over the loss of her son.

There was no bridge. Charlotte rowed across the Vasse River that separated the two properties when she paid her first visit to Georgiana. The two women, one fair and one dark-haired, embraced. Charlotte described in her diary how she was impressed by the neatness and charm of the Molloys' small wooden home. Georgiana had placed a bunch of wildflowers in a vase on the table. When Charlotte complimented her on the beauty of the arrangement, Georgiana said that she could not 'bear to be without flowers in the room'. She had planted anemonies, pinks and wallflowers in the garden and some of her yucca lilies.

Georgiana was now impatient to start sending Vasse flowers and seeds to Mangles. She had an enormous box made up measuring one metre by two to export her specimens. Like most women of the period she failed to realise her own worth and worried that she would not be able to do a good enough job documenting all the new species at the Vasse to satisfy Captain Mangles. She had written notes for a publication entitled the *Floral Calendar*, which was published at Captain Mangles' expense and under his own name, a practice now known as vanity publishing. It contained no acknowledgement of Georgiana's work.

Around this time there appeared a book by Professor Lindley, of London University's Botany Department who was also the Secretary of the Horticultural Society. He had received a complete set of Georgiana's seeds and copies of her notes. His publication was entitled *A Sketch of the Vegetation of the Swan River Colony* and was brought out in 1839 as part of Edwards' classic *Botanical Register* series. It contained much information taken directly from Georgiana's notes but did not acknowledge her work because the text had reached the author direct from Captain Mangles, who had incorporated it into his own research. However, Georgiana was delighted to receive a copy of Edward's publication, together with toys for the children and a mouth-organ.

Georgiana had no appreciation of the enormous value of her precise documentation of the Australian flora, and replied that she was most gratified 'to think how small an aid I have lent to your cause'. Had she been a modern academic she would have had cause to sue him, but women were second-class citizens in scientific life and their very eagerness to act as unpaid research assistants, combined with the traditional concept of feminine modesty, made them devalue their own efforts.

The German naturalist Ludwig Priess stayed with the Molloys for a month at the Vasse, absorbing as much as possible of Georgiana's knowledge while she took him collecting botanical specimens. In an amazing combination of bad manners and plagiarism, he never even wrote his hostess a note thanking her for her attention and hospitality, nor acknowledged the information she had given him for his research papers. He also failed to send her some specimens and seeds which he had initially promised in return for those she gave him.

By the end of July Georgiana was well enough to ride around the new countryside of the Vasse, accompanied by Vernon Bussell. John Bussell had recently made a census of the entire district and she learnt that 87 people were now resident in this vast area. She wrote to Captain Mangles, telling him that she hoped they would build a new house as theirs was very hot and even the plants became scorched in summer.

Georgiana had not seen her sister Mary for ten years. Mary Kennedy came out to the Vasse to help when Georgiana fell pregnant yet again. Mary was convinced that Georgiana was foolish to work like a slave and live without entertainments or amenities. Sophisticated Mary found colonial bush life both boring and repellent.

On 7 May 1840 the Molloys' cook left suddenly to work for the Bussells. Next day, assisted by Mary, Georgiana gave birth to her sixth child, another daughter, named Flora, the Latin name for flower. The delivery left her with a debilitating post-partum infection. (Before Semmelweiss's discoveries on infection were known, infection was often passed to the mother's vagina from the unwashed hands of a doctor or midwife).[14]

Kind-hearted Fanny Bussell helped Mary Kennedy nurse Georgiana, who though she had a fever, worried about the seeds of the magnificent golden orange flowers of *Nuytsia floribunda*, which were just ripening, which she still hoped to collect and send to Captain Mangles. Mary Kennedy had enough of bush life and botanising and as soon as her sister had recovered, she went home leaving Georgiana with an enormous amount of domestic drudgery.

When the Bussells and other male settlers went on a punitive raid and killed fourteen of the Nyungar, young Lenox Bussell claimed proudly that 'a lasting peace has been established without the loss of a single European'. The deterioration in the situation with the normally peaceful Nyungar people, who had so kindly shown the first settlers their waterholes and seen their food supply dry up as a result, distressed Georgiana very much. She realised that to them the land was their Dreaming while to settlers like the Bussells it was simply a commodity.[15]

Their neighbour George Layman became involved in a bitter quarrel over damper and flour and insulted a Nyungar elder by pulling his beard. The elder's son was in jail awaiting a charge of manslaughter and Layman was speared to death in retribution. John Molloy, as Police Magistrate, conducted an official enquiry and was made guardian of the four fatherless Layman children. Georgiana attempted to console the Layman children and their mother and had them to stay at *Fair Lawn*.

By now Georgiana had found a whaling ship to take her second consignment of seeds and notes to John Mangles. But Captain Molloy by now was less enthusiastic about his wife's hobby and kept suggesting she should spend more time at home mending his clothes and less in the bush.

When the second Vasse winter came, the Molloys still had no glass in their windows, which were nothing but large square holes cut out of the wooden walls. As some sort of protection against cold and the many flying insects, Georgiana made window screens out of unbleached calico, which she painstakingly stitched onto wooden frames.

The Reverend John Wollaston, clergyman to the Australind Settlement, was a keen amateur botanist. On a botanising expedition, he spent three days with the Molloys and noted that they were 'uncommonly generous and motivated by less self-interest than anyone else in the colony'. He wrote an account of his visit in his journal.[16] Wollaston's wife was also worn down with the enormous physical work of pioneering. In reality male freedom to explore and conquer meant female bondage as male pioneers needed cooks, cleaners, seamstresses and mothers, Wollaston realised.

Wollaston and his son John were drawn to Georgiana by their mutual passion for botany. The Reverend Wollaston noted how thin she was and how she was working harder than any maid since Governor Hutt had chosen that week to make an official visit to the Vasse. As Captain Molloy was Government Resident and Magistrate for the Vasse and Augusta, the Molloys had to host his visit, involving still more household duties for Georgiana. Wollaston noted how

> I could not help remarking to the Governor as Mrs Molloy continually passed from the house to the kitchen with the dinner dishes in one hand and her youngest daughter, without shoes or socks in the other, how distressing and laborious must be the female emigrant's lot, who has in her native country been used to the comforts and cleanliness . . . of genteel life.
>
> The Molloys are at present without servant of any kind . . . Mrs Molloy, assisted by her little girl, only nine years old, attended to everything in the cooking way. Although the dining room has a clay floor and opens into the dairy, the thatch appears overhead and there is not a single pane of glass on the premises, yet our entertainment, the style and manners of our host and hostess, their dress and conversation all showed . . . that genuine good breeding and gentlemanly deportment are not always lost sight of among English emigrants.

It is interesting that Governor Hutt's valet does not appear to have given assistance in clearing the table or washing the dinner dishes in the separate kitchen to the rear of the building, where there was no sink. Georgiana would have drawn the water from the well and tipped the heavy bucket of water into a large copper over the wood stove to heat it. She and her daughter washed the greasy dishes in a basin before she made butter, baked bread, cooked lunch and dinner for her guests, cleaned the house, and set the table and arranged the flowers for the evening meal.

Georgiana was responsible for the three girls' spiritual and temporal education. Mr Wollaston baptised the Molloys' youngest daughter with the eminently suitable name of Flora, and remarked in admiration that Georgiana 'is a perfect botanical dictionary'. In fact by this time she was more like a walking encyclopaedia, longing to increase her knowledge whenever she could tear herself away from her exhausting and unending round of what she termed 'domestic drudgery'.

In June 1841 she sent Captain Mangles her last parcel of over one hundred different specimens of seed, all neatly tied up in tiny brown muslin bags. Moves were afoot to name a flower species after Georgiana, since it had become apparent that her work was being published with no form of acknowledgement. It was proposed by the Western Australian botanist James Drummond to name a species of grevillea, Molloya, in her honour, but this never eventuated. However, the tall, scented *Boronia molloyae* has secured Georgiana Molloy botanical immortality. Georgiana confessed that she longed to go out collecting again. 'I should like nothing better than to kindle a fire and stay out all night . . . as I should be ready for my work early in the morning'—but by this time she was pregnant.

By the time spring came *Fair Lawn* deserved its name. The grass was sown down to the river's edge, and vines and fig trees had been planted. Three weeks before Christmas 1842, Georgiana's seventh child was born. Baby Georgiana was named after her mother. The birth was difficult and the local doctor was drunk. She haemorrhaged and lost a great deal of blood; the doctor proved manifestly incapable. Alfred Bussell rode on horseback to Leschenault to get another doctor and the following day returned with one who was sober, but Georgiana's condition did not improve and a blood clot paralysed both her legs.

Thereafter Georgiana, weak and exhausted, and realising she was dying, worried endlessly as to who would rear her young daughters. As the summer heat worsened, she endured further complications and her sufferings grew more intense. Her husband made pathetic attempts to make her a hydrostatic bed out of a waterproof coat to ease the ulcerated bed sores. Skilled medical care could have saved her but there was none. She never once blamed her husband for the fact that her last two pregnancies were responsible for her illness. To the last she loved him deeply and believed that her short life had been lived to the full through her family and her botanical research. In her last letter to Captain Mangles she wrote, 'I believe I have sent you everything worth sending'.

Georgiana died in April 1843 destroyed by the rigours of childbearing in the bush. She was only thirty-seven when she died but had she lived long enough would eventually have learned that the seeds she had sent to Captain Mangles would be in botanical gardens and plant nurseries all over Britain, Europe and North America.

John Molloy never remarried. He lived on for another twenty-five years. The women of the Vasse showed the spirit of care and cooperation for Georgiana's children that has always inspired Australian women in the bush. Her closest friend Charlotte Bussell looked after the three elder girls, acted as official hostess at their weddings and continued to visit the girls when they married. In a strange reversal of fate, the widow of George Layman (who Georgiana had befriended), brought up little Georgiana in her home.

Georgiana was buried in a paddock behind *Fair Lawn*, her grave surrounded by the white yucca lilies.

Kew Gardens and the rest of the world gained from her professionalism and dedication to the expansion of scientific knowledge. British horticulturalist George Hailes, who had grown magnificent show specimens from Georgiana's kangaroo paw seeds, wrote a moving epitaph in a letter of condolence to 'Handsome Jack': '*Not one in ten thousand who go out into distant lands has done what she did for gardens . . .*'

---

[1] Fraser, Antonia. *The Lives of the Kings and Queens of England*. Book Club Associates, London, 1975, p. 260.

[2] Georgiana Molloy has no separate entry in the *Australian Dictionary of Biography*, Volume 2, but receives a one-line entry under her husband's name. Captain John Molloy's entry notes that he was named after the man who brought him up, a penniless sea captain dismissed for cowardice in 1797, that 'Handsome Jack' Molloy resembled the Duke of York in looks and it seems significant that he named parts of his land grant at Augusta after the various titles of Frederick, Duke of York. It records that John Molloy's fees at Harrow and Oxford were paid by a firm of lawyers acting for an unknown benefactor and when Molloy turned 21 he was handed a sum of money to buy himself a commission as an officer. The paternity of Frederick, Duke of York, is also supported by Hasluck, A., in *Portrait with Background*, Oxford University Press, Melbourne, 1955 pp 256–7.

[3] Letter from Georgiana Molloy to Helen Story, 25 January 1830, Battye Library, Perth.

[4] Friend, Mary Ann. *Journal, 1834*. Cited in de Vries-Evans, Susanna, *Pioneer Women, Pioneer Land*. Angus and Robertson, Sydney, 1987.

[5] Letter from Georgiana Molloy to Helen Story, 1 October 1833. Battye Library, Perth.

[6] Georgiana Molloy to her family. Letter dated 15 April, Cumbria Record Office, Carlisle, cited in Lines, William J. *An All Consuming Passion*. Allen and Unwin, Sydney, 1994. A full account of the early settlers at the Vasse and at Augusta and their relations with the Nyungar people.

[7] Letter from Georgiana Molloy to Helen Story, 8 December 1836. Battye Library, Perth.

[8] Georgiana Molloy to Mrs Kennedy, 29 May 1833, Cumbria Record Office, Carlisle, cited W.J. Lines. *Op. cit.*

[9] Georgiana Molloy's letter to Helen Story, 8 December 1834. Battye Library, Perth.

[10] Lines, William J. *Op. cit.* Bessie Bussell's letter to her family at Augusta about arriving at Cattle Chosen is dated November 1835 and is in the Bussell Papers in the Battye Library, Perth. A full account of the Bussell family at Augusta and the Vasse is contained in Shann, E.O.G. *Cattle Chosen: the Story of the First Group Settlement in Western Australia*. Oxford University Press, London, 1926.

11 Letter from Georgiana Molloy to Captain Mangles, 25 January 1838. Battye Library, Perth. Cited in Hasluck, A. *Portrait with Background, A Life of Georgiana Molloy.* Oxford University Press, Melbourne, 1955.

12 Georgiana Molloy reminisced in a letter to Captain Mangles about 'dear Augusta'. Letter dated June 1840, Battye Library, Perth.

13 Lines, William. J. *Op. cit.*

14 Shorter, E. A. *History of Womens' Bodies.* Allen Lane, London, 1982 & 1983.

15 Green, Neville (ed.) *Nyungar—The People and Aboriginal Customs in the South West of Australia.* Creative Research, Perth, 1979. Cited in *Lines*, William. *Op. cit.*

16 The account of John Ramsden Wollaston's stay with the Molloys is contained in Wollaston's *Picton Journal.* Paterson Brokensha, Perth. 1948.

CHAPTER 8

Georgiana McCrae
(1804–1890)

PIONEER, PORTRAITIST AND WRITER

Georgiana Huntly McCrae was one of the most talented of the professional artists who arrived in Australia in the nineteenth century but she was unable to continue her profession because her domineering husband refused permission for her to continue painting portraits. Instead Georgiana wrote about the first days of Melbourne and her journal remains a valuable social document. The small homestead she designed at Arthurs Seat, on the Mornington Peninsula at McCrae, is visited by thousands every year. Georgiana's letters, journals, sketches, architectural plans and paintings reveal her talent—both her work and her life are unforgettable.

She was the illegitimate daughter of George, Marquis of Huntly (who would eventually succeed to the title of fifth Duke of Gordon), and Jane Graham, daughter of a Northumberland farmer. Jane Graham always maintained that she had gone through a marriage ceremony with the Marquis but no evidence of this was ever found.[1] When the Marquis was thirty-three and deep in debt he finally decided to marry Elizabeth Brodie, daughter of a Glasgow merchant and iron-founder. It was a marriage of convenience: Elizabeth was a plain and unsophisticated young woman with mousy ringlets and no conversational skills whose deep religious faith led her to spend much of her time at prayer circles and Bible study groups. Elizabeth Brodie's attraction for the dark and dashing Marquis of Huntly was her vast private income which he hoped would pay off his debts and support his three illegitimate children.[2] Brodie money from the counting house and iron foundry would allow the pleasure-loving Marquis to continue to live the life of a Georgian aristocrat.

The youngest of the Marquis's three illegitimate children, Georgiana was born and baptised as a Gordon when she was two-and-a-half years old; her Gordon kinsman Lord Reagh stood as godfather at her London christening which was also attended by her father.

She and her mother were supported financially by the Gordon family. Georgiana was educated at a school run by French-speaking nuns to become a young lady and take up a position in society in which she would have an ambiguous and insecure place. Georgiana's father's gambling and other debts had been paid off by her stepmother, who was at first Marchioness of Huntly and later the fifth Duchess of Gordon. Privately Georgiana always called her stepmother the 'Brodie' Duchess because her large private income came from the Brodie Iron Foundry, started by the Duchess's father. Money gave Georgiana's stepmother power in the marriage of convenience, with disastrous effects on Georgiana.

At the convent Georgiana was taught French and became bilingual. All her life she retained an attractive trace of a French accent. She was taught to be resourceful and became an excellent needlewoman. From an early age Georgiana showed a remarkable talent for painting and an appreciation of art and history. In the era before photography most young ladies dabbled in the art of watercolour drawing to record places and events, but Georgiana studied art seriously in order to become a professional artist. Her prospects of a suitable 'society' marriage at this stage were not good. Neither she nor her mother wanted her to stake her future on the appearance of a suitor prepared to propose to an illegitimate daughter of the nobility. She would work extremely hard and hope to become an artist or a musician and, if necessary, earn that important dowry necessary to achieve a 'good' marriage.

Due to Georgiana's outstanding artistic ability, it was agreed that she should leave school and concentrate on art and music. She and her mother lived at Somers Town, a relatively inexpensive part of north London now demolished, which then lay close to Paddington.[3] However, Georgiana's music did not progress as rapidly as her painting. She was beautiful, talented, had a lively intelligence, a strong and attractive personality and excellent sense of humour. Her music master fell in love with her and proposed marriage when Georgiana was only 15 years old. He was promptly sent packing by her protective mother and Georgiana's musical education was entrusted to a music mistress.

Through a friend, Georgiana made the acquaintance of the famous landscape artist John Varley and became his pupil. Encouraged by Varley, she sent her first painting to the prestigious Summer Exhibition of the Royal Academy in London. To her delight her landscape with a church was exhibited. In view of her youth, this was remarkable, since only a third of all the many paintings submitted were selected for exhibition by the committee. Records of the Royal Academy reveal that Georgiana exhibited two scenes at the Summer Exhibition in 1818 and 1819 respectively.[4]

In spite of the fact she was a woman in a male profession, fame seemed within her grasp. She became a pupil of two of the leading artists of her time, Dominic Serres and John Glover (an artist working in the classical traditional of Claude Le Lorrain, Glover would eventually emigrate and become one of Tasmania's most important colonial landscapists).

Circumstances had given Georgiana a desire to be independent and to earn her own living, at least until she married. She realised that the way to do this both pleasurably and profitably was to paint miniatures, which were much quicker to execute than full-length portraits and easier for a woman to carry about. Accordingly she became a pupil of Charles Hayter, the personal art instructor to Princess Charlotte. Hayter specialised in painting miniatures of the rich and famous in watercolours on ivory. He had written a book on the art of miniature painting which was very well regarded in art circles of the day.[5]

Hayter found Georgiana a charming, diligent and highly talented pupil, who was so keen to learn that she usually arrived early for her lessons in order to prepare her paints and brushes. From Louis Maueleon, a French artist in exile, she had learnt how to grind pigments, prepare colour washes and make quick life sketches in charcoal. Under Hayter's expert tuition she soon mastered one of the most demanding techniques, the art of painting in watercolours direct onto a thin wafer of ivory, using brushes containing only a few hairs. Georgiana had enormous patience and talent for colour and line as she acquired the true hallmark of an artist, the total mastery of her craft. However the lessons in miniature painting were abruptly terminated by her mother when Hayter tried to arrange a marriage between Georgiana and his clever but slightly deformed son.

In 1820, she was awarded a silver medal from the Royal Society of Arts for her portrait of her grandfather, Duke Alexander, fourth Duke of Gordon. She was only sixteen. The following year Georgiana won a silver palette award for a 'Portrait of a French Lady' making her one of the most promising young portrait artists in Britain. She received her award from the hands of the Duke of Sussex at a special ceremony in London.[6]

Her art training came to a sudden end around 1821 (Georgiana specifies no date in her 'Recollections' and even the date and details of her mother's parentage may have been deliberately omitted by her daughter Lucia, who copied out her mother's original manuscript journal).[7]

Georgiana's life changed when her mother Jane Graham suffered a carriage accident in which she was thrown to the ground and left with serious head injuries. Georgiana, who was only nineteen, showed considerable presence of mind, seizing the reins and bringing the frightened horses to a halt. Her mother never recovered from her fall. From then on she suffered a presenile dementia and was incapable of looking after herself. Her mother's sister, Margaret, who lived near Gravesend, took charge of the unfortunate Jane Graham until she died thirteen years later. (Georgiana is not clear about the circumstances and date of her mother's death in her journal).

Many years later, her aunt Margaret would later leave Georgiana a small sum of money to put towards buying a house.

Due to conventions of the period, no unmarried girl of any standing could live alone. So Georgiana was invited to live with her grandfather, Alexander, at Gordon Castle. Doubtless her stepmother, the Marchioness of Huntly, would not have welcomed a third illegitimate child of the Marquis, her husband, at Huntly Castle as a living reminder of his virility and her infertility.

Gordon Castle, in the north-east of Scotland, lies on the River Spey and near the village of Fochabers. The Gordons owned vast tracts of land but the family fortunes were heavily mortgaged to pay debts incurred in the past. Georgiana found that her grandfather, Duke Alexander, still lived in feudal splendour served by seventeen house servants, liveried coachmen, grooms for the horses and a small army of gardeners. Gordon Castle had three wings and was surrounded by 1500 acres of woodland and park. The Dukes of Gordon as clan chieftains had ruled over the north of Scotland like kings and even raised their own Highland Regiment, the Gordon Highlanders. Georgiana found Gordon Castle was an exciting place to live for an aspiring artist. The long galleries were hung with portraits by Van Dyck, Raeburn, Sir Joshua Reynolds and Angelica Kauffman, the sight of whose work may have acted as a spur to Georgiana's artistic ambitions. Meanwhile she helped her grandfather with his correspondence.

Engraving of a painting by Thomas Allom, Gordon Castle, Fochabers, Morayshire in 1837 showing Georgiana's father, the fifth Duke of Gordon, and her stepmother, the Duchess, out riding with their Highland servants. Private collection, courtesy John Simpson.

Georgiana would write letters dictated by the Duke in the mornings and have her afternoons free for painting. She maintained some degree of independence earning extra money by painting distinguished visitors to the castle. She also made pencil drawings and watercolours of Scottish scenery and other castles belonging to relatives like Lord Fyvie at Fyvie Castle, for her own amusement. She spent long hours with James Hoy, the Duke's librarian, a scholarly man, in the extensive library of the castle where Georgiana learned the colourful history of her Gordon ancestors. She made a written inventory of the family portraits and old masters on the walls of Gordon Castle.

At night Georgiana would dine with the Duke and his librarian in the Great Hall, lit by hundreds of candles. Dinner was always served by liveried footmen. She was given a large room of her own, high in one of the towers, known as the Crimson Bedroom where she had space to paint. Some of Georgiana's undated watercolours show the view from this window over trees and park with the battlements of Gordon Castle in front of the window. Georgiana was no longer an illegitimate girl living in genteel poverty and obscurity. To the servants who now surrounded her she was Miss Huntly Gordon of Gordon Castle. The old Duke, her grandfather, was charmed by the warmth of her personality, her elegance and her wit. She grew to love him and he became the father figure she had never had.

James Hoy was also fond of Georgiana and as a birthday present gave her an engraved stone heart.[8] Her grandfather, spoke French with her on occasions, enjoyed Georgiana's company and was proud of her artistic talent.

On 17 June 1827 Duke Alexander died at his London home in St James'. The Duke's body was brought back to Scotland and lay in state in Edinburgh's great stone Palace of Holyroodhouse as befitted one who had ruled over a large section of Scotland's wild and rugged north.[9] Georgiana's father, who had been holidaying in Switzerland on his wife's money, succeeded to the title as fifth Duke of Gordon as well as the heavy expenses of running a large estate with many old retainers and the burden of supporting them in old age.

As the Duke's body was brought back to Gordon Castle after the population of Edinburgh had paid their respects, without warning and like an omen, a fire erupted in the castle's east wing. The blaze burned fiercely; finally part of the wooden roof of the castle caved in. Georgiana's father could see clearly that his wife's fortune was vital to rebuild one entire wing.[10] The prospect of even more lavish spending of her money placed the Duchess, Georgiana's stepmother, in a far stronger position with her husband than before. He agreed to attend regular morning prayers—every inch the reformed rake.

Elizabeth, Duchess of Gordon, was a homely-featured woman, with mouse-brown hair. She was only ten years older than Georgiana, and it was natural she would be jealous of her husband's affection for his beautiful, talented and witty daughter. However, the Duchess's conversion from Anglicanism to evangelical Christianity prevented her from openly displaying resentment towards her stepdaughter.

The dour Duchess lost no time in changing the routines of Gordon Castle. She instituted morning and evening prayers which her husband and the staff had to attend, as well as Bible study sessions with a teacher imported from Edinburgh, a ban on all Sabbath travelling and what she termed 'frivolities' such as reading novels (a pastime Georgiana enjoyed), balls, and private theatricals. This absence of joy and culture, the Duchess's sanctimonious homilies, allied to her overbearing character and her many household economies made life unpleasant for Georgiana for five years.[11] The situation between the two women was not helped by the fact that the Duchess remained childless. To compensate for lack of a legal son and heir, Georgiana's father openly referred to Georgiana as his daughter and bought expensive presents for her, which must have infuriated the Duchess.

The definitive rupture between the two women occurred in 1828, when the

Duchess ended Georgiana's romance with her distant cousin Peter Charles, known as Perico Gordon, son of John David Gordon, one of the Catholic branch of the family, who were known as the Wardhouse Gordons. Perico was heir to the childless Charles Gordon, Laird of Wardhouse. He had spent much time with his Catholic uncle at the sherry-growing area of Jerez de la Frontera in southern Spain, where the Gordons are still famous as winegrowers.[12] Like Georgiana, Perico's mother was also dead. She was Catholic and Spanish, which damned him in the eyes of the Duchess, but this would have been an added attraction to Georgiana who loathed the cold, dour, evangelising version of Christianity forced on her by the Duchess. She was invited to visit Perico and his aunt, who acted as chaperone to the pair at Wardhouse Castle. Perico taught Georgiana some Spanish folk songs (which she wrote into the music book she eventually brought to Australia). They both spoke French and he too was fascinated by Gordon family history. Georgiana would alter describe this visit as the happiest days of her life—'*les plus heureux jours de ma vie*'.

Perico was two years younger than Georgiana and had been left slightly lame from a childhood illness. She found him both sensitive and artistic and described how she stood close to him, and that when he returned her portrait miniature (having had it copied) the ivory on which it was painted was still warm from his breast pocket.

The sexual chemistry between them was evident; Georgiana liked his wit and charm, he made her feel alive and desired. She loved Wardhouse and wanted to be Perico's wife. She gave him a portrait miniature of herself. In it her dark curly hair clusters around the pale oval face, and she wears over one shoulder the tartan sash of the Gordons for a Highland ball at the castle.

Perico was deeply attracted to Georgiana and he and his aunt who chaperoned them gave her to understand he intended to ask the Duke for her hand in marriage. However, the Duke, keen for domestic harmony, decided to leave the delicate matter of arranging Georgiana's marriage to the Duchess. When Perico asked permission to marry Georgiana, he was told that this was not possible. He was a Catholic and she was Protestant, and the Gordon family had already suffered much pain, financial loss and disgrace through legal separations and mixed marriages. (Georgiana never knew the whole truth about this interview for many years but it is unlikely the devout Perico would have renounced his Catholic faith to please the Duchess.)

The evangelical Duchess ordered Perico never to write to Georgiana again. The Duchess firmly controlled the purse strings. The Gordons had been rent by Catholic and Protestant fighting culminating in the anti-Catholic Gordon Riots in London led by the Duke's uncle, Lord George Gordon, which had cost the family a great deal of money in compensation to those injured. So the Duke was in no position to contradict his wife's religious prejudices against this marriage.

Georgiana must have suffered deeply. This was the first time she had been in love. In her precarious position in the Duke's household she was unable to force a showdown with her bigoted stepmother. For Georgiana keeping a journal became a way of expressing all the feelings she was forced to hide.

She was sent to live in Edinburgh in a house owned by an evangelising and rigidly disciplined friend of the Duchess, who Georgiana believed had been paid to spy on her and report back to the Duchess. Georgiana now supported herself by painting miniatures and full-length portraits on commission and, through Gordon connections and her own talent, made money at it. Pressure was brought to bear on her to comply with the Duchess's choice of husband, Andrew McCrae, a Protestant lawyer. Andrew was a distant cousin of the Gordons—his portrait by Georgiana shows a serious but handsome young man with a high forehead, a mass of black hair and intense, deep-set brooding eyes. Recovering from a romance where he had been jilted, he too was interested in the Gordon heritage. He was intelligent but had no family money as his father had forfeited an inheritance. Andrew both

Georgiana drew her second son, Willie (William Gordon McCrae), aged ten. Courtesy Mrs. Barbara Blomfield.

desired and rejected the idea of money. He had an impractical streak which led him into rash choices, was something of a recluse, but found Georgiana attractive and intriguing.

Andrew tried for two years to persuade Georgiana to marry him, urged on no doubt by the Duchess who promised, as was customary, a good dowry. Finally in 1830 Georgiana agreed. Between them Andrew and the Duchess finally wore down Georgiana's reluctance to a marriage that was convenient to everyone except her. Without the Duchess's support and the promise of a dowry the stigma of her illegitimacy would have limited Georgiana's prospect of a 'good' marriage. While her illegitimacy caused insecurity it gave her a fierce desire to own a home of her own, a desire that would not be granted for many years.[13]

On 20 January 1830 Georgiana described how 'Andrew McCrae proposed to me so very unexpectedly that I could not know my mind. He left Edinburgh to work in London on 26 January and then I ascertained the state of my feelings for him.' He wrote her a very awkward letter apologising for being 'abrupt and importunate' and begging her to reconsider. He said nothing at all about loving her.

She said nothing about loving Andrew either. But her portrait of him shows him as an attractive dark-haired young man and certainly his prospects in the law were good. His grandfather's considerable fortune, derived from a West Indian sugar plantation, had been forfeited by his father, who had offended his grandfather by writing an article about the evils of slave labour on West Indian sugar plantations. When her engagement to Andrew was announced Perico wrote her a stiff little note to congratulate her and signed himself in Spanish 'your true and sincere friend, Perico'.[14]

Georgiana may have been afraid the Duchess or her servants were spying on her. She wrote nothing down about her feelings and her only comment about her wedding was revealing: 'Left my easel at Gordon Castle and changed my name.'

Georgiana was married from Gordon Castle in September 1830 with all the ceremony of a daughter of the house. Pipers played, the kilted highlanders danced and bonfires blazed on the hills in the castle grounds in celebration. The Duke gave her one hundred pounds and a fitted leather dressing case, probably relieved to be free of the Duchess nagging him about Georgiana.

The Duchess's wedding gift was a small sum of money to buy furniture rather than a large dowry. Andrew had set up practice of Edinburgh initially, but moved to London in search of better career prospects while keeping on the rented Edinburgh house. In London, Andrew was offered a parliamentary position vetting the legal wording of new bills. Their living expenses were high in London: Andrew insisted on keeping on the Edinburgh home and some of his Scottish clients. Georgiana had had a daughter who died aged three which affected her deeply. She had then borne three healthy sons, George Gordon, William and Alexander (Sandy). But there was no money to spare for nurserymaids, so Georgiana had to give up her painting and care for her children full-time. She packed away all her equipment, saying she would return to it when the children were older.

The Duke died on 28 May 1836; his will containing a generous bequest to Georgiana was unsigned and so invalid. But in compensation she did receive a very small annuity from the Duchess which Georgiana always referred to, ironically, as her 'pay'. Perhaps she felt it was a compensation for the dowry which never eventuated.

Disappointment over the Duke of Gordon's will and the high cost of living and working in London and Edinburgh may have influenced Andrew's decision to emigrate to Australia. Georgiana showed no enthusiasm for the emigration plan which would take her away from her beloved Scotland, from art galleries, concerts and civilisation. For her, emigration represented an enormous sacrifice and she was reluctant to leave.

The eighth year of her marriage, 1838, brought many changes: when Georgiana

turned 34, she learned from her aunt that her mother had died leaving her some money. In this year Georgiana also noted in her diary that Perico Gordon had visited her 'to explain'. It is likely that he told her about the Duchess's intervention and that, according to Spanish custom, he had been officially betrothed to a Catholic fiancée or *novia*, a girl of 14 whom he had never seen alone without a chaperone, daughter of a Spanish Count. He had returned to southern Spain where he eventually married his *novia*. Perico's explanation must have been like coals of fire to Georgiana, as by now she and Andrew were drifting far apart.

That year Andrew booked passage to New South Wales for his wife and children. He believed Australia offered the opportunity to make enough capital to buy a home for their children and ensure them a good future. By borrowing Georgiana's savings from her work as a portrait artist and obtaining letters of introduction to Governor Gipps and other influential members of Sydney society, Andrew hoped to set up a legal practice there or in Melbourne and would accompany other members of the McCrae family to Australia.

At the time of their projected departure to Australia, Georgiana was seven months pregnant. She packed up their rented London house and prepared inventories for shipping agents. To save money Andrew moved to his club, while Georgiana lived with her aunt at Gravesend while they awaited their ship. The stress of the move brought on the premature birth of Farquhar, her fourth son, with the additional medical complication of puerperal fever.

A long sea voyage was now impossible for Georgiana, so Andrew sailed as planned, without his wife and children but with his surgeon brother, Dr Farquhar McCrae, and family, also bound for Australia. Andrew embarked on his great adventure and appeared to pay scant heed to his wife's needs: he neither wrote nor sent her money and she waited in vain for news.

On arrival in Australia, Andrew's brother had decided that the tiny pioneer settlement at Port Phillip, then four years old and just starting to call itself Melbourne, presented better opportunities for professional men than Sydney so he and his family remained in Melbourne instead of continuing their journey to join Andrew. Andrew's letters of introduction from Sir Thomas Mitchell to the Governor and other important men in Sydney failed to secure him a government position. Dejected, he spent all the money Georgiana had earned with her painting on a parcel of virgin land in New Zealand which proved an unwise gamble. Then, after a period of indecision, Andrew moved to Melbourne and bought into a partnership with a lawyer named James Montgomery, in offices in the centre of Port Phillip.

Meanwhile, Georgiana had rented another house in south London. She was still weak and exhausted and was also extremely short of money. Andrew had sent her nothing and did not even write to her, probably not wanting to disclose what he had done with her savings. The Duchess offered no help or sympathy, she insisted to Mr James Cummings, (the husband of Georgiana's close friend Lucia and a founding director of the Union Bank of Australia), who acted as mediator between the two women, that 'the sum set aside for me [Georgiana] would not be forthcoming until her decease'.[15]

By September 1839, Georgiana was reduced 'to her last shilling piece'. Never shy about selling her work, she took a basket of her beautiful portrait miniatures on ivory to Lucia Cummings, who displayed them in her house and acted as Georgiana's selling agent. Lucia may have obtained Georgiana more commissions for portraits to solve the problem of day-to-day expenses. To obtain the money for their passage to Australia Georgiana was forced to swallow her pride and ask the Duchess to pay the fares for herself and her children, since Andrew appeared unable to do so.

The Duchess gave her stepdaughter just enough money for their first-class fares, one way only, probably delighted she was emigrating. However, she once more gave Georgiana a firm promise that she would leave her a handsome sum in her will, in accordance with her late husband's wishes. Georgiana believed her and always imagined she would have enough money to return to her beloved Scotland after the Duchess was dead.

Her friends James and Lucia Cummings arranged a musical evening as Georgiana's farewell party on 23 October 1840. The following day she wrote in her diary, 'The most trying day of all'. On 25 October, accompanied by friends rather than family, Georgiana reluctantly boarded the ship with her four young boys, the Scottish nursemaid and a maid, whose passages were paid by the Government under the immigrant bounty scheme.

It was blowing a howling gale which reminded Georgiana of Aberdeen, 'where, to say the truth, I would rather have been than on an emigrant ship bound for the Antipodes'. She described her cabin on the sailing ship *Argyle* as 'a dark and gloomy den, damp, comfortless and strange . . . with a persistent odour of paint'.

On the voyage to Australia Georgiana ate at the captain's table while her two female servants travelled steerage class as bounty immigrants on an assisted passage. One was allowed to sleep in Georgiana's cabin should she require her.

Very practically Georgiana had purchased a cow so that her boys could have fresh milk on the journey, believing she could sell the animal for a handsome profit when she arrived in Australia. She enjoyed the voyage, writing and producing a play for the passengers to act. Her boys at this time ranged from three to eight years old. She gave them their lessons in her cabin and they made family excursions ashore at the ship's ports of call and she made a map of the long voyage to amuse and instruct them.

After four months at sea, the *Argyle* finally arrived at Williamstown where they landed. The McCrae finally reached Melbourne in a much smaller steamer three days later, tying up at a gumtree on the riverbank since there was as yet no wharf available in what was virtually a shanty town.

Sheltering her young children under her plaid cape, and hoping anxiously that her husband would be there, Georgiana walked up a plank onto the bank of the

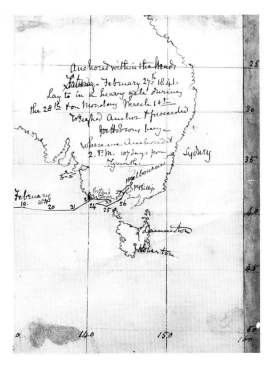

Georgiana McCrae drew this map of her voyage for her children in 1841. It shows how her ship took 107 days (three-and-a-half-months) to sail from London to Melbourne. La Trobe Library, Manuscripts Section, McCrae Collection.

Yarra at the bottom of the straggle of huts which made up present-day Flinders Street on a cold March day. Her diary has no entry describing her arrival on Australian soil but it appears Andrew was not waiting to meet them. They waded through an unsavoury mixture of mud and horse manure up the hill to her brother-in-law Dr Farquhar McCrae's tiny one-storey brick cottage in Great Bourke Street. Georgiana's only pair of good London boots were totally ruined by the mud. It was an inauspicious beginning for a new life and the future of their marriage.

Georgiana's heart must have sunk further when she saw the tiny prefabricated house that her husband had rented for them in Lonsdale Street, which at that time lay on the edge of the primitive settlement of early Melbourne. Her new home was nothing more than a wooden shell, unlined and raised on stumps above a sea of sticky mud and animal dung. There was 'one large room and several box-like bedrooms'. The kitchen was a tiny hut at the rear with a smoky firehole in the roof where the maid had somehow to cook for a family of six. The stinking privy was also situated outside in the muddy yard.

With the assistance of the maid to boil water and do the heavy cleaning and washing-up, Georgiana ran the tiny house, which she renamed *Argyle Cottage*, she supervised the children's education and made all their clothes. She rode out to see the nine acres (four hectares) of land on which their new house was to be built on the right bank of the Yarra River, at today's Studley Park near Abbotsford, about three kilometres from Melbourne. The land was 'thickly covered with boulders, of which the house is to be built'. She was determined that their new home would be beautiful, with lawns sloping down to the Yarra, and she drew up plans for the builders.

Meanwhile at *Argyle Cottage* she received and paid social calls, renewing acquaintance with some of the Scottish settlers, giving dinner parties for her in-laws and potential clients of her husband's legal practice. She made chair covers and sketched the muddy streets of infant Melbourne, where bullock drays bogged down and children drowned in the filthy gutters, which were sometimes more than a metre deep. Her rough pencil sketches are invaluable historical records of Melbourne's first days.

Georgiana was horrified to learn that a year's rent of their primitive cottage, due to Melbourne's extreme shortage of accommodation, would consume the whole of her small annuity from the Duchess. She was very disappointed that the Melbourne weather was not like the mild Mediterranean climate she had been led to expect. Heavy thunderstorms blew in the boys' bedroom windows and soaked the bedding, and in dry weather there were such severe dust storms it was almost impossible to breathe. Andrew or 'Mr McCrae' as she always called him seemed to enjoy the adventure and spent a great deal of drinking time with his friends in Melbourne's select 'gentlemen's clubs'.

In some respects Georgiana was luckier than the majority of pioneer women. Her servants adored her, staying with her through thick and thin. Her energy was prodigious and she never seemed to stop working. However, her journal contains regrets that life at primitive Port Phillip was so different to that in London or at Gordon Castle. In the six years from 1841 (in which she kept her now-famous journal), she sometimes wrote of her financial worries and her homesickness for Scotland. On hearing of a friend who was going 'home', she commented 'Lucky she!' When the little stone heart, given her by James Hoy, the Duke's librarian, fell on the floor and broke into tiny fragments, she commented sadly, using the old

French proverb *Tout passe, tout casse, tout lasse* (Everything changes, everything breaks, everything becomes wearisome).

But moments of despair were brief. To overcome these feelings, she threw herself into plans, projects, designs and entertainments with an infectious enjoyment of life that shows in much of her writing.

Georgiana had another child and this time her medico brother-in-law, Dr McCrae delivered it. Her insensitive husband slept through the entire birth and his brother had to wake him up to tell him that he had a fine daughter, whom they named Lucia.

The fact that Georgiana was a Duke's daughter, coupled with her striking good looks and lively personality, ensured that her debut into the snobbish, enclosed world of Melbourne society caused comment. She still had a graceful figure, gleaming dark hair and brilliant eyes under dark eyebrows that winged upwards towards her temples. Her sense of humour was undiminished and her laughter infectious. Her diary shows that she derived much amusement from the social climbing which went on in the tiny, cloistered circle that was Melbourne, but she was never bitter, malicious or judgmental about the behaviour of others. Her comments on the first days of the colony of Victoria are of enormous historical importance.

Georgiana described the social life of early Melbourne, which was very different from the splendour of the Highland balls at Gordon Castle. Four balls were held each year in Melbourne. Everyone wore full evening dress, and all applicants for tickets were vetted by a committee, to make certain they were free from the dreaded 'convict taint'. Georgiana recorded in her journal that

> At 10 pm we went en masse to the Mechanics Institute. All the elite of the colony assembled including Mr and Mrs La Trobe, Charles Hotson Ebden, the Mayor and his niece, dressed in Praying Mantis Green, looking not unlike the insect itself in the waltzing position.

Andrew McCrae had the misfortune to arrive with very little capital and to miss out on the first land sales, which made some of the people the McCraes associated with very rich indeed. Later Andrew attempted once again to speculate in land but lost money on most of his blocks[16] except for four small blocks of land at Alberton. He knew virtually nothing about sheep-farming, which was the other main way of acquiring wealth in the colony at the time. Although the McCraes never had much money to spend on entertaining, Georgiana was an excellent and imaginative hostess. She was so amusing and such a capable planner that people loved coming to her *fortune-du-pot* or pot luck dinners. After dinner she sang German and Scottish folk songs to her guests in her pleasing mezzo-soprano voice and played Schubert impromptus, Chopin preludes, and French ballades. Georgiana had guests to dinner practically every night but the high costs of bush hospitality used to worry her.

Georgiana engaged a tutor for her sons—John McLure, an Oxford arts graduate who was devoted to her. Later, when they were in financial trouble, she paid him his annual wages of fifty pounds and he insisted on returning ten pounds to her. He stayed with the family through all their troubles until the boys finished their schooling.

Knowing her sons' education was in good hands, Georgiana put all her creative energies into designing and building *Mayfield* using stone from the land and bricks specially imported from Scotland.[17] She also designed a superb garden which sloped down to the river. Lieutenant-Governor La Trobe, who had become a family friend, came to show the gardener how to set out Mr William Wentworth's vine cuttings and Charles La Trobe also gave her some Swiss vine cuttings from *Jolimont* to plant. She methodically listed in her diary all the plants and vegetables in the new garden.

By 1842, a year after her arrival, the house was finally habitable. They moved in

Lonsdale Street, Port Phillip, where Andrew McCrae rented a small shack for Georgiana and the children on her arrival. The hut in the centre where the maid is feeding poultry was occupied by their friend Captain William Lonsdale, other new arrivals are still in tents. Private collection, courtesy Christie's Sydney.

among the plasterers and painters but the main sitting room still had no floor or plastered walls. The doors and window frames were made of Manning River cedar, the skirting boards were cedar, the floors were pine, and the roof was covered in slate. All the glass for the windows had to be imported since none was available in Melbourne. While they were waiting for it to arrive, Georgiana stretched unbleached cotton over the windows to keep out the insects. The handsome house and property was named *Mayfield*, from the may trees planted in the garden. It had 610mm-thick walls to keep out the heat, and long French windows opening onto a wide verandah where she could draw and paint and the children could play. Unfinished and not very large, *Mayfield* seemed a mansion after the horrors of *Argyle Cottage*. At long last Georgiana had a home of her own, designed to her own plans. She was delighted.

The plasterers started work on 31 May and by the middle of September the plastered walls had dried out in the 'large room' and they were able to have pleasant dinner parties with music. Having her own home made Georgiana feel secure and contented. But other drawbacks associated with pioneering continued. It was impossible to buy an iron stove in early Melbourne and they had to order one from Britain. Until it arrived they cooked on a trivet over an open fire. According to Georgiana, the road to *Mayfield* was 'an everlasting chain of bog-holes, with figures of eight and many deviations due to fallen trees; only the first mile from town is in repair'.

Georgiana's closest friends were Governor La Trobe and his delicate Swiss wife, Sophie. She had first visited them at Jolimont, their prefabricated cottage two weeks after her arrival in Melbourne, as an obligatory social courtesy call, since Andrew McCrae, as an ambitious lawyer, was keen for her to make their acquaintance. Charles La Trobe had written several books about his travels in America, Switzerland and Mexico. He was a talented artist and a keen amateur musician, an unusual choice for a colonial governor, being more of a cultured intellectual and a creative man than a public servant. He was often pilloried by the Melbourne press for his elegant manners and desire to please everybody. Sophie La Trobe was homesick for Switzerland and her family home. She was delighted to find a friend who spoke

162

French fluently. The two women would sit in the Governor's cottage on warm afternoons sipping claret and water and talking in French. They gave each other support when dealing with the childhood illnesses with which Melbourne was plagued, since they both lacked the soothing counsel of older family members.

The McCrae children suffered from dysentery and the normal childhood ailments. Alexander (Sandy) also caught a disease similar to chickenpox, known by the Aborigines as 'dibble-dibble', and Georgiana nursed him devotedly, applying lotion to his face frequently to ward against scarring. She recorded in her diary that dysentery and cholera were the main causes of death of young children in the Melbourne area.

Shortly after *Mayfield* had been completed, Georgiana moved out of the matrimonial bedroom and started to use the former dining room as her bedroom, indicating considerable tension between her and Andrew. This step may have been the result of a bitter disagreement caused by Andrew's dismissal of Lizzie, her servant. Andrew believed Lizzie was trying to 'trap his tutor into matrimony' and that John McLure would marry her, leave them and establish his own school, so the poor girl was sent packing against Georgiana's wishes. She described how she did not dare to tell Lizzie the real cause of her dismissal and complained that she had 'lost her right hand helper and companion'. At the time Andrew was often away in town on business, dining at the Port Phillip Club and spending money which would have been wiser to have used to pay off their land. But they entertained frequently for Andrew's clients and her own friends. Georgiana painted the portrait of the thirty-two-year-old merchant and financier Octavius Browne, who was to marry the daughter of her friends James and Lucia Cummings. The portrait was not painted for money but as a wedding gift. Georgiana portrayed the engaging Octavius Browne as an energetic colonial bushman in a red flannel shirt and moleskin trousers with his waterbottle strapped to his belt. The costume was possibly intended as a joke for his fiancée by the young, art-loving merchant banker. Octavius was the brother of Dickens' artist, Hablot Browne (better known as Phiz), and a close friend and patron of Conrad Martens.[18] Georgiana made a quick and vivid preliminary watercolour sketch before she painted the full portrait in oils.

For the next year Georgiana was busy decorating her house and completing the garden. Then, at the end of 1842, Andrew's partner, James Montgomery, proposed a dissolution of their legal partnership. According to Montgomery's brother, who recorded Andrew speaking without caution after drinking too much wine at one of Georgiana's dinners, 'Mr Montgomery complains that he is left to do all the work, while Mr McCrae is amusing himself. Mr McCrae retorted that he himself created the business and kept it alive through civilities to all the clients.' This statement is recorded by Georgiana in her diary and indicates Andrew was spending too much time drinking with his chums in the Port Phillip Club (later he spent his time drinking and gambling with the gentlemen members of the Melbourne Club).

Georgiana was worried about the dissolution of the practice, but since it revived her hopes that the family might return to Scotland, she was not that displeased. She even wrote an amusing poem on the subject entitled 'Farewell mosquitos, ants and flies!'

Hope of returning home faded when Georgiana discovered their true financial position and that they would leave empty-handed as they were so heavily in debt. 'Mr McCrae, in a despondent mood, tells me what I had a suspicion of two days ago, that our prospects of ever leaving Australia Felix is becoming day by day more indistinct.'

When she wrote this, affairs in Melbourne were going from bad to worse because of the dramatic slump in wool prices. Finally Andrew had to break to her the dreadful news that they were on the verge of bankruptcy 'due to the insolvency of the clients of the firm [of McCrae and Montgomery]'. Melbourne's fragile, credit-based economy was dangerously near to collapse. Finally the practice of McCrae and Montgomery was dissolved in a welter of recriminations.

Things grew steadily worse. Andrew had been even more improvident than Georgiana had been led to believe. As he had arrived with very little capital, they had only leased the land *Mayfield* was built on, and paid the building costs with more money borrowed from Dr Charles Nicholson, the owner of the land. Andrew had gone deeper and deeper into debt and now Dr Nicholson claimed *Mayfield* in lieu of his unpaid rent, which amounted to the price of the land and two cash advances. The elusive Andrew had not told Georgiana the full extent of his borrowings. Legally a wife had no right to money of her own at this period and Georgiana had given her husband the small sum bequeathed by her mother's sister, Aunt Margaret, 'to invest in a house for me', and money she had saved when she was a professional artist. He had lost the entire amount.

Georgiana had longed for security—for a home of her own in which to bring up her children after so many rented houses. Designing her first real home had been an outlet for her creative energy and a display of her talent. But now it was clear that they did not have the money to pay for the rent to Dr Nicholson, much less their return passage to London. This caused more quarrels between Georgiana and Andrew, and a change in their mode of living.

Household expenses were drastically cut, Ellen, the maid, converted mutton fat into candles and slush lamps and Georgiana made all the family's clothes out of cast-off and second-hand garments. Even though they had no money, she continued to help those worse off than herself.

Andrew, stressed by their financial difficulties and the rupture with his partner, quarrelled with his brother, Farquhar and issued an edict that little Farquhar, named after his uncle, was now to be known by his second name of Peregrine, or Perry.

Eventually Georgiana realised that for the sake of the children, her only chance of retaining *Mayfield* was to write to the Duchess and ask her 'to purchase this house and land as a permanent home for myself and my children'. She enclosed a plan of the grounds and the house and told the Duchess that 'by advancing me the money for the property now, the outlay will be worth double to me what the sum would be at your decease'.

Andrew doubted that the Duchess would send her money and told her that they must become pioneers, taking up a cattle run of seven square miles on the Jamieson Survey at the foot of Arthurs Seat on the Mornington Peninsula. They were to leave *Mayfield* and their relatively civilised way of life and go off into the bush to try and make money. However, Andrew lacked farming experience; he had been a lawyer in an office for many years and had only the haziest notion of running cattle and living off the land.

Georgiana loathed the idea. She was five months pregnant but Andrew insisted that she ride the 85 kilometres out through dense bush to Arthurs Seat to look over their new 12,800 acre (5,820 hectare) run. She knew the two-day journey was dangerous for her and the unborn baby and was furious when Andrew said 'that he can't afford to pay for a conveyance, so that I and mine must take our chance'. She was even more angry when an overhanging branch swept her off her pony. She clung to the tree branch, waiting for Andrew to rescue her. He dragged her down so clumsily that she was injured. He then insisted that she remount and continue the journey to their nearest neighbour, Captain Reid, who lived 16 kilometres away.

'After seven hours in the saddle I had reason to dread the effects of the wrench in my side,' she wrote. The clumsy rescue attempt resulted in a difficult and painful pregnancy. Georgiana wrote that she 'suffered unusually' when she gave birth to

Margaret, or little Maggie, who was born at *Mayfield* after Andrew had departed for Arthurs Seat.

She was even more miserable to find that both her husband and her children had totally forgotten her fortieth birthday, always a critical age for a woman. The only thing to cheer her up was the arrival of a box, fortunately already paid for, containing clothes and books sent from England by daughter Lucia's godmother, Mrs Lucia Cummings, who had purchased for Georgiana a woollen dress and cape, a straw bonnet already trimmed, two dozen gloves, an umbrella, cotton, needles and pins—all difficult to obtain in early colonial Australia. Knowing they were dear to Georgiana's heart, Lucia had also sent her a large quantity of the latest books on art and architecture which could not be obtained locally.

Andrew received a lump sum payment for an outstanding debt from his Edinburgh practice. This enabled Georgiana to stay on at *Mayfield* until June 1844 with the youngest boys and the baby. Andrew, John McLure and the eldest boys set themselves up in primitive conditions at Arthurs Seat, happy as Boy Scouts on a camping trip. Meanwhile Georgiana prepared to leave behind three years' hard work with absolutely no financial gain to show for it. They were not unique in this situation as the spirit of the time made pioneer settlers invest everything in sheep and cattle and lease land rather than buy it.

Georgiana soon recovered her optimistic outlook and started to design the family's new home at Arthurs Seat. Once again she packed up all the household goods and some seeds for the new garden, and, even though she was leaving, methodically planted some melon seeds at *Mayfield*, wondering 'For whom will they bear fruit?' Life which had been settled and orderly with friends and family in the pleasant surroundings of *Mayfield* once again became disorganised and insecure.

There was a delay as the vessel on which they were to sail was held up by contrary winds. In her diary Georgiana wrote:

> We are to sail tonight. Thomas and Stribling have carted two loads of packages to the boat and a third load is now waiting for the dray. If I had a free choice in this matter I should remain at *Mayfield* until the house is sold or let. There is a living to be had here through my art of miniature painting, for which I have already several orders in hand, but I dare not oppose the family's [the McCraes] wishes that money must not be made in that way. At Arthurs Seat we have only huts and no house built for the reception of ourselves and our furniture and poultry, by this trip of the boat.

The passage about the family's opposition to her painting professionally is echoed in another letter where she commented that they violently opposed her idea of earning money by painting but noted wryly that they had not minded her doing it before she was married. The situation arose because Georgiana had received a request from Mrs Howitt to paint portraits of her children for a handsome fee. The denial of Georgiana's creativity fuelled more violent discussions with her husband.

But in the end Andrew triumphed. Since there were no roads, Georgiana embarked on the sailing boat *Jemima* bound for Arthurs Seat on the Mornington Peninsula. On board were three thousand bricks.

The Duchess coldly refused Georgiana's request for an advance against her legacy, informing her, through their mutual friend Mr Cummings, that she would send 'one hundred pounds for your immediate need as house purchase in such a depressed colony was a poor investment'.

Mayfield was sold by Dr Charles Nicholson, the owner of the leased land on which they had built. The McCraes received not one penny for all the money and hard work they had put into building *Mayfield* and improvements to the property. Although Georgiana did not know this at the time, Andrew had lied to her

Jolimont, the portable wooden cottage which acted as home to Georgiana's friends Governor Charles La Trobe and his wife Sophie, painted at the request of the Macarthur family by Conrad Martens, probably after a drawing by Edward La Trobe Bateman. Courtesy private collection.

Below: Georgiana McCrae's plans and the front elevation which she drew up for the builder of their small and inexpensive cottage on the Mornington Peninsula. Georgiana drew up the builders' plans for her homes at Mayfield and McCrae Cottage and detailed the position of the furniture in each room. Courtesy Mrs. Barbara Blomfield.

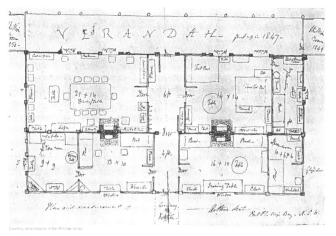

consistently about their finances. She must have been furious to discover he had used the money and speculated in land in New Zealand and lost it. Dr Nicholson (later Sir Charles) had also loaned Andrew money and been tolerant for a long time over Andrew's inability to repay the debt.

The new owner eventually subdivided the nine-acre block, sold half the land and made a handsome profit as Georgiana had wished to do. Georgiana's feelings towards the Duchess and her own future can only be guessed. It meant a fresh start with no capital when she and Andrew were in their forties, an age when the majority of her friends were established in a secure way of life.

She and her husband arrived at the cattle run at Arthurs Seat on a wild night, with the wind blowing a howling gale and driving the chilly rain into her face. She was horrified to find the tutor, the two eldest boys and a servant, living in a collection of smoky turf huts without chimneys, which were in constant danger of catching fire. It was even worse than *Argyle Cottage*. There was no neighbouring settlement even of bark huts or humpies; no shops and no friends or in-laws for comfort. She spent her first night at Arthurs Seat in a draughty bark hut sleeping on a damp mattress on a mud floor with insects crawling over her. She wrote:

> Neither Mr McCrae nor Mr McLure seem to have thought about hearths, each fireplace being hearthless, with great risk in a wind of the house burning down . . . The paths between the huts have become a mass of mire and there is nothing for us to do but stay inside . . . I am most unhappy . . . the last six months of suspense, worry, hurry, delays, packing and unpacking, detention in town [waiting for suitable wind for the ship to sail] and now this scattered way of living has worn me out.

She designed the kitchen, as was customary, well away from the house to avoid risk of fire, with an outside oven for baking and roasting. The primitive privy was also outside. To save money there were no covered walkways between them for protection against rain, wind or sun. The house had a superb view over Port Phillip Bay and a small dressing-room and studio combined for Georgiana off the main bedroom, which she named her Sanctum and where she set up her easel. An orchard was established and Georgiana continued to plant and cultivate vegetables for table use.

Georgiana McCrae's drawing of her cottage on the Mornington Peninsula. The kitchen is separate to minimise fire risks. A small bread oven is built into the wall to the left of one water barrel. La Trobe Library, Manuscrips Section, McCrae Collection.

Housekeeping in an area with the nearest shops 80 kilometres away presented its own problems and it was necessary to plan extremely well for the monthly shopping trips when the dray, drawn by four oxen, went to Melbourne for supplies.

With a family of eight boisterous children, Georgiana must have found *McCrae Cottage* hideously cramped, particularly during the winter when bad weather forced the children to remain indoors. Because of lack of space, the two youngest children had to sleep with the new baby in the matrimonial bedroom, which by modern standards seems very small. Two more girls named Frances Gordon (Fanny) born in June 1847 and her last child Agnes Thomasine, who arrived on 27 March 1851, were born in this tiny cottage. No doctor attended at their birth and Georgiana had only the servant girl to deliver her babies. Fortunately both of the births were uncomplicated.

The McCrae family became friendly with the Bunorong people who visited the area in summer—their finest hunter, Benbenjie, joined in the boys' hunting and boating expeditions and taught the boys a great deal about Aboriginal skills of tracking and hunting. Georgiana painted a sympathetic portrait of a fine-looking Bunorong girl, Eliza, who sometimes helped with the washing and other household tasks, and a companion miniature of Benbenjie. The Bunorong returned every year to fish and the McCraes grew especially fond of Eliza and Benbenjie and a younger boy named Johnnie.

In summer they moved the piano onto the verandah where the Bunorong people, when camped close to the cottage, enjoyed Georgiana playing Schubert, Schumann and Chopin from sheet music she had brought from Gordon Castle. She also enjoyed playing and singing hauntingly sad Scottish ballads. Georgiana and her favourite son George compiled a vocabulary of the language of the Bunorong. With her customary kindness Georgiana sheltered Myrnong, a young Aboriginal woman running away from an elderly husband to join her lover. Georgiana recorded that 'a young lubra in her possum rug, her eyes beseeching pity and her finger on her lip' had been discovered hiding in terror in her bedroom. 'I whispered to her asking what she did there . . . but all she said was "Moonie find me!" and in an almost inaudible cry, "Moonie kill me!" I could not bid her go out and be murdered.' Georgiana let Myrnong sleep with her in her bedroom and would have kept her longer but at dawn the girl stole out of the room so softly that Georgiana did not hear her.

When little Johnnie, his former playmate, died of tuberculosis, George Gordon was heartbroken. He and Georgiana built a cairn of stones in Johnnie's memory. In summer the children swam every morning and did their lessons while Georgiana sat in her little studio-dressing-room, painted delicate miniatures of her children and wrote up her journal. She described how different it all was to Gordon Castle:

> Our house is built of gum-tree slabs, supported by grooved corner posts. The biggest room has been furnished with a table and chairs but no pictures. Instead [of pictures] long lines of the actual landscape appear at the interstices between the planks.

The days passed pleasantly for the boys and Andrew, mustering horses and cattle, shooting and fishing. Georgiana was an excellent horsewoman and she sometimes joined her husband and the boys for the mustering. It was fortunate that her children and their future prospects were now far more important to her than acquiring wealth or possessions. Teaching George to draw and listening to him read some of his own writing was one of Georgiana's great pleasures. The children were all intelligent, healthy, high-spirited and good-looking. They fished by moonlight with the faithful McLure, and on still nights she heard the sound of their oars splash in the water as they manoeuvred their boat away from the shore.

Georgiana, the elegant and cultured Edinburgh artist, gradually adapted and lived happily enough as a pioneer in the wilds of the Australian bush. Andrew was the traditional father—reading prayers every morning with the family and servants in attendance. Georgiana described how he was in better health since he had taken to horseback riding and gardening. As always they had no spending money but bush housekeeping was cheap. They ate salted beef, varied by wild duck or roast kangaroo. She described how 'the fish commonly caught are flathead.

These dressed on the coals seem to my taste as good as Finnan haddies [smoked haddock]'.

Many friends came to visit the family including Governor Charles La Trobe. He found Georgiana in the kitchen with an apron full of coffee berries. He helped her grind them and make coffee. For some strange reason Andrew refused to meet the Governor and insisted on going away to a mountain hermitage he had constructed for himself. He only returned when the Governor had left which was signalled to him by means of the display of a white sheet. Could Andrew have been jealous? La Trobe often made long trips by himself due to his wife's poor health.

With her medicine chest brought from London, Georgiana rapidly acquired the skill of 'medicine woman' among the Aborigines, who brought their sick children to her for help. She was also forced to doctor her own children for childhood ailments. It was now impossible to take them the 80 kilometres to see Dr Thomas Cole in Melbourne who had previously delivered one of her children.[19] She became proficient at treating minor injuries, boils and ophthalmia or sandy-blight and even scarlatina. The worst emergency occurred when the powder flask blew up in George's hand, leaving the top joint of his little finger hanging by a thread. She put it back on and washed and dressed the wound, but eventually George had to be sent by dray to stay with Dr Cole, a distant relation by marriage.

Toothache could also be a problem and Georgiana recorded how she travelled with three children to Melbourne in 'our coach and six' which was a dray drawn by six bullocks. 'Willie was in misery because of the toothache and I had a difficult time keeping the wind off his face.' Two sea-chests covered with mattresses made comfortable seats for their journey but it was unbearably slow. They stayed overnight in a primitive shepherd's hut where they spread the mattresses over the floor, but finding these too hard Georgiana got up and crouched by the fire with Fanny, the baby, in her lap. She spent the rest of the night awake, ravaged by fleas, and envied the hut's owner, Grandmother Davey, who was fast asleep on a box of rags.

On Sunday, 11 November 1850, she arrived at *Jolimont*, the small wood and brick cottage owned by the La Trobes and which was to be used as Victoria's first Government House. She was to spend a short holiday with the Governor and his wife and had frequently visited Sophie La Trobe there when they lived in Melbourne and spent happy afternoons when Sophie was well, sipping claret and talking French.

The Mayor arrived while they were all at dinner to say that the Separation Bill, making Victoria an independent colony, had just passed through both Houses. La Trobe gave permission for the town to celebrate that night by lighting bonfires. Unfortunately the whole town went mad and many trees were burnt down by the excited populace.

Friday, 16 November was to be 'a historic day full of surprises and excitements', wrote Georgiana. 'Promptly at 6.00 am a band composed of horns and saxophones began to play a reveille to Charles La Trobe, who was about to be declared Lieutenant Governor of the infant colony of Victoria.' Out of courtesy he appeared to greet the band on the balcony at *Jolimont*, and Georgiana joined him there. They were both in their dressing-gowns. Sophie La Trobe had previously had a bad fall from her carriage and since then had suffered from violent migraines, triggered by noise and excitement. Sophie had 'one of her neuralgic headaches and would gladly have forgone that part of the programme' and asked her husband to stop the band playing. Georgiana recorded how 'he held my sleeve' (this intimate gesture appears in Hugh McCrae's edited version of the diary but not in Georgiana's expurgated copy). Was this a detail Georgiana had related to George, Hugh's father, which he added to spice up the story or was it a proof of the strength of her affection for La Trobe? There is never any mention of Andrew touching her, or of any of her emotions for

Georgiana's sympathetic portrait of Eliza, an Aboriginal girl who came to their home on the Mornington Peninsula every summer and helped her with the children. Private collection. Reproduction, courtesy Christopher Deutcher Fine Art, Melbourne.

Opposite: *Two very different unsigned lithographs show the opening of the Prince's Bridge in Melbourne, where Georgiana McCrae took the place of Charles La Trobe's wife Sophie. Georgiana's appearance at the Governor's lady caused spiteful comment and speculation over the extent of their relationship. Private collection.*

him, and the portrait that she painted of her husband lacks the deep insight of some of her paid commissions.

By now Sophie La Trobe, 'upset by the saxhorn and fearful of cannonading', asked Georgiana to act as her deputy at the historic opening of the Princes Bridge. Georgiana was delighted to deputise as La Trobe's official consort at the ceremony and wrote happily, 'Behold me now, equipped in Madame's black satin jacket, trimmed with Australian swansdown and my own grey silk bonnet'.

Charles La Trobe, tall and handsome in full ceremonial uniform handed Georgiana into the official carriage, followed by himself and his children and their French governess. 'Snugly packed together we drove to the Treasury,' she wrote. Here La Trobe took over the reins and they drove through Swanston and Collins Streets and took up their official position in front of the Prince of Wales Hotel. At midday the children's governess, who had been watching the hill through her opera glasses, exclaimed 'that she saw smoke and there was a prodigious noise of guns, the signal for them to set out for the bridge'. La Trobe gathered up the reins and proceeded at a majestic pace until they reached the middle of the bridge which La Trobe officially pronounced open, saying that 'it had been produced by Port Phillip materials and Port Phillip money'.

Georgiana was obviously thoroughly enjoying herself in the role of the Governor's lady. She recorded:

> We were passed by a procession of Freemasons, and each man as he went forward ducked his head to Madame, whose double, in the black satin jacket replied with the most gracious salaams. At the summit of the hill La Trobe alighted and, standing by the flap of the tent, again spoke a few words suitable to the occasion. On the return journey a few spots of rain made me anxious on account of Madame's best jacket which had already been stickied by Nellie's saved-up bun . . . When we arrived the wind blew through the house throwing the doors open and the children made so much noise shutting them again that poor Mrs La Trobe once more retired to bed. The servants were still absent enjoying the celebrations but the gardeners' helping-man brought in a round of roast beef with vegetables and on these we dined *en famille* most heartily.

Georgiana was still at *Jolimont* two weeks later and attended the official ball held to celebrate Victoria's separation from New South Wales. Presumably Andrew was with her but she does not mention him although he had been involved in preparations for this important event. All the guests were in fancy dress. The evening was a pleasant one with a large company, a good band and plenty to eat and drink—Geelong champagne, Harper's brandy and local wines and beer being served.

However, gossip and speculation had been generated by Georgiana standing in for the Governor's wife at such an important social function. La Trobe was extremely unpopular with some of the colonists and with members of the town council. The Governor had already been attacked in the press and in printed satirical lampoons and verses for failing to support Port Phillip's needs strongly enough in Sydney and London.

The newspapers took four days' holiday after the opening of the Princes Bridge, the highlight of Victoria's independence celebrations. During this time, while the printing presses were lying idle, a printed *pasquinade* or broadsheet appeared denouncing La Trobe for taking his mistress to the ceremony. Copies were circulated around the town, rolled up in tubes known as pipes. The pipes must have caused distress to both families. The lampoon was unsigned and even had they known who had printed it, legal action would have meant more unwelcome publicity.[20]

Presumably both the McCraes and the La Trobes decided to ignore the pipes and to take no further action so that the scandal would die a natural death. While Georgiana may have found La Trobe highly attractive, he loved Sophie and Georgiana was good friends with both of them. Even though her own marriage was now unravelling fast, an affair between her and the Governor seems unlikely.

Some time after returning to Arthurs Seat Georgiana was injured during a storm. As the storm arrived, Georgiana locked the door. Her husband, finding it locked, angrily beat the door in with his bare fists, not realising that she was standing behind it holding baby Maggie in her right arm. She wrote:

> The door burst inwards and, striking my forehead with terrific force, threw me on to the ground. Mr McCrae did all he could for me, Sarah being too shocked at the appearance of the wound to dress it. Had I carried dear little Maggie on my left arm, instead of my right, she must have been killed on the spot, for Mr McCrae had struck the heavy blackwood door a tremendous blow, as the blood upon his knuckles could attest.

She suffered a black eye which swelled up and she had blinding headaches for several days. After that there were no ill effects, but she must have blamed her husband for it.

Georgiana and her family spent seven years at Arthurs Seat. She worked hard, continually making and remaking clothes, organising the house and the children's free time, ordering stores, painting and writing when she had time between household and motherly duties. One dreadful night a lamp overturned and the bedroom curtains caught fire and charred a self-portrait of Georgiana, painted at Gordon Castle. Fortunately the fire was put out before it burnt the house down. The house was threatened again on 'Black Thursday' in 1851 when bushfires blazed along the entire coast of Victoria from Cape How to the South Australian border and the air was filled with acrid smoke and wood-ash. George Gordon McCrae was then eighteen, and went to fight the fire. Fortunately their house was spared.

Seven years after Georgiana's bleak arrival, Arthurs Seat had become a delightful home and Georgiana felt secure again. The little house had a rustic charm and atmosphere enhanced by their fine Georgian furniture and some pieces that bush carpenters had made for them. Friends who came by sea or on horseback to visit them found the view over the crescent of the bay delightful and *McCrae Cottage* charming and comfortable, even though it was much smaller than *Mayfield*.

After so much effort expended on designing and building their little homestead, life on the land did not succeed financially for the McCraes. Andrew was a poor cattle farmer: there are continuous references in letters and Georgiana's diary to cattle breaking their legs and having to be shot, or wandering away and getting lost. One of the bullocks succeeded in hanging himself from a cherry tree while trapped between the shafts of the dray when no-one was watching the poor beast.

Then on 6 October 1851, Georgiana related how the whole secure world she had built around her family was about to collapse again, leaving only more financial worry.

> A deeper sorrow has fastened at my heart, since the time has now arrived when I must say good-bye to my mountain home, the house I have built and lived in, the trees I have planted, the garden I have formed. This run of ours would do for a flock . . . but, without four or five hundred pounds, one cannot purchase sheep free from disease. What our own, or our children's future prospect here, or at home, are likely to be remains in the clouds.

Andrew had decided that they would never make money as pioneer cattle farmers on the Mornington Peninsula. He joined the ranks of other 'unfortunate squatters and ruined gentlemen' who obtained official positions as police magistrates on the goldfields, through the patronage of Governor La Trobe.

This was no sinecure. Andrew was overqualified for such a position with his legal experience and the pay was certainly not enormous. However, a basic dwelling without water supply came with the position. The boys visited their father in October 1852 and described his residence as 'a miserable place consisting of twenty habitations huddled together, a low marshy coast covered in mangrove'. In summer Andrew's servant had to go over a kilometre to fetch water.

It was at this juncture that the McCraes' lives began to divide. Arthurs Seat was sold for one thousand pounds, not an enormous sum, and Georgiana and the children returned to Melbourne on the chartered ketch *Diamond*. With their limited capital and the children's education to think about, they could not afford to buy a home and rented a terrace house at La Trobe Street West. In January 1852 Georgiana wrote to friends in Scotland saying that she hoped to remain in Melbourne 'for the little girls' sakes'. This was now their sixth matrimonial home and she had borne Andrew nine children.

There was a probability that they would all have to go to Alberton where Andrew was installed in a primitive government dwelling. It was the parting of the ways. Georgiana considered that she and the growing girls had had enough of pioneering, living in houses without sanitation or water, in areas lacking medical facilities. Agnes, the baby of the family, had always been a delicate child and in Melbourne Georgiana had doctors in her husband's family whom she could call upon. She had no shortage of friends in Melbourne, she was longing for a more stable life and a permanent home for her children and was tired of fighting with Andrew.

By the time Georgiana returned to Melbourne, it had changed considerably. She recounted how prices for food and housing had more than doubled and how 'every man must be his own footman, shoeblack and knife-cleaner', (since the blades of knives were not stainless steel, they blackened after every meal).

Georgiana's beloved youngest daughter, Agnes, brought Georgiana great sorrow and suffering when she died in Melbourne a few weeks before her third birthday. At the time Andrew was away on the goldfields and Georgiana had to cope alone. It brought back the agony of her first-born daughter dying at approximately the same age in Scotland. As Agnes lay dying her mother made a beautiful and poignant sketch of the daughter she was unable to save. As a further record of her last child a plaster portrait medallion by the well-known pre-Raphaelite sculptor Thomas Woolner was commissioned by Georgiana. Woolner had arrived in Victoria with Edward La Trobe Bateman to seek his fortune on the goldfields but returned to Melbourne disillusioned and penniless. Georgiana invited him to her artistic dinners and, generous as ever, she and her friend Edith Howitt helped Woolner find commissions in order to pay his return passage back to London, where he eventually became a famous sculptor.

As a police magistrate, Andrew was constantly being transferred from place to place. Finally he settled at Kilmore, where he became Warden of the Goldfields for 17 years as well as Commissioner for Crown Lands. He visited Melbourne whenever he could to see their children. Georgiana had decided that their marriage was definitely not harmonious enough to join him on the goldfields and stayed on in North Melbourne, where her little terrace house was always full of visitors. She no longer had a studio, but played an important role in the Melbourne art scene encouraging younger artists like Edward La Trobe Bateman and Nicholas Chevalier. It is interesting that Louisa Meredith, the artist and writer, visited Georgiana on her trip to Melbourne. Introduced through her neighbour, the mother of Arthur Loureiro, the Portuguese artist who painted Georgiana's portrait, the two creative women found they shared many ideas in common including their remarkable intelligence and power over words as well as paint. Louisa's portrait by Georgiana is a tribute to the friendship of two extraordinary women of achievement. But Louisa's husband placed no obstacles in the way of her creativity.

Just as Georgiana returned to Melbourne, Sophie La Trobe's headaches grew unbearable and she was advised to return home to Switzerland for specialised medical treatment. Charles La Trobe offered his resignation as Governor since he wished to accompany his beloved wife. However, it was not accepted as no suitable replacement could be found for him at short notice. The control of crime both on the goldfields and in the goldrush town of Melbourne, and the issue of miners' licences which brought about the Eureka Stockade rebellion, gave La Trobe enormous administrative problems. He was caught between the demands of the squatters, his social peer group, who demanded undisturbed possession of the runs they had leased or purchased, and the demands of the diggers to go anywhere they liked in search of gold. Charles La Trobe incurred the anger of both groups, losing some friends and his beloved wife at the time he needed them most.

Sophie died at her family home in Switzerland in January 1854, but Charles La Trobe had already been a virtual widower for a protracted period. He had no background of administration and, although highly intelligent, he often lacked self-confidence. Georgiana, with her warm and compassionate nature, would undoubtedly have offered her sympathies. Since they were both alone their long friendship was of great comfort to them during the long and lonely period before La Trobe was able to return to Switzerland. Charles La Trobe was several years younger than her, and in some ways resembled Perico Gordon. Possibly she thought he represented the type of creative, artistic man she should have married.

Following the deaths of Agnes and Sophie and a bad fall in 1859 which left her lame, her creativity appears to have withered and she did not paint for a long period. Georgiana was now fifty-five and for part of the year she suffered intense pain in her hip. Her published journal tails away on her return to Melbourne. But family members relate how a second journal which, at her request, was burnt by her son George, because it might hurt the descendants of important people. A series of intimate letters were also burnt by an unmarried female descendant.[21] What light they may have thrown on her feelings for Perico Gordon or Governor La Trobe and the reasons she finally decided on a separation from Andrew will never be known.

Although Georgiana made over eighty miniatures and pencil portraits in Australia, as well as numerous landscape and botanical sketches, she never attained the fame which should have been hers. Undoubtedly she was one of the best, if not the best, portrait artist in the colony of Victoria during the nineteenth century. She exhibited again in 1857 with the Victorian Society of Fine Arts in the company of Chevalier, von Guerard and other talented artists. On 4 December 1857 Georgiana was praised by the *Argus* for the quality of her work. 'We have seen no miniatures in the colony comparable with those exhibited by Mrs McCrae, while the pencil and water-colour drawings that accompany them are full of talent.'[22]

Nicholas Chevalier was such a good friend that Georgiana jestingly referred to him as 'her adopted son'. The two artists met when she visited his studio where they discussed techniques of painting. Chevalier was tall and handsome, a clever and amusing raconteur. He could speak French fluently and had lived in Switzerland. Like Georgiana he too had exhibited at the Royal Academy in London, and she enjoyed a feast of art gossip. When back in London, Nicholas Chevalier sent Georgiana vivid accounts of his own success in the Royal Academy Summer Exhibitions and the visit of Queen Victoria to his studio. The friendship between Georgiana, Nicholas and his wife Carrie, who was a prolific correspondent, continued for twenty years. Georgiana was also friendly with the Portuguese-born

Portrait of Louisa Anne Meredith, 1860. Georgina McCrae (born in England 1804, arrived in Australia 1841, and died in 1890) has presented her fellow writer and artist as an intelligent woman with considerable strength of character. Watercolour and pencil, 19.8 x 16.0 cm (oval format). Presented through The Art Foundation of Victoria by Mrs James Evans, Governor, 1989. National Gallery of Victoria, Melbourne.

artist Arthur de Souza Loureiro, who was married to a sister of the Australian writer Jessie Couvreur.

Until his marriage, Georgiana's favourite son George Gordon lived at home. Through him she had a great deal of contact with his friends from the Yorick Club, including poets and writers Henry Kendall, Marcus Clarke and Adam Lindsay Gordon, a distant kinsman. At this period the McCrae home was the centre of a group of amusing and intelligent young writers and artists. Money was always short but Georgiana's *fortune-du-pot* dinners were still greatly appreciated and her lively, witty comments at table made her a welcome member of their circle. George was a great source of comfort to her and took over the role of man about the house. She continued to spend a great deal of time with him and his wife after they were married. George was a gentle, kind man with the temperament of an artist who, for financial reasons, was forced into a career in the public service. Both George Gordon and his son Hugh (the Bohemian poet and writer who edited Georgiana's diary for publication) were creative artists and carried Georgiana's talents into wider fields. Her descendants form a distinguished dynasty of artists, architects and writers. Georgiana's sons and grandsons inherited the aristocratic Gordon good looks and charm; the girls were replicas of their mother with long dark hair, dark eyebrows and a natural charm and dignity of manner.

Georgiana's stepmother, Elizabeth, Duchess of Gordon never remarried. She travelled frequently to the Continent and became fat, imperious and totally obsessed by religion and missionary work, donating vast sums to various evangelical groups. When she died at Huntly Lodge on 31 January 1864 the news of her death took four months to reach Australia via her solicitors. Georgiana was devastated by the news that the Duchess had deceived her totally and left her fortune to the church, with no bequests whatsoever to her stepdaughter or her husband's grandchildren and, above all, nothing to George Gordon McCrae the Duke's favourite godson. The Duchess left money to the Duke's other illegitimate children, Susan and Charles, but failed to honour the promise she had made to Georgiana that on her death she would be amply recompensed for the loss of the bequest to her made by the Duke of Gordon in his unsigned will.

To make matters worse Andrew and Georgiana quarrelled and he was tactless enough to blame Georgiana for her illegitimacy. This hurtful blow on a sensitive matter sounded the death knell of their marriage. Georgiana started noting down opinions in her Commonplace Book on marriage and the rights of women. She found a book published in 1854 by an early American feminist author, Margaret Fuller Ossoli, on *Women in the Nineteenth Century* concerning the importance of a husband respecting his wife's actions and trying to understand her mind. It was fuel for her cause. She copied out passages from Margaret Fuller into her Commonplace Book as well as others which dealt with the breakdown of marriage

> whenever it clearly appears that man and wife can no longer live in peace and harmony, their separation would be far more beneficial to themselves and favourable to morals, than their compulsory union . . . if the union does not confer happiness it is an undoubted proof that they ought never to have been married.[23]

Public rejection in the Duchess's will in favour of the Duke's other illegitimate children, Mrs Susan Sordet and Admiral Charles Gordon, distressed Georgiana enormously. Not only had she believed the Duchess's promises that she would receive the legacy withheld from her father's will but she realised her omission from the Duchess's will would cause doubts in the minds of others about her right to be seen as a member of the Gordon family. The result was that Georgiana now became obsessional about the Gordons and their family history, copying out notes she had made in her adolescence from conversations with

James Hoy, the Duke's librarian. She wrote a family tree of the Gordon family and listed paintings in Gordon Castle which had been bequeathed to the fifth Duke's nephew, the former Duke of Richmond, who had subsequently taken the title of Duke of Richmond and Gordon and to William Brodie of Brodie Castle.[24]

At her insistence George Gordon McCrae took his long service leave and went to Britain to try to claim some portion of the inheritance his mother had been promised from the Duke's original bequest. His father's legal friends in Edinburgh dissuaded him from suing for a part of the Gordon estate because, although George searched diligently for missing documents to prove the existence of Jane Graham's marriage to the Duke, he found none. George Gordon McCrae returned to Melbourne having registered a claim to a small annuity. Even allowing for inflation it was only a fraction of the amount promised by the Duchess. It was to be all that Georgiana and her children received from the deceased estate of one of the richest women in Scotland, who had faithfully promised her husband that she would leave money to Georgiana but, instead, bequeathed it to various religious organisations.

Years later Andrew retired from the public service. By now they had drifted apart completely. The children had grown up. On 10 January 1867 nineteen-year-old Fanny, the youngest, had married the handsome Irishman George Watton Moore at a wedding attended by both parents.[25] But these appearances of family unity were merely social niceties, papering over the cracks in the McCraes' thirty-six years of marriage. Her daughters' marriage marked a watershed and now Georgiana knew she wanted a divorce or a legal separation. She had had enough of the McCraes whose pride had prevented her becoming a professional portrait painter. She had had more than enough of Andrew McCrae and his money-making schemes.

Georgiana consulted a lawyer about her marriage problems and a possible solution. Two weeks later Andrew told his niece, Thomas Anne Ward Cole,[26] that Georgiana was applying for a judicial separation. She may even have wanted a divorce, unusual though this was at the period. But with Charles La Trobe gone, there seems to have been no man in Melbourne who shared her interests other than her sons' friends, all decades younger than herself. There is no indication she had anyone else in mind when requesting a separation.

However, the McCrae family were outraged at Georgiana's conduct. Divorce or legal separation would have created a scandal leading to social ostracism and they were already facing another possible judicial separation in the family. Two would be disastrous. It could also have been very costly had Georgiana had someone else in mind. According to Halsbury's law on colonial marriage, Andrew would have had the option to sue any new man in Georgiana's life for alienation of his wife's affections. By now the Victorian Marriages and Matrimonial Causes Statute of 1864 had been in force for three years. In practice, the courts were still very cautious about granting legal separations to women. Andrew was a lawyer and knew how to work the system: he had not deserted his wife but gone to the goldfields with her consent. There were no grounds for adultery and such cruelty as there was had happened a long time ago while the new matrimonial laws were so heavily weighted against women that it allowed husbands to plead 'provocation by the wife' as grounds for their cruelty.

The tricky situation was resolved by Andrew McCrae returning to Scotland, although for years they continued to correspond regularly about matters relating to the children. Ironically, when Andrew finally retired from government service his pension was sufficient for him to travel overseas and visit France. It must have been galling to Georgiana, who spoke fluent French and loved French culture, that she lacked the money to fulfil her dream and travel there or revisit Gordon Castle and the scenes of her youth.

In 1874 Andrew returned to Victoria. He had mellowed considerably and derived enormous pleasure from the visits of his children and grandchildren. When he fell ill Georgiana nursed him devotedly through illness and pain until, months later, he died.

Georgiana decided that the time had come to take up painting professionally once again. She unpacked her folding palette and made several miniatures. However, she found it considerably more difficult to do the fine and delicate work in her seventies now that her eyesight was fading. She made several portraits and pen drawings, which were printed in Sydney and Melbourne magazines and newspapers and some larger watercolours.

By now she had little money, so gave up her rented house and stayed with old friends and with her children. She made frequent visits to *Barragunda*, the homestead at Cape Schank near Arthurs Seat, belonging to her great friend Edith Howitt, now married to Robert Anderson. The house was influenced by the French style and had architectural decorations and an exquisite formal garden designed by Georgiana's friend Edward La Trobe Bateman. In these gracious and happy surroundings both Georgiana and Louisa Meredith made a series of sketches, although by now Georgiana appears to have had arthritis or rheumatism in her fingers. At the age of seventy-four she talked about her fingers 'feeling dead'. Georgiana also stayed with her son George and his wife Augusta at Hawthorn but found the house cramped and noisy due to the presence of many young children. Occasionally she talked to her daughters about 'the happiest days of my life', referring to her broken romance with Perico Gordon and the happy days when she had visited him and his aunt at Wardhouse. Georgiana must have continually reflected how different her life would have been had the Duchess not ruined her chance of marrying Perico Gordon.

Georgiana's daughter Margaret lived nearby and had married Nicholas Maine, a solicitor. In her eighties, Georgiana, still an upright and erect lady but lame from the accident she had had in 1859, went to live with the Maines. When Louisa Meredith came to Melbourne in 1888 the two artists visited a large exhibition of paintings by Louis Buvelot and both of these remarkable women, at various times, stayed with Edith Howitt Anderson at *Barragunda*, where Georgiana was horrified to learn that the cottage she had designed at Arthurs Seat had been allowed to run to rack and ruin.[27]

In her eighties Georgiana was as independent and determined as ever. Her daughter Margaret Maine studied drawing with Loureiro, and when she was eighty-three Georgiana sat for Loureiro, who lived nearby and had admired some of her portrait miniatures. Georgiana had no money to pay for her portrait in watercolours so it was intended as a gift from one talented artist to another. The *Age* art critic commented on the 'soft silvery hair and eyes in which the sensitive and intelligent [expression] has been very happily rendered'.

On receiving a small legacy from her old friend, Mr William Westgarth, another pioneer writer of the first days of Melbourne[28] who had paid her a visit shortly before his death, Georgiana thought of leaving the Maines' home and renting Loureiro's house. Unlike the Maines', this house had no stairs to climb, and it was free as the artist and his wife were about to return to Europe.

Her children were horrified by this plan: Georgiana could scarcely stand with pain from her hip and an infected foot and had chronic bronchitis. She made her will on 6 May 1890, near her eighty-sixth birthday, but the Duke's daughter had little to leave anyone except her paintings and her jewellery.[29]

She died on a cold May day. Her obituary praised her both as an artist and a writer, saying 'It was largely due to the influence of such a woman as Mrs McCrae that ideas of refinement and principles of taste were kept alive during the dark ages of our colonial history'.

On her deathbed Georgiana's grandchildren were brought to see her. To

Hugh, her favourite, she gave a silver coin telling him to buy a book by which to remember her.

Family legend[30] has it that to her favourite son George, her sole executor, she gave her original diary, which she had never shown to anyone, containing her deepest emotions and the full story of her broken marriage, along with the shorter edited journal. George read both versions and burnt the original. Fortunately, as a writer himself, he recognised the literary value of her edited memoirs of Melbourne's early days. They were published many years later by Georgiana's grandson Hugh McCrae. *Georgiana's Journal* is a witty, memorable and historic document, illustrated by Georgiana's own paintings and drawings and delights all those who read it.

Portrait of Georgiana McCrae at the age of 83 by Arthur Loureiro emphasises her aristocratic features and intelligence. Georgiana's eyes appear almost black in the self-portrait which she painted just before her 21st birthday. In contrast Loueiro has made Georgiana's eyes reflect the lavender ribbon which softens her silver hair. The miniature self-portrait was owned by Georgiana's great-granddaughter Lady Cowper (who allowed me to reproduce it in Pioneer Women*) and is now in the State Library of Victoria's La Trobe Collection. Loureiro's portrait was inherited by Andrew McCrae, who subsequently donated it to the National Trust of Victoria.*

[1] Information supplied by Claire Mack, a descendant of Georgiana McCrae and her mother Mrs Barbara Blomfield, who supplied watercolours and much valuable information for the chapter on Georgiana McCrae in de Vries-Evans, Susanna, *Pioneer Women, Pioneer Land*. Angus and Robertson, Sydney, 1987.

[2] Charles Gordon was born in 1798 to Ann Thomson, a housemaid employed at Gordon Castle, entered the Navy and subsequently became an Admiral. Susan Thomson (later Sordet) was born in 1805 and when she married and went to live in Switzerland was given a dowry by the Duchess of Gordon. Georgiana's grandfather, Duke Alexander, fourth Duke of Gordon, sired nine illegitimate children and seven legitimate children. The Gordons acknowledged and provided for their illegitimate children. It was Georgiana's tragedy that due to the antipathy of her jealous stepmother she received less than the other illegitimate children but did receive an annuity of one hundred pounds after her father's death.

[3] Niall, Brenda. *Georgiana*. Melbourne University Press, Melbourne, 1994.

[4] For titles and dates of paintings exhibited by Georgiana see Graves, Algernon, *The Royal Academy of Arts*, London, 1982, and *Works Exhibited at the Royal Society of British Artists 1823–1893*. Antique Collectors' Club, Woodbridge, Suffolk. n.d. circa 1981.

[5] Hayter, Charles. *An Introduction to Perspective, Practical Geometry, Drawing and Painting . . . Addressed to his Pupils*. London 1813 and reprinted in several different editions.

[6] McCrae, Hugh, ed. *Georgiana's Journal, Melbourne, 1841–1865*, 2nd and 3rd editions. Angus and Robertson, Sydney, 1966 and 1994. This is an annotated and abridged version of

Georgiana's second diary. Family legend runs that Georgiana copied out her original journal removing various references to her mother's parentage, presumed to be more lowly than she made it, her own illegitimacy, her love for her cousin Perico Gordon of Wardhouse, her deteriorating relationship with her husband Andrew McCrae and her affection for Lieutenant Governor Charles La Trobe.

[7] The original of Georgiana's recollections describing her early life is yet another missing document by Georgiana. The copy made by Georgiana's daughter, Lucia Hyndman, circa 1891, is in the Charles Stuart Perry Papers, La Trobe Library, State Library of Victoria, cited by Niall, Brenda. *Op. cit.*

[8] *Georgiana's Journal* records that in Melbourne she dropped the little heart on the floor where it broke.

[9] Niall, Brenda. *Op. cit.*

[10] *Morning Chronicle*, London, 17 July 1827.

[11] Niall, Brenda. *Op. cit.*

[12] Georgiana refers to Jerez by the eighteenth-century name of Xeres de la Frontera, now officially replaced by Jerez.

[13] I feel considerable sympathy with Georgiana as I am the illegitimate daughter of an Irish peer and grew up during the 1930s–1950s when illegitimacy was seen as shameful. This is why I related Georgiana's story at length in *Pioneer Women, Pioneer Land*.

[14] Georgiana McCrae. 1830 Diary (unpublished). Marsden Campbell Papers privately held.

[15] Georgiana McCrae. MS Journal, July 1840. McCrae Papers. La Trobe Library, State Library of Victoria. This is a significant statement and explains why both Andrew and Georgiana thought that their children would be provided for out of the Duke's will. They had done what the Duchess wanted and married so it was reasonable for them to suppose that she would keep her promise to them.

[16] When he died Andrew left practically nothing and had not paid off money owed on various blocks of land which had been forfeited. This reveals a disturbing aspect of his character.

[17] Georgiana's original floor plans and side elevations for *Mayfield* are currently owned by her great-grandaughter, Mrs Barbara Blomfield.

[18] De Vries-Evans, Susanna. *Conrad Martens on the Beagle and in Australia*. Pandanus Press, Brisbane, 1993. Contains an account of Octavius Browne's visits to Martens.

[19] Dame Mabel Brooks, *Riders of Time* quoted this incident as told to her by her grandmother, Mrs Balcolmbe of The Briars. Cited in Niall, Brenda. *Op. cit.*

[20] A copy of this pasquinade was brought in for sale when I was head of the Rare Book Department in James R. Lawsons, auctioneers of Sydney, along with some convict pardons. Unfortunately the owners thought the documents worth far more than my estimate and decided not to sell.

[21] Information from Mrs Claire Mack, Georgiana's great-great-grandaughter.

[22] Cited in *Dictionary of Australian Artists* , ed. Joan Kerr, Oxford University Press, Melbourne, 1992. Entry on Georgiana McCrae by Katrina Alford and Candice Bruce.

[23] Georgiana McCrae. Commonplace Book, McCrae Papers, Harry F. Chaplin Collection Fischer Library, University of Sydney in which Georgiana cites T. A. St John as writing a commentary on Milton and marriage and divorce. Passage cited in Niall, Brenda, *Op. cit.*

[24] The Duke of Richmond and Gordon and the Brodie family inherited paintings and furniture from Gordon Castle that Georgiana believed to be rightfully hers. Gordon Castle is inhabited by a distant relative of the present Duke, who when I wrote to her in 1987 had never heard of Georgiana. Georgiana was right, being omitted from the Duchess's will had effectively cut her off from the Gordon family in Britain.

[25] Niall, Brenda, *Op. cit.*

[26] T. A. Cole Diaries, 22 January 1867, MS 10570/10973, La Trobe Library, State Library of Victoria.

[27] The house was later bought by one of Georgiana's descendants and is now a house museum run by the National Trust of Victoria, filled with Georgiana's possessions.

[28] Westgarth, William. *Personal Memoirs of Early Melbourne and Victoria*. George Robertson, Melbourne, 1988.

[29] Probate granted Supreme Court of Victoria, 1 September 1890, to George Gordon McCrae as sole executor. See Niall, Brenda, *Op. cit.* for a full account of Georgiana's last years.

[30] Mrs Claire Mack and Mrs Barbara Blomfield are the sources for this. Another interesting account of Georgiana's life and work is in Hancock, Marguerite, *The Reluctant Colonist*. In Kelly et al. *Double Time, a History of Women in Victoria*. Penguin Books, Melbourne, 1986.

CHAPTER 9

Louisa Meredith
(1812–1895)

WRITER, BOTANIST, ARTIST AND CONSERVATIONIST

The resourceful and talented Louisa Meredith was an award-winning artist as well as an adult and children's author whose books achieved enormous popularity in her own lifetime, in Britain as well as Australia, and are now eagerly sought by Australian collectors. Her engravings of Australian flowers are sold today in art galleries and adorn the walls of many Australian homes. Her vivid, and sometimes caustic, writing revealed New South Wales and Tasmania in a new light to world scientific and literary circles.

She charmed critics and readers with amusing descriptions of the hazards and frustrations of bush housekeeping and turned what could have been a disastrous life into one of triumph over adversity through courage and determination. She was the mother of four sons, who cared for them without the benefit of medical assistance in an era when bush children suffered high mortality from childhood illnesses. She was responsible for her husband's entry into Tasmanian politics and his eventual rise to Cabinet, as Treasurer and Minister for Lands. She helped him write his speeches and was an extremely able political hostess.

This was the portrait photograph Louisa Meredith preferred. Here she looks romantic enough to forsake a promising literary and artistic career for a life of deprivation and isolation with the man she loved. The smaller photograph shows Louisa in old age, her strong character worn down by deaths of children, deprivation and the long struggle to survive financially. State Archives of Tasmania.

Louisa Meredith was born Louisa Anne Twamley in Newhall Street, Birmingham, England, in 1812. Her mother was a Meredith from a distinguished family who prided themselves on their descent from the kings of Wales. Louisa's paternal grandfather was a highly intelligent barrister. She had married, totally against the wishes of her family, a man both socially and intellectually beneath her, and the marriage was not happy. Louisa was brought up in extremely modest circumstances and Mrs Twamley put all her effort into educating Louisa so that she could return to the strata of society from which her mother had come.

Louisa's uncle and future father-in-law, George Meredith, a successful but domineering Tasmanian squatter, known as the King of Swanport, helpfully offered Louisa the position of governess to the children of his second marriage to Mary Evans, his former housemaid. Louisa felt that as a successful writer and book illustrator who was supporting herself from her books and paintings, she was capable of a significant literary career in England, and turned down her uncle's offer rather curtly. 'Where would my literature be in Van Diemen's Land, writing sonnets to whales and porpoises?' she wrote back to him. George Meredith was to bear a grudge against her for the rest of his life.

At this time Louisa was nearly twenty-one and life in England seemed bright with promise. She continued writing and painting until she had published five books, all illustrated by herself (these are highly thought of by collectors today for their beauty).[1] She held a number of exhibitions of her paintings, including an exhibition of 26 works at the Royal Birmingham Society of Artists,[2] and achieved a reputation as a successful young artist, writer and political journalist. She had been introduced to the poet William Wordsworth to whom she dedicated her second book. Her articles on the Chartist movement were to influence the young Henry Parkes, the future Premier of New South Wales, who later became her friend. At 26 Louisa was a attractive and highly intelligent woman with a strong will of her own who had had an unhappy love affair with one of her editors, and was ready for a more stable relationship.

Watercolour of native flowers painted for Louisa Meredith's most popular children's book, Some of my Bush Friends in Tasmania. *This was re-issued in 1891 as* Bush Friends in Tasmania *in a limited edition of 700 copies. Private collection.*

Meanwhile her cousin Charles, the eldest son of George Meredith's first marriage, had established a small sheep farm near Bathurst, New South Wales, with money borrowed from his father. It was started in partnership with the author-squatter William Brodribb, who then went to Victoria. Charles was a delightful and handsome young man, but a hopeless businessman and farmer. As his father, the arrogant George Meredith, had quarrelled with the Governor of Tasmania, Charles realised that his only hope of receiving a large land grant was to petition the British Government directly. Naturally, when in Britain he went to visit his aunt and cousin Louisa in Birmingham. Amiable, handsome, weak-willed, intelligent and starved of affection and education since the death of his mother, Charles fell deeply in love with Louisa. Equally smitten, Louisa realised that she would have to leave her cultured, artistic and literary circle of friends and move to a new and still uncivilised colony. Her love for Charles was so strong that she was prepared to make any sacrifice for him, and spent the rest of her life protecting him through a series of failed ventures.

Louisa and Charles were married in April 1839 and left Birmingham for Sydney two months later, intending to stay for five years only and then return. After a long voyage in cramped conditions, during which Louisa spent much of the time prostrate with seasickness, the young couple arrived in Sydney.

> In an absolute whirl of delight and excitement I hastened to put a few packages ready to take ashore. The agitation on board was universal, and the transformations little short of miraculous; passenger chrysalids were turning into butterflies every instant. Gentlemen, whose outer vestments for the past month would have scarcely brought half-a-crown in Ragfair [a second-hand clothes market] in England,

suddenly emerged from their cabins exquisites of the first order. Ladies, whose bronzed and scorched straw-bonnets would have been discarded long before by a match-girl, now appeared in delicate silks or satins of the latest London fashion.

When the boat came to take us ashore, my joy was complete. Seated in the slung chair, wrapped in the British flag, I gladly bade adieu to the good ship that had so long seemed to me a weary prison, and soon, with a delight that must be felt to be understood, stepped again on land.

How happy are the first few days on shore. After such a voyage, every action is an enjoyment. I could walk, without the floor jumping about and pitching me over; could use both hands to brush my hair, instead of keeping one to hold on by; could set my wineglass on the table without fear of its upsetting into my plate, though I often caught myself carefully propping it up against something. The abundant supply of water for ablutionary purposes is a priceless luxury when first enjoyed after the limited allowance on board ship. Few ship-stewards are very clean and therefore our exquisite enjoyment of clean cups, glasses, plates and forks, may be imagined. Vegetables too, after a long diet of pork and rice, were most acceptable.

They rented surgeon D'Arcy Wentworth's former house at Homebush. Louisa suffered dreadfully from the heat at Christmas and, when pregnant, visited drought-stricken Bathurst en route to Charles's sheep station. She kept a journal and made sketches which became the background for her first and most famous Australian book, *Notes and Sketches of New South Wales, From 1839–1844*. This was written in Tasmania years later and contains some extremely well written descriptive passages about the colony and its inhabitants. Her descriptions of the filthy bedroom at the inn, where the blankets were black with dirt and the staff drank most of the time and the dinner party where the men talked about nothing but wool, are classics of Australian literature.

Most gentlemen have their whole souls so felted up in wools, fleeces, flocks, and stock, that I have often sat through a weary dinner and evening of incessant talking, without hearing a single syllable on any other subject. Far be it from me, to imply want of respect for the worthy enthusiasts in wool; still there are times and places for everything. In English society the lawyer does not carry his briefs and special pleadings into the drawing room; the physician dreams not of occupying an [entire] dinner party with his last wonderful cure; even the author refrains from volunteering a recitation of his new book. Surely, according to our old-world notions of propriety, the wool-merchant also should sometimes divest himself of [talking] shop, and not always be engrossed by his bales and fleeces. However fascinating may be the company of his fine woolled sheep and peerless breed of merinos, he should not insist on taking them out to dinner. I had to endure a perpetuity of mutton and wool; whilst choice samples, [of wool] tied and labelled with most fond accuracy, were passed from hand to hand, and contemplated with the profound and critical air of a connoisseur passing judgement on a masterpiece of art. So long as the conversation conveyed intelligence respecting different parts of the Colony, connected with sheep-farming or other occupations, I could derive amusement and knowledge from it, but the eternity of wool, wool, wool—wearied my very soul.

Louisa's eldest son, George Campbell Meredith, was born in Sydney the following year. The depression of 1840 reduced the price of Charles's animals so much that they were sent to the boiling-down works.[3] After selling the run, the Merediths did not receive their share of purchase money because their agent went bankrupt before he had paid them. Forced by lack of funds to go to Tasmania and live with Charles's father, to whom the couple still owed money, Louisa once again suffered agonies of seasickness as they crossed Bass Strait in a cabin full of lice where 'dirty water dropped through chinks in the deck on to the bed'. They arrived in *Cambria*, George Meredith's remote but large and comfortable homestead, after a terrible journey during which the cart containing Louisa and her baby was often in danger of falling over a precipice. Only thin ropes tied to the sides prevented this.[4]

At Cambria Louisa felt comfortable in the cooler climate and could relax on the wide verandahs and write up the journal which would later become part of her next book, *My Home in Tasmania*. As the wife of George's eldest surviving son and heir, and the mother of his grandchild, Louisa expected to be made welcome. However, although eager to help Charles reorganise his financial affairs, George Meredith was not enthusiastic about his eldest son's arrival, practically penniless, accompanied by Louisa and her child. From his two marriages, to Sarah Meredith and Mary the housemaid, George Meredith had to provide for another six children as well as Charles. There was already a substantial rift between the children of the two wives because Mary had a child by George before the death of Sarah.

From the outset George and Louisa had a strained relationship, probably because she would not allow her father-in-law to dominate her husband as he did the rest of the family. Louisa must have resented the harsh treatment his father had given Charles in his boyhood. In one of her books she recounted how, as a delicate child of 12, he was sent out alone to live in the bush hunting down kangaroos for their meat and, although intelligent, was denied access to an education. His father's sheep were expensive merinos and he refused to slaughter them for mutton to feed his family and servants and made his son Charles kill kangaroos instead. The gentle, affectionate Charles hated kangaroo hunting. He and his eldest brother, George, were then sent off in charge of two convicts and a thousand sheep 120 miles (192 km) on foot to Hobart without either food or money and spent days without anything to eat. Charles's older brother so loathed his despotic father that he ran away from home and lived on Maria Island, where he was eventually murdered by Aborigines.[6]

Louisa and her father clashed repeatedly. Finally Charles and Louisa moved out of *Cambria* to *Riversdale*, a small and primitive wooden house on George Meredith's property. Louisa took over the management of stock records and stores, acted as tailor and dressmaker to her family, and still managed to find several hours each day in which to write and paint.

Louisa had grave problems with convict servants who stole food and clothing. Reliable servants stayed for only a short time before leaving to get married. Charles inserted a humorous advertisement in the paper which read 'How to Get Married! Engage with Charles Meredith as cook or housemaid'. The couple had some bizarre experiences with their servants. One convict nursemaid took the key of the larder from under Louisa's pillow as she slept and, aided by the groom, stole eight dozen bottles of wine from the cellar. They were discovered drunk in bed together. Another maid swore, smoked tobacco, and after drinking an entire bottle of rum had a violent fit and was carted off to hospital, where she spent the night in the bed of a male patient and then married him! Another touch of drama was supplied by the numerous snakes that entered the house. A nursemaid, carrying George in her arms, even tried to pick one up, thinking it was an eel! As a writer, Louisa noted down these incidents and used them in subsequent books.

There was no piped water at Riversdale. Clothes were washed by hand with water boiled in a copper and were ironed by flatirons filled with heated coals. Cooking was done over an open fire in great iron pots hung on trivets. When there were no servants all the burdens fell on Louisa's capable shoulders. There was no sewing machine; pregnant Louisa sewed everything by hand. Domestic pilfering was so bad that she was forced to keep all the rations under lock and key and distribute them herself to their hired farmhands, servants and convicts. Dairying, jam-making, and providing hospitality for other squatters and their families also occupied her time.

Charles and Louisa borrowed more money from his father and started to build their own small cottage named *Springvale*. Their second son, Charles Henry, born in November 1841, died of chronic dysentery three months later. Charles realised that to help Louisa forget her grief, they must leave *Riversdale* as soon as possible and move into the still half-built *Springvale*. The piano was hoisted up on the dray and padded with bags full of straw; piglets and even more luggage occupied the next cart. Weak from the effects of giving birth without a midwife, depressed and grieving, Louisa climbed into the cart with her precious piano and moved three miles (4.8 km) away to *Springvale*. This was the first home she had ever owned. Here she recovered her customary optimism, finished her book on New South Wales, reared chickens, ducks and turkeys, and made butter, cream and cheese. At *Riversdale* she had expended enormous energy on a house belonging to her father-in-law, designing and creating garden beds, curved paths, a fishpond and a thatched octagonal summerhouse. She was determined that their own cottage and garden would be even better and coped well with the problems of living in isolation.

At *Springvale* a third son, Charles Twamley, was born in 1844. They kept pet lambs and their horses and cows were treated with great kindness. Other pets included a baby opossum which slept inside an old top hat, and a pair of bandicoots. There was always a tabby cat in the house and Louisa had a fine Arabian mare to ride. Surrounded by her family and her animals, this was the happiest and most fulfilling time of her life and she made a large number of drawings and paintings of distinctively Australian trees, plants, flowers and animals.

Sadly enough, all the money spent on clearing land and building dams and fences proved an unwise investment. Through no fault of his own, Charles simply could not make the property pay. Tasmania was in the middle of a deep depression. The couple was once again without capital or sufficient income to support their growing family. They lost their fences, an entire apple orchard and many sheep, in one of the worst floods ever experienced on the east coast. 'The broad sandy beaches near the river mouth were strewn for miles with carcasses washed up in heaps by the tides,' Louisa wrote. She described how two of their farm workers' wives, washed out of the cottage they shared, spent the rest of the stormy night in a tree to escape the rising flood; one wife clutching her baby and the other a kitten. Charles and Louisa had carved *Springvale* out of virgin bush, contrary to George Meredith's advice, so he refused to help his son again and Louisa and Charles were on the verge of bankruptcy. Finally, through

Happy to have escaped from the horrors of Lath Hall *to* Poyston, *the house the Merediths built at Port Sorrell in 1845, Louisa's drawing shows the house with her boys playing by the stream. Lithographed for* My Home in Tasmania, *which Louisa wrote while living at* Poyston.

Louisa Meredith's pencil sketch made at Poyston, shows tame echidnas, who amused the boys when one fell in the milk churn. Lithograph from My Home in Tasmania, *published 1852. Private collection.*

Lath Hall *was a damp wooden hovel at Port Sorrel which Louisa Meredith described as 'dismal' and where she felt depressed and isolated. Note the snake in the foreground, another constant worry to pioneer women. Frontispiece to Louisa Meredith's* My Home in Tasmania, *published 1852.*

Louisa's friendship with Governor John Eardley-Wilmot, Charles was offered the locum position of Assistant Magistrate at Port Sorrell on the north coast.

All the upheaval of moving again, in torrential rain, greatly upset Louisa. Baby Charles Twamley was only four months old and nearly died when blood streamed from his throat after a leech fell on him from an overhanging branch on the journey. The house that went with the job was named *Lath Hall* by Louisa. It turned out to be a run-down cottage made of flimsy wooden laths, and it was damp and desolate, the skirtings and floors covered in mould. Louisa spent two miserable weeks camping there without her household equipment, which arrived later by sea. She found many items were broken or damaged beyond repair, since the crew had been drunk when they loaded it aboard. Her precious wedding presents of china and glass were now in fragments and were irreplaceable in colonial Tasmania.[7]

Many of the local settlers were semi-illiterate, trying to live by felling the densely packed trees and, aided by their wives, clearing the ground. Louisa felt isolated and friendless, 'as though there were some evil spell upon us, dooming us always to go on wandering'.

The only successful thing about the Merediths' pioneering life so far had been Louisa's writing. *Notes and Sketches of New South Wales* was now the best-seller of Murray's Home Library, widely read in Australia and overseas; but Louisa had signed a bad contract with her London publishers and her meagre royalties only paid for a few housekeeping expenses. Her frank, but sometimes caustic, descriptions of the crudities of colonial life also made her enemies among those who recognised themselves in her books.

In 1845 Louisa derived great comfort from a visit to Government House in Hobart as a guest of Governor John Eardley-Wilmot where she found that, due to the visit of English artist and art teacher John Skinner Prout, painting was now greatly in vogue among colonial ladies. She attended concerts, regattas, picnics, theatres and dinner parties. She was delighted to find here people who had topics of conversation other than wool and enjoyed herself away from the isolation of Port Sorrell, even taking part in some amateur theatricals at which she showed great talent.

On her return the couple purchased land near the sea, and built themselves a new house named *Poyston* after Charles's birthplace in Wales. Here her son, Owen, was born in 1847. The resourceful Louisa once again designed and created a garden, full of roses and raspberry canes, and took up beekeeping. She kept goats for milk and meat. She studied and drew frogs (which she wrote about), sketched birds and made a collection of sea shells which she illustrated and she also drew a beautiful series of Tasmanian fish. Since the garden sloped down to the water, Louisa and her boys swam and went boating during the summer. But the autocratic George Meredith was aging.

Charles was summoned back to *Cambria* by his father to take over the management of the estates with his half-brother, Edwin, while his half-brother John, the previous manager, went off to try pioneering in South Australia. Charles and Edwin had never been friendly as children and they found it impossible to work together. George Meredith, who wished to retire, agreed to lease the property to Charles until his death. Charles and Louisa naturally expected to inherit it since, after his full-brother's death on Maria Island, Charles was the eldest son. However, in 1853 John, who had made his fortune in South Australia, returned to Cambria and offered George Meredith a substantial sum to purchase the entire estate. His father curtly informed Charles in writing that he had accepted John's offer for financial and personal reasons. George Meredith's dislike of the strong-willed Louisa, his affection for John's wife, Maria (who had made a point of befriending the daughters of George's second marriage who were jealous of Louisa), and his own avarice, made him accept John's good financial offer and he remained John's guest at *Cambria* until his death.

Louisa was heartbroken that her family would never inherit *Cambria* where they could live in style and elegance, or be able to return to her England. Her parents were dead and she had inherited nothing from them. Disappointment and financial worry hardened her character, and made her all the more determined to succeed on her own terms.

Any hope of a reconciliation between Charles and his half-brother disappeared when John, who had bought the lease of *Riversdale*, forced them to move once again. In the middle of the continuing family feud, George Meredith died. His estate was equally divided amongst his children, with an additional amount for his unmarried daughters. This meant that Charles, the eldest, received far less than his half-sisters. Once again Louisa seemed 'under a dark star' in coming to the colony. She now had to face years of financial insecurity, family estrangement and deprivation when isolated in the bush. She loathed the fact that the Meredith family was a subject of gossip and speculation all over Tasmania. However, she was still in good health, strong and attractive, with a fine bone structure inherited from her distinguished ancestors, and a mass of dark hair. While Louisa could be arrogant and snobbish, she was also a woman of exceptional charm and wit. Cultured men, like Premier Sir Henry Parkes and Governor John Eardley-Wilmot, found her conversation amusing and interesting and were honoured by her friendship.

This original pencil sketch reveals Louisa Meredith's mastery of composition and shading. The detailed drawing was made in 1845 on Louisa's hazardous journey menaced by escaped convict bushrangers on the way to stay in Government House, Hobart, as the guest of Governor Eardley-Wilmot. Private collection.

Reconciled to the fact that she would never be the wife of a squatter with unlimited leisure and freedom for creative pursuits, Louisa still managed to complete her second most important Australian book, *My Home in Tasmania*, which was published in London in 1852. It was so successful in England and Australia that it was republished in America. By this time the Merediths were living at *Twamley*, a bleak, isolated homestead in the middle of a forest at Prosser's Plains, north of Hobart, where they remained for nine years. Charles ran a few sheep and cattle and was a small-crop farmer earning only a subsistence from this. Louisa saw no way of sending her three boys to a school on their meagre income and wanted to move to Hobart, where the educational opportunities were better, as she was now her children's only teacher.[8]

The Merediths' social position, considered so important in colonial days, had suffered as Charles had been virtually disinherited by his father. Louisa decided that Charles should enter politics where his intelligence, wit and charm could find some useful outlet, and where he might eventually gain a lucrative position in the Cabinet, since his lack of schooling after the age of 12 precluded him from most commercial positions.

They rented out the farm at Prosser's Plains for a small sum and moved to Hobart. Charles was elected Member of Parliament for Glamorgan; now freed from farm and domestic work the determined and energetic Louisa produced, in 1860, her beautifully illustrated volume, *Bush Friends in Tasmania*, containing ten plates of flowers, including the lovely waratah. They visited Melbourne hoping Charles might find more lucrative work but were disappointed. *Over the Straits, A Visit to Victoria*, published the following year, contains four engravings of Tasmanian scenes made from drawings by Louisa, as well as interesting descriptions of early Melbourne. Here, sandwiched between handsome bluestone buildings, she found tumbledown wooden cottages and shops like dolls' houses, 'displaying goods that might be put in a small trunk'. She was delighted by their visit to the office of the Electric Telegraph and it was probably her influence that encouraged Charles to press the Tasmanian Parliament to have a cable laid across Bass Strait. She also visited Georgiana McCrae in North Melbourne and had her portrait painted.[9] In the comparative sophistication of gas-lit Melbourne she found people interested in art and literature, elements which she missed so much since she left England.

In *Over the Straits* the animal-loving Louisa indignantly exposed the lack of care for animals that she saw around her in Melbourne. She cited the cases of large fat ladies who, knowing that their horses had saddle sores like open boils, still rode every day for pleasure regardless of the pain caused to their poor animals; and of housewives who left bush turkeys with their throats slit to bleed to death upside down so that the meat would be white and tender.

In 1878 she became joint founder of the first Tasmanian branch of the Society for the Prevention of Cruelty to Animals. She urged Charles to introduce a number of bills into the Tasmanian Parliament to prevent cruelty to animals. She was instrumental in stamping out the repellent practice of keeping captured black swans without food for weeks on end, cooped up in a tiny cage until, just before their deaths, their down could be easily removed from the withered flesh and sold for profit.

It is also a credit to their loving and supportive relationship that for Louisa's sake, Charles put up with the taunts and jeers of his fellow politicians when he presented these bills in Parliament, since the sitting members were all keen hunters and shooters. Through Louisa's humane influence various acts were passed for the protection of Tasmanian wildlife. Throughout her books there are constant references to the dangers of ruining the natural environment and killing native fauna.

All Louisa's books reflect her love of native animals, many of which she adopted as household pets when she found them wounded in the bush. Her description of a native possum is particularly interesting and vivid:

> The full-grown opossum is larger and heavier than a very large cat, with a pretty innocent-looking face, which is both like that of the deer and the mouse, the shape of the nose and whiskers strongly resembling the latter. The eyes are very dark and brilliant, the ears soft and delicate, the legs short and strong, with monkey-like feet and long sharp claws. They sit up, holding their food in their fore-paws like a monkey. The tail is 18 or 20 inches long, the underside is quite smooth and devoid of hair, the upper covered with thick woolly fur, the colour being either black, dark grey, dark brown or deep golden brown like yellow sable.
>
> The tail is strongly prehensile and holds so tightly that they often swing their whole weight upon it and when shot dead, sometimes hang for a minute by it, before falling. Fine moonlight nights often prove fatal to the poor creatures, being the time chosen for shooting them by scores, either for the sake of their warm skins for rugs or to feed dogs with their luckless bodies. Sometimes they commit sad ravages among the young corn and then the war waged among them has certainly a fraction more of justice but too often they are the victims of human cruelty.

Together the Merediths ensured that the lives of literally thousands of animals were saved. This conservationist philosophy was reflected in Louisa's book *Tasmanian Friends and Foes, Feathered, Furred and Finned*, published in 1880, when she was 68 years old.

This same book also recounted the story of Charles's deprived childhood. Intelligent but poorly educated, Charles never encouraged his children to gain a good education or a profession, which always saddened Louisa and was their only bone of contention in an otherwise perfect marriage.

All the hardships which Louisa had to endure in her pioneering days, together with the loss of *Cambria*, were insignificant compared to the blow she suffered when Charles died of heart failure in March 1880. His political career had blossomed with her help. She had been a loyal and devoted wife and mother, giving birth to all her children under difficult circumstances and enduring the loss of two of them. Charles had been forced to spend much of his Cabinet salary on entertaining to keep up his Parliamentary position, and he left only a few hundred pounds to her and the children, and even these small savings were later lost in a bank crash.

Louisa Meredith received a small pension from the Tasmanian Government in recognition of her outstanding contribution to the literature of her adopted land, the first Australian writer to be accorded this distinction. She published 19 major books in her lifetime, many of which were reprinted several times, as well as numerous articles in British and Australian newspapers, and the royalties she earned from writing were a vital contribution to the Meredith family income. Few colonial women, other than Georgiana McCrae and Caroline Louisa Atkinson, were talented enough to write and illustrate their own work, and her words are still widely quoted in many contemporary publications. She won awards for her watercolours and oil sketches at the 1866 Melbourne Intercolonial Exhibition; at the 1870 Sydney Intercolonial Exhibition; the 1880 Melbourne Intercolonial and the 1884 Calcutta International Exhibition. When in reduced financial circumstances, Louisa was helped by her friend Lady Gormanston, wife of the Governor of Tasmania, who arranged for some of Louisa's original drawings and watercolours to be purchased from her by the Royal Society of Tasmania, who still own them.

After the shock of Charles's death, her own health deteriorated but in spite of her sciatica Louisa continued to lead an active life, writing, editing, drawing and painting. Her friend, Premier Sir Henry Parkes, found her a cheap passage to England

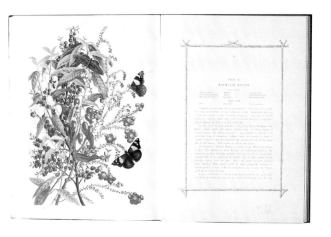

in 1889 to enable her to edit and launch *Last Series—Bush Friends in Tasmania*, with a cover by Edward La Trobe Bateman, and 13 colour plates from her own drawings. It also contains some of her own poems, with black-and-white illustrations based on her drawings.[10]

Louisa Meredith died in Victoria six years later in 1895, aged 83. Her obituary praised the quality of the books she had created and her unfailing determination and industry up to the very end of her life. One stated that 'her most enduring monument was in her numerous writings, paintings and etchings, which will stand out in bold relief to inspire others who take up literary and artistic pursuits'. The following passage from one of her own books sums up the philosophy and dauntless spirit of such a remarkable pioneer woman. 'I believe . . . that, to appreciate fully the blessings of a happy home, children, friends and books, a trial of lonely bush life for a few years is indispensable.'

A copy of Bush Friends in Tasmania, *Louisa's most popular book was republished in Britain when she was in her eighties. To launch it she sailed to London. The illustrated limited edition is now very valuable. Courtesy James R. Lawson.*

1   Scourse, N. *The Victorians and their Flowers*. Beckenham, U.K., 1988. Gives details of Louisa's artistic career in England.
2   Rae Ellis, Vivienne, entry on Louisa Meredith in *Dictionary of Australian Artists*. Oxford University Press, Melbourne, 1994.
3   Meredith, Mrs Charles, *Notes and Sketches of New South Wales*, London, 1844.
4   *Ibid*.
5   Clark, C. M. H. *A History of Australia*. Melbourne University Press, Melbourne, 1968. Provides a general background on New South Wales and Tasmania in Louisa Meredith's time.
6   Rae Ellis, Vivienne, *Louisa Anne Meredith, A Tigress in Exile*. Blubber Head Press, Sandy Bay, Tasmania, 1979. An excellent and comprehensive biography, the standard work on this author.
7   *Ibid*.

The most popular illustration in Louisa Meredith's Bush Friends in Tasmania. *Louisa's work resembles one of Beatrix Potter's watercolours. In her text Louisa described Australian gold frogs, sitting in their moist floating bowers . . . more beautiful than English frogs. Private collection.*

8 *Ibid.*
9 Niall, Brenda. *Georgiana*, Melbourne University Press, Melbourne, 1994.
10 Meredith, Louisa. My *Home in Tasmania*, London, 1852.
Louisa Meredith wrote 14 books while in Australia. Her story has been compiled from the
    following:
Meredith, Mrs Charles, *Notes and Sketches of New South Wales from 1839–1844.* John Murray,
    London, 1844. This volume is not illustrated, and extracts are quoted in the preceding chapter.
Meredith, Louisa Anne, My *Home in Tasmania during a Residence of Nine Years.* John Murray,
    London, 1852.
Meredith, Louisa Anne, *Over the Straits: A Visit to Victoria.* London, 1861. The original artwork
    for this is in the Mitchell Library.
Meredith, Louisa Anne, *First Series—Bush Friends in Tasmania* (1860). *Last Series—Bush Friends
    in Tasmania* (1891) John Murray, London. Two folio volumes.
Meredith, Louisa Anne, *Tasmanian Friends and Foes, Feathered, Furred and Finned.* John Murray,
    London, 1880.
Additional information on Louisa kindly supplied by Geoffrey Stilwell, formerly Curator of the
    Allport Library and Museum of Fine Arts, Hobart.
Pictorial works by Louisa Meredith are held by the Mitchell Library, Sydney; The Australian
    National Library, Canberra; Tasmanian Art Gallery and Museum and Van Diemen's Land
    Folk Museum and several private collections.

CHAPTER 10

Ann Caldwell
(1820–1890)

AUSTRALIA'S MOTHER COURAGE

On one of my lecture tours around New South Wales, I met Belinda and Ann Cox descendants of Martha Cox. They asked me to edit and annotate Martha Cox's memoirs, written in 1937, nine years before her death. From Martha's memoirs the remarkable story of her pioneering mother, Ann Caldwell, emerges. Martha wrote down incidents on scraps of paper as they occurred and when she had time, but kept no journal. She dictated her memoirs towards the end of her life when living in retirement in Wagga. She incorporates into them the extraordinary history of her mother's early life. Martha was a keen reader all her life and she writes clearly and well, using the occasional vivid metaphor and simile. She follows the golden rule for writers and writes about what she knows—pioneer selectors living on the land without capital, at the mercy of drought, flood, fire and a constant shortage of money.

Ann Caldwell's story is representative of a major group of women who have not had their due in Australian history. These women, often penniless immigrants from Ireland, had an oral culture and their stories were rarely written down as most could not read or write and have left little behind them to record their importance in Australian history. A statue recently erected on Sydney's Circular Quay commemorates a token *Pioneer Woman*. But there should be a statue in every town or city in Australia to commemorate women of the calibre of Ann Caldwell, and the statues should show their faces lined by the sun and wind and their bodies battered by hard work and frequent child-bearing.

She endured a hard life so that her children would have a better one. Eventually her dream was fulfilled by her children, but only after many years of backbreaking struggle on her part. Her heart-warming story honours all those nameless women who travelled across dusty plains in a covered wagon (spelt *waggon* in the memoirs—the spelling used in Martha's day), lived in huts of split logs and rusting corrugated iron with a dirt floor, their kitchens rickety lean-to sheds partitioned off with sacking, their sinks old kerosene tins. No contraceptives helped them limit their families and they watched infants die with monotonous regularity. But Annie, as she was known, was hardworking, determined and organised and exceptionally well informed for the times on the importance of hygiene. None of her children died young. On her mammoth trek across Australia, she insisted that her children wash themselves and their clothes in creeks at a time when many people on the road wore their dusty clothes until they literally fell apart.

Ann Caldwell was from Irish peasant farming stock. Her death certificate records her father's name as Thomas Mooney and that her mother was born Elizabeth Cozzen, that she married Matthew Caldwell when she turned twenty-one, just before they emigrated to South Australia. Marriages at this period were usually delayed among the Irish peasantry so that older siblings could marry first.

Annie and her husband would have had little hope of owning land had they

stayed in Ireland. In 1841 they arrived in Adelaide (several years before the great Irish potato famine). But times were already very hard in Ireland for working-class people and between 1839 and 1842, some 23,705 Irish immigrants arrived in Australia compared with 5,986 Scots and 12,227 English and Welsh.[1]

In Adelaide, initially Annie and Matthew Caldwell worked for others, possibly as housekeeper and labourer, to earn enough to take up a small landholding. Unfortunately their stock never prospered due to lack of water. No picture of Ann's bush hut remains, if one was ever made. A typical South Australian settler's hut at this time was a one or two-room windowless dwelling made from wooden slabs or brush, roofed with bark or corrugated iron, sometimes lined with yellowing newspaper to keep out insects and winter winds. Glass was too expensive for settlers and a simple shutter which opened outwards would have served for ventilation. There were no cupboards—clothes, frying pan and pannikins were hung from pegs, and the sink and washtub were made from kerosine tins. The kitchen was a shed with open walls carefully sited apart from the house to avoid fire danger.

The Caldwell's food was monotonous but they had the compensation that on the land meat was cheap. Meals consisted of beef salted down by Ann, or oily roast mutton, the eternal Irish dish of boiled potatoes, as well as bread and lashings of butter, with jam as a special treat. Some settlers ate roast kangaroo, parrot or cockatoo pie, roast bush turkey (very tough) or the more tender flying fox which, boiled, tasted like chicken. Ann probably experimented with anything available to vary the endless monotony of mutton and beef. But vegetables were rarely eaten when water was scarce; in a drought all the water went to their precious sheep and cattle or to make tea. When Martha, Ann's daughter, became a farmer she nearly died of scurvy following a long drought. Meals were washed down by copious mugs of black billy tea.

But limited as the Caldwell family's diet would have been by today's standards, it represented an improvement on the usual meals of Irish peasant farmers, where meat was only eaten on high days and holidays during Ann's childhood. In Ireland tea, bread and potatoes were staple fare. In Australia, if times were bad, the

The camera captures rural poverty in dwellings of pioneer settlers like Ann Caldwell. Reproduced with permission from Tyrell Collection, National Library of Australia, Canberra.

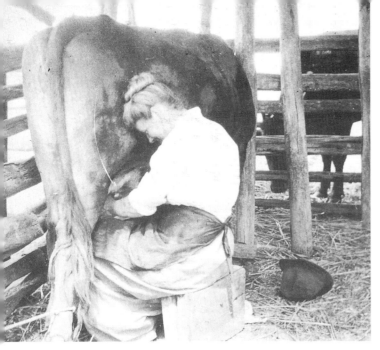

Caldwells could still afford a hunk of bread smeared with beef or mutton drippings, and black tea.[2]

Life was hard on the land without a proper water supply. So Ann, Matthew or the children would have walked or taken a cart to the nearest spring or dam for water. Drinking water for humans and stock was precious. Washing up was done in a bucket. Bathing was a weekly event in a tin bath in front of the fire, the water later being used to soak dirty sheets and clothes.

It was not unusual for boys to leave school early to help with the farm work. In Australia many selectors' children left school at thirteen or younger. In addition, school would be missed to help with the harvest, the shearing and dipping of sheep, or the mustering and branding of cattle. For selectors without capital, farming was a family affair. Martha relates how her mother gave each of them special tasks on the farm from an early age. At night they used home-made slush lamps made from a twist of rag floating in a saucer of smelly mutton fat, the cheapest form of lighting for poor selectors.

Hard work took its toll and Matthew Caldwell died in 1856. Ann was left a widow in her mid-thirties with seven children to support ranging in age from fourteen years to eighteen months, and pregnant with her eighth child. It was difficult surviving in a marginal farming area in the days before social security or welfare benefits provided a safety net for families in emergencies. But, as with so many of these colonial women, adversity was the spur to action—all the more so in Ann's case because she had no husband to protect her. It was dangerous for a woman to travel alone as women were frequently raped and robbed by bushrangers in the bush.

Although educated women with capital, like Ann Drysdale, Caroline Newcomb, Fanny Buntine and Eliza Forlonge became squatters and pastoral managers, Annie Caldwell is a rare exception in taking up a selection without capital, albeit under her younger son's name.

In 1864, when Ann Caldwell was forty-four, she made the momentous decision to take her brood ranging in age from eight to twenty years on a journey of several hundred miles into the wilds of New South Wales to become a selector, or small landowner, under the terms of the Selection Acts of 1860–61. These Selection Acts were designed to benefit immigrants without capital.

Martha's account of her mother's eight-week trek from South Australia to the western foothills of the Great Dividing Range in New South Wales, in a covered wagon with seven of her children, is unique in Australian literature: it is reminiscent of the sagas of American pioneers heading west. Annie Caldwell planned and undertook this arduous journey from Gumeracha (48km north-east of Adelaide, near today's Mount Pleasant winery) to *The Billabong*, the property they selected in

New South Wales (10km from modern-day Holbrook, and not to be confused with the present-day village of Little Billabong 25km north east of Holbrook). Ann and her children covered a distance of approximately 900km on this epic journey. From Martha's account, the children covered much of the ground on foot to ease the horses and she remembers their feet bleeding until the soles toughened up. Ann's aim was to acquire good land which had been opened up for selection and establish her family on the land

At *The Billabong*, Ann Caldwell and her children once again started from scratch—first building a rough shelter for themselves and their stock. The climate in the area is one of extremes: bitterly cold winters and searingly hot summers. Ann worked alongside the boys in the arduous task of establishing a farm from scratch. In Martha's admiring words, 'Mother seemed able to turn her hand to any sort of man's work'.

They lived under the most primitive conditions. On top of the farm chores, there were the labour-intensive, time-consuming household tasks. Baking and cooking in the hot Australian summers was an ordeal. Clothes were sewn and mended by hand. Wash day was dreaded. On these days, Ann and the children carried water from a stream or well in buckets to the copper. The 'copper', which often was not made of copper at all but of thin cast iron, was a hemispherical vessel that would hold between one to two thousand litres (twenty to forty gallons) of water. The clothes would be boiled, then lifted out with a pot or dip stick, rinsed with a blue-bag, starched with flour, mangled and finally ironed with flatirons heated in the fire or on top of the range. Women like Ann frequently burned hands grasping the burning hot metal handle of irons fresh from the fire. Each household needed several irons, which were heated turn and turn about. Life with children and no money was desperately hard on the selector's wife as was summed up by Manning Clark[3]

> For poor selectors, life . . . [was] not worth the conventional farthing on dairy farms [where] mothers and daughters got up between two and four in the morning to milk the cows. Fathers and sons at the same time got ready to transport the milk to the nearby town. The men fought the land . . . the women were enslaved to the kitchen and the backyard . . . They churned the milk into butter, baked bread, made soaps with saltfree fat, caustic soda and resin . . . In the backyard they tanned and dyed sheepskins, cattle hides, kangaroo skins, rabbit skins and possum skins and used them for floor covering, winter clothing, bedding and for decorating the house . . . The [female] inhabitants of these rural slums used old kerosene tins as their wash tubs, mud and pebbles for soap, their hands as wringers . . .

Unlike many women of the period, who saw themselves purely as wives and mothers, Ann undertook overall family responsibilities as the head of the household. By spending every penny earned on developing the property, Ann Caldwell finally achieved financial security for her family. While there are many memoirs and diaries by squatters' wives like Georgiana McCrae and Emmeline Leslie, who complete with piano, fine china dinner service, family silver and domestic staff trekked out to new homes in the bush, this account of the life of a penniless selector, Ann Caldwell, is unique. The farming experience of Ann Caldwell is, to the best of my knowledge, the only detailed record of a working-class woman in Australian literature who becomes a selector and establishes a farm in virgin bush. Her remarkable story deserves to be better known.

Here Martha Caldwell recounts the story of her mother's struggles to establish her children. Martha was born on the Caldwell's property at Gumeracha in 1854, in the Torrens River Valley north-east of Adelaide. She would later marry a young farmer named David Cox and suffer hardships similar to her mother. Undoubtedly her mother's example gave Martha the strength to continue to manage her farm when she in turn was widowed. Martha begins her account by relating:

> My parents, Matthew and Ann Caldwell, were born in County Armagh, in the north of Ireland. My mother said little about her early life. Shortly after their marriage they took an emigrant ship bound for Adelaide, where they arrived in 1841 with little more than the clothes they stood up in. At first both of them worked in Adelaide [most Irish unskilled immigrants went in for labouring or domestic service on arrival].
>
> My parents Mr and Mrs Caldwell, took up a couple of leases at Gumeracha in the Torrens River district, then very remote from Adelaide, but the principles used for farming in Ireland did not respond well to Australian conditions of soil and climate. They soon found that much of their land was without water and my father had to sink wells so the sheep and cattle could survive. They had no diversions or amusements to console them in their hard daily round of work and family. For small settlers with no capital like my parents, life consisted of felling trees, grubbing out stumps, building fences of brush or logs and sinking tanks for water—working, waiting, living by grit, zeal and enterprise.
>
> In cases of medical emergency or illness, my father had to ride a saddle-horse at break-neck speed over tracks that were rough and risky in the extreme to seek counsel of a doctor in Adelaide, which was well over a day's ride away. Our family consisted then of Elizabeth the eldest, the two boys William and John, and four girls, Olivia, Sophia, Agnes and myself. I was only a toddler when father died in the prime of his life and Priscilla was born a few months after my father's death. It was a dire blow to poor mother and us all. The entire responsibility of farm and seven children to support fell on my mother as William and John, however willing, were too young to render much assistance as William was 12, John 10, and Elizabeth 14 years of age.
>
> Mixed farming makes enormous demands upon the energy and resource-fulness of a competent and industrious couple. For a widow, burdened by a large family of young children, the task can become too grievous to bear. But my mother had courage, foresight and determination. If she felt despair for the future she never gave in to it.[4] Mother explained, 'It's not for myself but for you fatherless children, that I must fight on. And with God's help I shall do my best to see things through'.
>
> To bring in extra income Mother sent eggs and home churned butter for sale to a settlement called Blomberg, about three miles away as money was always scarce.

Lack of water meant that many sheep and cattle died during dry years. Income from the butter making was vital and meant hours churning away with a wooden plunger. There were no drum churns at this date; to get the butter to set it was often necessary to wait until the heat of the day was over and do the work at night. She would also have milked, fed calves, pigs, fowls, got breakfast of cold salt beef, porridge and tea, washed up, prepared children for school, carried water in kerosene tins from the dam, set the house in order, made bread, scrubbed and washed frequently as their clothes were few (the clothes boiled away in those eternally useful kerosene tins), and then dinner had to be prepared and the cows milked once again. Hire labour was out of the question and the Caldwell family pulled together and struggled to make ends meet.

> The farm produce was taken to the store on foot by the bigger children and they brought home groceries in exchange. In the good seasons our sheep and cattle

gradually increased in numbers but the fenced portion of our land was only sufficient to retain the cattle. Fencing was expensive, so the boys used to shepherd the sheep on the hills and hurdle [pen the sheep in with hurdles or barriers] them at night.

At the age of seven I was sent to the small school at Mount Torrens, four miles away. When I burst into tears and said I could walk no further, the older children would take turns to carry me on their backs. When we got home Mother allotted each of us a special task. Mine was minding baby Priscilla and keeping her out of mischief. There were certainly no drones in the Caldwell hive but the seasons were dry and unfavourable and things were not too prosperous with us in South Australia.

Like many Australians, Martha is prone to laconic understatement. Ann Caldwell had to feed and clothe eight children on the earnings from poor quality land without a good water supply and the family probably hovered around the poverty line as their stock sickened and died around them. Ann would have realised that the bitter struggle would have continued throughout her life unless she went in search of better land and it must have been sheer desperation that made her decide to make the long wagon trek eastwards described in her daughter's memoirs.

> Mother heard stories about all the good land available in New South Wales under the Free Selection Act, sometimes known as the Robertson Land Act.

Premier John Robertson's Crown Land Acts were passed in 1860 and 1861, under which leasehold areas, whether surveyed or not, were thrown open for selection and sale. Selectors (small farmers) could purchase for one pound an acre any block of Crown Land from 16–129 hectares in size. Each selector was only required to pay a deposit of one-quarter of the purchase price. They had to occupy the land for three years and 'improve' the property by erecting buildings, usually huts made of slab or bark. The balance of the purchase price plus interest could be paid over an extended period. Robertson's Selection Acts were intended to encourage small settlers with limited capital, like Ann Caldwell and in turn Martha and her husband, to own their own land and become yeoman farmers. Martha continues the story of the great trek east.

> It was 1864 when we started our eight weeks' journey in the tilted [covered] waggon [a lumbering vehicle—sometimes with eight wheels or more and drawn by as many as ten horses—used to transport goods when speed was no object, as they travelled at between ten and fifteen kilometres per hour depending on the type of country traversed and how much bush had to be cleared to allow the passage of the wagon].
>
> William and John were now twenty and eighteen years of age respectively while Olivia was fourteen and I was ten [Elizabeth, the eldest daughter, was twenty-two and not a member of the family group at this point]. Mother called a family conference and it was decided we should make for land beyond the Murray River and set about making a new home for ourselves.
>
> Although only ten, I was pretty sharp on the uptake and apprehensive about such a long journey through wild and lonely bush. A lot of strange men came to see my mother about selling the stock and the property. But what concerned me most was that Lassie, our favourite black cattle dog, might be sold along with the rest of the stock. Lass was my pet and playmate. I was greatly relieved when Mother told me Lassie was far too precious to be left behind.
>
> Finally Mother had sold everything we owned except the covered waggon, five horses and the camping requirements for our journey.

It would take the Caldwells eight weeks to travel from South Australia to Albury via Victoria over an unknown and unformed track in a wagon with seven children—a severe ordeal for anyone, let alone a woman without a husband and with no guide.

> The weather had been dry for months, but we took no risks of a drenching. Our tarpaulin tilt was rainproof [a tilt was a canvas cover, curved and stretched round an interior wooden frame, similar to the covered wagons used by American and South African pioneers].
>
> We had just enough bedding and space [in the wagon] to accommodate the eight of us [including the mother] at a pinch. Many others had gone the eastward trail, usually two or more migrant families travelling in company, but, unlike most of them, Mother who was good at navigating through the bush actually chose to travel alone.

Ann seems to have acquired a great deal of bush lore and navigational skills, making her unusual for her time. In both Australian and America[5] during the great Pacific migrations of 1837–1840 to California and Oregon, women usually left all the work of navigating on pioneer treks to the men. The women stayed in the rear of the wagons with the children during the day (while the men drove) and emerged to cook in the evening. Women then packed up the cooking utensils for the next day's journey and struggled to maintain an acceptable standard of cleanliness. Many hated it. Many American women saw the wagon journey as a hellish but necessary transition to a new land where they could renew their domestic life once more.

> My mother always insisted that fire to cook with, water to drink, and food were the main requirements on a long journey into unknown country. We had a stock of wooden matches in longish brown tins: mother took her flint and tinder-box in case we ran out of matches.[6] We carried a barrel of water to be replenished at streams on the way. As for food, we started with fresh and salted meat, tinned fish and jam, a bag of potatoes and plenty of flour, tea, sugar, and not forgetting a good lump of suet in the flour bag for dumplings on special occasions, mostly on Sundays, when we would always rest from travel. Of course mother had her little stock of medicines, not omitting the hateful castor oil, medicinal salts and senna [a powerful laxative brewed up with water into senna tea and rightly or wrongly used as a bush remedy for a variety of ailments]—how we youngsters hated the lot of them!
>
> My older brothers, William and John, took turns with mother in driving while the girls walked before the waggon lopping low-hanging limbs of trees and removing logs and other obstructions.
>
> Our teams consisted of five fine strong horses. I can see them now, Duke and Sultan, a brown horse and a bay; Punch, a heavy coacher; Captain, a heavy draughthorse and Prince, a fine chestnut horse taking the lead. A pile of chaff in the waggon served as bedding for us as well as fodder for our team of horses. They were always hobbled at night so they could not stray and leave us stranded. The boys took turns to keep watch over our cattle.
>
> Mother kept us well supplied with tasty camp oven bread made with grape-stone yeast. Mrs Greig, a Gumeracha neighbour, gave our mother a bag of grape stones before we left. Mrs Greig's husband made his own wine and the grape stones came from the strainings. With flour and sugar they supplied the ferment. Mother would let the sponge rise during the day and bake at night; it was lovely bread, and when we ran out of meat and vegetables our meals were composed of fried bread alone. But usually we had a bit of beef or mutton and perhaps a bit of butter and a drop of precious milk when we were favoured by good luck and found a settler's home along the track, who would give or sell us milk.
>
> Sometimes Mother made a johnny cake, or what we'd call a soda loaf

The strain of the long wagon journey with young children to feed and keep clean shows on this woman's face. While many American women made the trek across the plains of the mid-west in wagons, few widows like Irish-born Annie Caldwell in Australia did the same without the protection of a husband.

James A. Turner's painting shows a typical tilted or covered wagon in which children are sleeping. Annie Caldwell's journey would have been very similar but her eldest sons were in their teens and she had a further seven younger children with her. Private collection.

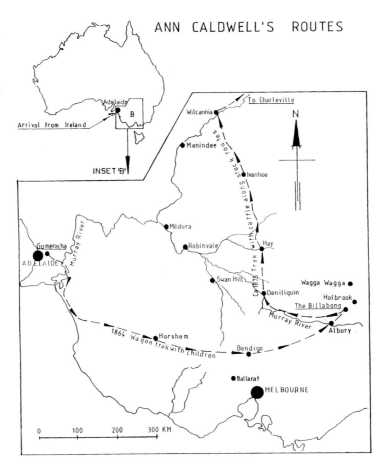

now, and she would fry it in the pan. There was no baking powder but Mother mixed soda and acid with a little cream of tartar instead and showed us how to toss the 'johnny' and catch it in the pan as it turned. But none of us children could manage it.

Our waggon crossed the Murray River on a punt. My brothers caught a twelve-pound cod there which mother promptly salted for the road.

I shall never forget the long and trying journey over the dry bed of Coorong Lake. Ordinarily it is a stretch of about 90 miles of water, with flocks of pelicans and other wild fowl and even sea gulls; but drought had absorbed all the water, and we chose to follow the lake bed rather than tackle the even more difficult sandhill route. The stench of rotting fish was almost insufferable. We youngsters, with the exception of Priscilla, the baby [of the family], used to walk to lighten the load on the horses. We walked, until our feet became chafed and sore from the sand and how good it was when night finally came to escape from the heat.

At length, we crossed the border into Victoria. When informed of the fact, I looked about expecting to see a big town, but nothing more than bush appeared in view. We had no road maps or guides, and judged our location mainly by guesswork. When we struck the Wimmera River, the country was delightfully green, a treat to our sand-dazzled eyes. I thought it must be our 'Promised Land', and asked Mother if the journey was over, but she only shook her head and smiled.

The boys shot three wild ducks which provided quite a feast, and once they even shot a wild turkey. They had two old-fashioned muzzle-loading muskets with iron ramrods. The boys used to let me fire off a cap now and again and I became quite a good shot. Rabbits had not invaded the country in 1864, or we could have turned them to good account when our mutton ran out.

When we reached a creek near nightfall we always camped. Many a time there was no creek, although the boys nearly always managed to reach water on a Saturday night so that Mother and the two eldest girls could do the family washing, and get the things dried and folded over Sunday—it was not possible to do any ironing.

Flat irons were heated over a fire or other more complicated varieties had detachable handles and were filled with burning coals. A third type was designed to take kerosene, which would have been difficult to obtain on the road. Presumably the children also bathed in the creek. Keeping clothes clean must have been impossible, as the dust of the road would have become ground into trailing hemlines and men's sweatladen shirts. Despite this, Ann Caldwell instilled into her daughters the principles of good order and hygiene on the wagon trail.

However, we managed to keep things clean. Once, at a small lake, the water was so brackish that the cake of soap floated on the salty water.

If a stranger had come along after our supper was over and peeped in through the back flap of the waggon he would have seen our mother reading from a novel to entertain us, while the boys sheltered the candle from the wind. How we all looked forward to those readings—popular romances, Mr. Dickens' latest work and some poetry from the old country.

Although Martha does not mention this, her mother must have had some education in the Irish National or free school before she emigrated as she used to read novels to her children at night on the long wagon journey. This made her unusual for a selector's wife in the 1840s when only some thirty per cent of women could read and write.

One night Mother's reading was interrupted by the thunder of hundreds of cattle hooves in a mad stampede from their camp a mile from us. We huddled together in the waggon for safety peering out through the canvas of the tilt. On the cattle came in a mad rush, roaring and bellowing and amidst them, and on their flanks came the drovers at full gallop, cracking their whips and yelling in an effort to turn the herd. We thought the great beasts would wreck us, waggon and all, and trample us underfoot, but the waggon slowed them down and split them into two streams that divided around us. Our horses took fright and bolted in their hobbles. Without the horses we could not continue and it took the two boys a whole day to find them and bring them back.

I shall never forget the first time a mob of blacks visited our camp. I thought we were doomed. One lubra kept putting her little finger into the bowl of her black clay pipe as a hint that she was out of tobacco. Mother had brought a stock to please them should they put in an appearance. The boys handed some sticks of tobacco round which put them all in a good, friendly humor. They told us of the road ahead and the creeks. But I was scared and dreamed about them all night long. The boys teased me. They told me that if I didn't behave mother would leave me with the blacks and I would have to eat roast possum and goanna.

We passed through Big and Little Bendigo. I don't remember much about the streets or houses, but I can still see great heaps of clay and gravel thrown up from the holes left deserted by the gold miners. Mother's brother, Tom, had made a fortune there in the early days of the fields. He had gone back to Ireland to live at his ease.

The weeks rolled by as we journeyed on in our waggon, crossing the Campaspe, the Goulburn, the Broken Rivers, and fording the Ovens River at Wangaratta.

From there our course lay north-east over dry, lonely country and brought us at long last to the Murray River with the thriving town of Albury on the opposite side.

By now we were all weary after the long and toilsome journey. There were repairs to be made to the waggon and harness, which were beyond the scope and skill of the two boys. The team badly needed a spell and improved conditions. Now that we had reached the boundary of the wild country and we were about to explore for a new home, it was necessary to make inquiries as to where land might be available for selection, so we decided to rest by the river for a fortnight.

The horses picked up condition quickly on the fine grass along the riverside. The boys made good use of their rods and lines and we all caught some fine fish. Food supplies including meat were now regular, and baker's bread from Albury relieved mother of the work of baking for us all, at least for a time. It was a treat to get fresh eggs, milk and fruit from a settler a short distance away.

At length our rest was over. Mother crowded us all into the waggon so as to reduce the toll fee as much as possible at the bridge. In Albury a good supply of rations was obtained at one of the stores. Having heard that there was a good camping ground at the Twelve Mile [Mullenjandera] we made our way in that direction reaching there about sundown. I remember there was a beautiful golden sunset. Thousands of other lovely sunsets I have forgotten, and yet that particular one became fixed in my mind because my mother said, 'Look children, at the gold in the sky!' I believe she thought it a good omen.

Next morning she gave John and William, the two boys money and food and told them to have a good look round the country. They were to find a place where we could select a block. It must have water and they were not to come back till they had found a place.

Each night, when seated round the table made from a packing box at which we children ate our supper, Mother would be troubled, wondering how the boys were getting on and where they were that night.

A week passed without word. But just as we were going to commence supper, back they came, tired and dusty, but in good spirits.

They had found a place called Big Billabong, nearly six miles from a place called The Ten Mile [later known as Germanton after J. B. Pabst, a German pioneer settler in the area. In World War I, due to anti-German feeling, the name 'Germanton' was changed to Holbrook].

William described the land as good grazing country and recounted how they had struck a selector near The Ten Mile, named Palmer, 'a really good man', who took them round to a fine place on Green's Run. Mother, practical as ever asked whether the 'Billabong' was a creek but was told that it was really a string of waterholes, which according to Mr Palmer could keep the stock going.

The next day was Thursday and land court day at Albury. The camp was early astir. After breakfast the horses were harnessed to the waggon, and back went mother and the boys to Albury, where a block was selected in John's name.

Ann Caldwell had to obtain the land in the name of her son, even though he was under twenty-one and she was paying: but it was Ann who would be manager on *The Billabong*, helped by her sons until they married and took up properties of their own.

Further household necessaries were then bought, and, by nightfall, the boys were back again with us at the camp. Mother explained that five shillings per acre had to be paid as deposit and the balance of fifteen shillings per acre would be paid yearly at the rate of one shilling per year, part of that going to pay the interest, which was at the rate of five per cent, and part to go off the principal. In 28 years

the land would be freehold, Mother said, and we would get the deeds from the Government. [Ann Caldwell obviously had a shrewd business head and realised the financial benefits of this scheme].

In two days we reached *The Billabong* and settled down on our selection. The weather was warm and fine, and we lost no time in building a slab hut to shelter us.

There was no stringy bark timber about, as bad luck would have it, so we had to use box bark for the roof and walls. Box was not as easy to strip as stringy bark, but Mother and us girls lent a hand and before long we had a rough dwelling erected. Like most of the early settler-type of cabins, it was barely sufficient to give us all sleeping and living accommodation so someone still had to sleep in the waggon each night. Even if the place was not very stylish, we thought it wonderful after being housed in a dusty waggon riddled with roaches for so long. The sheets of bark were secured to the rafters by means of greenhide thongs.

The boys were real proud when they had finished the hut, and next they put up a shed and a stockyard. Those things had to come before we could think about buying cattle. How hard we all did work! Mother seemed able to turn her hand to any sort of man's work after her ten years as sole manageress.

Ann Caldwell was a remarkable pioneer and farm manager. Irish women were used to hard physical labour on farms where they did much of the work in the fields and cut peat for fuel, in addition to the usual household chores involved in bringing up children—cooking; the arduous laundry routine; continual washing of greasy plates and other utensils in water that also had to be fetched and boiled; sweeping out the slab hut with its dirt floor and shutter for a window and the strip of linoleum or oil cloth on the floor of the central passageway.

Ann made butter in a wooden churn by laboriously beating it with a pounder, and made curd cheese to earn extra money. Poddy calves and sick lambs had to be cared for, cows milked night and morning, the hens fed and eggs collected. Doubtless she learned to mend fences as well as to keep farm accounts.

Mother was 'the boss' and kept us children well up to our jobs. The place had to bring in money, mother decided, so twelve cows with calves at foot were purchased. Into the yard they went, with their calves in pens near by. All that bellowing and bleating made it [the first night] the rowdiest night of our lives. Mounted bareback on a quiet pony a neighbour had lent us, I used to ride around the mob as they grazed in the day. At night they lay round the yard chewing their cuds while the calves were in the pens. We now had lots of milk and cream and butter for our cheesemaking. Each of us youngsters was given a cow to name and to make us take a sort of owner's interest in the property.

About ten acres of land was now cleared hurriedly in order to get in a crop of wheat. The ploughing of that new and not too cleanly grubbed ground was tough work with the old single-wheeled plough. The harrowing was done with the head of a green tree for harrow, and many a spill I had trying to stand on the dragging limbs to get a ride.

At last the paddock was sown. We all helped to put up a rough bush fence with the aid of the strong horses to draw the foundation logs into place. Kangaroo grass was the main feed; it was everywhere in those days. The cows liked the heads of the seed and the sweet, green pickings low down on the ground. Straying bulls often got into fights. They would tear holes in the ground, and when rain came the grass shot up to the stirrup irons of your saddle. Many a time I got a nasty spill when a horse put his foot into one of those 'bull-holes'.

It was a wild free life, and we all felt very happy in our new home. Mother used to sing as she flew round doing her many jobs through the day including the butter and cheese making. When night came she was always sewing and mending and darning for us. She never complained.

It was not long before our loneliness was relieved by the arrival of our friends, the Ross family from Gumeracha, who selected an adjoining block and settled down to farming. When we first arrived at *The Billabong* there was no school of any kind available. It was quite a time before a man named Boreham opened a little school in a public house at Fern Hill. Our schoolmaster was, no doubt, capable enough as a teacher, but the conditions were much against him. Our schoolroom was in the rear of the premises and our master often found his way round to the bar. We were not granted any play at 11 o'clock, although Mr Boreham took himself off for ten minutes every day at that time during which the more studious among us read our books, or worked our sums. We worked on slates, but always had to copy our figuring work into an exercise book and take it home each night, I suppose to show our parents some evidence of our progress.

It was five miles to school, and I rode there on Cocky, my bay pony. With me rode William and Bob Ross, two fine boys who were my guardians along the track. I rode side-saddle fashion, although mounted on a man's saddle [it was thought highly improper for females to ride astride at that time, but must have been a difficult balancing feat without a proper side-saddle].

A steady demand for our cheese at Albury kept mother hard at work. She said that the cheese should never be less than six months old to be of satisfactory flavour [sic], but our cheese could never wait to reach that age. We girls and Mother made it with rennet prepared from the stomach of a calf killed at six weeks old which had been constantly penned, and never allowed to eat grass. The milk was placed in a large tub and kept at blood heat. The rennet matured in a week, and was mixed with the milk, in the proportion of a dessertspoonful to a gallon of milk. That curdled the milk. After an hour the curd was sliced with a long knife, first one way and then across at right angles. In another hour the whey had risen to the surface and was taken out with a saucer, dipping and pressing down to get the last drop available.

Next we would wring the curd through cheese-cloth into a large basin, getting the last drop of whey. Then a piece of cheese-cloth was fitted into a round wooden vat, and the curd, having been well rubbed up with the hands, was salted and a little coloring added, then put into the vat and folded over with the cheese-cloth. A round, neat-fitting lid was inserted in the vat and pressure applied by means of a heavy beam-lever and block. I remember that an old boiler [cauldron] full of bricks or stones hung at the end of the beam to increase the pressure. The cheeses would be taken out and turned every three days, and pressed for about three weeks, after which they were stood on a bench and turned every day, each receiving a good rubbing with butter, top and bottom, at the first turning.

We were all fond of curds and whey. Mother also made fine butter, but there were no separators or patent drum churns then, the cream being beaten to the turn entirely by hand in a big wooden churn with a plunger.[7] Every settler made a bit of butter; the big factories were never dreamt of in those days.

With the passing years came family partings. My sister, Elizabeth was married and living in South Australia. Olivia married a farmer named Crouch and resided at Dry Timber Plain, six miles from The Ten Mile; my sister Sophia married a man named John Bates, and went to live on a station in Queensland. I was nineteen years of age when a young selector named David Cox came to claim my hand.

Martha married David Cox, son of the leaseholder of Livingstone Gully near Wagga and he and Martha set off to make a new life, ending up, after a number of false starts, in north-western New South Wales as pioneer settlers at Corongo Peak in the Bourke/Cobar area. From this point Martha's memoirs are concerned with her own family and their story. She is isolated on the land, has a son, and only sees her mother in Queensland, when years later in her fifties, Ann Caldwell moved to join her sons in a new farming venture near Charleville.[8]

Martha and her husband and children also took up a property near Charleville but following the birth of their second child her health broke down under the harsh conditions and poor diet. David took Martha to rejoin her mother and brothers. Ann Caldwell cared for Martha and the baby, which Ann weaned as Martha was too ill to feed it. Ann was still involved with farming herself and was the mainstay of her daughters-in-law in times of childbirth or illness. Martha and her family moved to the Wagga Wagga region and established themselves there. Ann Caldwell went to live a Tea-tree Creek, Kyeamba with a married daughter, Agnes (Mrs Lawrence Cox), where she remained until she died at age sixty-nine, surrounded by her family. Martha Cox died many years after her mother, in March 1947, and was buried in the Cox family's extensive burial plot in the cemetery in Wagga Wagga, which served both the Protestant and Catholic communities. Ann Caldwell is buried nearby in the same plot but while the men are commemorated by headstones these remarkable pioneer women have none.

[1] Madgewick, R. B. *Immigration into Eastern Australia.* 1937. Cited in Kiddle, M. *Caroline Chisholm*, Melbourne University Press.

[2] *Argus*, 13 January 1902, pp. 5–6. Anon. 'Hard Lot of Farmers' Wives'.

[3] Clark, C.M.H. *A History of Australia*, Volume IV, p. 171. Melbourne University Press, 1979.

[4] Ann Caldwell may have seen other married women or widows succumb to depression, drink or suicide and determined this would not happen to her. The popular myth of pioneer women is that they were all heroically brave while today's women are made of less stern stuff and seek consolation in Valium and counselling. Reality was somewhat different. Many convict women found themselves trapped in monotonous lives in rural slums in the bush because

they believed a loveless marriage to a poor farmer was better than a lifetime of domestic drudgery as servant to a squatter's family. Lea-Scarlett's research indicates that 'isolation and loneliness were large factors in the drink craze' that was recorded as affecting some female pioneers. Godden and others state that women were driven by harsh circumstances to suicide or even murder in the bush. See Lea-Scarlett, E. *Gundaroo*. Canberra Roebuck Society, 1972, p. 23, cited in Godden, Judith. *A New Look at Pioneer Women*. From *Hecate*, Volume v, Number 2, 1979, pp. 6–21.

[5] It is interesting to compare Martha Caldwell's account of her mother's spirited leadership of their pioneer trek with a study of American unwilling 'waggon trail' women in Faragher, Johnny and Stansell, Christine, *A Heritage of Her Own*, Chapter 10 in the monograph *Women and their Families on the Overland Trail to California and Oregon, 1842–1867*. Simon and Schuster, New York, 1979.

[6] At the age of ten, Martha was probably told little of the dangers of such a journey through wild country. With many ex-convict bushrangers at large, Ann's sons, who had guns to shoot game, would have been prepared to use them to defend their lives should that need have arisen.

[7] Ann Caldwell used the oldest and the simplest device, a plunge churn consisting of a timber cylinder fitted with a lid and a plunger. The operator used a 'plunger' (a broom handle, fitted with a perforated disk at the end—somewhat like a potato masher) up and down in the timber churn full of cream which was at a temperature of 68°F or 20°C. If conditions were right the butter would 'come'. Cold water was added and the operator kept churning for a few more minutes. Buttermilk, a highly prized, delicious drink, was carefully poured off. Clean cold water was then poured into the churn in large quantities to wash the butter of any residual buttermilk. The butter was placed into a 'butter worker', a scrupulously clean shallow wooden tray or trough with a wooden roller that was rolled up and down. More water was poured on while the butter was rolled and 'cleaned'. Unless the butter was absolutely clean, 'off' flavours would develop. Once the buttermilk had been washed out, the butter was salted and worked again and stored in an earthenware crock in which it was 'rammed' hard with a mushroom-shaped tool to expel all the water and air to stop it going rancid. The salt could be washed out before eating the butter. In the heat of the Australian summer, butter making would be undertaken at night when the temperatures were cooler so the butter would not immediately turn to oil.

[8] John Oxley Library, Brisbane, has no separate entry for Caldwell and it has not been possible to trace exactly where the Caldwell family property was located but it is believed to have been between Thargomondah and Charleville.

CHAPTER 11

Mary McConnel
(1824–1910)

FOUNDER OF THE BRISBANE CHILDREN'S HOSPITAL

Dark-haired, demure Mary McLeod met her future husband, David McConnel, when visiting her brother, who was a medical practitioner in Yorkshire. David McConnel was also visiting his brother, who farmed near Mary's brother. David McConnel, a typical Scots Presbyterian, well-built, athletic and with sandy blonde hair, had just returned from Queensland, then known as Northern New South Wales, where he had established by hard work and initiative the first sheep station on the upper Brisbane River, called Cressbrook.[1] He came from a farming background. Her parents were city dwellers from Edinburgh and the rest of her family were either in medicine or the church. There was instant attraction between the blonde young squatter and the raven-haired Mary, whose engagement portrait shows her with her long dark hair demurely fastened into an elegant chignon. She was religious, idealistic but surprisingly practical for one so young and had a quality of gentleness and sympathy which was to make her loved by everyone who knew her. Alexander McLeod gave David permission to marry his daughter the following year on the understanding that the young couple would remain in England to farm near Nottingham but, a few months later, David was urgently summoned back to Cressbrook by his brother John for financial reasons.

In 1848, Mary McConnel, then aged 24 was faced with the difficult dilemma of whether to let her husband return to Australia without her and stay behind to look after her elderly parents, or accompany David, who had originally promised her parents that he would stay on in England and let his brother John run the Australian Cressbrook property in his place. If she accompanied her husband to the Brisbane River Valley she would be one of the few white women for hundreds of miles. With her deep faith that God was guiding her life for a special purpose, she chose to go with her husband aboard the *Chasely*, a leaky rat-infested old vessel. Mary recounts how

> . . . I was led to decide in favour of going to Australia. The cup was a bitter one, but it had its own sweetness. I wrote to my dear parents, telling them that I must go, and asking them to commend me to God's care. Their hurt, reluctant consent was given and we left our friends and beloved Scotland. Then we went to London to make preparations for our departure on 31 December 1848.

> The ship *Chasely* had been chartered, along with two others, by Dr John Dunmore Lang, whose

Mary McConnel, demure, determined and attractive, poses for this signed photograph just after her marriage to David McConnel. John Oxley Library, Brisbane.

church was in Sydney, New South Wales.[2] These three ships were to convey well-chosen superior emigrants, intended to populate the towns that had been formed about 20 years before in the newly opened district of Moreton Bay. My husband took cabins in the *Chasely* for ourselves and our maid [Hannah].

We found a number of nice people among the emigrants, who had availed themselves of Dr Lang's arrangement with the British Government that on payment of 200 pounds they should have land privileges on arrival in Brisbane. The evening before sailing, Dr Lang came on board, and addressed the emigrants in a fatherly manner, reminding them of their responsibilities in making their home in a new land, and bidding them to be true to their religious principles. My husband made our large cabin in the stern most comfortable. Our bookshelf was well filled; two swinging candle lamps gave a fair light. We had a large double sofa that shut up into a single one for the day.

There was snow and sleet that night and the wind blew hard. Next morning we set sail on a voyage which was to take four months. The weather continued boisterous, and we crossed the Bay of Biscay in a gale. There we had the misfortune to lose overboard in a giant wave all our poultry and our sheep we had brought with us, save one which was reserved for a sumptuous repast when we arrived in Moreton Bay!

We had a disagreeable experience of rats both by day and night. My husband knew my antipathy to these rodents, and had brought two terriers with us, one from Skye, the other English. One we always had in our cabin; the other was invariably out on loan! At meals I always sat with my heels under me, the only protection I could have at these times. These rats became so numerous that water had to be put out for them to drink as it was found they were gnawing the ship, seeking for water since they were so thirsty.

There was real hardship when our fresh provisions were finished. Salt beef and pork were not at all appetising. We were very badly off for vegetables, milk and butter, as the art of preserving these items was at a very rudimentary stage. The bread was always heavy and dark, so we had to fall back upon mouldy ships' biscuits. We were each restricted to three pints of fresh water daily, for all purposes. We had a saltwater bath, which it would have been hard to do without.

In spite of all these drawbacks, we had pleasant times. Among the emigrants were some very nice people, well connected and well read. Their wives were very pleasant and one of them played the harp. We all did needlework, and often we sat together in my cabin, where we spent happy hours. We were all young married women, full of wonderment about the faraway land that was to be our home.[3]

They arrived in Moreton Bay on 1 May 1849. Mary reminisces:

My husband, self and maid were invited to leave the ship in the Customs boat. We took our two terriers with us. We were some hours going up the river to Brisbane. What a dismal waterway it was! Neither sign of house nor man and mangroves the only vegetation visible. Soon we were near Brisbane. The first building by the river was the Customs House, and close by lay Mr Thornton's cottage, from which there was a jetty. In the cottage we could see two ladies using a telescopic spyglass to see who was in the boat. An immigrant vessel landing in the Bay was an object of great excitement in those days. The landing took place and we were introduced to Mr Thornton's wife and stepdaughter. After me came my traps, [suitcases etc.] just such things as ladies in England travel with. One lady looked at them in amazement and pointed out to me that they would be of little use in Brisbane as there were no roads. My heart sank.

The former convict settlement of Moreton Bay with its stone buildings along North Quay that became the straggling frontier town known as Brisbane when Mary McConnel arrived in May 1849. Watercolour by Henry Boucher Bowerman. Photograph by the author who purchased the painting from Christie's, London. Now in John Oxley Library, Brisbane.

The houses did not have the luxury of spare rooms, so my husband secured accommodation for us in the only hotel which Brisbane could boast, the Bowes Inn. There Dr Ballow brought his young wife to see me. There were no ladies travelling, so the landlord thought it useless to provide public sitting rooms which would not be used. We were shown into a bare dining room, with a long table and many chairs. Several men were there who left when we entered. The verandah was the great rendezvous. I went into our rooms but when I wanted to shut the door I found that I had to put a chair against it as there was no handle, lock, nor bolt! I looked for a blind to the window, but it was innocent of such a luxury, and I could not spare the one towel to give the room privacy. Other things were equally unpleasant and we decided that we must leave the hotel.

My brother-in-law, Mr John McConnel, was also in the Colony. At the time of our arrival he had two rooms in Brisbane Town. When he heard that his brother David was just married and was bringing his wife to Moreton Bay, he had at once come to Sydney to look out for us. Although John had been told by letter that we were sailing direct for Moreton Bay, it was long after our arrival that he received that letter. Meanwhile we took possession of his two private rooms in a cottage belonging to Mr Swan, a quiet and respectable man, former owner of the *Courier*. The cottage was in George Street, where it crossed Queen Street, the principal thoroughfare.

The cottage was weatherboard, with a narrow verandah. A French window opened from the verandah into the sitting room. Another door, at the opposite end, led into the bedroom. They were sorry apartments. The sitting room had as its only contents, a table, some chairs, and two large packing cases containing the skins of birds and animals which John had preserved with evil-smelling arsenic, to send away to a museum. In this room there was no fireplace. I had become accustomed to bad cooking on board ship. Here it was no better, but at least the food was fresh, which was a decided improvement. It was all very rough and I had not learned to cope with this. Brisbane was a township with no general store. One does not easily get accustomed to such things.

In the evening of the day we moved into the rooms I heard a rustling noise, and a swarm of large, black flying insects hit me on the face. They came from behind the chest of drawers. I called out to my husband in terror. He said they were flying cockroaches! We had no protection from them that night. But next day we made net curtains to hang around the bed. Everything was unpleasant, although my dear husband made the best of it all for me.

There had been no rain for some months; now it began to fall in torrents. No one had a carriage of any sort, not even Captain John Wickham, the Government Resident. His house, Newstead, at Breakfast Creek, was some miles down the river. He rode on horseback into town along what is now Wickham Street, but everyone

Cressbrook Homestead on the McConnel's cattle property in the Brisbane Valley painted by Conrad Martens when he stayed there in 1851. Mary McConnel befriended Aboriginal women and some Aborigines appear in the foreground. The painting, once owned by the McConnel family, is now in a major private collection of Queensland art.

else came and went by river. There were no proper roads, and in such weather a carriage would have been of little use. My husband had gone to the ship to get our belongings on shore and his absence made it more dark and cheerless, and I was glad to find a fireplace in our bedroom.

When the rain cleared people came to call on me—Captain and Mrs Wickham, Dr and Mrs Ballow, Mr Duncan, Collector of Customs, with his wife and daughter. They were all most cordial in their expressions of welcome. Mrs Annie Wickham was a daughter of Hannibal Hayes Macarthur, of Vineyard, Sydney, who I think was the first to introduce sheep into the Moreton Bay district. Mrs Wickham was young and very charming. Later she became a good friend to me. [Anna Wickham was married to Captain John Wickham, formerly on the voyage of the *Beagle* with Charles Darwin and Conrad Martens. Their home, Newstead House, was then Brisbane's unofficial Government House.]

Before long our brother returned from Sydney. He was glad to have a sister in this new and faraway land, and nothing could exceed the heartiness of his welcome. We had to vacate his apartments and we found a small, wooden, five-roomed cottage on Kangaroo Point, on the south side of the river. The walls were unlined weatherboards and the shingled roof was very leaky. There was a 4 foot (1.2 m) wide verandah along the front, enclosed by a wooden paling. We were forced to put most of our imported furniture in a shed, but we had to find room for the piano, one of our wedding gifts. This could only be done by blocking the door that gave access to the verandah, so that all our visitors had to enter through the kitchen. The roof of the sitting room was so leaky that when a shower came I had to place utensils to catch the raindrops to save my pretty things. And yet, how happy we were in that rough little place!

My husband bought acres of land at Bulimba, a few miles down the river on the south side, and set about clearing and building. I accompanied him and the surveyor when they went down to inspect the land. It was too rough for me to go all the way, so they seated me on a log to await their return. It was then that I made my first acquaintance with a snake, lying in a heap of withered leaves. It raised its head, showing a beautiful scarlet throat. I seemed hypnotised and could not take my eyes away from it, but I did not feel any fear.

The work of clearing the land and building *Bulimba House* became an unfailing object of interest to us. Our only way of going to the spot was by river, so my husband purchased a boat. We took many boat trips, spending days watching the progress of our new home. The house was built of white freestone, brought up in punts from a quarry some miles down the river.

While we were waiting for our new home to be ready we paid a visit to Cressbrook, my husband's station about 90 miles (144 km) up the Brisbane River. It was a sheep and cattle station found and taken up by him in 1841–2. The journey was a formidable one for a lady to take in those days, especially for me as I could not ride. We had brought out with us a heavy, four-wheeled phaeton which we had used during the few months that we lived in Nottinghamshire, and we travelled in that. It seated four. My husband and I sat in front, and Hannah, with the smallest amount of luggage we could possibly do with, sat behind. The groom led spare horses, carrying saddlebags filled with clothing. As there were neither made roads nor bridges, we had some rough experiences. To save the phaeton's springs, they were bound up with green hide, the untanned hide of a bullock cut up in strips, not very elegant in appearance, but answering our purpose well.

Half way along our journey was a small township called Woogaroo, now the site of an enormous lunatic asylum [Woolston Park Hospital]. The place is beautifully situated on the Brisbane River. A pretty cottage in this early township was the home of Dr Stephen Simpson, the first Commissioner of Crown Lands for the Moreton Bay district. He was a man past middle life and a widower, a doctor of medicine, who had travelled much. We greatly enjoyed his interesting accounts of his travels. This was my first experience of bush hospitality; his hearty welcome was delightful. We were made most comfortable; his arrangements were simple but with an air of refinement.

From here it was an easy journey to Ipswich, or Limestone as it was then called. Being the head of navigation, it was a busy little town. Goods came up from Brisbane by river and the streets were lined with long teams of bullocks and drays that had brought wool, tallow, and hides from the interior. They were reloaded with necessary goods for the stations: flour, tea and sugar, as well as all the contents of a bush store.

The Ipswich Inn we stayed at was a rough little place and very rowdy. We started early next day, a rough way over miles of black soil. It was a feat of dexterity to keep clear of the ruts made by the great wheels of the heavily laden bullock drays. We crossed impossible looking gullies with steep and often slippery banks! I used to shut my eyes, abandoning myself to God. Then we came to 'wattle-tree country', poor soil, but so pretty, for the trees were in bloom, and the air fragrant with their sweet scent. We had to keep zigzagging to avoid fallen trees.

It had been a long, weary day, and it was quite late when we arrived at Wivenhoe Inn. Many drays were camped all about, their drivers carousing inside. The man and his wife who kept the Wivenhoe Inn seemed quite respectable. We had a private room, if one could call such a room private, for the partition separating it from the public room was of wooden boards 6 feet high! It was the same in our bedroom. The landlady brought in our supper of a fine ham, new-laid eggs, good bread and delicious fresh butter. We were very tired, and glad to rest.

Through the space between the partition and the shingled roof every single sound was heard, and, as the night wore on, the obscene talk of the bullock-drivers became unbearable. My husband went to the landlord to ask if he could quiet them. It was no use. Their money was just as good as other people's, they replied so we had to endure it.

We were off early next morning. A long journey was before us, with nowhere that we could stay the night till we reached Cressbrook. We stopped at the house of Major and Mrs North for lunch. The Major had lost a good deal of money by standing as security for a member of his family. He honourably paid his debt and came to Australia trying to retrieve his fortune. Their cottage was bark, with an earthen floor which was very uneven. His wife went to a box and took out a snow-white damask tablecloth, spread it on the rickety pine table, unsteady because of holes in the floor, and laid out on it some beautiful old silver. I was even more amazed when I saw her take a great pot off the fire, carry it outside and drain the water from the boiled fowls.

After the meal we hurried away as we had to reach Cressbrook before dark. About 8 miles [12.8 km] from the head station my husband stopped and bade me welcome to Cressbrook. Neither white man nor black did I see, nor hoof nor stock, and the stories about his sheep and cattle seemed to me all a myth, and I said so. My husband only laughed. As we neared the station the country became very pretty, and the road grew much better.

The crossing of Cressbrook Creek was beautiful. However, the banks were steep and the crossing difficult. Two and a half miles [4 km] further we came to a chain of lagoons. Here we were met by the super [superintendent or farm manager], Alpin Cameron, a big burly Scotsman, who gave us a hearty welcome. It cheered me to see a pretty, neat cottage and a well-stocked garden with a grapevine. Just in front of the house was a bunya tree planted by my husband in 1843. It is now a giant, called grandfather's tree. I felt rested, glad and thankful, for after the experience of the last two days I did not know what to expect.

We had a suite composed of sitting, sleeping and dressing rooms. The house was quiet and comfortable, though terribly bare. We took our meals in the common dining room. Our first meal was in the evening. The super [farm manager] presided. I sat beside my husband. There was an enormous tin teapot that held at least 8 quarts (9 litres) and it took both hands to lift it. There was an apology made for the sugar, which was as near black as could be. When the super learnt that I was coming to Cressbrook he had ridden to the various stations around, none of them nearer than 12 miles (19.2 km), to try in vain to get white sugar. Master and men shared alike what food was available. In the middle of the long table there was a huge mutton fat lamp which was not pleasant to smell but it gave a fairly good light. I often sat down with 14 men, most of them travellers arriving at sundown, which is never later than 7 o'clock. Cressbrook was on the main road. We often had very pleasant people to dinner, but I was always the only woman.

During that time I witnessed the most sudden and severe storm that I have ever experienced. Everybody was at the woolshed and I was alone in the house. Suddenly the sky become overcast, then black. It was almost dark when the rain, accompanied by hail, came down in torrents. The roofs were not sealed, and through the dry shingles the storm spouted down. There was not a dry spot or thing in the house. I was terrified. My husband and brother-in-law ran as fast as they could since the woolshed was some distance off and the water in places was already up to their knees, incredible as it may seem. They were much concerned as everything was dripping wet. Big woodfires were soon blazing, and Hannah, together with the married couple in the kitchen, set to work to make things better. Of course I did my share, and was glad to be busy. Many sheep were killed [as a result of the storm].

I was troubled by the extreme bareness and shabbiness of our sitting room, which had a very old sofa, six old cane chairs, and a square cedar table, but nothing more. One afternoon while my husband had gone to town to see how our house at Bulimba was progressing, my brother-in-law showed me the stores. There were bags of flour and sugar, chests of tea, saddles, bridles, hobbles, men's clothing and tobacco. In the corner of a shelf I spied a roll of unbleached thin grey linen. On my request it was brought into the house.

Mary goes on to tell how she used this linen to cover the sofa and chairs and her husband's crimson silk handkerchiefs as piping for the covers. Expecting her husband to be angry, Mary rushed to finish the room before he returned from work. Much to her surprise he was delighted with the results of her resourcefulness. In December they were able to move into *Bulimba House*, which was still not complete.

We moved into one large room, making a dividing partition of strong unbleached calico, the inner division [became] our bedroom, while we made the front part as nice a living room as possible. Beyond this was the store. The servant's room was overhead. No servants could be procured nearer than Sydney, although very soon after immigrant ships came directly to Moreton Bay. Our servants, a man and his wife, seemed respectable and capable. The woman was cook and laundress, the man was an indoor servant and also helped his wife. Hannah was housemaid and generally useful.

As the hot weather increased the mosquitoes became intolerable. I took refuge in our large bed, safely tucked inside the net curtains with my work, books and writing materials. With a swamp close by, the pests could not have been worse. Early in 1850 an immigrant ship arrived. From it we obtained an excellent gardener, James Johnston from Edinburgh. He had a nice young wife and a baby. The interesting work of gardening began and several acres of ornamental grounds in front and at the sides of the house were created. There was also a large and useful kitchen garden. My husband encouraged settlement of respectable families near to him. He had bought a good deal of land, and portions of this he sold to his work people. They had it on easy terms, making regular payment from their wages. Then from time to time they were let off work, allowing them to begin clearing and making their homes. I think our gardener was the first one to start. He was delighted with the new country and wished to bring his father and mother out. To have a house ready for them he worked hard all his spare hours.

Just about this time my first baby was born, and Mrs Johnston was my nurse as there were no special nurses available in those early days. I had a good doctor and all went well. James Johnston, our gardener, rose to own a sugar mill, built on his own land. He was a very intelligent man and well read, a grand type of my own countrymen. Ultimately he became a member of Parliament. These people, who remained with us down to the third generation, were invaluable. About this time my husband set up a large dairy at Cressbrook and had a milking herd of beautiful Devon cows. Another Scottish family was that of Thomas Cairns. Aided by his wife he took over the poultry yard and their daughter became our nursery-maid.

Among Dr Lang's immigrants was a first class cabinet-maker named Towell. My husband engaged him to come to Bulimba to make the furniture for the house, all except the beds which we brought from England. He used cedar and stained pine, and it was much admired by our visitors.

It was a busy time, clearing, draining, ploughing, with everything growing like mushrooms. Thus began the thriving district now called Bulimba. We began to have a considerable population around us. Among them were a number of children and we cast about to devise means for education and Sabbath observance. All the young people and their elders that came from the old country knew their three r's and were very intelligent. There was no teacher to be had in Brisbane, although there were one or two schools. My husband and I each had a large Sunday School class, he of boys and I of girls, and all except the little ones read to us. They were very regular in attendance, prepared their lessons well, and were quiet and attentive.

We also had frequent services on Sunday afternoons. There were two ministers in Brisbane, one Church of England, the other Independent.

They held regular Sunday services at Bulimba. About this time Mary's second son was born, although she does not mention the date of the birth.

On the north side the way was very rough, without a formed road. My enterprising husband bought a strip of land running from our ferry to North Brisbane, fenced it on both sides, and made a road. He also built stables, a little coach-house and a dwelling. There we put our conveyance, two horses and a man in charge, who also had charge of the ferry boat. This arrangement added greatly to our comfort and convenience.

In South Brisbane much business was being done with Ipswich and the bush, so it became a busy place. The Rev Mr Mowbray, who lived in Kangaroo Point, used to have services in South Brisbane when his health allowed him. He suggested to my husband that a Presbyterian church might be built there. A wooden church was erected, seating about 200 people.

In 1852 my youngest brother, Rev Walter Mcleod, arrived unexpectedly from Scotland. My joy was unbounded for not one familiar face had I seen since I came to this far off land. In those days when a steamer was coming up the river a bell was rung to announce the event a long way below our reach of the Brisbane River. On the day when this bell heralded my brother's arrival, we hastened down with our little son; and he and I stood by the boat-shed while the boat was rowed out into mid-stream by my husband to meet the steamer. I could scarcely bear my joy when I watched my brother leave it and enter the boat. As it neared the bank I came out of the darkness, and then the moment arrived when we were locked in each other's arms. He was three years younger than I, always delicate and needing tender care.

We had grown a great many pineapples, and I wished to send a hundredweight of pineapple jam to my relatives in England and Scotland. This caused a busy time, the pineapples first had to be reduced to pulp, placed in large earthenware jars and sprinkled with sugar. The work was done in my beautiful large storeroom.

At about one or two o'clock in the morning I awoke and found myself standing on the floor of our room, some way from the bed. I did not return to bed, but was impelled to walk towards the nursery. The moon shone brightly when I entered it. I passed Harry's cot, with its net curtains drawn and tucked in. I then passed the nurse's bed. All seemed still and peaceful. I watched the moon beams playing on the water and then turned again. Repassing Harry's cot I thought the moonbeams were too strong on it, and I went to draw the dimity curtain, when I thought the child looked strange. I instantly threw back the curtain and found he was in a fit, with his face dark purple, foam all round his mouth, his eyes glazed and his body rigid and cold. I took him in my arms, awakened the nurse and called my husband. The nurse went at once for hot water.

My kind friend and neighbour, Mrs Wickham had written for my benefit a list of rules useful for a young mother. One rule was never to be without hot water. [Mrs Wickham lived at Newstead House.] This I adhered to most faithfully, so that our darling child was soon in a hot bath and he became less rigid. We tried to give him castor oil, the only thing we had for an emetic, but his teeth were clenched and we could not open them. Soon there was no need of an emetic for he brought up a great quantity of pineapple pulp. After this he quickly recovered, and the life of our child was saved! Unobserved, the child had been running backwards and forwards taking each time a handful of the delicious pineapple pulp. He was under two years of age but was very precocious, walking at ten months and speaking early. How glad and thankful I was that I kept the rules given to me by my dear friend Annie [Wickham, who would, shortly after, die of some tropical fever].

I had begun to feel contented and happy in my far-away home. The distance caused the one heartache in my otherwise happy life. I had one of the best and kindest of husbands, two boys and my beloved brother. My new home was beautiful, and there was much in which I could take a real interest. Our people were very dependent upon us, and it was in our power to help them.

Mary grew into a confident, well-organised and hard-working woman who came to love her adopted land and coped well with the trials of pioneering. Since her brother was a doctor she had some medical knowledge and visited any sick woman or child within riding distance. Mary dispensed sensible medical counsel, books to read and medicine when suitable. However, when she developed a lump on her own knee an alcoholic doctor informed her husband she was dying with gangrene and left her to her own devices. Mary relates the progress of her severe illness:

One day there was a regatta in Moreton Bay. My husband was very fond of boating. I was feeling better, and I persuaded him to go to the regatta while my brother remained with me. Towards evening I became very ill, fainting continually. My brother was anxious and sent one of our men for my husband and for the doctor, who also was sailing on the bay. My husband arrived and every restoration was tried, but still I continued fainting. The doctor was long in coming, so my husband sent again and again. At last he came but was quite tipsy. When he entered my room, the smell of drink made me sick. He looked at me, felt my pulse, and then took my husband aside to tell him I was dying and would not live till morning. He left some foolish prescription, and took his departure.

When day was breaking my brother carried me downstairs to the drawing room. I was laid on a couch by the open French windows. It was haymaking time. The farm servants, who were Germans, sang while they worked. The fresh early morning, the scent of hay and the rhythmic merry singing seemed to work as a charm on me. There gradually came longer intervals between the faintings. My husband, after consultation with my brother, decided to ride to Ipswich, some 30 miles (48 km) away, and fetch Dr Sachs to see me. We parted with the probability of not meeting again on earth. I commended him to God and he started off.

On arrival in Ipswich my husband begged the doctor to come to Bulimba. But the doctor had a most important case on hand and could not leave and suggested that I come to Ipswich to see him. My husband decided to engage a river steamer to go to Toogooloowah [the Bulimba property, as it was also known] to fetch me and he found a furnished cottage with four very small rooms. He returned home to find me no worse. Next morning the steamer arrived and I was carried on board in my bed. A widowed sister of James Johnston came with me as nurse and Harry and a maid also accompanied me. I had to leave my baby behind with his nurse, who was a good and tender woman. My brother, who came also, lodged with my husband at a hotel close by.

I bore the journey well, and my bed was put in the largest of the four little rooms. Dr Sachs came as soon as possible. After examination he took my husband aside and said, 'I cannot undertake this case. Your wife probably will die and I will be blamed for it. I have a reputation to make.' At last he yielded to earnest pleading. On the following day he took charge of my almost hopeless case. The leg was much worse than he had anticipated and he proposed amputation. My dear husband tenderly broke this painful alternative to me. When I said that I would rather die, Dr Sachs agreed to try and save my leg [without amputation].

For many weeks he poured liquid caustic down my leg [which should have burned the flesh] but to me it felt just like water. However he persevered and twice a day applied the caustic and bandages. I had a cane lounge chair put on wheels and was kept out in the open air all day long, and scarcely had any food, only bread dipped in champagne and herb tea made by the doctor.

One day, while having the caustic poured down my let, it felt as if a little red hot cinder was rolling down my limb. Dr Sachs threw down what was in his hand, gave a skip across the floor and excitedly cried, 'Now I can give you hope. Life is coming back to the limb!' From that day there was a steady though slow improvement.

Now I felt stronger I had a great longing to see my baby. He came up from Bulimba with his nurse and he looked so bonnie! It was good for me to have him with me again. However teething problems went hard with him. I do not think the good doctor understood the treatment of infants and my beautiful boy died when he was only seven months old. I tried not to fret and, sought to be resigned to our Father's will. His little forlorn brother wept and fretted. His father brought him a little toy from Brisbane. He looked at it, burst into tears, and returning it to his father said, 'Papa give it to God, and ask Him to give it to my little brother Alick'.

Then the day came when I was allowed to use crutches, but my foot scarcely touched the floor. Gradually it improved and one day I told the Doctor that, if I had a high-heeled shoe, I probably could walk. He replied that I should never have high-heeled shoes since I must compel my leg to get straight and he was right. After about a year and a half I walked as well as ever and my heart was full of gratitude. I prayed that I might become a better woman, with a heart alive to the sufferings of others and able to help them.[4]

Undoubtedly these painful experiences caused Mary to become the motivating force in the founding of what is now the Royal Brisbane Children's Hospital and increased Mary's faith that God had sent her to Queensland with a special mission in life. Mary's eldest daughter, Mary McLeod (Banks) described how at Cressbrook a laundry maid got into difficulties in the creek at Cressbrook while the children were bathing. While all around her panicked, Mary, who could not swim, quietly waded out to her in water up to her chin in spite of her heavy skirts and crinoline and saved the hysterical girl from drowning by dragging her to safety.[5] She had that quiet day-to-day courage which characterised so many Australian pioneer women.

Bulimba House by Conrad Martens, the first stone house in Brisbane, built by the McConnels beside the Brisbane River. John Oxley Library, Brisbane.

Mary McConnel was descended from two ancient Highland Scots families, the McLeods and the Roses. Open hospitality was as much part of life in the Highlands of Scotland as in the Australian bush and she entertained all travellers who sought hospitality at Cressbrook with care and kindness. She had been brought up in a cultured, academic and sheltered world but at Cressbrook and at *Bulimba House* she coped with daily emergencies, hard physical work in sub-tropical surroundings, illness and isolation, acting as manager of all household and dairy activities as well as unpaid social worker to their numerous tenants and employees, behaving as 'to the manor born' since her husband was indeed one of the largest landowners and employers in Queensland at that time. In the era long before the welfare state Mary fulfilled many roles: teacher, counsellor and even medical advisor sustained by her religious faith that her role in life was to help those less fortunate than herself. Some time after recovering from her gangrenous leg she had another accident when her horse bolted and she was thrown from the trap—again she went to Ipswich but she was only badly shaken. Her husband decided they would sell Bulimba House and visit England to give Mary a rest.

After all was settled we went almost immediately to Sydney, where we embarked. Harry had his fourth birthday at sea, and his friend little Willie Wilson his fifth.

We took a little Aboriginal orphan boy home with us. Our Cressbrook Super found him abandoned at Durundur, a station nearer the coast which also belonged to us. The boy was about seven years old. We decided to call him Alpin. He could not speak any English but he very readily adapted himself to the change of circumstances. He did not give us much trouble, and became quite a favourite on board. When we arrived in England he was a seven days' wonder; particularly in my brother's village in Yorkshire, where we went for a short time. We treated him in every way as we would have done a white boy.

The following seven years were spent in England, Scotland and on the Continent. Four more children were born to us during that time, two sons and two daughters, and my husband went once to Australia. While he was away my ten months old baby boy died, which was a great grief to me. [This was her second child to die.]

When we returned from our trip abroad we put Alpin, the Aboriginal boy, into school in Edinburgh and he made excellent progress. He was now getting on to be 16 years of age, and we wished him to learn a trade. Eventually my husband found it necessary to return to Queensland. As the length of his stay was indefinite, I desired to go with him. Since the summer heat in Australia had such a disastrous effect on my health, it was thought better that I should stay in Europe. My doctor said that I was in perfect health and that he could not see any reason why I should not go with my husband. However he advised that, if my health began to suffer, I should return home without delay. We decided Alpin should return with us.

In 1862 we again sailed for Australia in a sailing vessel bound for Sydney. I had an excellent nurse for the baby and we had quite a comfortable voyage. About a year before, the Moreton Bay District and all to the north of it had been formed into a new colony called Queensland, with Brisbane for its capital. Sir George Bowen was our first Governor.

On our return we found a great change for the better in things generally, although Brisbane was still in a very crude state. There were more people but no good hotel. Queensland now had its own Parliament and my husband was asked to become member of the Legislative Council. However he respectfully declined the honour. There was no easy way of getting to town in these days, so to accept meant he would have to live in Brisbane while the House was sitting. He did not wish to be so long away from Cressbrook, especially as he had been absent for nearly eight years. In declining he said he would leave the honour to one of his sons [in the future].

My husband and I, and the three children, the governess Miss Sargent and the nurse commenced the journey as soon as everything was ready. We had brought out a good dog-cart [a type of two-wheeled cart with a dog box under the seat] and the phaeton [a heavier open carriage with four seats] which carried us all. The luggage followed close behind in a covered waggon. The weather was fine, but the roads were so bad that progress was slow. We made Wivenhoe the first night. The inn was not comfortable, but it was clean and quiet. We made an early start next morning and reached Sandy Creek, where Esk now stands. We could not make the remaining 15 miles [24 km] to Cressbrook till long after dark, so there was nothing to do but to camp out. Two children with their governess slept in the dog-cart, the seats being removed, while nurse, baby and I were in the phaeton. The men camped on the ground beside the fire. The bush sounds in the night were very eerie. The notes of numerous birds, the screaming cockatoos, the howl of the dingo, and the buzz and chirrup of many insects were disquieting, but the children slept soundly.

We were glad when day broke, and all was bustle to get away. We went along at a good pace and soon arrived at Cressbrook. The necessary arrangements were made for us to move in. Alpin [the Aboriginal boy named after their farm manager] had so long enjoyed a civilised state in Britain that we thought he would not care to return to his old life. But the old scenes and his tribe who lionised him, were too much for him and he became restless. So we thought it best to send him back to the Old Country. My husband made good arrangements with a very kind captain to take him home in his ship. We did not tell Alpin till he was on board. I had packed his box, putting in little things I knew he would like. My husband took him to Brisbane the evening before the ship sailed, went on board with him, told him that he was going back to his friends who had been so kind to him and that he would come back in two or three years. He gave him a half-a-sovereign, said goodbye and left him with the captain. But the same night Alpin swam ashore, bought a tomahawk, and went into the far-away bush. He never came back, which was a grief to me. Perhaps we ought not to have taken him back to the scenes and people of his old life. We did it all for the best, wishing to keep him under our own eyes.

My husband set himself to make friends with the different tribes that lived on the land of Cressbrook and they soon got to like and trust him. He never failed to do what he promised. I know that one or two of the Aboriginal men speared cattle, once an imported bull from England, but of course they had no idea of the value of the animal.

Mary was an efficient manager at Cressbrook where the storeroom was kept locked and groceries that were running short were noted down by her on a slate, as they had to be brought once a month by bullock wagon from Brisbane. Soap, tea, flour and working clothes for the men on the property were all dispensed from the storeroom by Mary. The storeroom was constantly plagued by ants and she insisted that all sweet things were placed on stands with their feet in saucers of water which the ants would not cross. Behind the house lay the outbuildings with stables for the draught horses and the pure-bred stock, barns for hay and corncobs, a school house where a morning and midday bell was rung to summon the children, a blacksmith's forge and a row of little wooden houses where the stockmen, the ploughmen, the blacksmith and an old Irish carpenter lived with their wives and children.

Mary grew attached to some of the Aboriginal women and was distressed when they were ill-treated by their menfolk.

My little Harry, when he was a baby, was very fond of an Aboriginal woman named Long Kitty. She was very affectionate and liked to have charge of him, so I let her go to the river and bathe him. I gave her a comb and a loose red gown and she would come up very smart, with her hair parted—'likit missus'—and ask for the baby. Another interesting native woman was also called Kitty, the wife of Piggie Nerang. Kitty was very pretty, she came from Durundur, and grew very fond of me and the children; she was very affectionate. Polly was another fine 'gin' who was very cruelly abused by her husband, who had knocked out her front teeth. She was a gentle creature with a little daughter named Clara. Kitty also had a little daughter named Topsy, who was full of mischief. I tried to separate these children a little from the tribes. I arranged a room for them where their clothes were kept and where they had a tepid bath every morning, for although I had provided warm beds I could not prevent them from going off to the camp at night to sleep by the camp-fire. They learned to read a little and to sew, to repeat and sing verses and hymns, but when the tribe went on their nomadic excursions leaving their clothes behind and wearing nothing but possum skins nothing would induce them to leave the little girls behind. So on their return everything had to be learned again. The Aboriginal mothers are certainly very fond of their children.

We had another station, Durundur, about 30 miles [48 km] away. It had been agreed that by giving a year's notice on either side the partnership would be dissolved and my brother-in-law would have Durundur if he wished, while Cressbrook was to be my husband's property. After the dissolution of the partnership we built a large addition to the old Cressbrook homestead[6] making it our permanent home. When my brother-in-law went to Durundur we made the cottage into bachelor's quarters. [After her husband's death Mary lived for an extended period in the cottage.]

After Sunday school each week we gave the children numbers of *Sunday Magazine* and *Sunday at Home* for their parents. The children got plenty of books and we took a great deal of pains in teaching them to sing. After school they joined their parents in a walk by the river. Many changes took place. Sandy Creek [Esk], 15 miles [24 km] away was made a township and most of our people bought land there. The conditions of sale were that the purchasers must reside on their allotments and improve the land. The men had not enough money to do that as they could not give up work, so as soon as possible they moved their wives and families down and joined them from Saturday till early Monday morning. But there were neither church nor schools.

Our silver wedding took place about this time, and my husband bought, cleared and fenced land in Esk for a church and parsonage, in commemoration of our silver wedding. Then we set about building the church and parsonage. State schools were being established and, as there was a sufficient number of children to warrant a school at Esk, we at once applied and got one. Soon the school was built and a teacher placed in it so the children were all right. At Cressbrook there were also enough children to enable us to apply for a provisional school. The conditions were that a schoolhouse and house for the teacher should be provided by the applicants, also that the teacher should be provided with food, firewood, etc. We made application for the teacher we already had at Cressbrook. Her certificates were accepted and she continued for some year.

There was a good deal of immigration from England, Scotland and Ireland, and a number of the immigrants took up land around us. I was interested to visit them and see just how hard they worked homemaking when money was scarce. Trees had to be felled and slabs prepared for the huts. Wives bravely helped their husbands with the cross-cut saw and when the roots of the trees were laid bare to be burnt out, they helped to keep the fire going. Meanwhile the families lived in tents loaned by the government. Fortunately the climate was favourable to outdoor life. There were frequent accidents and sickness among the children of these migrants, sometimes necessitating them to be taken to town. This could be difficult and bad for the patient when transported by a springless cart over rough roads. When they arrived in town there was often a long period of waiting before the doctor saw the patient, prescribed and got his fee of ten shillings.[7]

Due to the tragic death of her babies and her own illness Mary had long been interested in infant and child welfare. While overseas she had visited both the Sick Children's Hospital in Edinburgh and the famous Great Ormond Street Hospital for Sick Children and observed their methods. She had seen that Queensland during the pioneering days was no place for a sick child; for many children failed to survive to the age of five because of the outmoded attitudes towards child care and nourishment. There was no Children's Hospital and no special wards for children between the ages of five and adulthood.

Today when adequate medical care is seen as the birthright of every Australian, it is difficult to imagine the heavy burden of responsibility carried by pioneer mothers. They struggled single-handed to cope with the task of raising large families in remote areas with little recourse to medical or hospital assistance in an emergency. Lack of proper facilities certainly contributed to the appallingly high infant mortality in Queensland. Accidents were common, and when a child from the bush required medical treatment it meant a harrowing journey by bullock cart over rough tracks to Brisbane and many young patients died on the journey.

Mary McConnel was the first person to be deeply convinced of the urgent need for a children's hospital and she was the instigator of fundraising although later she was helped by other volunteers. Her reasons for this were given in her second book, published at her own expense, entitled *Our Children's Hospital*, which was written to raise additional funding for the hospital. Her own writings reveal a woman of great compassion and determination whose religious faith expressed itself in a practical way.

Before Mary's campaign for a children's hospital began, sick children under five were never admitted to hospital in any state except Victoria. It was believed that sick children were exclusively the responsibility of their mothers and should be prevented from entering hospitals, as this deprived parents of one of their most sacred duties: to nurse their children. This attitude was responsible for the premature death of a great many children. Mary set out to change public opinion and awareness in favour of a special hospital where children from the bush and local children would have good clean accommodation and specialist nursing. 'They forgot that mothers, however affectionate, are often totally ignorant of how to cure any kind of disease and when accidents occur are helpless in the treatment of them' she wrote in a book describing the first 21 years of the hospital she had virtually founded.[9] Although she raised an enormous amount of funds for the hospital over the course of the years and contributed a great deal herself, she believed that the Children's Hospital should not only be a charity but also an institution for children of any nationality or creed, in return for which parents should pay something for the welfare of others, no matter how small, or should contribute help to the running of the wards. Mary was powerfully affected by the words of Jesus, 'Suffer the little children to come unto me'. She believed she had a mission to found the Brisbane Children's Hospital for children of *all* creeds and races.

From the garden of *Witton Manor*, Indooroopilly, she ran the charity fetes and bazaars which raised so much of the money necessary for the building of the hospital. She was helped by a ladies' committee which organised a display of articles for sale at the Annual Exhibition in Bowen Park in August 1877. Mary had undertaken the task of obtaining trained staff for the new hospital, which was extremely difficult because the only other Australian children's hospital was in Melbourne. Qualified

This 1887 photograph of the McConnel family, taken after David had died shows the dynasty which the McConnels founded in Queensland. Photographed at their Cressbrook property in the Brisbane Valley. John Oxley Library.

sisters and a matron were impossible to find in Brisbane she soon realised. So using the resourcefulness and ingenuity which characterised her actions she wrote to her brother who worked as a doctor in Yorkshire. His wife became very involved in the project and personally interviewed and selected the first matron, a Miss Hellicar, an Australian sister who had trained at the Westminster Hospital in London, and two further nursing sisters. The necessary medical equipment was purchased and, since funds were low, the McConnels personally paid the matron's fare to Australia.

On 11 March 1878 the new hospital was officially opened in a converted private house in Spring Hill. Mothers from the city and the bush were deeply thankful for the work of Mary and her committee of fundraising helpers. The little hospital rapidly outgrew its premises and moved to its current site in Bowen Hills, where it now forms part of the Royal Brisbane Hospital complex, the largest in the southern hemisphere. Mary McConnel remained the Patroness of the Children's Hospital and was deeply involved with its work until her death in 1910. In view of her remarkable achievements it is surprising that she is not better known.

Today the Royal Brisbane Children's Hospital has a McConnel ward with a bronze plaque in memory of Mary and a women's committee which raises money for vital projects which has been renamed the Cressbrook Committee in her honour. A large brass plaque adorns the wall of the little church at Sandy Creek, now Esk, which she and her husband built with their own money. *Cressbrook* still stands almost in the original form and on the same acreage as when it was built, making the third memorial to this important Queensland pioneer woman, two of whose descendants are practising as doctors today.

She survived her beloved husband David by 21 years and lived on at the cottage at Cressbrook, which is still occupied by her descendants.

Mary's obituary in the *Brisbane Courier* praised her accomplishments both in developing Cressbrook and the surrounding town of Esk, and her outstanding achievement in securing a Children's Hospital for Queensland. Somewhat surprisingly she never managed to rate even a brief entry in the *Australian Dictionary of Biography* but many parents whose sick children have been cured in the hospital she founded must look at her memorial plaque and feel gratitude for her dedicated devotion to Queensland's children.

[1] McConnel, David Cannon, *Facts and Traditions collected for a Family Record*. Edinburgh, 1861. Gives a history of the McConnel family.

[2] Fox, M.J., *The History of Queensland*. Brisbane, 1921.

[3] All extracts are from McConnel, Mary, *Memories of Days Long Gone By*. London, 1905. Mary's own memoirs.

[4] *Ibid.*

[5] Banks, Mary McLeod, *Pioneering Life in Queensland*. London, 1931. This book, written by Mary McConnel's daughter, whose married name was Banks, describes her mother's heroism to save the life of a domestic servant.

[6] Australian Council of National Trusts, *Historic Homesteads of Australia*, Vol. 1. Reed, Sydney, 1985. Contains photographs of Cressbrook Station still owned by the McConnel family today.

[7] McConnel, Mary. *Op. cit.*

CHAPTER 12

Elizabeth Macarthur (1766–1850)
Emily Macarthur (Stone) (1806–1880)
Elizabeth Macarthur Onslow (1840–1911)

THREE GENERATIONS OF REMARKABLE WOMEN

Elizabeth Macarthur

'Few of my friends . . . when I married thought that either of us had taken a prudent step. I was considered indolent and inactive; Mr Macarthur too proud and haughty for our humble fortune or expectations,' wrote Elizabeth Macarthur to her childhood companion, Bridget Kingdon, the daughter of the local vicar at Bridgerule, Devon. She added, 'And yet you see how bountifully Providence has dealt with us. At this time I can truly say that no two people on earth can be happier than we are'. She was only 26, and ignorant of the extremes of fortune and misfortune which fate held in store for her.

Elizabeth Veale's father was a farmer who died when she was only six. Her mother was widowed twice more, money was scarce at home, and for family reasons the young girl divided her time between the home of her grandmother and the vicarage at Bridgerule.[1] Bridget Kingdon and Elizabeth became the closest of friends and they shared their daily lessons with Bridget's father, the Reverend Mr Kingdon, in the vicarage schoolroom. This intensive private tuition with an excellent and concerned teacher was to make her one of the best-educated women in colonial New South Wales.

Elizabeth had a soft, English-rose type of prettiness, but was a steel butterfly in terms of brains and bravery. She was intelligent enough to realise that, without a dowry from her dead father, in an era when women of marriageable age greatly outnumbered men in Britain, her prospects of a 'good' marriage were uncertain. The arrival of the handsome young Lieutenant John Macarthur, even though he was on half-pay and had no inheritance, probably threw the young unmarried girls of the district into a flurry of excitement.

John Macarthur was highly ambitious. Army commissions were valuable assets in wartime, but in peacetime they paid little and were virtually unsaleable. He was living in a farmhouse near Bridgerule and thinking of taking up farming in the rich Devon countryside, when he probably paid a social call on the vicar at the rectory where he would have met Elizabeth. At this time he was embittered by his lack of money and future prospects in peacetime England. Perhaps farming without the capital to buy land lacked appeal, once his keen financial brain had examined the possibilities. He was already thinking of enrolling in the New South Wales Corps, and falling passionately in love with Elizabeth, who returned his emotions and wanted to bear his children, made emigration seem even more desirable. Elizabeth was already two months' pregnant when they were married in October 1788. The Reverend Mr Kingdon conducted the ceremony and little Edward was born seven months later, but the eighteenth century was nearly as permissive as the twentieth and this would have aroused little adverse comment. It was probably the only time in her long and sensible life that Elizabeth lost her head and yielded totally to her emotions.

Against the advice of friends and family, she married John for love rather than for money. Even in their early, frugal days he was irrational and aggressive, seemingly always searching for a fight. In spite of many dismal forebodings, their union, strange as it was in many aspects, was a true love match for most of its 46 years. It was Elizabeth's strength of character and loyalty which made the marriage successful, and her fortitude was to make her one of the most important pioneers of the Australian wool industry.

Elizabeth endured a terrible sea voyage aboard a ship of the infamous Second Fleet. She wrote: 'My poor little boy was taken very ill and continued in the most pitiable weak state during our passage to the Cape.' Her servant caught a fever from the women convicts who were chained up in rags on the other side of the cabin bulkhead. Her only exit to the deck was through a narrow, dark passage which had been turned into a hospital for fever-ridden convicts, who were highly contagious, and the ship was riddled with vermin. For the sake of her baby, Elizabeth could not risk catching the same fever as her servant. Even in the intense heat as they crossed the equator, she was forced to remain below decks where the terrible smell, of bodies unwashed for several months and slop pails full of urine and excrement, invaded her cabin. At night the air was rent by cries and curses, combined with the sounds of the sailors fornicating with the convict women of their choice.[2]

At the Cape of Good Hope they changed ships, which resulted in the Macarthurs gaining a better cabin, but John fell overboard into the harbour and became very ill with rheumatic fever. His wife nursed him devotedly, even when 'every sense was lost', and baby Edward's condition worsened so that she did not expect him to survive. She was also pregnant with their second child. She gave birth prematurely and with inadequate medical care the baby died. After six months of worry and illness, they arrived in their new country.

At Sydney Cove the convicts, riddled with scurvy, lice, dysentery and venereal disease, were off-loaded like freight since many of them could not walk.[3] Elizabeth and her convalescent husband and sickly baby were confronted by a pioneer settlement of wattle-and-daub windowless cottages. Dirt, dust, flies and drunken men and women were everywhere. When she first arrived there were constant thunderstorms before the summer weather turned to drought. She observed everything, alternately repelled by the brutality and obscenity around her and fascinated by the native birds and flowers which she saw for the first time she wrote in a letter home:

> Save for the natural setting around the finest harbour in the world, everything was wretched, the tents . . . sagging in a downpour, the night fires in the direction of The Rocks, a sink of evil already and more like a gypsy encampment, with stumps, fallen trees and boggy tracks wending their way around rocks and precipices

At this time The Rocks resembled nothing more than a vast brothel. Convict women were turned loose to earn their living at the oldest profession in the world. Elizabeth

Macarthur visited The Rocks, when Lieutenant William Dawes took her to see his observatory at Dawes Point in the course of her lessons in astronomy.

There were no other educated women with her interests to share her lonely leisure hours while her husband was on duty, so Elizabeth wrote long letters home and read books. She had had an excellent grounding in English literature and for the rest of her life she was a vivid and conscientious correspondent. Unfortunately many of her letters have been lost, but she would have made a good author had she not been cast in a different role.

Elizabeth's Devonshire farming background and her own common sense made her far more successful than many of the men who attempted to farm in the pioneering days of New South Wales. At first the Macarthurs lived in Sydney, where she complained of 'having no female friend to unbend my mind to, nor a single woman with whom I can converse with any satisfaction', but there was plenty of social life with the young officers. The first educated white woman to arrive in Australia, she also had a natural charm, and the officers flocked to the Macarthurs' small cottage. Food was rationed and everyone invited to Government House had to take their own bread with them, with the exception of Elizabeth. Governor Phillip said, 'There will always be a roll for Mrs Macarthur', and there was. He also sent her fresh fruit daily from the Government House gardens. Throughout her husband's brawls with various governors, Elizabeth always remained on good terms with them and their wives, exchanging gifts of books or baby clothes, and gradually she came to be regarded as the permanent first lady of the colony, since the governors' ladies changed so often.

In Sydney she learned to give the elegant dinners expected of the wife of an officer and a gentleman. There were delightful evenings 'in boats up and down the inlets of the Harbour, taking refreshments and dining out under an awning . . . in some of the creeks or coves'.[4] She was taught a little astronomy by Lieutenant Dawes, and learned to play a few simple tunes on the piano. The instrument's owner, a young captain, found her so enchanting that he made her a present of the piano when he left. She became pregnant again, and wrote home saying that she was 'abundantly content'.

John Macarthur had no intention of remaining poor. Three years after their arrival he was granted 100 acres of land close to the Parramatta River. 'It is some of the best ground that has been discovered and ten men are allowed us for the purpose of cleaning and cultivating,' Elizabeth wrote. She worked hard, supervising the men, and within three years they had the whole area under cultivation and over 2,000 barrels of wheat in store, in a land that was desperate for food. As a reward for being the first man in Australia to clear and cultivate 50 acres (22.7 ha) her husband was granted an extra hundred acres at Parramatta, where they had by now built *Elizabeth Farm*, which John named in honour of his hard-working and entrepreneurial wife.

Elizabeth Farm was a long brick cottage with four rooms, a large central hall, a cellar and a beautiful verandah with a view over the river. Elizabeth softened the raw woods of the posts with creeping vines. The kitchen, the servants' quarters, the stables and the sheds were separated from the main body of the house. It was Elizabeth's home for the rest of her life, the place where she felt happiest and the true centre of the Macarthur family.[5]

Unlike many other pioneer women, Elizabeth never wanted to return to England and considered Australia her home. She came to Australia when she was 27 and had been married for five years. By the time they built *Elizabeth Farm*, she had given birth to three children and buried one of them. She had travelled half round the world, lived in a tent or windowless hut in the first days of Sydney and then a small cottage. She was tired of moving her children and their possessions from one spot to the next and wanted to put down her roots in Australia and make a success of their pioneering life. She bore nine children, seven of whom survived infancy.

For twelve of her forty-six years of married life she was separated from her husband, living at *Elizabeth Farm* with the children's governess. The Macarthurs were builders of taste and discretion and *Elizabeth Farm* was always a charming home. However, there were a few disasters. Once the kitchen caught fire and burnt down. Eventually the cottage was to need much renovation and extension, but Elizabeth gave it a sense of style and it still reflects her personality. She had 'a room of her own' in which to run her own business affairs when her husband was in England, complete with a small writing desk and her favourite books. Here she wrote the long and interesting letters which kept her sons informed of her progress when they went away to England to school. Today, the house, the oldest private home in Australia, has been restored by the Historic Houses Trust of New South Wales, and Elizabeth Macarthur's writing desk, with a small posy of flowers and writing implements, stands much as it did in her lifetime.

In Sydney, as a farmer's daughter, the young Mrs Macarthur had often been bored and lonely and had to look for hobbies to fill in her time. At *Elizabeth Farm* she was in her element. They had a convict servant in charge of a dozen greyhounds for hunting and the larder was abundantly supplied with wild ducks and kangaroo meat. Elizabeth ran the dairy and was usually able to supply her growing family with butter and milk. It is important to realise that she saw herself as a professional farmer rather than an amateur. In 1794 she wrote to her mother, 'My stock consists of a horse, two mares, two cows, 130 goats and over 100 hogs. Poultry of all kinds I have in great abundance. The farm being near the Barracks I can without difficulty attend to the duties of my profession.'[6] She saw sheep breeding and farming as a fascinating career rather than a dilettante way of filling in time for an officer's wife whose husband was busy with his own career. In 1797 they purchased Spanish merino sheep imported from the Cape and crossed them with their own stock.[7]

By 1798 Elizabeth had a large orchard with almonds, apricots, pears and apples, and 'extensive gardens with fruit and vegetables' as well as a vineyard. She loved the climate, saying that it was one of the finest in the world, 'where the fruitful soil affords us many luxuries'. She told Bridget Kingdon that there was an excellent road for carriages over the 14 miles (22.5 km) between Elizabeth Farm and Sydney, and she extolled the beauties of the Hawkesbury River, which she had visited on horseback and by boat.[8]

Her one great problem was the education of her four sons. Edward, aged eight, had to be sent 'home' to school, which must have caused her considerable heartbreak, since he had always been delicate and without her devoted nursing would have died in infancy of an illness caused by teething.[9] She lost another baby named James when he was only 11 months old. Three more children, Elizabeth, Mary, and Emmeline, were born.

Her letters to her mother in England show her quick intelligence. She adapted quickly to the rigours of colonial life and threw herself enthusiastically into the role of farm manager in her husband's absence. She supervised the younger children's education and created around her the harmonious lifestyle of the English landed gentry while surrounded by the alcoholism and sexual depravity of early New South Wales.

The timid young girl had been forced by circumstances to become a very strong woman. This businesslike impression was softened by her quick wit, high spirits and cultured mind. However, she never complained of the deficiencies of the colonial existence where many basic necessities of life were often in short supply. When young, she loved entertaining or going to social events and seeing for herself the remarkable developments that were taking place all around her.

In 1801, when John Macarthur was sent to England for court-martial in connection with his duel with Lieutenant Governor William Paterson, he took with him his daughter Elizabeth and his son John so that they might go to school. Four

years later the young Elizabeth, now aged thirteen, returned with her father and a governess named Penelope Lucas, who took charge of the girls' education. Miss Lucas was similar in age to her pupils' mother and for the next 38 years she was to be Elizabeth's closest friend and confidante. In contrast to many squatters and landowners of the period, Elizabeth Macarthur saw that her convict servants were always well cared for and well housed, and they were never sternly punished by colonial standards.

Late that same year, after her husband's disastrous involvement in the Rum Rebellion, when he acted as Colonial Secretary under the governorship of his friend, George Johnston, John Macarthur left for England with Johnston; the threat of trial for treason hung over them both. This delicate legal situation dragged on for eight years, with Macarthur in virtual exile until 1817 when he was granted permission to return to New South Wales, provided he did not involve himself in political matters. During this long period Elizabeth was responsible for the care of the valuable merino flocks at Elizabeth Farm, the house and its extensive fruit and flower gardens, the estate's numerous farm servants and shepherds, and the direction of the convict labourers. She was assisted by John's young nephew, Hannibal Hawkins Macarthur, but, since he had only just arrived in the colony, he was considerably less experienced in Australian farming methods than she was.

Elizabeth Macarthur became deeply involved with the crossbreeding of merinos for their wool. This was a new departure, since up to the time of John's leaving, New South Wales farmers had only thought about sheep in terms of mutton. Five years after he left, his wife was growing wheat, barley and oats as well as overseeing the difficult and novel business of shearing and wool washing and having the clip dressed, baled and shipped. In spite of her family duties, she was an excellent manager, exporting high-quality wool to England, where her husband sold it. Her improvements of the breed and the wool yield of the Macarthur flocks so impressed Governor Macquarie that he gave her a further

At the request of James Macarthur, Conrad Martens painted the slab hut on the Camden Park property where courageously Elizabeth used to risk attack by bushrangers and stay overnight when making tours of inspection on horseback when her husband was in England. Private collection.

600 acres (272 ha) of land at Parramatta as a reward. Her convict labourers admired her, and during a particularly severe drought, when the lambs of most of the other farmers died, Elizabeth managed to save more than half of the Macarthur lambs. In effect she became her husband's business partner as much as his wife. Her social conscience extended to her own convict servants, whom she treated benevolently and humanely. Hers was a household of women when her husband was away: the convict and other servants, a Chinese cook and a Scottish gardener and a 'Mussalman' or Mohammedan footman (the latter two unmarried) had their own small cottages in the grounds.

For eight years Elizabeth Macarthur ran the Camden Park estates, Elizabeth Farm and the Seven Hills Farm and its staff of 90 convicts and emancipists by herself with conspicuous success. She visited Camden Park regularly on horseback, sometimes completely alone and sometimes accompanied by her devoted and trustworthy ex-convict overseer, Thomas Herbert, who was to remain with her for 40 years. At Camden Park before the homestead was built she spent lonely nights in a dirty, spider- and insect-infested slab hut without running water or sanitation. She was often at risk from escaped convict bushrangers and sporadic bursts of retaliatory violence from the Aborigines. On 16 May 1814 she wrote to her husband and mentioned how troublesome the natives had become. The wife of shepherd William Baker had been murdered in her hut by Aborigines at the Upper Camden yards.[10] Up to 1816 there were reports of violent murders of shepherds, women and children, flocks depleted and homesteads ransacked, but Elizabeth seems to have been fearless in her journeys of inspection at Camden.

After each journey Elizabeth sent detailed reports about her inspections to her husband. On receiving his replies, often as much as a year later, she carried out his suggestions for the development of their joint flocks. However she was forced to make many major decisions by herself and proved to be an excellent farmer in her own right on both properties. She was the first woman in Australia to make hay for sale, although she noted that Mrs Macquarie was also ordering this to be done. 'We feed hogs, have cattle, keep a dairy, fatten beef and mutton,' she wrote.[11] She was one of the first to adopt the policy of removing tree stumps when land was cleared, in order to make ploughing easier.

Throughout Elizabeth Macarthur's married life she was constantly loyal to her husband, a man whom practically everyone other than herself and his children found abrasive, quarrelsome and infuriating. She looked beneath the turbulent surface and realised that he was a man of great vision and determination. Only to her did he show real affection. He constantly wrote her loving letters starting, 'My dearest Elizabeth', 'My beloved wife', and continuing 'Believe me, my Elizabeth, the period of separation from you has been an almost uninterrupted scene of indescribable wretchedness', and 'Dearest beloved, how great are my obligations to you'.

In May 1812, after he had been parted from Elizabeth for three years, John wrote her one of the most touching letters of admiration for a woman's management skills that remains from the nineteenth century

> I cannot express how pleased I am at the account you give of the state of our affairs under your excellent and prudent management. I trust the return of Hannibal will relieve you from the necessity of attending to the laborious and more disagreeable part of an undertaking that not many men would be capable of conducting so successfully as you have, much to your own credit and the advantage of your Family. My beloved Wife, when I reflect on the many adverse circumstances to which you have been exposed and the extraordinary trials that you have born, without sinking under the accumulated pressure, but with the most active fortitude and good sense, it is impossible for me to express all my admiration.[12]

Their devotion was deep and moving but perhaps in some ways life was easier for Elizabeth when he was not there. Unlike her husband she was always on excellent terms with everybody in their circle. After her husband returned to England she avoided Sydney society and lived quietly at Parramatta with her children and the faithful Miss Lucas. However, she became very friendly with Mrs Macquarie, with whom she had much in common. As a result, additional land grants were forthcoming and new leases arranged.

Under Elizabeth's capable supervision the pure merino breeding flocks increased and the quality and weight of their wool continued to improve. The wool buyers, alerted to the merits of Australian wool by John Macarthur in London, started a vogue for the Australian fleece because of its excellent quality. The great pastoral age of Australian agriculture arrived, due in large part to the vision and hard work of the Macarthurs. Elizabeth Macarthur reaped the benefits and sold her crossbred merino sheep to the squatters who were moving out beyond the known boundaries. The export trade in wool turned Australia from an unprofitable dumping ground for convicts into a viable settlement for enterprising pioneers.

Elizabeth seemed to have an instinctive flair for business and for the social niceties which foster close relationships with those in powerful positions, whereas her husband was either suspicious or supercilious with everyone. She had high standards and educated her children to be the natural leaders of the new society. Perhaps because her standards were so exacting, her sons and daughters were slow to marry. She saw William Charles Wentworth as a 'rugged and untidy person' with a convict mother, and did not regard him as a suitable husband for her daughter, Elizabeth, so the proposed marriage of convenience suggested by Wentworth's father fell through. John Oxley, the discoverer of Brisbane River, was also an unsuccessful suitor. It was disclosed he had a mass of debts and was therefore considered unsuitable to provide for a wife who had been delicate since she was a girl. In 1810, the year after John Macarthur's second departure from Sydney, the young Elizabeth had suffered a severe illness and lost the use of her limbs. It was probably a mild attack of poliomyelitis, but without proper medical attention it must have been extremely worrying to her mother, who cared tenderly for her. This daughter was to remain unmarried, living with her mother at Elizabeth Farm for the rest of her life, writing letters, gardening and painting.

Most of Elizabeth's letters to her husband are missing today since it was probably difficult for him to keep them while travelling. They were often written both across and up and down the page, which made them difficult to read, but saved money, because postage to England was exorbitant at that time. From his replies it is apparent that she cared deeply for the welfare of her sons and their education.

In one letter dated December 8th, 1814, her appreciative husband told Elizabeth that 'It will be the study of my life to requite you for all you have suffered on my accounts', and in another, depressed, lonely and missing her company, he suggested that she abandon her pioneering life in Australia and return to England. The 'timid and irresolute girl', as she once described herself to Bridget Kingdon, would not think of leaving her adopted land, and battled on alone until her husband returned in 1817. She realised that their beloved children had a far better future in Australia than in Britain. She was 51 years old when her husband returned from England for the second time, bringing home two of their sons, James and William, with him and wrote to Bridget Kingdon saying 'I am scarcely sensible of the extent of my happiness and I can hardly persuade myself that so many of the dear members of our family are united again under the same roof'.

Her son John, who entered the legal profession and lived a bachelor life in London, was of invaluable assistance to the whole Macarthur family. He was in effect their agent, responsible for the purchase and shipment of all their clothes, household goods, books and stationery, and for the working clothes of their convict servants.

He sent out dresses to his mother and the girls, and Elizabeth told him that

> What we have for our personal use should be of superior quality. We wear out our things and therefore we wear them for a long time. At this distance from the Mother Country mere articles of show are ridiculous. Our household linen and clothes should be of good quality, because in the end they are more useful. [This indicates her modest and frugal nature which wealth did not change.]

However, her husband was not able to fully enjoy their joint triumph. His manic depression which had previously been controllable and had made him so energetic and enterprising, gradually became more pronounced. A consensus of psychiatric opinion today classes him as a typical manic depressive, whose illness could be controlled with lithium carbonate but, tragically, at that time there was no formal diagnosis of manic depression and no known cure. Elizabeth was forced to witness the slow disintegration in personality of the man she loved and who had loved her so devotedly.

After the shock of the death of their son John in London in 1831, her husband's illness accelerated. He now seemed much more obsessed with extending Elizabeth Farm and building Camden Park than with the wool business which provided their income. Once again Elizabeth coped magnificently with everything. In May 1838 she wrote to Edward, saying how preoccupied his father was with his grandiose building schemes. 'I do not hear that he makes any enquiries or notices anything in relation to the sheep' was her slightly worried comment. She had always allowed her husband to have his way in the redesigning and furnishing of their home with marble mantelpieces and Indian carpets, since her own interests lay more in reading and the management of the household and its gardens and estates and, whatever his faults, John Macarthur had always had the cultivated tastes of an eighteenth-century gentleman.

In 1832, when his health and mind had begun to deteriorate, Governor Sir Richard Bourke had him removed from the New South Wales Legislative Council because he had been pronounced 'a lunatic'. Elizabeth was forced to admit that she had 'long previous apprehensions'. John Macarthur suffered from obsessional delusions that Elizabeth, the perfect wife and mother, had been unfaithful to him during his long absences. He accused her of infidelity, disowned his own daughters and drove her closest friend and confidante, Penelope Lucas, out of Elizabeth Farm so that she and her daughters, Elizabeth and Emmeline, were forced to live in a cottage on the estate. The house was 'thrown into confusion. Pistols, swords and offensive weapons in his hands. I need make no further comment', Elizabeth wrote, discreet even in the midst of her desolation, the day after he had attacked her savagely with a cutlass. John Macarthur had now become totally paranoid, believing that his daughters were robbing him and that his son-in-law, Dr James Bowman, had tried to poison him.

For Elizabeth it must have seemed like a nightmare that her husband's love could turn to unreasoning hatred under the influence of a mental illness that, at that time, no doctor knew how to cure. She took refuge with her married daughter, Mary Bowman, at *Lyndhurst* in Glebe, Sydney. James and William took charge of their violent and agitated father at Parramatta, and his bed was moved into the library. She wrote to Edward, saying 'at times I can hardly believe what has happened. I have been banished from home a year'.[13] Eventually, both for his own protection and her peace of mind, John Macarthur was moved to a cottage in the grounds of Camden Park and in September 1833 Elizabeth was able to return to her 'beloved home' to live there with her daughters Elizabeth and Emmeline.[7]

After John Macarthur's death in 1834, Edward, the eldest son, inherited Elizabeth Farm, with the proviso that his mother could live there for the rest of her life, and she retained a permanent income from the estate's wool business. Edward continued to send her books and periodicals from England, and she wrote frequently to him, telling him details of her life in New South Wales, family affairs and any matters which she thought might tempt him to return to Australia. Mary and James Bowman and her grandchildren were frequent visitors, and until the Bowmans' financial crash due to unwise speculation, she visited them at *Lyndhurst*, where a special chair was built for her, which can still be seen there today. 'Lady Gipps frequently favours us with a visit and sometimes the Governor', she wrote to Edward in 1840, proudly informing him that 'Elizabeth Farm and the old Cottage, Garden and Grounds attract great attention from strangers'.

Elizabeth's life continued tranquilly, with much intellectual stimulation from her reading and writing and great support from her loving family. After her death her library was catalogued by Henry Curzon Allport, the noted artist who had lived for a time at Elizabeth Farm when he worked for the Macarthurs. The catalogue lists a large number of books in French, many titles on gardening and plant species as well as cultivation of the vine, both *Blackwoods Magazine* and the *Edinburgh Review*, the leading literary periodicals of the day, and bound volumes on English, Roman and European history. It is significant that there were no Gothic horror novels or the light, frothy reading matter deemed suitable for ladies of the Georgian period, indicating Elizabeth's cultured and informed taste.

Her youngest and favourite daughter, Emmeline, married Henry Parker, a cousin of Lady Gipps and private secretary to the Governor. Lady Gipps was a regular caller during the social season when the Governor was in residence at Parramatta. Elizabeth was never given to idle gossip in her letters, but a picture of the various governors' wives whom she knew so intimately emerges from a study of her letters.

William Nicholas painted a portrait of Elizabeth Macarthur when she was 78 years old, and shows her as a regal lady. Private collection.

She was on very friendly terms with Mrs Grose and Mrs Macquarie and she described her friend Lady Brisbane as 'in every way an acquisition to the colony'.[14] She saw very little, however, of Lady Darling; whether this was through personal antipathy or because Lady Darling was in poor health after childbirth, she does not say.

She commented, however, that Governor Bourke and his wife were not altogether popular with the more socially minded inhabitants of Sydney, since they entertained very rarely due to Mrs Bourke's ill-health; and in fact she died during her husband's term of office. Perhaps the Bourkes were reluctant to meet her after her husband's forced removal from the Legislative Council? Other Governor's wives saw her as entirely her own person, and she was accepted socially in spite of her husband's rash actions. Lady Gipps was probably Elizabeth's favourite, after Mrs Macquarie. In style the Gipps were a great contrast to the homely Bourkes, and the ladies of New South Wales proceeded to refurbish their wardrobes to visit Government House. Elizabeth and her daughter made new muslin dresses for the summer season at Parramatta. Emmeline and her husband had a room at Government House in Sydney for the periods when he was on duty, and another was kept free for Elizabeth whenever she might want to visit.

Of all her sons, only James married in her lifetime, but she resisted most of his invitations to make her home with him and his wife Emily at Camden Park, preferring her own happy and tranquil life at Elizabeth Farm. When she was seventy-five she suffered much sadness when her unmarried daughter Elizabeth died unexpectedly. She consoled her grief by caring for her daughter Mary's children when Mary became ill, energetically helping James in his electioneering campaign for the seat of Cumberland, and taking a keen interest in the shearing of the family's flocks. When the weather was fine she attended church, and evening prayers for the servants and tenants were held regularly in her dining room.

After Emmeline's marriage to Henry Parker, Elizabeth spent happy summer holidays with members of the Parker family at *Clovelly*, Watsons Bay.[15] From here she went on long walks to Camp Cove and the Gap and went boating on the harbour. At *Clovelly*, the house she had come to love in old age, she suffered a stroke and was nursed by the faithful Emmeline Parker until she died in February 1850, at the age of 83. In accordance with Elizabeth Macarthur's own request, she was buried at Camden Park beside her beloved husband, a great lady to the end of her life.

Emily Macarthur (1806–1880)

Emily Stone was born in India, the daughter of Henry Stone, a civil servant in the employment of the Bengal Government. Her mother was Mary Roxburgh, the daughter of Dr William Roxburgh, Superintendent of the Calcutta Botanical Gardens. Dr Roxburgh was a noted Scottish-born botanist and author of *Flora Indica*, the definitive work on Indian plants and flowers.[9]

Christened Amelia, but always known as Emily, the little girl was sent back to England by ship at the age of five along with her older sister, Mary. Their separation from their parents was normal at this period because the humid Indian climate was regarded as unhealthy for children. Emily's mother returned to England with the other two children a year later and moved the whole family to Edinburgh. But the Indian climate had given her a series of fevers and weakened her constitution so that she died in 1814, leaving little Emily motherless at the age of eight. Emily's grandfather returned from India to act as guardian but died a year later as did Emily's younger brother Henry.

Emily's father was devastated by the loss of his wife, father-in-law and younger son in such a short space of time. He resigned from the Bengal public service and entered the family banking firm of Stone & Company in the heart of the City of London. He remarried and finally settled the children of his second marriage,

Macarthur Family Tree

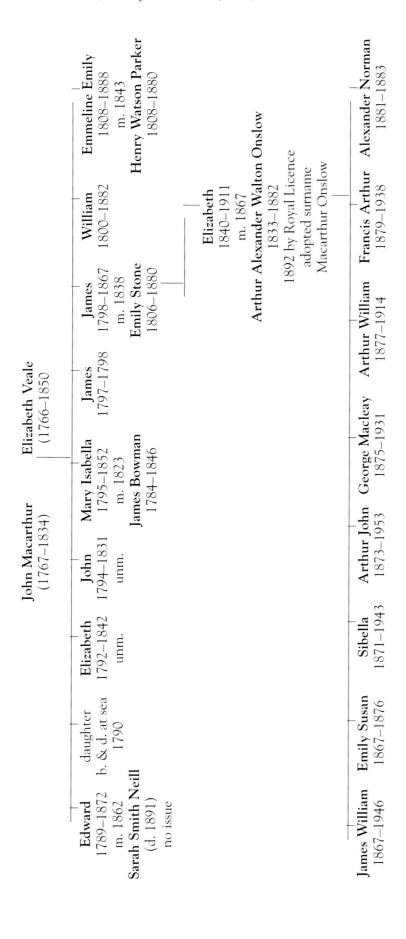

Lithograph dated 1824 after a painting by Joseph Lycett. Shows Elizabeth Macarthur and her husband dressed like British aristocrats, gazing with delight at an idealised rendering of Elizabeth Farm with its barns and surrounding pastures, from which sheep and cows are remarkably absent. Courtesy Rare Book Dept., James R Lawson, Sydney.

Below & Opposite: Watercolour portraits by Emily Macarthur (neé Stone) of her only daughter, Elizabeth (Macarthur Onslow). From an album owned by the late Mrs. F. Rothe, now in the National Library of Australia.

together with Emily, her older sister and younger sister Sibella, at Stanmore, now part of London but, at that time, a rural area in Middlesex.

While living in Stanmore, Emily who had firm ideas about education, particularly the role of religious education, taught part-time at the small school at Harrow Weald. In 1836 with a group of young women of similar educational background, she made what was, for that period, a daring all-woman tour of the British Isles and Europe, and recorded her travels in a series of sketches.

Due to family difficulties with her stepsisters and stepmother, Emily went to stay with her younger sister, Sibella, who had married a member of the Norman family, a banking dynasty which owned a handsome mansion in Chislehurst, Kent. The road which ran round the boundary of the Norman estate has subsequently been renamed Camden Park Road in Emily's honour.[16]

In 1838, at the Normans' Chislehurst home, Emily, who loved the idea of travel and adventure, met James Macarthur.[17] James had just turned forty but had delayed marriage in New South Wales, hoping to find a wife as strong-minded and intelligent as his remarkable mother, Elizabeth Macarthur. The courtship was necessarily swift as James was due to return home within a few months. They were married on June 14, 1838, and after a brief Scottish honeymoon embarked for New South Wales. Their marriage, by the standards of the time, was very late in life: Emily was now over thirty-two, a committed teacher who had perhaps scared off other suitors with a reputation of being a 'blue-stocking' (as intellectual women were often known at the time). James was intelligent, a large landowner and unlike many men of his time, not afraid of marrying a woman as clever as himself.

Emily, attractive, intelligent and with a handsome dowry[18] and excellent family connections among the great banking families of England through her sister Sibella, was regarded as an ideal daughter-in-law by the Macarthurs. Through Emily's connections to the Stones, the Normans and their friends the Barings, the Macarthur family now had access to credit from major British merchant banks on extremely favourable terms, a factor which would play a vital role in their continuing economic, social and political dominance of the colony of New South Wales.

Before they set sail for Australia Emily and James had been assured of a greatly increased overdraft from Stones' and Barings' banks. With this credit facility, during the depressed period of the 1840s when credit was not freely available, James was able to relend borrowed money at a profit in Australia. Money borrowed from British banks at low rates of interest enabled him to complete his building program on his extensive Camden Park estates and saved the Macarthurs from the depression which left several other members of the family (including Emmeline Leslie's father, Hannibal Macarthur) in a reduced financial state or bankrupt.

Emily's political connections in Britain were also significant. The Macarthur grazing interests had previously been identified with the Tory party, now they had access to a circle of rich, middle-class Liberals and aristocratic Whigs like the Bonham-Carters and the Cavendish-Bentincks.

The newlyweds arrived in New South Wales in March 1839, in the middle of a severe drought which must have contrasted sharply with the greenness of the lush English countryside they had so recently left behind. Emily adjusted well to her new homeland and settled in as a highly competent châtelaine of the newly finished Camden Park mansion with its square Georgian portico, cedar doors and handsome library.

She found herself married to a prominent member of the colony's political and social establishment. Life at *Camden Park* was stimulating with visitors from all walks of life, including many English naval officers who came as guests from ships in Sydney Harbour. Emily worked hard on many different projects at Camden Park including the wine and dairying concerns which her dowry had funded and which brought profit and prestige to the estate.

During Emily's and James's lifetime, *Camden Park* was renowned for its exemplary treatment of workers, both convict and free. They worked hard but they were well fed and clothed. Farm labourers were also imported from Scotland.

Emily's interest in education was revived when she became involved with the school on the Camden Park estate founded by William, her bachelor brother-in-law, who had his own suite of rooms in Camden Park. Emily helped to teach the children of their workers, convict and free, to read and write and gave them lessons in history and geography. The school expanded and was her pride and joy. She made a delightful drawing of the small weatherboard building.

Elizabeth, Emily's only daughter, named after her famous grandmother, was born in 1840 and no effort was spared on her education. Emily painted her only daughter frequently as a child. She ensured that Elizabeth had extensive formal training in painting and drawing, copying first from her mother's drawings and watercolours then being tutored by various governesses. From 1860 to 1864 the family lived abroad. From their London base they toured the British Isles and the Continent.

Emily was a talented and sensitive watercolourist who left an invaluable record of their family life in her diaries, notebooks, ledgers and the sketches which she made and which date from 1839 to her death in 1880.

These drawings and sketches in pen, pencil or watercolour are mainly held in Macarthur family collections. Her early work consists of about 137 drawings and paintings—such as landscapes of Scotland—and the subjects include castles owned by Roxburgh relatives, views at Chislehurst and Stanmore and sights seen on her travels in Europe. They fill six large sketchbooks and several albums, some of which

This handsome Coalbrookdale dinner service was specially commissioned in England for James Macarthur on his marriage to banker's daughter Emily Stone. It bears the Macarthur family crest. Private collection.

also contain works by Conrad Martens, who was a frequent house guest at Camden Park.[19] Martens sold views of *Camden Park* in watercolour to James but donated several smaller works (which do not appear in his account books) to Emily, probably when he was a house guest. Martens often brought his daughter Rebecca to play with Emily's daughter, Elizabeth, who as an only child may well have been lonely for playmates.

Emily painted views of *Camden Park* and Sydney scenes on her visits there. One watercolour shows the magnificent library at *Camden Park*, which was previously attributed to her daughter Elizabeth, whose work fails to equal that of her mother in composition and technique.

Elizabeth Macarthur-Onslow (1840–1911)

Born in 1840 at *Camden Park*, little Elizabeth was initially educated at home by her mother. As an only child who would eventually have to take over the management of one of Australia's most substantial farming enterprises, Emily wished her daughter to have a chance to see wider horizons than *Camden Park* and to meet a wide variety of people.

In 1860, at the age of 20, Elizabeth accompanied her parents to England. As already noted, they rented a house in London and travelled extensively in the British Isles visiting Norman and Roxburgh relatives and toured France, Germany and Italy in summer. Both Elizabeth and Emily made a number of watercolour sketches and drawings of their European tour.

During their stay in London, Elizabeth attended classes at the Normal Central School of Art (which was part of the South Kensington Museum) and took painting private lessons from William Collingwood Smith, a founder member of the Royal Watercolour Society.

The family returned to Camden Park in 1864 partly because Elizabeth was homesick. While Elizabeth may have enjoyed a few flirtations with suitable young men in London, she finally married someone from her own circle. On 31 January 1867 she became the wife of Captain Arthur Alexander Walton Onslow. His mother, Rosa Roberta, was one of the daughters of Alexander Macleay, who built Elizabeth Bay House, Colonial Secretary from 1825 to 1837 and Speaker of the Legislative Council.

Photograph showing Elizabeth Macarthur Onslow (daughter of James and Emily) with her eldest children, James and Emily Susan. From a Macarthur family album now in the National Library of Australia.

Captain Arthur Onslow came from an aristocratic British family but lacked a private income and had spent his early years in India, where his father was a public servant. He retired in 1871 from the Navy. He and Elizabeth lived at *Camden Park* and in Sydney. Theirs was a very happy marriage. They had six sons and two daughters; a daughter and a son died in infancy. When not preoccupied with the day-to-day business problems of running her large estate, Elizabeth's interests centred around their friends and family.

Elizabeth and her husband, Arthur Onslow were friends and supporters of Lucy Osburn in the campaign mounted against her by the medical establishment of Sydney Hospital. Onslow was responsible for the royal commission into public charities that dismissed charges against Sister Lucy Osburn in 1873.

Elizabeth Macarthur Onslow employed women on her Camden silk farm to tend the valuable silkworms. This copper engraving shows that tending silkworms was traditionally women's work while men gathered mulberry leaves.

On her father's death in 1867 Elizabeth had inherited a share in *Camden Park*, blocks of valuable city land and properties at Taralga and Sutton Forest. Emily continued to live at *Camden Park* and her relationship with her daughter was an affectionate and close one. Elizabeth was heir to the remaining Macarthur interests and these passed to her on the death of her uncles Sir Edward and Sir William Macarthur, who died in 1872 and in 1882 respectively. She also inherited money on the death of her mother in November 1880.

Elizabeth received a terrible blow when her husband died on 31 January 1882, on their fifteenth wedding anniversary. But the years ahead were to be full of new challenges and activities.

Emily had passed on to her daughter her own deep-seated belief in the importance of a well-rounded education. Five years after her husband's death, in 1887, Elizabeth moved herself and their six children to England to live at the home of her husband's family while continuing their education. In the succeeding years she travelled frequently from Australia to Europe to study dairy farming in Britain, and *métayage* or share-farming in France. This study of dairy farming resulted in Elizabeth setting up twelve 'cooperative' dairies and a central creamery to process cream into butter on the Camden Park estate. This highly successful 'cooperative' functioned under a share-farming arrangement by which the Macarthurs provided the housing, farming equipment and the cows which were allocated in herds of sixty to each farming family. The dairies which separated the cream from the milk were equipped with steam and great attention was paid to hygiene. A piggery was set up to use surplus milk and milk by-products.[20]

Elizabeth was also innovative in her other agricultural undertakings. She consulted with the Department of Agriculture and introduced phylloxera-resistant grapevines and experimented in sericulture—planting mulberry cuttings at Camden with the idea that farmers' daughters could work in the silk-growing industry on a share basis. She joined the Women's Co-operative Silk-Growing and Industrial Association and the Victorian Silk Culture Association.[21]

Camden Park House, 1843. Watercolour by Conrad Martens. Martens was a frequent guest of Emily and James Macarthur. Photograph courtesy the late Mrs. F. Rothe. Painting is now in the Dixson Galleries, State Library of New South Wales.

Emily Macarthur had been a teacher before her marriage. She painted this delightful watercolour showing the schoolhouse on the Camden Park estate, where she taught local children. From a Macarthur family album now in the National Library of Australia.

Elizabeth was not closely involved in the women's movement but through the Women's Co-operative Silk Growing Association she came into contact with those rare women who ran businesses and were part of the move for votes and power for women. She was a member and generous supporter of a number of organisations and good causes: the Society for the Prevention of Cruelty to Animals (its local patron), the Camden School of Arts, the Agriculture Society and Macarthur Park.[22] She donated a set of memorial bells to St John's Church as well as a clock. Her personal intervention with New South Wales ministers, and her son James's offer to pay for the first one hundred horses, is reputed to have decided the Government to offer the British a detachment of troops in the Boer War, where four of her sons also served. According to her daughter Sibella, it was Elizabeth who compiled the family history.[23]

From her mother she had inherited a love of drawing and of watercolour in particular, and she painted landscapes and recorded her travels with sketches. There is a large collection of Emily's and Elizabeth's sketchbooks at *Camden Park*. (In one of Elizabeth's sketchbooks there are two drawings which are clearly by her teacher Conrad Martens and facsimiles of work attributed to her at Elizabeth Farm, Parramatta, New South Wales).

She died aged seventy-one on 2 August 1911, while on a visit to England. Her estate was recorded as being worth £196,668 (at her husband's death, Arthur Alexander Walton Onslow's estate was less than £500).

Elizabeth Macarthur had inherited the bulk of the Macarthur estates and with the shrewd business sense inherited from her grandmother, she had consolidated the Macarthur fortune. Following her death much of it was lost by her male successors. In 1899 she had been canny enough to have formed a company, Camden Park Estate Limited, making her six children shareholders. However, she did not let the business rule her life and in later years, as both mother and father to her children, her main concerns centred around her family. In 1892 to perpetuate the Macarthur name, she sought royal approval to have it prefixed by deed poll to that of Onslow. This name is still borne with pride by many of her descendants today and in Australia the name Elizabeth Macarthur is always linked with female achievement.

---

[1] Bridgerule Marriage Register gives marriage date of Elizabeth Veale and John Macarthur as 6 Oct, 1788. Inscription at Camden Park reveals Edward's date of birth as March 1789. Cited King, Hazel, *Elizabeth Macarthur and her World*, Macarthur Press, 1980.

[2] Letter to Brigid Kingdon, Bridgerule, Devon dated 23 August, 1794 reproduced in Sibella Macarthur Onslow's edited documents entitled *Some Early Records of the Macarthurs of Camden*, n.d. The preface proves that most of the work was done by her mother Elizabeth Macarthur Onslow.

[3] Shipboard Journal of Elizabeth Macarthur in Macarthur Onslow, S. *Op. cit.* pp 4–14. *Ibid.*

[4] Collins, David. An Account of the English Colony in New South Wales. London, 1798, 1802 and facsim. ed. 1975.

[5] Macarthur Papers, Mitchell Library, State Library of New South Wales.

[6] E. Macarthur. Letter dated 21 December 1793 in Macarthur Onslow, S. [ed]. p. 44. *Op. cit.*

[7] Garran, J. C. W. *White Bampton and the Australian Merino*, JRAHS, Sydney, Vol 58, Pt. 1, 1972 p. 2. Cited King, Hazel. *Op. cit.*

[8] E. Macarthur to B. Kingdon, 21 December 1793. Macarthur Papers, Mitchell Library, State Library of New South Wales, Sydney.

[9] E. Macarthur to B. Kingdon, 23 August, 1794. Macarthur Papers.

[10] E. Macarthur to J. Macarthur. May 16 1814. Cited Macarthur S. [ed]. p. 301. *Op. cit.*

[11] Elizabeth Macarthur to Eliza Kingdon, March 1816. Macarthur Papers, cited King, Hazel. *Op. cit.*

[12] John Macarthur to Elizabeth Macarthur, n.d. *Ibid.*

[13] Elizabeth Macarthur to Edward Macarthur. 6 January and 9 February both refer to John Macarthur's disturbed state of min. *Ibid.*

[14] Elizabeth Macarthur's relationship with governor's wives as well as those of her husband has been covered in detail in King, Hazel. *Op. cit.*

[15] Following the bankruptcy of Hannibal Macarthur, Elizabeth's son-in-law Henry Parker had purchased *Clovelly* from Hannibal's estate.

[16] Information about Elizabeth Macarthur-Onslow and Emily Macarthur is taken from discussions with Quentin Macarthur-Stanham, Annette Macarthur-Onslow and her entry on Emily in *The Dictionary of Australian Artists*, Oxford University Press, 1994, and Radi, H. *Two Hundred Australian Women*. Women's Redress Press, Sydney, 1988. The main source of information on Emily (Stone) is her descendant Annette Macarthur-Onslow, author, artist and historical researcher, who has written brief details of Emily's life in *The Dictionary of Colonial Artists*, ed. Joan Kerr, Oxford University Press, Melbourne, 1993 and the Norman family.

Information about Emily and her sister when living in Chislehurst was given to me by

Quentin Macarthur-Stanham when I visited Camden Park and saw sketchbooks with Emily and Elizabeth's paintings. Having grown up in Chislehurst myself, I was fascinated to learn of its connection with Emily, and Camden Park Road, Chislehurst, commemorates her today.

17 Emily's brother-in-law, banker G. W. Norman was a fellow director with Macarthur family members of the Australian Agricultural Co., so he probably introduced James to Emily.

18 Emily's marriage settlement was £10,000, then a considerable sum. (Norman Family papers 0310 C144/20 Kent County Archives). It was partly used to create a vineyard and a dairy and help extend the school at which Emily and an assistant taught. (102 Dorset workers, their wives and children emigrated onthe ship with James and Emily and, as an experienced teacher, she took responsibility for their children's education.)

19 De Vries-Evans. *Conrad Martens on the Beagle and in Australia*, Pandanus Press, Brisbane 1993 refers to Martens' painting of The Ghost Horse (illus. page 98, courtesy Macarthur family) and other smaller works painted as gifts for Emily in return for hospitality and Martens' tuition of Elizabeth when young.

20 Radi, Heather. *200 Australian Women*. Entry on Macarthur women by Annette Macarthur Onslow. Women's Redress Press, Sydney, 1988.

21 *Ibid.*

22 Information on Elizabeth Macarthur Onslow as family historian taken from the Preface to *Some Early Records of the Macarthurs of Camden. Op. cit.* in which Elizabeth's daughter, Sibella, as editor, acknowledges that the compiling of family documents and letters and '*connecting them with other papers and books*' was the work of her mother, who had recently died. Sibella refers to this important reference book as '*the work my Mother had so nearly finished*'. [Italics are mine].

CHAPTER 13

Mary Penfold
(1820–1896)

FOUNDER OF A GREAT AUSTRALIAN WINERY

It seems unjust that Mary Penfold, who ranks with Elizabeth Macarthur for her part in founding a great Australian export industry, does not rate an entry under her own name in the *Dictionary of Australian Biography*[1] but is included as an afterthought to her husband's entry. Mary Penfold founded and ran what is now a multi-million dollar business—Penfolds Wines. Unfortunately Mary's own letters were not preserved but one major source of information are letters her mother wrote to Australia.

'The wind blew in gales and our days and nights were spent in tears and prayers for your safety,' wrote Mrs Julius Holt, a London physician's wife, to her daughter Mary, who had just arrived in South Australia after a nightmare voyage aboard the *Taglioni* in 1844. Terrible storms had lashed the ship and Mary's parents feared that their much-loved only daughter might have drowned. At the time Mary's ship was due to sail Dr Julius Holt was very ill and Mary's mother had accompanied her to the docks to see her off. Mrs Holt goes on to recount her husband's anguish over the fact that he might never see his daughter again, and his fears for the deprivation and hardship which could await her in the new country. In this same letter Mrs Holt deplores the fact that Mary's husband, Christopher, 'would listen to no one but the emigration agents'.

In a letter Mary received in May 1845 from her mother-in-law it becomes apparent that one of the reasons for the young Penfolds leaving England was a debt problem between Christopher and his brother Tom, and possibly other creditors.

> . . . how different everything turns out to be in Adelaide to what we anticipated but you know it was contemplated that you should go to the Bush and you must have endured many hardships from which you are now exempt. Indeed I hear nothing that should induce you to wish to leave Adelaide (excepting to be with those dear to you) and I can say with truth that all our happiness is in your's. Therefore I cannot wish your return at present if I love you or those near and dear to you, because it must be to poverty . . .
>
> It is very gratifying to hear that Christopher likes the change and is so determined to put his shoulder to the wheel. You say he works so very hard, I trust he will reap the benefit and that your crops will turn out very profitable . . . I do hope that Christopher will not recover only his profits but think as well of the losses he may meet with as I attribute all his failures in life to have arisen from his being too sanguine . . .
>
> We went to Notting Hill to see Emma [Mary's sister-in-law] and they tell me they are going out to you the first of June. Emma is all life and spirits with the expectation of seeing you again. I wish you to have her society but I do not know what to say [about] Tom. He says he is forgetting all that has passed and with a good feeling towards Christopher and would be willing to lend him money again

if he will but pay the interest—this Emma tells me—but I would advise you to have nothing to do with his money however advantageous it may appear to you. Do pray strive to overcome all difficulties and be independent of him. Remember his irritability he will always take with him and although I would say we must forgive and forget all injuries, you must avoid having your reputation injured as it was at Brighton . . . There must be something wrong in the man who is at variance with all his brothers and sisters (excepting James) as Tom is . . . if the musquitoes bite you much put a bit of honey on as this almost instantaneously cures wasp stings.

I saw the Adelaide Observer of December at Tom's [home]. It had the account of your purchase of the farm and the sale that was to take place of a robe and cap and two dressing cases. We expect they were yours.

I shall dine with Tom and Emma on Saturday next and tell them that you say not to bring out more than they want. I tell them only to take one servant, she wants two.[2]

From this letter it became apparent Tom had fallen out with other siblings apart from Mary's husband. Ironically, having been partly responsible for their emigration, he and his wife were now proposing to join the Penfolds in Adelaide.

Mary Penfold had been accompanied to South Australia by her husband, Dr Christopher Rawson Penfold, their four-year-old daughter Georgina, and their mother's help and companion Ellen Timbrell, orphaned daughter of an army captain. The decision to emigrate appears to have been made entirely by Christopher Penfold, and Mary, an only child, was obviously torn between her love for her parents and her husband and child. The Penfolds arrived in South Australia on 18 June 1844. With them they brought precious vine cuttings from the Rhône area of France.

At the start of settlement in Adelaide, all ships were forced to anchor a mile downstream and female passengers were carried unceremoniously ashore, slung like sacks of potatoes over the shoulders of burly sailors. They also had to endure the sight of their precious baggage and irreplaceable household possessions thrown ashore onto the muddy beach, where crates and boxes sank into the oozy slime and many items were broken or damaged beyond repair. For many pioneer women it was not an auspicious beginning to life in a new land, but fortunately for Mary a new wharf had just been built at Port Adelaide and they were able to land in more normal fashion.[3] However some of their household goods were damaged. Mary's family had given her expensive wedding presents and the Penfolds owned Wedgwood and Sevrès porcelain, handsome mahogany furniture and a piano.

On 3 October 1844 the *Observer* recorded that

Mr [not Dr] Penfold is the fortunate purchaser of the delightfully situated and truly valuable estate of Mackgill [named after Sir Maitland Mackgill, now known as Magill], for the sum of one thousand, two hundred pounds . . . comprising 500 acres [220 ha] of the choicest land, 200 acres [90 ha] of which are under crops. The site of the residence is worthy of a noble mansion . . . its woodlands offer a most agreeable background to this highly picturesque and desirable property.

Mary Penfold must have been delighted to live in such a beautiful place, nestling in the foothills of the Mount Lofty ranges, surrounded by birds and trees but only four miles due east of the new town of Adelaide. *Grange Cottage*, with its white-washed walls and tiny rooms panelled in red cedar, was to be her home and office for the next 45 years.

Local gossips whispered that Christopher Penfold had emigrated because he was in financial trouble through over-speculation. This gossip seems to be substantiated by Mrs Holt's letters. Mary Penfold's missing diary would, no doubt, have thrown further light on the subject but it mysteriously disappeared after her death, possibly destroyed by heirs to the Penfold name who feared damage to the Penfolds' reputation. In another letter to Mary, her mother repeats her belief that Christopher Penfold had always been over-confident, which might possibly confirm this conjecture but, on the other hand Mrs Holt obviously resented her only daughter's forced departure to Australia, so was not a strictly impartial witness. She clearly did not approve of Christopher's brother Thomas, his financial exploits and the way in which he treated his wife. She warned Mary not to become involved with him financially again or she would have problems with him again, and her remarks suggest that Christopher had suffered as a result of previous financial dealing with his brother.

While Mary was a beloved and privileged only child and had received every advantage in the way of education and upbringing, Christopher was a member of a struggling family of thirteen children. His father was the hardworking vicar of the Sussex village of Steyning, only 16km from Brighton, where Christopher eventually went into practice. Although books and education were greatly valued at Steyning Vicarage, there could never have been much money from a vicar's meagre stipend for Christopher's expensive medical books and living expenses when he was studying at the prestigious St Bartholomew's Hospital Medical School. Perhaps Christopher Penfold wished to become a specialist, but the first years of hospital medicine were unpaid and young medical residents worked there for the honour of post-graduate study under a famous consultant.

The Penfolds married in 1835, when Mary was only fifteen. We do not know how Mary met her husband, but in the early Victorian period girls married far younger than today; however, rarely did girls from a middle-class family marry as young as fifteen. At fifteen she would not have 'come out' into the affluent middle-class society in which her parents moved. Three years later Dr Penfold set up in general practice in the fashionable seaside town of Brighton, rendered expensive by the patronage of the Prince Regent who had used it as an elegant health resort. In order to make the right impression on his wealthy patients, Christopher was forced to rent or purchase an expensive home with suitable accommodation for his surgery and waiting room. With no family funds available, he would have had to borrow money to finance setting himself up in practice. Presumably he borrowed from his elder brother Tom, and failed to pay back the interest. There was certainly ill-feeling between the two brothers.

It was rumoured that during Christopher's childhood a sister had been sent to live with an elderly aunt to cut the family's housekeeping expenses, and later she had been married off to an elderly man for his money. Obviously there must have been great financial pressures on the Penfold family for them to allow this to happen. Christopher had to make his own way in the world. This may have been one of the major motivating forces for his emigration. Possibly he was too proud to seek financial help from Mary's parents and wished to be totally independent, although young doctors have always had to rely on loans to establish themselves in private practice. He would have studied at 'Barts' with the sons of the wealthy, and become accustomed to the expectation that his training would enable him to establish himself and Mary in surroundings of which he felt her parents would approve.

Whatever happened to the Penfolds in England that caused them to emigrate, Christopher Penfold redeemed himself in Adelaide. They took over *Grange Cottage* on the Magill property, a stone one-storey cottage with a low-hipped roof and a long verandah. They installed their beautiful furniture and fine porcelain, probably wedding presents from Mary's parents and friends, in the tiny sitting room.

Portraits of Mary and Christopher Penfold are still at their cottage. Dr Penfold was painted in 1835, the year of his marriage, when he was twenty-four. He holds a book in one hand, and appears handsome as well as intelligent, with expressive, gentle eyes and a warm and generous mouth. The only existing picture of Mary Penfold shows her as an elderly widow, but she was obviously very attractive when younger. In widowhood she looks kind, rather careworn, but with a very determined set to her chin. The Penfolds were a devoted couple and had an extremely happy marriage. They had true pioneering spirit and both worked enormously hard to make a success of the farm and the practice.

Once they had moved into *Grange Cottage*, Mary sent her parents a picture of the little house and the outbuildings, showing young Georgina wearing red shoes and stockings and striding 'stick in hand, among the poultry and animals: pigs, cows, turkeys, fowls and pigeons'.[4]

Mary also sent home a small piece of metal for testing, which her father told her in his next letter was a mixture of lead and zinc. South Australia was then in the grip of a mining boom.[5] Christopher was still interested in mining and investments but Mary's father cautioned them not to 'neglect the fleece and the farmyard to dig a will-o'-the-wisp out of the earth'. Attached to her father's letter was a most moving letter from Mrs Holt to her son-in-law saying

> I sincerely hope you may realise your expectations. Many thanks for your assurance that you do and will take care of my idolised Mary. I place implicit confidence in your promise and will do my best to be happy. You can judge of my affection by your own for your lovely darling infant.

Mary's parents were obviously worried that Christopher Penfold would once again do something rash, and a later letter to Mary from her mother says how

> I am glad that Chris, who has always been a little too sanguine, would not give the man fifty pounds [a large sum at that time] to tell him [the whereabouts] of the mine.

Obviously freight was expensive to Australia as in the same letter Mary's mother described how she had passed on Mary's message to Tom Penfold, her brother-in-law, to bring out only essentials with him, including feather beds.

The Magill estate gradually prospered though Mary's hard work as farm manager in all but name. All the administration fell on her as her husband was deeply involved in building up his practice and doing the rounds of his sick patients on horseback. He did not have an assistant and like any other doctor's wife, Mary would have taken messages and given practical advice to patients in his absence. Surgery was held in their dining room. Mary was often busy supervising both Ellen Timbrell in her domestic duties and their manservant, Elijah Lovelock, who helped with the ploughing, sowing and harvesting. She was also involved with her daughter's education. A page from her day-book contains varied entries showing her bank accounts, payments to a man for additional ploughing, the purchase of new plough shares in Adelaide, receipt of cash for a surgery visit from a sick child, and other farm work.

Most important of all is her brief statement 'Began making wine'. Winemaking was Mary's special interest rather than her husband's although his scientific knowledge would have been very useful when it came to the wine-making process. He prescribed their wine to his anaemic patients, being firmly convinced of the medicinal powers of red wine. Having chosen land with wine-making in mind, they started with port and sherry, but soon discovered clarets and rieslings sold better. They certainly planned the vineyard together, as did many other couples. But what had been originally conceived as an adjunct to the medical practice, medicinal wine to be prescribed to patients of Dr Penfold, under Mary's stewardship developed into a thriving and prestigious business.

By the end of the 1860s, Penfolds Wines had become a flourishing concern.

Because of her husband's heavy workload, Mary continued to manage the business virtually single-handed. This fact was not widely known for in colonial Australia a middle-class woman was not expected to be in charge of any business venture, but to occupy herself with home and children, except when her husband was absent. Dr Penfold was a dedicated and popular doctor, although at that time medicine had few cures for major diseases, and general practitioners were seldom wealthy. Like other country doctors, he would also have had many poorer patients who were unable to pay his fees during bad years and whom he treated free. He worked long hours and was also involved with the founding of St George's Church at Woodeford, north of Magill, and chaired the meetings of the Burnside District Council. With so many commitments, the doctor had little time available to involve himself in the day-to-day running of the farm and the wine business, although many thought the success of the winery was due to him.

At first the Penfolds made wine for their own use and to prescribe to patients, leading to the company's slogan '1844 to evermore'. The Penfolds sold their wine in Adelaide and won prizes at local shows, so that gradually the fame of their product spread. With a keen entrepreneurial instinct, Mary found another marketing outlet for their excellent wines in Melbourne. It was only the high interstate customs duty imposed on South Australian wine in Victoria that prevented greater expansion of the business. Before Federation, each state levied tariffs on the others' produce.

Dr Penfold's medical practice prospered and their daughter grew into an attractive and intelligent girl, taught many of her lessons by her mother. They made an extended visit to Melbourne to find new markets for their wine. It was there that Georgina, when nineteen years old, met and married a public servant and capable administrator named Thomas Hyland. He acted as the Victorian sales agent for Penfolds as he and Georgina were living in Melbourne. The wine business grew and prospered, but at this time Mary probably saw herself as the wife of a respected doctor with a business sideline, rather than as a successful entrepreneur in her own right.

In March 1870 Mary Penfold suffered a major tragedy when her husband died at the age of fifty-nine after a long illness, possibly cancer. Dr Penfold was held in great esteem by his patients and when his funeral cortege passed through Magill the flags which were flying for a local election were lowered to half-mast, and all the stores closed out of respect.

Thomas Hyland himself underestimated his mother-in-law's role in the winery. In a letter to Mary written just after her husband's death he advised her that he had been building up good sales of Penfolds Grange and other wines in Victoria as a sideline to his public service appointment. Rather patronisingly, he added that Mary should now sell out the property and be 'pensioned off'. It appears that at this time Thomas Hyland had not realised that Mary Penfold had been managing the vineyard and winemaking process prior to her husband's long illness, and he seriously under-estimated her business acumen. He wondered if 'you could manage things for six months [as] it would give us more time to sell the property', and suggested that 'if the Border Duty gets settled, we could then sell it [the Grange estate] well in Melbourne'.

Mary had absolutely no intention of selling the home and business she had worked so hard to create. She replied brusquely to her son-in-law's discouraging letter with a well-written and concise report on the prospects for the Penfolds wine business and included a balance sheet setting out the financial situation.

Two months later she received this letter from Thomas Hyland:

> I am quite pleased at the practical way in which you are taking the business in hand and your resolutions, determination and instructions could not be better. In fact if you go at it determinedly . . . you will be alright.

This letter also contained a proposal for a formal partnership between them. He sensibly proposed that Mary should continue to manage the Grange Estate vineyards and that he and Georgina would continue to sell Penfolds wines in Melbourne. Mary Penfold accepted his proposals and a most successful partnership was con-tracted. By now Ellen Timbrell, who had originally helped her with the winemaking, was dead, but Mary Penfold's domestic burdens were far lighter since there were no patients to take up her time. Mary continued to work hard; she could no longer be regarded as a doctor's wife making pin-money, she was in fact a skilled vigneron running a successful enterprise. Thomas Hyland grew to respect Mary Penfold's business acumen and management skills.

The relationship between Mary, Georgina and her husband was close. In 1872, two years after Dr Penfold's death, he and Georgina entrusted their delicate little daughter, Inez, to Mary, believing that the clear country air of Magill would help her to regain her health while staying with her beloved grandmother. The arrangement was a great success for grandmother and granddaughter, and Thomas would later adopt the name Penfold and call himself Hyland-Penfold.

Two years later, at the beginning of June 1874, a journalist from the *Adelaide Register* inspected the Penfold vineyards and cited the Grange estate as an example of good management. From his article it is evident that the writer was impressed by Mary Penfold's personal supervision of the winery and her extensive knowledge of the winemaking process. The reporter described how

> Mrs Penfold makes four varieties of wine, sweet and dry red and sweet and dry white. Grapes of all kinds are used and the uniformity which is so great a consideration is secured by blending the wines when they are two or three years old. This is done under Mrs Penfold's personal supervision, not in conformity with any fixed and definite rule but entirely according to her judgment and taste. Mrs

> Penfold is aiming to get such a stock that she need not sell any which is under four years of age. There are now in the cellars about 20,000 gallons of wine of that age ready for market but the total stock is close upon 90,000 gallons [more than 400,000 litres].[6]

Mary Penfold had expanded into winemaking in a most professional and organised way. The *Adelaide Register* described the exact procedures that she used, together with the type of machinery, and went into some detail about the enormous oak casks which Mary had purchased in spite of gloomy predictions of disaster from her rivals. The cellar contained casks holding some 5,000 gallons (22,700 litres) each; these stood twelve foot (3.6m) high. There were seven gigantic casks made of Australian red gum or English oak. From the *Adelaide Register*'s article it appears that Mary was experimenting with many new varieties of grapes, apart from the Grenache which she and Christopher had originally brought with them on the voyage. New varieties included Tokay, Madeira, Frontignac, Verdelho, Mataró, the Spanish Pedro Ximenez, and Muscat; to obtain these Mary must have been involved in correspondence with vignerons all over Europe. She read widely about new methods of wine production and, maintenance of vinestocks as she was keen to avoid phylloxera and other diseases that ravaged vineyards in Europe.[7]

After Christopher's death Mary kept herself constantly busy. Unlike many widows of the period, she did not appear to suffer from a sense of isolation or depression. She had the companionship of Inez, her intelligent and creative grandchild, and her beloved pug dogs, Toby and Beppo. The Hyland-Penfolds often visited her when they could get away from Melbourne and in turn she wrote the family long and amusing letters. Frequently these were addressed to Inez's brother Leslie. In one letter to Leslie she recounted how, with his father and sister Inez, she had taken a trip to the Adelaide Hills. Here they had encountered men panning for gold. 'I wanted to get out and see what they had got but directly they caught sight of our wagonette they took us for a wedding party and yelled at us in a very Colonial fashion,' she wrote.

Mary was progressive in her ideas and evidently welcomed the technological advancement of the time. Rather than taking the steamer on her visits to the married daughter and children, she was one of the first passengers aboard the newly instituted train service between Adelaide and Melbourne.

By 1869 the Grange had sixty acres (27.3 ha) of vines under cultivation. On 14 September 1881 a further partnership agreement was signed between Mary, Thomas Hyland and her cellar manager, Joseph Gillard, by which she would receive ten per cent of the profit and in which she agreed to continue to act as winemaker and wineseller under the name of Penfold & Co for the next seven years. Thomas Hyland was to be the accountant for the partnership. Mary's son-in-law, due to the success of the business and his confidence in its future, left his secure public service job to devote his time and energy to the family enterprise but remained in Victoria while she ran the winery. This historic document is still in *Grange Cottage* today.

The Penfold company by 1881 were producing over 107,000 gallons, equal to one-third of all the wine stored in South Australia's at that time[8] and selling all around the country. They went on to exhibit successfully at the Colonial Exhibition in London. In 1884, when Mary turned sixty-eight, she finally handed over the management of the thriving business to Joseph Gillard. He did not retire until 1905, at which time Mary's grandson, Herbert Leslie Hyland-Penfold took control. By this time Penfolds had become one of Australia's major winemakers and Mary's 'Grange' trademark had won world renown for its quality as one of Australia's greatest wines.

In 1892, Mary's beloved granddaughter and companion, Inez, died. She and Inez had shared *Grange Cottage* happily for twenty years. Although Inez had been shy and retiring, she was well read and an excellent conversationalist with a passion for literature. She had given Mary great joy and mental stimulation in her later years. Inez had written some poems in the rather charming whimsical style, later made popular by the fantasies of Walter de la Mare. Mary devoted her time and energies to collecting her granddaughter's poems and stories and publishing them under the title *In Sunshine and Shadow*, hoping that 'whatever their faults they will meet with no harsh criticism for her dear sake'.

After Inez died Mary no longer wished to remain alone at *Grange Cottage* and in January 1892, when her garden was at the height of its beauty, she packed up a few treasures to take with her to Georgina's home in Melbourne. She could not bear to witness the disposal of the beautiful Regency furniture which she and Christopher had commissioned in the first years of their marriage; her much-loved ebony piano and the Dresden, Sèvres and Wedgwood china which had given her so much pleasure. They were sold under the auctioneer's hammer after her departure and most were scattered beyond trace.

Mary Penfold died in her mid-seventies on a mild January day in Melbourne in 1896. Her body was brought back to be buried at St George's Cemetery, Magill.

It is a significant comment on the way women were viewed in Australian colonial society that her obituary in the *Adelaide Register* of 4 January 1896 mentioned that 'she resided for forty-eight years at the Grange Vineyards'. Neither the journalist who wrote it nor any of the Melbourne papers mentioned her contribution to the wine industry. She was not given any credit for pioneering South Australian wine growing and wine-making, for trying to lower the tariff barriers between South Australia and Victoria, or for her successful initiation and management of one of the largest and important wineries in Australia.

Mary Penfold wearing widows' weeds. The portrait photograph of this determined and enterprising businesswoman hangs at Grange Cottage today.

Over the next fifty years *Grange Cottage* deteriorated badly and was about to be demolished after World War II. It was saved by the exertions of Mary's great-grand-daughter and other members of the family. In 1949, *Grange Cottage*, from which the most famous of the Penfold wines, Grange Hermitage, takes its name, was opened as a private museum commemorating the achievements of Mary and Christopher Penfold. Today (1995) the museum is no longer open to the public and most of the original Grange vineyard has been subdivided for a housing estate and sold. Penfolds wines have won international fame in wine circles due to the vision and enterprise of this remarkable woman.

1   *Australian Dictionary of Biography*, Douglas Pike ed. Volume 5. Entry on Dr Christopher Rawson Penfold (1811–1870) refers to Mary Penfold in the last three paragraphs written by D.I. MacDonald, but she had no entry under her own name in spite of her importance in Australian winemaking history. See also Mills, S.A. ed. *Wine Story of Australia*, Sydney, 1908; Keane, E. ed. *The Penfold Story*, Sydney, 1951; Mayo, Oliver, *The Wines of South Australia*, Penguin Books, Ringwood, Vic, 1986; Lake, Dr Max, *Vine and Scalpel*, Brisbane, 1967.
2   Jolly, E. *The Penfold Cottage Story*. Adelaide, n.d.
3   *Adelaide Register*, 8 August 1842.
4   Warburton, Elizabeth. *The Paddocks Beneath*, Burnside City Council, Burnside S.A. 1981.
5   Cited in *The Penfold Cottage Story. Op cit.*
6   *Adelaide Register*, 4 June 1874. Story headed 'Mrs Penfold's Wine Manufactory'.
7   'The Phylloxera Scare', Supplement to *Adelaide Chronicle*, 15 November 1879.

8 Norrie, Phillip, *Penfold Time Honoured*, Apollo Books, Sydney, 1994. This book follows the long-established Australian tradition of minimising the contributions of women to Australia's development. Mary Penfold's contribution in this slanted book is mentioned on pp. 23–4 as occurring only after the onset of Dr Penfold's illness sometime in 1860 '. . . his ailing health meant his wife Mary, aided by a servant Ellen Timbrell, increasingly managed the vineyard alone. [After a long illness Dr Penfold died in March 1870] . . . Mary assumed control of the wine business. Helped by Joseph Gillard . . . and her son-in-law Thomas Hyland, Mary built up the business to one of the largest wine companies in Australia. In 1880 the Hyland family moved back to Melbourne . . . [from which] Thomas Hyland . . . oversaw the expansion of Penfolds Wines from Magill into Victoria . . .'. Three of the conclusions drawn by the author about Mary misrepresent her vital contribution to the company:

i) Without detracting from Joseph Gillard's contribution, he joined the Penfold business in 1869, only months before Dr Penfold's death. Dr Penfold's involvement had been minimal for some years due to illness. Prior to that he had been kept busy running his thriving medical practice.

ii) Under a 1869 agreement, Thomas Hyland was the accountant and the marketing agent for Penfolds in Victoria where he continued to live.

iii) Mary remained on the site of the winery at *Grange Cottage* and it was Mary Penfold who continued to run and oversee the expansion of the Adelaide winery and vineyards, not Thomas Hyland, as this book suggests.

CHAPTER 14

Mary Watson
(1860–1881)

HEROINE OF LIZARD ISLAND

The Barrier Reef has been the scene of many shipping disasters and deaths but none of these events concern a story as heroic as that of twenty-one-year-old Mary Watson, who lived on Lizard Island for one year of her brief life.

My fascination with Mary's story began in 1975 when, newly arrived from England, I visited the pinnacled red-and-white brick edifice in the Brisbane suburb of Bowen Hills that housed the old Queensland Museum. The building was as extravagantly Victorian Gothic as some of the displays. I found myself in a time warp, wandering through aisles of dusty cedar-framed glass cases occupied by stuffed birds, gigantic hairy-legged spiders, lethal stonefish and blue-ringed octopuses.

One exhibit fired my imagination: an enormous blackened tank over one metre square. Against it lay a piece of pasteboard brown with age inscribed in faded ink:

> In this iron tank twenty-one year old Mrs Mary Watson, her baby and their Chinese servant escaped from hostile Aborigines on Lizard Island only to die of thirst on the Reef.

Here was a fascinating story of female heroism but there was no brochure or bookshop to tell me more about Mary Watson. An elderly museum attendant volunteered information that Mary came from central Cornwall and had kept a diary, which was now in the John Oxley Library. I went to the old State Library building, ascended in a rickety lift to the top floor, read the poignant entries Mary pencilled in just before she died, and saw her portrait in an ancient yellowing copy of *The Australasian Sketcher*.

Mary had now become overpoweringly real. Thoughts of her agonising days cramped in that dreadful tank while slowly dying of thirst haunted me. A few months later I was a guest at a symposium in Cairns and from there flew to the small deserted airstrip on tiny Lizard Island, nearly one hundred kilometres north of Cooktown, to see where Mary had lived.

We went in a four-wheel-drive to Watsons Bay, which was named after Mary. All that remained was three rough granite walls, listed by the National Trust as part of Mary's cottage. This is a romantic attribution but unfortunately untrue. The granite was used for the smokehouse: Mary's primitive living accommodation had thin wooden walls through which for several nights she lay awake listening to marauding Aborigines.[1]

The stone smokehouse was the hub of Mary's husband's highly profitable fishing station where they processed bêche-de-mer or sea cucumbers. Captain Watson had purchased the lease of the fishing station from Captain Bowman, who had built the smokehouse. Bowman, who had become rich from the concession, had obtained the lease from the Queensland Government. Frank Reid, schooner captain-turned-author, recorded that part of the fireproof walls of the smokehouse was still there in 1954 when he visited Lizard Island.[2]

A spring of water close beside the ruins is the one at which Mary filled a tin can with fresh water before embarking in that uncomfortable cramped iron tank with her baby and the wounded Chinese man.

I wanted to uncover the reasons why an educated, twenty-one-year-old girl from Cornwall would have done something as unusual for the Victorian age as running a lucrative business on a tropical island.

Years later I was invited to speak at the Cornish International Literary Festival, held at Looe, a Cornish fishing port to the south of the area where Mary grew up. I discovered that Mary's father had owned *Nanhellan*, a farm high on the bleak moors near the tiny village of Newlyn (now known as St Newlyn East to distinguish it from the fishing port of Newlyn, on the coast between Penzance and Land's End). Nineteenth-century maps of Cornwall show Nanhellan as a large estate. They fail to mention the present hamlet of Fiddlers Green close by. *Nanhellan* lies in a rough triangle between the fishing village and holiday resort of Perranporth to the west, Truro to the south (where Mary's mother was born) and the larger town of St Austell to the east, where the Oxnams, Mary's family, would have sold their cattle and sheep.

Mary was a Celt. She had dark hair with reddish highlights, dark expressive eyes and the typical Celtic love of words. She grew up in a beautiful but isolated part of England where Celts had fled when persecuted centuries before—an area steeped in Arthurian legend. On her grandfather's large estate the land was harsh, with rough granite outcrops and boulders. The fields could only support a few sheep, rabbits and goats plus a few hardy sure-footed cattle.

Mary's birth certificate registered her name as Mary Phillips, daughter of Mary Martha Phillips, spinster, and Thomas Oxnam, bachelor, aged twenty-three. Mary's mother was a village girl living just outside Truro. It is likely that she was a domestic servant, employed by Thomas's widowed father or another local landowner.

Rumours that Thomas Oxnam, up at the big house on the moors, had got one of the local girls pregnant and married her after the birth of his baby must have set tongues wagging. At that time a vast gulf separated simple villagers and educated gentry. Uneducated girls without a penny to their name, working as maids like Mary Martha Phillips, simply did not marry gentlemen, even if they were the fathers of their children. Sons of the landed gentry were expected to gain sexual experience from obliging village girls and then to marry daughters of other landowners who had dowries in money or land. Village girls who became pregnant were usually paid off by the family with a lump sum or a regular income arranged through lawyers.

But for reasons never explained, twenty-three-year-old Thomas Oxnam broke the male chauvinistic pattern of his time and class. He married his penniless lover exactly eight weeks after their daughter's birth. Thomas was certainly not cut out for farming the granite backbone of Cornwall that runs down to Land's End: the only really fertile portion of the Nanhellan estate was rented out to a tenant farmer, whose monthly rent enabled the Oxnams, father and son, to live like gentlemen.

Thomas Oxnam's mother was dead and his only sister had recently married and moved away. So after their delayed and probably very quiet wedding, Mary Martha and her baby moved into Thomas's family home of *Nanhellan* with his widowed father.

Cornish farmers benefited from the economic boom created by tin mining. The mining boom made farming this harsh land profitable and combined with tenants' rents enabled Thomas and his father to live the life of country gentlemen, shooting, fishing and dabbling, without great success, in cattle breeding. This agreeable way of life continued for the next eleven years while Mary Martha had nine more children and ran the family home.

Mary grew into an affectionate, placid and highly intelligent child and from an early age showed a love of reading and music. Her grandfather paid for her to attend a private school where she learned reading, writing and arithmetic. Her grandfather bought her an expensive Collard piano on which she soon became an accomplished pianist. He expected his grandaughters would have dowries and marry the son of a local farmer or one of the local gentry.

But as Mary grew older, the tin mines, including the one close to *Nanhellan*, were forced to close: tin was being produced far more cheaply in Malaysia which robbed Cornwall of its home and export markets.[3] By the time Mary turned sixteen, the Cornish economy had virtually collapsed: mining companies folded, the price of land fell, farmers found it difficult to sell their produce and ten thousand Cornish miners and their families faced starvation. Many emigrated to South Australia and North America, while others hung on in grim poverty. (After a decade of recession and desperate poverty Cornwall was saved by the china-clay industry and a brief revival of tin mining.[4])

Early in 1877, when Mary was nearly seventeen, her grandfather died. Thomas inherited *Nanhellan* and an estate burdened with debt. The only tenanted farm that brought in reasonable money was left to Thomas's married sister. Thomas was now asset-rich but short of cash.

Desperate for income, Thomas started a shop in the nearest village but in a depressed economy it lost money. With ten children to feed and clothe and a determination to retain his family's ancestral home and land, Thomas started speculating using money borrowed from the bank against the security of *Nanhellan*. Mary knew nothing of this. She was a quiet, bookish girl with a sweet, rather grave face and dark reddish-brown hair parted in the middle and tied back. She loved the idea of being a schoolteacher and was a devoted sister to her younger siblings.

Shortly after Mary's seventeenth birthday she learned her father faced bankruptcy. *Nanhellan* would have to be sold to pay the bank. For Mary and her younger siblings this not only meant the loss of the home and comfortable way of life but would affect their marriage prospects substantially. In the eyes of snobbish, class-ridden Victorian England, having a bankrupt for a father made Mary and her seven younger sisters unsuitable as potential brides for the sons of large farmers or the once-wealthy Cornish gentry such as the Godolphins, Carew-Poles, Courtenays or Grevilles. The Oxnams had definitely gone down in the world.[5]

At this unsettling juncture, Mary's father read in a newspaper about the booming frontier state of Queensland, with its Palmer River goldfields and vast cattle industry. Like so many of the unemployed Cornish tin miners, Thomas Oxnam decided that emigration to Australia would solve his financial problems: he may also have felt that in a land with so many single men, his eight daughters would find good husbands easily, dowry or no dowry.

The family packed the few personal possessions the bailiffs permitted them to remove, while *Nanhellan* and its furniture was advertised for sale along with Mary's beloved Collard piano.[6] The house and furniture brought good prices but all the money was taken by the bank to pay off debts. The Oxnams and their ten children were left with little but their clothes when, in 1878, they boarded the *City of Agra* bound for the Queensland coastal town of Maryborough. During the long voyage, Mary dutifully gave reading and writing and history lessons to the nine Oxnam children—and others—to bring in extra money. For Mary, this was no hardship; she loved the company of children and enjoyed teaching them.

The Oxnam family landed at Maryborough, Queensland's sugar cane and cattle port. But the rush to find gold on the Palmer River was almost over. Jobs were in short supply. Thomas Oxnam managed to find a job as assistant manager of a boiling-down works. Thomas soon realised he could buy cattle bound for the slaughter yards on his own account, sell them at a profit and work for himself. He resigned from the job at the smelly boiling-down works, borrowed money, bought cattle for slaughter, sent the carcasses to be boiled down for tallow and sold the hides to the tannery. Soon the family were able to move to a much larger weatherboard house with a verandah. At long last it seemed that their luck had changed.

Just as Thomas Oxnam was starting to pay off his bank loan, severe drought struck Queensland. When his bank called in the loan, leaving him in debt once again, Oxnam became deeply depressed by yet another commercial failure and Mary Martha, who was expecting her eleventh child, miscarried and nearly died.

Mary tried valiantly to bring in much-needed funds by setting up a school for infants and young children. In order to obtain permission to start her own school, she was required to show the authorities her birth certificates. This was when she suddenly discovered she was illegitimate—something to be deeply ashamed of at that period. From this time onwards Mary became shyer and more reserved but more self-reliant. She now signed her name as Mary Phillips Oxnam on all official documents.

The effects of the drought meant that many parents could no longer afford Mary's teaching fees so she took a paid position as a resident governess on the property of Mr C. Bond of Cooktown.[7] Mary was told she would be treated as one of the family but instead found herself treated contemptuously as a servant. She missed her younger brothers and sisters and parents and felt isolated, lonely and miserable.

Between 1874 and 1884 Cooktown was the second-largest town in Queensland and the second-wealthiest due to an influx of goldseekers for the neighbouring Palmer Fields gold rush. Hearing that Cooktown still lacked a good private school, Mary resigned from her hated position as governess. Cooktown was a large shanty-town filled with ninety-four pubs, and about the same number of brothels, restaurants and dance halls where raddled women fleeced men of their money. Out of a total population of 30,000 nearly half were Chinese, most of whom were refused permission to bring in wives under the White Australia policy for fear that they would soon outnumber the white population. Men, white and Chinese, outnumbered women by four to one.[8]

Constant worry over finance had the effect of making Mary, now aged twenty, slim down and lose her puppy fat. She was now an attractive young woman with a mind of her own. Setbacks in her young life had given her an indomitable spirit and a will to survive. She was determined not to return to the overcrowded family home and be yet another mouth for her parents to feed.[9] She knew they were struggling to support so many young children and felt she must fend for herself.

Out of desperation, Mary did something quite daring: she took a job playing light popular piano music in a Cooktown restaurant owned by a Frenchman named Monsieur Bonel.

A visitor to the restaurant described Mary as 'a good pianist. She was very reserved, delicate looking and seemed nervous. Often it is such people who, when face to face with danger and death, prove themselves the bravest.' (See note 24). Small wonder Mary was nervous. Educated young ladies in the Victorian era did not normally play the piano in hotels or pubs in a gold rush town—a place a respectable woman would not dream of entering and any woman working there was thought a 'woman of easy virtue'. But Mary's talent as a pianist and her natural charm attracted patrons to the restaurant. It was here that she met a Captain Robert Watson, a man twice her age who had led an adventurous life and in whom she may have seen some of the characteristics of her own father.

Unfortunately Mary's diary reveals nothing of her courtship by Captain Watson or her subsequent engagement. Her future husband, known to his friends as Captain Bob, was a rolling stone but a more practical one than Mary's father. Born in Aberdeen, Scotland, Captain Bob resembled a character in a novel by Joseph Conrad, having captained tramp steamers all round the Pacific.

At the time of their meeting, bluff Captain Bob was running a sea cucumber fishing station on Lizard Island on land leased from the Queensland government, having bought the lease of the highly profitable fishing station from the first owner, Captain Bowman, who had retired wealthy after years of hard work.

Bêche-de-mer, also known as sea cucumbers from their curved shape and greenish colour, are fished from rocks or from the seabed by divers. At that time, they were found in large numbers on the Barrier Reef and in Torres Strait and fetched enormous sums—between eighty and one hundred pounds a ton.

Following the rush to the Palmer River before 1873, Cooktown had a large Chinese population who cheerfully paid high prices for cooked and dried bêche-de-mer. Chinese men believed these sea creatures with their phallic shape restored fading virility: an optimistic supposition that appears to lack supporting medical evidence.

Mary learned that Captain Watson's fishing operation was a two-man partnership. They did not employ Aboriginal or Malay divers like many of the lugger or schooner owners but sailed around removing the sea cucumbers from the rock and coral outcrops along the reef at low tide. He and his partner Percy Fuller employed two Chinese men in the smokehouse close by their hut.

Captain Watson was forty-two—old enough to be Mary's father. He was slight in build, with blue eyes, a fair, tanned complexion and brown hair thinning on top. Like many of the wanderers who had finished up in Cooktown, Captain Bob drank more than was good for him. He was something of a rough diamond and Mary, who was used to caring for others, may have felt her motherly instincts aroused by him. He was fascinated by Mary, who was very different to the type of women he normally met in bars and hotel restaurants.

Engraved portrait of Mary Watson as a young woman, taken from a photograph made around the time of her marriage. (The photograph was engraved to be reproduced in The Queenslander *after her heroic death). John Oxley Library, Brisbane.*

After years of wandering the Pacific, Captain Watson felt ready to settle down. In Mary, with her commonsense, love of children and quiet determination, he sensed he had found an ideal partner. Their courtship was brief. Captain Watson had no intention of running the bêche-de-mer station for the rest of his life. Lugger owners like Captain Edwards at Frederick Point on Albany Island and Captain Bowman, the previous lessee at Lizard Island, had lived rough for some years, worked hard and sold out for a good profit, while another lease holder, Phil Garland, had become a millionaire recently.[10] Captain Watson offered Mary his name and a new and interesting life and the chance to retire in comfort to a place of her choice after a few years of isolation. It was a lonely life that most city girls could not have endured but Mary was country-bred and in her twenty years had been through 'the school of hard knocks'. On 30 May 1880 at Cooktown's Christ Church, Captain Bob Watson, bachelor, married Miss Mary Phillips Oxnam, spinster.

Mary's family were not at the wedding. Having failed as a cattle dealer in Maryborough, Thomas had been employed in Rockhampton, in charge of the public bar at the Red Lion Hotel. He probably could not afford the fare to Cooktown. Besides, Mary's second sister, Nellie, was also getting married later that month: money was required for Nellie's dress and reception and Mary probably had to pay for her own wedding. A studio photograph[11] shows pretty Nellie wearing a pale dress with a long pleated skirt and flowers in her hair, standing beside her handsome young husband with her hand resting on his shoulder. There are no known photos of Mary's wedding, which was probably a quiet one.

Mary spent her honeymoon aboard her husband's fishing lugger, sailing to Lizard Island, where they and Percy Fuller were the only white inhabitants. Lizard Island has few trees and its peak, like the land around Nanhellan, is formed of granite. While the smokehouse was certainly made of stone the storeroom was built of wood and it is likely Mary's dwelling was also made of wood, possibly brought over prefabricated from the mainland. In front of her in the bay was a sandy beach sloping down to a shallow half-moon bay where green turtles, gigantic clams and angel and parrot fish swam among the coral. Lizard Island was and is a tropical paradise of white sand set in a sea that varies from turquoise to navy blue depending on the angle of the sun on the coral reef. The island's underwater coral gardens are among the most colourful and varied in the world. On land Mary saw for the first time huge but harmless grey-green monitor lizards with enormous forked tongues that darted out when disturbed. It was an uninhabited paradise.

Ah Sam and the older man, Ah Leong, did the heavy work and carried water for drinking and washing from the stream. Directly Watson and Fuller sailed in close and moored the lugger, their two Chinese employees, both unmarried because hardly any Chinese women were allowed entry to Australia, would collect the bags of greenish or blue-black sea slugs or cucumbers, which could vary from four inches to three feet in length, depending on the species. They then placed the sea cucumbers in the iron tank and boiled them for twenty minutes, stirring them with long paddles. Once killed the creatures were removed from the tank and split lengthwise with a sharp knife, gutted and then dried in the sun. When most of the moisture had evaporated the sea cucumbers were carried into the smokehouse with its tin roof and stone walls, laid on racks of wire netting and smoked for twenty-four hours over mangrove branches. By this time they resembled charred sausages and had something of the rubbery consistency of fried calamari but had a delicate and unusual taste.[12]

When Captain Bob and his partner were away fishing, Mary was in charge of Ah Sam and Ah Leong. It was a lonely life with few creature comforts, but Mary and her husband were working hard to build financial security for themselves and were sure they would return to the mainland as a wealthy couple.

Drinking water had to be brought from a nearby spring and stored in tin cans in the hut. They lived off fresh fish, tinned food and rice carried over by ship from the mainland and probably the Chinese men did the cooking. To avoid scurvy, Ah Leong grew vegetables in his small plot at some distance away from the beach, where the soil was more fertile.

That first year, just before Christmas, Mary found she was pregnant. There was no other white woman to help her and no medical services nearer than Cooktown; so in March 1881 she returned there to await the birth of her baby, who was named Thomas Ferrier after her father.

Ferrier, as she called the baby in her diary, was born on 3 June 1881 and Mary, the proud mother, returned to Lizard Island with her infant son at the end of the month. Perhaps she planned to write a book about her experiences on a tropical island. At any event she now kept a finished diary and wrote down jottings in another scribbling diary.

On 1 September, Captain Bob and his partner departed north to Knight Island[13] as they had almost depleted the reef around Lizard Island of sea cucumbers. They never employed Aboriginal divers to fish the seabed, possibly because there had been incidents where Aboriginal divers had mutinied and killed the lugger owners.[14]

Watson and Fuller intended to set up a second fishing station at Knight Island, and then sell out and retire. Mary did not go with them on their trip but she fully supported their aims and did not mind being left alone for a while.[15] Knight Island was nearly two hundred miles from Lizard. The trip would last several weeks and it was decided that when her husband returned they would take a short holiday together in Cooktown.[16]

Unknown to Watson and Fuller, the cottage and smokehouse had been built by Captain Bowman close to a stream which, at infrequent intervals (dating back long before Captain Cook had observed the presence of Aborigines) had been the site of Aboriginal secret initiation rites. The Aborigines who came there were not the tribe that had once inhabited Cooktown; they roamed the land further north and around one year in every five or six also used the stream at Watson's Bay as part of the initiation ceremonies of their young men. Prior to the cutting ceremonies which were reserved for men alone, the boys were immersed for hours in a stream, which had the effect of numbing the flesh slightly before the tribal elders made a series of incisions in the skin.[17]

The Aborigines must have noted the lull in the fishing operations on Lizard Island and may have seen Watson and Fuller's boat sailing north for Knight Island.

The Aboriginal elders were angry that the stream they regarded as sacred had been desecrated by the presence of white and Chinese men.[18]

On 27 September Mary wrote in her diary that Ah Leong had told her about smoke coming from a southerly direction and felt sure that it came from an Aboriginal campfire. The Aborigines, keen for revenge, must have rowed across to the island in canoes.

On the night of 28 September Mary was awakened by muttering in an unknown tongue which she could hear clearly through the thin wooden walls of the hut. She also heard footsteps and thought men were prowling around the cottage. She sat up in bed, rigid with fear, her husband's revolver in her lap and her baby pressed tight against her chest, but nothing more happened.

On 29 September Ah Leong failed to return from working in his vegetable garden at some distance from the beach. When Ah Sam searched for his friend he found only the man's straw hat on the ground.[19] Ah Sam told Mary that Ah Leong had been speared to death and his body taken by the Aborigines. Later this was proved correct.

The following day, 30 September 1881, the Aborigines ambushed Ah Sam who was working in the smokehouse, and speared him in the right side and shoulder. Ah Sam lay half-dead outside the hut, his body speared in seven places. Mary opened the door of the cottage with the revolver cocked, waving it so that the Aborigines would see she was armed. Then she dragged Ah Sam, screaming with pain, inside the cottage. The Aborigines made threatening gestures but, afraid of the revolver, did not touch her or Ah Sam.

Back inside her dwelling, Mary pulled the spearheads out of the groaning man and bandaged Ah Sam's wounds with strips of her petticoat. For the rest of the day she sat in the stifling heat of her hut with the door open and the gun on her lap waiting to see if the Aborigines would reappear, but there was no sign of them. She spent the next day also in the hut, watching and waiting to see if they would return.

That night Mary bolted the door of the hut and closed the shutters. It was hot and airless inside. Once more the Aborigines prowled around the cottage as Ah Sam lay groaning in pain. Sensing his mother's fear, baby Ferrier sobbed uncontrollably. Mary summoned up courage to open the door and fire off a round with her husband's revolver over the Aborigines' heads. They were painting in red and ochre on the wooden walls of the shed that was used as a storeroom, creating large stylised forms of fish and turtles.[20] Although Mary did not realise it at the time, these paintings of sea creatures were connected with the Dreamtime spirits and had a deep significance for the local Aborigines, still angry that their sacred places had been desecrated.

Captain Watson was not due back for at least another two weeks. Mary was alone with a helpless baby and a severely wounded man. She knew they must leave the island immediately and hope to be picked up by a passing ship or by her husband, should he return soon enough.

But how could they leave? There were no other settlers, no other boats. Then she thought of the iron boiling-down tank. It was four foot, or about 120 centimetres, square, just large enough to hold all three of them. It had no keel or fins, which would make it extremely unstable, but it would float. That grimy tank, cut down from a ship's water tank, blackened with grease and smoke, represented their sole means of survival.

Early next morning, even under severe stress Mary showed her courage, determination and imagination. The hut was now stiflingly hot with the window shutters closed for fear of a spear being thrown in. Systematically she collected all the equipment and provisions possible for a short sea voyage—her husband's revolver and ammunition, a tin of condensed milk, one of patent groats or baby cereal, some rice and tinned sardines, a pillow on which to rest baby Ferrier's head, his striped wrap, an umbrella to shield him from the sun, and a Chinese wooden neck pillow for Ah Sam. She also took her previous diaries and her few bits of jewellery, a fob watch, money, a change of clothing, some sharp pencils and a can to hold fresh water.

Hearing no more muttering or footsteps Mary opened the door and peered out. She saw the Aborigines sitting peaceably on the far side of the stream. It was obviously dangerous to approach them but she knew she and her baby must have fresh water if they were to survive. She ran quickly across to her side of the stream and filled a large tin can with drinking water. The Aborigines ignored her, occupied with chanting.

Fear lent Mary unaccustomed strength. Weighed down with long skirts and helped by the wounded Ah Sam, she managed to drag the heavy iron bêche-de-mer tank down the beach from the smokehouse, push it into the water and load provisions and equipment. With difficulty Ah Sam must have hauled himself over the edge of the tank and taken the baby from his mother.

The Aborigines watched Mary as she prepared to leave. Satisfied with having removed her and Ah Sam from their sacred ground and concentrating on the initiation rites, the Aborigines did not try to stop them leaving the island. Mary clambered over the edge of the dirty tank, hindered by long, water-logged skirts.

She grabbed one of the paddles used to stir the sea cucumbers and paddled away from Lizard Island. Doubtless the Aborigines watched her depart with relief and made no attempt to follow. Once their ceremonies were over they lit a number of fires which burned for several weeks, ransacked the hut and storeroom, and broke many of the remaining objects but did not remove them.

The tank was almost impossible to steer as it had a flat bottom and no rudder. Outside the bay the current took them into its power. There was no room to move in the tank which proved so cramped that it was impossible for Mary or wounded Ah Sam to lie down.[21] They were forced to sit bolt upright, Mary nursing Ferrier, facing each other diagonally to stop the tank tipping over and avoiding any sudden movements. The tank drifted on as they became numb with sitting on the hard iron, and occasionally they massaged their limbs to bring back the blood flow.

From 2 to 7 October the weather was calm and clear. For five hot, dry days, the flat-bottomed tank drifted north, sometimes turning round like a cockleshell on the water with the current. Mary must have known that if the tank had overturned it would have tipped them into the shark-infested ocean. Once the sun was up it was painful to touch the blackened iron which must have acted as a hotplate, absorbing heat reflected back from the glass-like expanse of the Pacific Ocean.

Mary pencilled entries into her increasingly battered and water-stained diary as they drifted in the unstable craft. They drifted nearly seventy kilometres north enduring blinding sun by day and a damp chill by night.

Mary rationed the drinking water, hoping they would discover an island with a spring of fresh water or a ship would find them. She constantly scanned the skyline for ships and worried as little Ferrier fretted and became dehydrated.

Slowly their precious water supply grew lower and lower.

Those dying of thirst report seeing mirages, usually of springs of water as well as images from their past. Perhaps Mary had visions of her childhood in Cornwall or in mirages glimpsed tantalising streams of fresh water. But throughout her painful ordeal, as her body and that of her baby slowly dehydrated, Mary remained calm and practical. In the pages of her diary there is no sense of panic or ranting recriminations against her husband for leaving her or any complaints against the Aborigines. Showing great presence of mind, like a captain on a sinking ship, Mary calmly recorded events in pencil, doubtless intending her diary to act as a log, should her husband find her.

> **4 October** Made for the sandbank off the Lizard. Could not reach it and got on the reef.

> **October 5**. Remained on the reef all day on the look out for a boat but saw none.

> **October 6**. Very calm morning. Able to pull the tank up an island with three small mountains on it. Ah Sam went ashore to try and get water as ours was done. There were natives camped there so we were afraid to go far away. We had to wait until the return of the tide. Anchored under the mangroves. Very calm.

> [Obviously the presence of more Aborigines greatly alarmed Mary and Ah Sam and they decided to paddle on to the next small island, hoping to find drinking water there.]

> **October 7**. Made for an Island about four or five miles from the one spoken of yesterday. Ashore—but could not find any water. Cooked some rice, clams and fish. Moderate S.E. breeze. Stayed here all night. Saw a steamer bound north. Hoisted Ferrier's pink and white wrap but it did not answer us.

> [This must have been a despairing moment for Mary. She was glad to leave the cramped confines of the tank and explore the island, which was uninhabited, but

found no fresh water. Their water supply from Lizard Island and the condensed milk was almost exhausted. She must have realised that she could not last much longer.]

October 8. Changed the anchorage of the boat as the wind was freshening. Went down to a kind of little lake on the same island. [This was a saltwater lagoon.] Remained here all day looking for a boat, did not see any. Very cold night, blowing very hard. No water.

October 9. Brought the tank ashore as far as possible with the morning's tide. Made camp all day under the trees. Blowing very hard. No water. Gave Ferrier a dip in the sea. He is showing symptoms of thirst. Took a dip myself. Ah Sam and self parched with thirst. Ferrier is showing symptoms.

October 10. Sunday. Ferrier very bad with inflammation, am very much alarmed. No fresh water and no more milk but condensed. [Presumably lack of water had made her breast milk dry up.] Self very weak: really thought I should have died last night.

October 11. Still alive. Ferrier much better this morning. Self feeling very weak. Think it will rain today. Clouds very heavy and wind not quite so high.

By now Mary's lips were cracked with thirst while her tongue had swollen and turned black as she wrote a poignant last entry in her diary. She did not waste her failing strength on describing her symptoms. Like Captain Scott recording the fate of his failed polar expedition, she was stoically brave in the face of death and blamed no-one for her fate. She may have hoped for a miracle that a passing ship might appear and save the three of them. But she was a realist and deep in her heart she knew it was unlikely as few ships sailed through the Reef. Her final entry was written to record the truth for her husband or those she hoped would find her body.

> No rain. [All this] morning fine. Ah Sam preparing to die. Have not seen him since nine. Ferrier more cheerful. Self not feeling at all well. Have not seen any boat of any description. No water. Near death with thirst.[22]

This is the final entry in the diary and we do not know if she or her baby died first.

Three weeks later, Captain Watson and his partner returned to Lizard Island. They found one wall of the cottage and the door and walls of the small wooden storeroom covered with designs of fish and turtles,[23] the tank gone and no signs of Mary, her baby or the two Chinese employees. Frantic with fear, they searched the island but found no traces. Next they scoured the adjacent coastline and islands for the next two weeks, never realising that Mary could have drifted forty miles to the north of Lizard Island in that unstable, uncomfortable iron tank.

It was not until 22 January of the following year that Ah Sam's corpse was found by one of the Aboriginal divers from another bêche-de-mer ship, the fishing schooner *Kate Kearney*. It was now the cyclone season and the schooner was sheltering from rough weather in the lee of Island No. 5 of the Howick Group (now renamed Watson Island). An Aboriginal diver employed on the ship had gone ashore to search for gull's eggs. On the far side of the island he was amazed to discover the emaciated and partially decomposed corpse of one of the Chinese.

The diver returned to his ship and in some agitation informed Captain Bremner about the dead man. Bremner had been advised by Captain Watson that his wife and baby and two Chinese men were missing, so Captain Bremner ordered his crew to scour the island.

They found the iron tank moored among mangroves. Mary's head was slumped against the side of the tank, her baby cuddled protectively to her breast. Her diary lay open on her lap. Mary's skeletally thin fingers were tightly entwined with those of her baby. By a strange irony of fate, a tropical storm had deluged the tank with rain soon after Mary and her baby had died of thirst.

The *Cooktown Courier* for January 1882 reported that

> Mrs Watson was lying on her back with her dead baby resting on her decomposed arm. The diary which the poor lady had managed to write till the last tells how . . . she bravely entrusted herself to the elements and the mercy of God in one of the frailest barques which ever bore a living freight. This brave woman drifted over the torrid sea to die of thirst on an arid uninhabited coral isle within ten miles of the mainland. The diary tells of her wonderful presence of mind that she took a pillow for her babe's head to rest on and an umbrella to shield him from the burning tropical sun.

When Captain Watson heard how his wife and baby had died, his hair is reputed to have turned white with grief and guilt.[24]

He sold his share of the boat, the buildings and the fishing lease for Lizard Island to his partner and moved to Cooktown, where he suffered a nervous breakdown. He became a familiar figure in waterfront bars, endlessly telling and retelling the tragic details of Mary's death to anyone who would listen. He is believed to have died of liver failure.[25]

The bodies of Mary, Ah Sam and baby Ferrier and the iron tank were brought back to Cooktown aboard the *Kate Kearney*.

On 29 January 1882 Mary's flower-bedecked coffin and the tiny satin-lined one that housed her baby were carried through silent streets in a horse-drawn hearse with nodding plumes. The hearse was followed by over six hundred black-clad mourners, the largest funeral ever to take place in Cooktown. The next day Ah Sam was buried by the Chinese community in traditional fashion.

Mary's lichen-covered grave can still be seen in Cooktown Cemetery and her simple granite headstone bears the engraved legend '*Mrs Watson, Heroine of the Lizard Island Tragedy*'.

Mary is one of the very few Australian women to have been honoured with a public monument. Engraved on the base of the joint memorial to Mary and Ah Sam in the main street of Cooktown is a poem celebrating Mary's bravery written by a former Mayor, which ends with her final words:

'Near death with thirst'

---

[1] The lucrative Queensland bêche-de-mer, trepang or sea slug fishing industry was thriving before the arrival of Europeans. Aboriginal cave paintings on Cape York attest to the presence of Maccassan trepang fishermen from Sulawesi in the area centuries before the arrival of Captain Cook. This trade was taken over by British captains of schooners or luggers on the Barrier Reef often using Malay or Aboriginal divers. Frank Reid's informative *Romance on the Barrier Reef*. Angus and Robertson, 1954, details this lucrative trade. The introduction to this book is by an author who actually worked on a fishing lugger on the reef: W.L. Russell, former Honorary Secretary of the Thursday Island branch of the Queensland Royal Geographical Society. See also Saville-Kent, William, *Great Barrier Reef: Production and Potential*. W.H. Allen, London, 1893, the 1908 Report by the Queensland Government into *Pearl Shell and Bêche-de-Mer Fishing, 1908*.

Sea slugs or sea cucumbers (the name was changed to make them sound more appetising) were smoked in stone smokehouses. Mary and her husband probably lived in a wooden dwelling which could have been brought in sections by boat and assembled on site.

On Lizard Island today there is no trace of a wooden hut or their storeroom with wooden walls and door; only some stones from the smokehouse remain. Photos in the John Oxley Library attributing the stone walls at Watsons Bay to Mary Watson's cottage is more romantic but according to Reid incorrect.

²   Watsons Bay, Lizard Island, is sited near the stone foundations of Watson and Fuller's fishing station and has a National Trust Heritage listing. It is now a camping site administered by the Queensland National Parks and Wildlife Dept. Lizard Island was named by Joseph Banks. Captain Cook surveyed Lizard Island from the peak known as Cooks Lookout, in order to find a passage through the Barrier Reef. The Aborigines rowed across to Watsons Bay at certain times of the year to fish, visit their sacred site and conduct secret initiation ceremonies.

³   du Maurier, Daphne. *Vanishing Cornwall*. Penguin Books. London, 1967.

⁴   Jenkin, A.K.H. *The Story of Cornwall*. George Nelson and Sons, London, 1934; *Guide to Cornwall*. Adam and Charles Black, London and Edinburgh, 1892.

⁵   For the enormous importance of dowries in the family dynamics of the Victorian period see the section on dowries in Pool, Daniel, *What Jane Austin Wore and Charles Dickens Ate*. Simon and Schuster, London and New York, 1994.

⁶   Robertson, Jillian. *Lizard Island, a reconstruction of the life of Mary Watson*. Hutchinson, Victoria. 1981.

⁷   Reid, F. *Romance of the Barrier Reef. Op. cit.*

⁸   Cilento, Raphael. *Triumph in the Tropics*. Brisbane. [n.d.c. 1950.] And *Encyclopaedia of Australia*, Grolier Society, 1983.

⁹   The analysis of Mary's handwriting was made in December 1978 by Joan Cambridge, Member of the Society of Graphologists (England) from Mary Watson's diary and is in the John Oxley Library, Brisbane, along with her diary.

¹⁰ Reid, R. *Romance of the Barrier Reef. Op. cit.*

¹¹ Now in John Oxley Library, Brisbane. Formerly labelled as being Mary's wedding portrait, it is now re-attributed as that of her sister.

¹² See chapter devoted to the history of bêche-de-mer fishing in Reid, F., *Romance of the Barrier Reef, op. cit.*, and *Barrier Reef Bêche-de-Mer Fishing Ventures*, Australian Fisheries Journal, Vol 39, No. 8, 1980.

¹³ *Cooktown Courier*, October 1881.

¹⁴ Reid, F. *Op. cit.*, and Cilento, R. *op. cit.* [a somewhat biased history].

¹⁵ Reid, F. *Op. cit.*

¹⁶ Reid, F. *Op. cit.*

¹⁷ Information kindly supplied by Ian McKenna, Curator of the Cooktown Museum.

¹⁸ *Ibid.*

¹⁹ The Coroner's Inquest, rightly or wrongly, indicated that the court believed Ah Leong was roasted and eaten. Also cited in Reid, F. *Op. cit.*

²⁰ Drawings, copies of the Aboriginal art believed to have been made by A.H. Fullwood, who was touring north Queensland 1886–1887, are now in the Cooktown Museum and are reproduced in Hogan, J. *Op. cit.*

²¹ Information kindly supplied by the tank's former curator, Ian McKenna, who spent five uncomfortable working days sitting in it in the Cooktown Museum, while painting a scenic background when the tank was going on display. The tank is now in the Townsville Museum (part of the Queensland Museum, whose property it remains).

²² The annotations are those of the author but Mary Watson's diary is reproduced in full in Reid, F. *Ibid.* p. 72–3.

²³ According to Ian McKenna, Curator of the Cooktown Museum, the Aboriginal drawings were copied by artist A.H. Fullwood, who was in Queensland in 1887 to make pictures to be reproduced in black-and-white for the *Picturesque Atlas of Australia*, Sydney, 1887–1888. Fullwood's black-and-white copies of the Aboriginal drawings are on the back of a map of the area. The map belongs to the National Trust of Queensland and is now in the Cooktown Museum.

²⁴ The account of Captain Watson's hair turning white overnight is cited by a contemporary, Robert S. Browne, in his book *A Journalist's Memories*, Brisbane, 1927. He also described Mary playing the piano in the restaurant at Cooktown. Additional accounts of Mary's life are contained in a book published anonymously, whose publication may have been funded by Captain Watson, entitled *Mrs Watson, a Cooktown Heroine*. Published at Port Douglas around 1891. A full account of the discovery of Mary's body is contained in Coroner's Inquest, No. 373, Cooktown Court Records. A brief account of Mary's life by S.E. Stephens ed. Bede Nairn appears in the *Australian Dictionary of Biography*, Vol. 6, Melbourne University Press, Vic, 1976 and in Hogan, J., *National Trust of Queensland Journal*, Vol. 4, No. 1 (April 1980).

²⁵ Information supplied by Ian McKenna, Curator, Cooktown Museum.

CHAPTER 15

Sister Lucy Osburn
(1835–1891)

AUSTRALIA'S FLORENCE NIGHTINGALE

Lucy Osburn, raven-haired, petite and delicately pretty, was widely travelled in an era when most women rarely left the country of their birth. She accompanied her academic father, a well-known Egyptologist, on several study tours to Egypt, the Middle East and Europe. From childhood Lucy suffered chest infections during the British winter, had spent many winters in warmer climes and was fluent in several European languages and, through working as unpaid secretary for her father, William Osburn, had a wider education that most women of her time.

In her mid-twenties when most of her friends were married and raising numerous children, Lucy amazed her family by announcing she wished to take up nursing as a career. Her father was unaware of the enormous changes currently taking place in British hospitals as a result of Florence Nightingale's reforms. He was horrified at the thought of his cultured, intelligent daughter working with the illiterate and sluttish women who were, prior to Florence Nightingale's reforms, employed to nurse the sick and dying in dirty, overcrowded public hospitals.

Lucy's desire to become a highly trained professional nurse started when she had accompanied her father to Germany. While he carried out his research in museums, Lucy undertook voluntary work for four months in the important Kaiserwerth Hospital, Dusseldorf, and visited hospitals in Holland and Vienna. Her father did not object to her unpaid work, which he viewed as a genteel philanthropic gesture. Like many others of his time, he did not see nursing as a suitable occupation for a young lady and wanted Lucy to continue helping him with his research.

As Lucy had inherited a small legacy, she was able to defy her father. In 1866, she enrolled in the Nightingale Training School of Nursing attached to London's prestigious St Thomas's Hospital, where she gained valuable experience working in both men's and women's surgical, medical and accident wards. Lucy greatly admired Florence Nightingale and for both these dedicated women nursing the sick and dying was more than a job, it was a mission. Previously hospitals had been dirty places where only the poor went to die. The wealthy were nursed by family members at home but Florence Nightingale's insistence on 'hygienic principles' was slowly changing the attitudes of patients and doctors towards the profession of nursing.

Lucy was a steel magnolia with a mind of her own. Against a background of family hostility she steadfastly continued her nursing studies even though her father turned her portrait to the wall in a gesture of disgust. Her sole support in her professional endeavours was her sister Ann, a teacher who dreamed of leaving home and founding her own school on modern principles.

Lucy finished her nursing training in September 1867 and was proud to be known as Sister Osburn, one of Miss Nightingale's nurses. She went on to study midwifery at another great London teaching hospital, King's College Hospital.

After a personal appeal by New South Wales Colonial Secretary Henry Parkes to Florence Nightingale for trained nurses to staff the Sydney Infirmary and

Dispensary, Sister Osburn, now in her early thirties, was invited to apply for the job of Lady Superintendent of the Sydney Hospital. Her constitution was not strong and she hoped that the milder winters of Sydney would alleviate her health problems with bronchitis and chest infections. She knew little of the conditions at the old Sydney or Rum Hospital (so-called because it had been built with a levy raised on the sale of rum). She was told that she was expected to establish a training school for nurses in the colony based on Nightingale principles of hygienic nursing and train those nurses currently employed there.

Lucy said a sad farewell to her family and she and the five nursing sisters under her charge endured a long and uncomfortable voyage to Australia.

On March 5 1868 the *Dunbar Castle* sailed into Sydney Cove and all six Nightingale nurses disembarked. Wearing their white starched caps and nurse's uniforms they found that cheering crowds had lined Circular Quay and Macquarie Street to greet their arrival.

Lucy soon discovered that the Sydney Hospital in Macquarie Street, founded by Governor Macquarie and his wife in 1816, over half a century before, was old and dilapidated. There had been criticism in Parliament and in the Sydney newspapers of the poor administration of the hospital by the House Committee and the Superintendent.

On their arrival at the long hospital building with its wide verandahs, Lucy and her nurses were shown round. They were horrified to find no running water, wards riddled with vermin and kitchens thick with grease. Cockroaches scuttled out of every crevice and were even seen in the patient's bandages. Ventilation was poor and the stench was overpowering. Patients lay unwashed, covered in bedsores, on unmade beds with mattresses rotten from urine and faeces. The fetid odour of putrefying flesh, open sewers and makeshift latrines permeated the hospital. Lucy was appalled and several nurses could not prevent themselves from vomiting. It was not a good start.

To counteract such an unhealthy working environment Lucy knew that she and her nurses must have good living conditions—but found that the new Nurses' Residence, promised by Henry Parkes in her letter of appointment, was not yet complete. They were hastily found damp and dirty rooms in the already overcrowded hospital. Later that night Lucy's lamplight tour of the hospital revealed black rats who swarmed onto the wards, ran across the patients' beds, invaded the mortuary and even gnawed on the corpses.

There was no going back to England. Lucy knew she must stay and fight for better conditions for her patients. Desperate to initiate reform, she found herself trapped between the dreadful conditions for patients and corrupt and unco-operative administrative staff. The 'nurses' she was expected to train to become health professionals were underpaid and clearly unsuitable. Some had been hospital cleaners, others, with raddled complexions, greasy hair and bawdy language, Lucy suspected were part-time prostitutes.[1] She discovered some of these nurses smuggled alcohol into the patients for a fee; they would sit on the beds and drink with the patients or even have sex with them. Sometimes the 'nurses' became so drunk on the wards that a desperately sick patient's anguished cries for help fell on very deaf ears.

Lucy knew she must act swiftly to establish discipline. She was a fireball in character but from childhood she had never been physically strong and tired easily. She set about her task of reform immediately but had to stop due to frequent vomiting attacks. This turned out to be severe dysentery which lasted for two months, probably brought on because the hospital's kitchens were insanitary and running with roaches.[2] Lucy felt depressed and isolated. When she remonstrated with both the Medical Superintendent and the doctors, they ignored all her suggestions for change, obviously threatened by the presence of a woman in a senior position.

Sister Osburn's proposed reforms were obstructed at every turn: the cooks, cleaners and storeman ignored her authority and would only deal with the male Superintendent. In a despairing letter to Florence Nightingale.[3] Lucy described the Sydney nurses as 'dirty frowsy looking women'. She wrote how 'the younger ones had long greasy hair hanging down their backs' and ragged overalls in place of nursing uniforms. She also confided to Florence Nightingale how lonely she found herself, isolated by her position of command.

Lucy's main rival for power and prestige was the very man who should have helped her to reform the nursing service. The Sydney Hospital Board had appointed Superintendent John Blackstone to administer all aspects of the hospital and he bitterly resented a woman telling him what to do. Unknown to the Hospital Board, Superintendent Blackstone had become an alcoholic: he was far more interested in the bottle than in his work and his supervision of patients and staff was minimal. Hospital gossips told her that, when a patient from the Solomon Islands died, Blackstone had been drunk and no attendant had been instructed to remove the corpse to the mortuary. The dead man's fellow Islanders, who, according to one account, had a long tradition of cannibalism, simply pulled the blankets from the bed, placed the corpse on top and began to roast it for a funeral feast.[4]

Photograph of Sister Lucy Osburn.

Superintendent Blackstone felt threatened by a woman issuing orders that showed up his own inefficiency. His sphere of control under the rules of the Hospital Board clashed with the list of duties Lucy had been given by Premier Parkes and Florence Nightingale. He took a positive delight in encouraging his staff to defy Sister Osburn and frustrate her as she attempted to clean up the wards. Lucy and her nurses spent hours spraying disinfectant onto walls and floor but the bugs lurked in crevices or under the floor. All Lucy's appeals for help to the Hospital Board had to go through Superintendent Blackstone's office and were ignored. To make matters worse, Blackstone continually ran down her work and her character when chatting informally to members of the Hospital Board.

But Lucy worked on doggedly. By the end of the year she had dismissed the worst of the local nurses and trained sixteen more local girls in their place. But some of her British nurses became jealous. She poured out her heart in long letters home and to Florence Nightingale describing her achievements[5] 'a nice staff of nurses now—eighteen have passed as nurses and six probationers. I would greatly like to have more sisters. At present we have only four.' She was able to send trained nurses to the bush and received glowing reports from country doctors praising them. The foundations of nursing training in Australia were being laid.

In her letters home Lucy described how lonely she was so she bought herself a small black and tan terrier, who proved a faithful companion and a deterrent to the rats that infested the nurses' quarters. Superintendent Blackstone seized on her fondness for the dog to harass Lucy further. He demanded she remove her dog from the hospital. Lucy just smiled sweetly at him but continued to keep her dog in her room.

Another dangerous enemy was visiting surgeon Alfred Roberts (later Sir Alfred), with whom Lucy clashed time and time again over the vermin problem. Alfred Roberts operated at the Sydney Hospital and other places and made a handsome living at it. But Roberts resented Lucy's zeal for reform because he thought it cast a slur on his capabilities and so did everything in his power to get her removed from the job.

On a visit to London Roberts visited Florence Nightingale who, he discovered, had received unfavourable letters about Lucy from two of her English 'Nightingale' nurses, Sister Bessie Chant and Sister Annie Miller, (who had previously been disciplined by Lucy because Sister Miller allowed a married house surgeon to visit her bedroom at night and she feared reprisals from his wife).

On his return to Sydney Roberts spread rumours that Florence Nightingale was disappointed with Sister Osburn's work. Fortunately the Colonial Secretary of New South Wales Henry Parkes championed Lucy. He wrote to Florence Nightingale defending her. Parkes described how 'Mr Roberts is a respectable professional man . . . but he is . . . a fusy [sic], officious diletente [sic] in all matters of sanitary reform, who spoils his own efforts to be useful by his desire to be the authority on all occasions'.

In fact Roberts did want reform but he wanted to effect it himself without consulting a mere nurse. He visited London in 1871 with a view to designing a model hospital[5] but, like many medical men who would later object to employing female doctors (see in Volume 2 of this series about Dr Constance Stokes), he could not bear to share power with a woman and especially one younger than himself.

Capable but power-hungry, Sister Haldane Turriff (later to become the first matron of the Alfred Hospital, Melbourne) saw herself as Lucy's successor and wrote letters of complaint to Florence Nightingale, hoping that if Lucy was dismissed she would be appointed Nursing Supervisor in her place.

Medicine was then an exclusively male profession. There were, as yet, no female doctors working on the wards to support Lucy. Many male doctors supported Alfred Roberts in his campaign to make life so difficult for Sister Osburn that she would resign and go back to England. Some even refused to write essential information about patients' disease on the chart that hung at the end of each hospital bed. When Lucy tried to hold lectures for her trainee nurses Alfred Roberts or one of his medical colleagues would arrive unexpectedly and disrupt her lectures by demanding the nurses go back on the wards and prepare patients for operating immediately.

Lucy's order to a staff member to burn a cockroach-infested box of damaged and mouldy books and magazines that contained pages torn from an old Bible was 'magnified into a systematic and determined burning of Bibles on my part', Lucy wrote angrily. Distorted accounts, in which Lucy had taken a devilish delight in burning a box of Bibles, were spread by Sister Miller. Further damage to Lucy's reputation ensued when the Bible-burning story was printed in the *Protestant Standard*.

Following publication of the article, a subcommittee was hastily convened to judge Lucy's actions. They deliberated for six weeks before finally clearing her of the charges. The whole farcical incident seriously affected both staff morale and Sister Osburn's disciplinary powers but she carried on working tirelessly, at great cost to her own health. However, Parkes and others in political and philanthropic circles admired Lucy for her ideas and her dedication and they began to voice a growing discontent with the incompetent and corrupt hospital administrators. The Legislative Assembly appointed a Royal Commission of Enquiry which examined 58 witnesses as well as Lucy herself.

In 1873 the Public Charities Committee under Judge William Windeyer was convened and Alfred Roberts gave evidence stating that Lucy had failed in her duties. Windeyer was not convinced by Roberts' statement and his wife, Lady Mary Windeyer, a great champion of woman, may have helped Windeyer see things from a balanced perspective and pleaded Lucy's case.

After an exhaustive enquiry Windeyer and his Commission of Enquiry condemned the Sydney Hospital's 'horrible' operating room, the stench of rotting flesh and the lice and cockroaches on the wards. The Commission accused the House Committee of 'utter neglect' and 'interfering between the head of the nursing establishment and her nurses'. The Commission of Enquiry blamed the Hospital's Board of Directors and the House Committee and said they were making every mistake in hospital management that Florence Nightingale had warned against in her writings. Sister Osburn was totally vindicated. The final report praised the 'vast improvement in the nursing services' and raised Sister Osburn's salary.[6]

The report on the Sydney Hospital led to a public scandal when it called for the sacking of Superintendent Blackburn. Major reforms were slow to be implemented but with Blackburn gone Lucy Osburn was now officially in charge of wards, patients, nurses, cooking and domestic staff. By now she had made firm friends with Lady Windeyer and her daughter Lucy and with Emily Macarthur and her daughter Elizabeth Macarthur Onslow, but Lucy found that even supportive friends in high places were no substitute for her sister Ann. It was now over a decade since Lucy had left England and she longed to return home to see Ann.

By 1884 she had spent sixteen productive years in Sydney. She felt that she had reformed the nursing service in New South Wales and laid the foundations of one of the best nursing training systems in the world. Lucy was now in her forties and was suffering from diabetes.

She returned to London to seek a specialist opinion for her illness, intending to come back once her health improved. From 1886–88 Lucy succeeded in managing her diabetic condition relatively well. A workaholic, she could not leave nursing although earning money was never her main aim. She worked as an underpaid district nurse among the sick poor in London's Bloomsbury and was eventually promoted Superintendent to the Southwark, Newington and Walworth District Nursing Association.[7]

Lucy still talked of returning to New South Wales but her diabetes became more acute and her doctors advised against this. She became frailer and suffered fainting fits. In 1891, aged only fifty-six, on a visit to her sister's boarding school in Harrogate, Lucy collapsed and died of complications of diabetes.

Money she had left behind in New South Wales awaiting her return was bequeathed in her will to her namesake, young Lucy Windeyer. Lady Mary Windeyer and other friends raised funds for a plaque to be placed in the Sydney Hospital in memory of Sister Lucy Osburn and the reforms she initiated.

Now that nurses have won their fight to have their training recognised as a university degree course, they should never forget that Sister Lucy Osburn's fierce battle for professional status for nurses and better conditions in hospitals forged the basis of Australia's highly regarded nursing services.

---

[1] *Australian Dictionary of Biography.* Volume 5. Entry on Lucy Osburn by John Griffith. Melbourne University Press, Melbourne.

[2] Watson, J.F. *History of the Sydney Hospital 1811–1911*, Sydney, 1911, and Florence Nightingale Papers, British Museum, London.

[3] Prostitutes were employed in several Australian colonial hospitals. Former prostitutes employed as nurses at the Woogaroo Asylum are detailed in Evans, S., *Historic Brisbane and its early Artists*, Boolarong Publications, Brisbane, 1982; this also happened in some British hospitals prior to Florence Nightingale's reforms.

[4] Borowski, Eva, A Nice Staff of Nurses, *This Australia*, A.C.P., Sydney, 1987.

[5] Lucy Osburn's letter describing the poor standards of nursing staff to Florence Nightingale was dated 4 December 1864. Florence Nightingale Papers, British Museum, London.

[6] *Ibid.*

[7] *Australian Dictionary of Biography.* Volume 6. Entry on Sir Alfred Roberts by Martha Rutledge. Melbourne University Press, Melbourne 1974. Borowski, A Nice Staff of Nurses. *Op. cit.*

[8] See also Evans, E.P. Nursing in Australia in *International Nursing Review*, 12, 1936 and Sussman, M.P., Lucy Osburn and her five Nightingale Nurses *Medical Journal of Australia*. 1 May 1965 and Watson, J.F. *History of the Sydney Hospital 1811–1911*. Sydney, 1911.

Chronology

The following notes are intended to assist readers to place the lives of the selected women into perspective against the general background of events affecting the lives of all Australian women.

1788   Arrival of First Fleet at Port Jackson. Age of sexual consent based on British law is set at twelve allowing child prostitution: one woman to every ten male convicts and alcoholism rampant in the new penal colony. Esther Julian (Johnston) arrives aboard the *Lady Penrhyn*, then sails to Norfolk Island penal colony.

1790   Arrival of Second Fleet including Lieut John Macarthur and his wife Elizabeth. They encounter a famine in Sydney.

1792   First land grant to John Macarthur and other officers. Mary Haydock arrives in Sydney as a convicted thief but can read and write and is assigned as a domestic to the Assistant Governor.

1794   Mary Haydock marries Thomas Raby (Reibey) and sets up in business as a trader.

1798   Sealing begins in Bass Strait. Aboriginal women kidnapped by white sealers: used to catch seals, beaten and abused by their captors.

1801   John Macarthur takes first wool samples to London.

1803   The *Sydney Gazette*, the first Australian newspaper published. First white settlement in Tasmania, at Risdon Cove, opposite today's Hobart. Matthew Flinders finishes circumnavigating Australia.

1804   David Collins, having failed to settle at Port Phillip, establishes a settlement at Hobart, Van Diemen's Land.

1805   Birth of Georgiana Kennedy (Molloy) in Cumberland, England.

1807   Elizabeth Macarthur ships her first consignment of merino wool to London.

1808   Deposing of Governor Bligh by George Johnston, who becomes Acting Governor. Esther, his de facto wife, remains at Annandale and accepts no official duties.

1809   Isaac Nichols, son-in-law of Esther Johnston, appointed to be in charge of incoming sea mail.

1810   Governor Macquarie takes office.

1812   Birth of Truganini in Tasmania.

1816   Georgiana Gordon (McCrae) exhibits at London's Royal Academy from now until 1821 and again in 1825.

1817   First bank in Australia opens, the Bank of New South Wales.

1820   First officially recognised Catholic priests arrive. Birth of Mary Holt (Penfold) in London. Georgiana Gordon (McCrae) awarded the Silver Medal at the Royal Academy for her portraits.

1821   Sir Thomas Brisbane succeeds Macquarie as Governor of NSW. Mary Reibey takes her daughters to England hoping to find husbands for them.

1822–3   John Macarthur receives Society of Arts Gold Medal for the quality of his Camden wool. Elizabeth Macarthur's name is not mentioned in the award.

1824   First NSW Legislative Council meets. Fanny Macleay exhibits a flower painting at London's Royal Academy. Her father is Colonial Secretary of NSW.

1825   Van Diemen's Land penal settlement becomes the colony of Tasmania, which along with NSW initiates a scheme of establishing free men with enough capital to buy stock to take up land leased from the Government, proportional to the amount of stock they own.

1826 Arrival of Fanny Macleay in Sydney. Arrival of Sir Ralph Darling as Governor of NSW accompanied by the philanthropic Lady Eliza Darling. Fanny and Lady Eliza Darling found the Industrial School for Girls.

1827 Alan Cunningham, Government Botanist, notes the fertile grazing lands of the Darling Downs, then part of northern New South Wales, and later shows his map of the Downs to Patrick Leslie, who with his brother George (husband of Emmeline Macarthur) become the first farmers on the Darling Downs, followed shortly after by Arthur Hodgson, husband of Eliza (nee Dowling). They are first female settlers on Darling Downs.

1829 Captain Charles Fremantle establishes the Swan River Settlement, to which Governor Stirling's friend, Captain John Molloy, and his wife Georgiana, emigrate the following year and endure pioneering hardships when they move to Augusta, where Georgiana's first child dies. From now until 1838 Louisa Meredith will exhibit annually at the Royal Birmingham Society of Artists.

1830 Start of the infamous 'Black War' against the Tasmanian Aborigines in which many are exterminated. Walyer, the Aboriginal freedom fighter, uses guerrilla war tactics to defend her people but is eventually captured. Georgiana Gordon, illegitimate daughter of the fifth Duke of Gordon, makes a marriage of convenience to her cousin, Andrew McCrae.

1831 Walyer dies in captivity. Free land grants to settlers with capital for stock abolished. Sales by auction introduced: revenue to be used to pay to bring migrants from Britain to take up land. Penal settlement founded at Port Arthur.

1832 Assisted immigration schemes begin with money raised from sales of government land. Bounty agents scour British and Irish workhouses for adult migrants promising them work and accommodation in NSW, but no provisions for migrant accommodation are made in Sydney.

1834 Fanny Cochrane (Smith) born at Wybalenna Aboriginal Settlement, Flinders Island. Colony of South Australia founded

1835 Port Phillip (Melbourne) settled by John Batman and J.P. Fawkner. Literacy rate still low among convict and working class migrants: there are no government schools so NSW government subsidises church schools. Most children leave school between 12 and 14. Louisa Meredith publishes her first illustrated book of poems in England.

1836 Height of wool boom. Established graziers have become wealthy from selling sheep to land-hungry migrants who need stock to obtain land grants.

1838 NSW economy still booming for the first half of the year. Caroline Chisholm and family arrive in Sydney. The world's first stamped 'covers' for pre-paid postage on sale in Sydney at one shilling and three pence a dozen—imitating Rowland Hill's 'penny' post. They lower the previously exorbitant cost of mail carried by shipping companies. These new postal charges bring letter-writing within the reach of women able to read and write (about 40% of the female population of New South Wales).

1839 The worst drought in human memory in NSW plus keen competition from German wool in British markets leads to a slump in wool prices in New South Wales. But emigration from Britain continues unabated. Caroline Chisholm finds destitute immigrant women sleeping in the streets as no one wants to employ them in the recession, believing they are prostitutes. Children's Visitation Act ensures divorced or separated wives obtain limited access to their children, provided the court declares them the innocent party. In exceptional cases divorced or separated women permitted to have custody of children under seven. Women's activist and author Caroline Helen Spence arrives in Adelaide. Louisa Meredith accepts the marriage proposal of her cousin, Charles Meredith and the couple arrive in Sydney. Newly-married Emily Macarthur arrives in Sydney with her husband James and takes over the running of the school on the property at Camden Park.

1840 Transportation of convicts to New South Wales abolished. Emily Macarthur of Camden Park gives birth to a daughter named Elizabeth after her husband's mother Elizabeth who still runs Elizabeth Farm, Parramatta.

1841 Caroline Chisholm granted permission to use Sydney's Immigration Barracks to set up a hostel for migrant and homeless women. Sydney homes can now be lit by gas. Artist Georgiana McCrae arrives by sea in the primitive settlement of Port Phillip to join her lawyer husband. Landmark law suit in Britain the previous year allows a husband 'to restrain her wife from liberty for an indefinite time' if he felt 'the sanctity of the marriage to be threatened'. (This decision, valid under Australian law, affected battered women trapped in violent marriages but in spite of protests was not revoked until 1891.) Charlotte Barton (Atkinson) writes Australia's first children's book *A Mother's Offering to her Children*, published in Sydney, and finally secures a legal separation rather than a divorce.

1843   Wool price depression continues causing widespread financial loss on the land and a slump in property. Those heavily mortgaged to banks lose their land and homes including Alexander Macleay, Colonial Treasurer and father of Fanny Macleay. Bank of New South Wales fails; Hannibal Macarthur, cousin by marriage of Elizabeth Macarthur and a director of the Bank is bankrupted and forced to sell his home. Death of Georgiana Molloy on the Vasse River, Western Australia.

1844   Mary Penfold emigrates from England. She and her husband Dr. Christopher Penfold settle at Magill, outside Adelaide, where she starts a winery, assisted by Ellen Timbrell, to provide wine for her husband's patients.

1845   All Government assistance to migrants temporarily suspended due to continuing recession and high unemployment. Andrew McCrae takes up land at Arthurs Seat and moves his wife, Georgiana, and children there against their wishes. Eliza Thurston is awarded the Silver Medal of the Society of British Artists.

1846   Caroline Chisholm revisits England, where she lobbies the British Government to fund the passage of children of convicts and free settlers to New South Wales to ensure family reunions. Death of Esther Johnston.

1847   British Government resumes assistance for migrants and Caroline Chisholm makes public speeches demanding washing and laundry facilities, individual bunks and better treatment for migrants on government-sponsored ships. Wybalenna Aboriginal Settlement closed and the inmates (including Truganini and Fanny Cochrane Smith) transferred to Oyster Cove.

1848   Caroline Chisholm and her husband form their own Family Colonization Loan Society in London, chartering their own ships with money raised by loans from prospective migrants. Caroline Chisholm personally oversees better conditions for women aboard emigrant ships. Order in council abolishing transportation of convicts to NSW revoked because squatters demand cheap labour to work their cattle and sheep properties.

1849   Transportation of convicts to NSW recommences but the arrival of two convict ships in Melbourne and Sydney causes anti-transportation riots among free settlers there. Mary McConnel arrives with her husband in primitive frontier settlement of Brisbane and takes up residence at Cressbrook Station.

1850   Transportation to NSW suspended but commences in Western Australia. Death of Elizabeth Macarthur.

1851   Victoria proclaimed a separate colony. Georgiana McCrae stands in as Governor's lady for the Independence Day celebrations due to the illness of the Governor's wife Sophie La Trobe. Gold discovered in NSW near Bathurst and at Clunes, in Victoria, leading to gold rushes.

1853   Arrival of the last convicts transported to Van Diemen's Land and of widowed artist Eliza Thurston and her daughters in Sydney. Eliza opens a school and 'drawing academy'.

1854   Eureka Stockade at Ballarat, Victoria, 3 December.

1855   Responsible government established in NSW, Victoria and Tasmania. Van Diemen's Land renamed Tasmania. Death of Mary Reibey, rich and respected as a business woman.

1856   Responsible government proclaimed in South Australia.

1857   Only 15 of the original Aboriginal inhabitants remain alive at the Oyster Cove Aboriginal Settlement, Tasmania. Caroline Louisa Atkinson becomes the first Australian-born woman to publish a novel in the Antipodes but *Gertrude the Emigrant* is published anonymously.

1858   Male householders only are given the right to vote in NSW.

1859   Northern New South Wales renamed Queensland and proclaimed a separate colony from NSW with its own responsible government.

1860   Premier John Robertson introduces in two Selection Acts (1860 and 1861) encouraged by Caroline Chisholm. This effectively creates a new class of smallholders or 'selectors'. Lack of capital, poor soil, low rainfall and relative inexperience with farming in Australia ensure most selectors and their wives and children face desperate lives in rural poverty. Louisa Meredith's lavishly illustrated book, *Bush Friends in Tasmania*, published in Britain.

1861   Australia's first public art gallery opened in Melbourne.

1862   Louisa Meredith exhibits watercolours at the London International Exhibition.

1863 First Kanaka labour transported to Queensland, including a small percentage of 'blackbirded' women, some of whom are sold into prostitution.

1864 Widowed Annie Caldwell treks in a covered wagon from Gumeracha, South Australia, to The Billabong, near Holbrook, NSW, with seven children and starts her own small cattle farm there in virgin bush on a small selection.

1866 *The Lancet*, a British medical journal widely read by Australian medical practitioners, carries an article defending female circumcision on the grounds that circumcision could relieve epilepsy and sterility. Caroline Chisholm returns to London where she lobbies the British Government for better conditions for all emigrants to Australia.

1867 The Reform Bill passed in London extending vote to male householders (previously they needed to own property or land of high value). Widows and unmarried women owning homes or land find their rates increased but fail to receive the vote. Widowed Eliza Thurston wins a Silver Medal at the Paris International Exhibition for her watercolours.

1868 The arrival of Lucy Osburn and her Nightingale nurses at Sydney Hospital leads to reform of that male-dominated and vermin-ridden institution, resulting in intense hostility among some doctors to Sister Osburn.

1869 British social reformer John Stuart Mill publishes *The Subjugation of Women* arguing that not only women but the whole nation would benefit from educating women who are trained from childhood to a life of submission to men. British Contagious Diseases Act ensures that prostitutes in garrison towns forced to attend inspections at Lock Hospitals. If found to be carrying venereal disease, the women are locked up for nine months in the Lock Hospital. This law is designed to protect their customers, soldiers and male civilians, and outrages many women's groups, who believe that it condones prostitution. This law is enacted in various states in Australia.

1870 Mary Penfold's husband dies. She is advised by her son-in-law to sell her winery but refuses. She continues running it successfully and exhibits Penfolds wines in London. Louisa Meredith wins a bronze medal at the 1880 Melbourne Intercolonial Exhibition. Florence Nightingale and Harriet Martineau protest against the Contagious Diseases Act, claiming prostitutes are often single mothers with no other means of income to support their children.

1872 First comprehensive system of state education in Victoria. Heart attack causes premature death of author and journalist Caroline Louisa Calvert (Atkinson), daughter of Charlotte Atkinson.

1873 Brettena Smyth (Volume 2) causes a public outcry when she sells imported contraceptives to women from her general store in North Melbourne and from a travelling cart.

1875 VD cases so numerous that women's movements in Britain and in Australia lobby for age of sexual consent for women to be raised to sixteen. Male opposition ensures it is only raised to thirteen which means girls of fourteen can work in brothels without the owner being prosecuted. NSW's first art gallery established in Sydney by the Government.

1876 Death of Truganini in Hobart, followed by attempts to claim her skeleton by medics and research scientists.

1877 Population of Australia reaches two million.

1878 Opening of the Brisbane's Children's Hospital, the first and only children's hospital in the entire north of Australia, founded by Mary McConnel, who supervises the engagement of staff and pays the salary of the first matron. Conservationist and author Louisa Meredith becomes co-founder of the Tasmanian Society for the Prevention of Cruelty to Animals.

1880 First public telephone exchanges opened in Australian cities. The Bulletin uses the slogan *Australia for the White Man* on its masthead in support of the official White Australia policy and this racist slogan will not be removed until 1960. Immigration to Australia was still denied to women of non-Anglo-Saxon or Celtic origin through the infamous 'dictation test'. Indentured labourers can only enter if single due to fears of overpopulation under the White Australia policy. Death of widowed Emily Macarthur and the Camden Park estate passes to her daughter Elizabeth, who becomes an innovative farmer. The first three women graduates in the British Empire awarded arts degrees by London University.

1881 Chinese Immigration Restriction Acts passed in Queensland, NSW and Victoria. First Salvation Army Corps founded. Australia's population now 2,250,000. Mary Watson dies of thirst on Howick Island when fleeing from Lizard Island in an iron tank. Population of Australia now 2,250,194.

1882 British Married Women's Property Act enables women to own land, houses or money brought to the marriage in the form of a dowry or bequeathed to them later.

1883 Julia Bella Guerin (Lavender) becomes the first woman to graduate from an Australian university with a Bachelor of Arts from the University of Melbourne. Over 1,000 Melbourne tailoresses strike for more wages but factory owners circumvent paying increased wages by employing a large number of out-workers, working from home. Henrietta Dugdale publishes Australia's first feminist tract, *A Few Hours in a Far-Off Age*, a biting satire on discrimination against women, male ignorance and denial of women's potential and their intelligence.

1884 Widowed Louisa Meredith, desperately short of money is forced to sell her own collection of her paintings and drawings. She is given a government pension in recognition of her outstanding services to Australian literature, art and science. The Tasmanian government grants Fanny Cochrane Smith title to 300 acres of land. She remains at Nichols River until her death in 1905, having donated some of her land to build a Methodist Church. Annie Lowe and Henrietta Dugdale form the Victorian Women's Suffrage Society.

1885 Federal Council formed, the first move towards Federation of all Australian states.

1887 Agitation for raising of age of sexual consent blocked by male MPs. Euphemia Bowes of Women's Christian Temperance Union (WCTU) agitates for votes for women. Against fierce opposition from some, but not all, male professors, the University of Melbourne declares medicine open to women students, the first university medical school in Australia to admit women.

1888 White Australians celebrate one hundred years of settlement—yet Aboriginal people and white women still have no vote. Louisa Lawson (See Vol 2 of this series) launches *The Dawn, the Australian Women's Journal*, which lobbies for the female vote. Other women work to set up the Women's Suffrage Group.

1888 Draft Constitution Bill accepted.

1901 Commonwealth of Australia established and Federal constitution proclaimed by Lord Hopetoun, Governor General.

Index